WOMEN IN PUBLIC RELATIONS

THE GUILFORD COMMUNICATION SERIES

Recent Volumes

WOMEN
IN
PUBLIC
RELATIONS

How Gender Influences Practice

Larissa A. Grunig
Elizabeth Lance Toth
Linda Childers Hon

Foreword by Kathleen Larey Lewton

THE GUILFORD PRESS
New York   London

© 2001 The Guilford Press
A Division of Guilford Publications, Inc.
72 Spring Street, New York, NY 10012
www.guilford.com

Printed in the United States of America

This book is printed on acid-free paper.

Last digit is print number: 9   8   7   6   5   4   3   2   1

Library of Congress Cataloging-in-Publication Data
Grunig, Larissa A.
    Women in public realtions: how gender influences practice /
Larissa A. Grunig, Elizabeth Lance Toth, Linda Childers Hon.
        p. cm. — (Guilford communication series)
    Includes bibliographical references and index.
    ISBN 1-57230-626-2 (cloth)
        1. Public relations.   2. Sex role in the work environment.
I. Toth, Elizabeth L.   II. Hon, Linda Childers.   III. Title.
IV. Series.

HD59 .G78 2001
331.4'816592—dc21
                                                                00-052088

Foreword

At a time when the world needs effective public relations more than ever before—when individuals, organizations, corporations, governments, and nations are seeking to find common ground and mutual understanding—the role and stature of public relations professionals take on new significance. Equally significant are the factors that influence the success or failure of public relations professionals. Gender-based inequalities continue to exist decades after the term "women's lib" was coined. This situation must be analyzed, understood, and addressed.

The bottom line is straightforward. Because the public relations profession is now predominantly a female profession, situations that negatively affect women have a negative impact on the entire profession and on the ability of public relations professionals to be effective.

This book, and the massive research effort that led to development of this book, represent a significant contribution to the public relations profession, to public relations professionals, and to the organizations, companies, and causes that we serve. For this, we owe a debt of gratitude to the authors, Elizabeth Toth, Larissa Grunig, and Linda Childers Hon.

Liz and Lauri have been the heart, soul, and brains of the "status of women in public relations" effort since it began as a Public Relations Society of America Task Force in 1989. They were the driving force behind the groundbreaking research, first in terms of insisting that efforts to address the gender inequality situation must be grounded in solid scientific research and then in marshalling the resources needed to support that research. They made the ultimate contribution of their own time, energy, and wisdom. They maintained their enthusiasm for the project in all of its iterations, over more than a decade. Faced with people who questioned the value of the effort, who questioned its very premise, and who even resorted to personal attacks in very public venues, they never flinched. Throughout a myriad of changes and challenges in their personal lives, and their careers, they stayed the course, kept the faith, and inspired all of us who worked with them. With the addition of Linda Hon to the team, they have created a book that truly enlightens each of us, and in doing so advances our profession and our ability to serve our organizations, our clients, and the people of a world that sorely needs help in building relationships.

KATHLEEN LAREY LEWTON, APR, Fellow PRSA
Senior Vice President, Fleishman–Hillard
Chair and CEO, Public Relations Society
of America

Acknowledgments

Collaboration has become the hallmark of women's work style in the academy. In particular, women writing about gender tend to coauthor more frequently than do scholars writing on other topics.

Sociologists have suggested three reasons for this propensity toward coauthorship and away from the individualistic production of scholarship more characteristic of men: Women are more likely than men to collaborate because women prefer a group work environment, they evaluate communal efforts more highly, and they consider collaboration a survival strategy.

Our reasons for joining together to produce this book on women in public relations may include all of the above. A simpler and truer explanation lies in friendship. We, the authors, have sought collaboration with each other as friends and colleagues in academia.

We also value our friendship with our colleague in industry, Kathleen Larey Lewton, whose affirming and insightful Foreword adds the real-world dimension we consider vital. We gratefully acknowledge her contribution here. Perhaps more important, we salute Kathy Lewton as the first chair of the Women's Task Force of the Public Relations Society of America (PRSA).

That group, of course, is largely responsible for the survey that provided much of the data cited in this volume. So we thank the members of the first Women's Task Force that served as the impetus behind the survey. We also acknowledge with gratitude then-PRSA president John Paluszek, who formed the Task Force, and also PRSA's Research Foundation that provided the money to conduct and publish the results of the two-stage study.

We especially acknowledge with gratitude our colleagues Donald K. Wright, Jeffrey K. Springston, Shirley Serini, and Arthur Emig—coauthors with Elizabeth and Larissa of the PRSA research that explored gender bias in our field. Don, as project director of the initial glass ceiling study, deserves special thanks. Thanks go also to our universities—South Alabama, Syracuse, and Maryland—for their support, especially in the data analysis.

Our students in the S. I. Newhouse School of Public Communications at Syracuse, in the College of Journalism at the University of Maryland, and in the humanities and public relations departments of the Florida Institute of Technology and the University of Florida also deserve our thanks for their (albeit unwitting) collaboration. Our concern for these women and men, the future practitioners of public relations, has provided the sense of urgency with which we wrote the book. We are particularly indebted to one doctoral student at Syracuse, Linda Aldoory, for her research assistance.

We recognize, too, the contributions of the many women and men who served as participants in the research that you will read about here. Some responded to the lengthy survey instrument, filling out page after page of closed-ended questions that may or may not have dealt with concerns central to their busy lives. Others bared their souls in focus groups held around the country. Still others spent hours in one-on-one interviews.

We also want to acknowledge our collaborator at The Guilford Press, Peter Wissoker. We are grateful for his initial interest in the project, and especially for his forbearance throughout its execution. We may explain his patience in the words of Vauvenargues: "Patience is the art of hoping." Stated more positively, we look at patience as the Chinese proverb that compared patience with power, reminding us that with time and patience the mulberry leaf becomes silk.

*   *   *

If this book truly is more like silk than some rougher, less elegant, and less durable substance, then we need to acknowledge the value of our collaboration with each other as authors. Cicero believed that a friend is a second self. In our case, we had three selves. Another feature of true friendship that Cicero described was the fact that we gave counsel as well as received counsel. So to Liz and Linda, my dear collaborators in this effort, I say "thank you." And here I'd like to quote Shakespeare, who reminded us that "words are easy, like the wind; faithful friends are hard to find."

Each of us would like to acknowledge the help and support that has come to us from various sources. In my case, I thank my husband, James E.

Grunig. Here I think of Kahlil Gibran, who advised that "there be spaces in your togetherness." Cliched though it may sound, Jim gave me that space. I am grateful.

—LARISSA A. GRUNIG

I would like to thank my colleagues Lauri and Linda for their friendship and encouragement in assisting with my part of putting this book together. I appreciate very much the many hours of support of Linda Aldoory, our research assistant. I thank the S. I. Newhouse School of Public Communications at Syracuse University for giving me the needed research support; and I thank my husband, Rich, and son, Joe, for making my life so full.

—ELIZABETH LANCE TOTH

I would like to extend my appreciation to my coauthors, Lauri and Elizabeth, for providing me the opportunity to write this book about women in public relations, a subject that is both professionally and personally of paramount importance in my life. Your friendship, support, and guidance throughout the process have been my beacon. I also want to thank all of the female practitioners who so willingly shared their time and knowledge with me during our interviews and focus groups. Their individual and collective wisdom benefits all of those who care about public relations. Most of all, I am deeply grateful to my husband, David, and my son, Gregory, for filling my life with love and my cherished friends at the University of Florida for filling my life with laughter.

—LINDA CHILDERS HON

Preface

THE PURPOSE OF THIS BOOK

This book integrates the theoretical literature of public relations and gender with the findings of the largest study to date on women in public relations. Its unique focus is on the large data set of responses to a host of questions from about 2,000 public relations professionals from across the country. The two-stage study, funded by the Public Relations Society of America (PRSA), included a mail survey and focus groups of both male and female practitioners who manage public relations programs.

In addition, the extensive personal interviews reported here provide a forum for women to speak for themselves. Through this participatory, collaborative component of the study's combined methodology, we shorten the distance between subject and researcher. Through this approach, we also "get under" the common conceptions—or misconceptions—of women's experience in contemporary public relations. In all of these ways, we attempt to delve deeply into the perplexities of women's subjugation in public relations.

The book, which compares the situation for women in public relations with women in other fields, tackles questions that include how gender affects salary in this field, what factors contribute to the glass ceiling barring women from advancement into management, and what other ways women experience sexual discrimination in public relations. The solutions for overcoming sexism we propose grow out of our review of relevant literature, focus-group data, and lengthy personal interviews with women around the country. With the influx of women into public relations has come increasing concern for how they, and members of racioethnic minorities, are faring in the field.

With the feminization of the field and of the typical public relations classroom has come increasing interest in how educators can meet the needs of their female and minority students. Recent research conducted by other scholars suggests that an understanding of public relations must be reconstructed by bringing gender and race fully into the center of teaching. We acknowledge the importance of accepting cultural and gender pluralism as a goal in teaching, but until the manuscript of this book was complete we wondered how to proceed. Without an appropriate text, incorporating the new scholarship about women into the curricula of public relations is arduous.

We consider this book, written for our legions of students in public relations and for young professionals in search of resources for their career advancement, a "text" rather than a "textbook." What's the distinction? Textbooks usually are written for didactic purposes. As a result, they are rarely "discussable." By contrast, we see our text as eminently discussable. The ideas, values, issues, and data presented here are rich in complexity and ambiguity.

Analyzing the field of public relations from a feminist standpoint results in two main conclusions. First, no existing textbook focuses on women in public relations—a curious gap in the literature, considering that there are books on women in other communication industries, such as television, film, broadcast news, and print journalism. Second, students relying on existing texts and contemporary coursework in public relations come away ill equipped to understand the relationship between the feminization of the field and their own chances for a successful, rewarding career in public relations.

Men and women alike, both graduate students and undergraduates, need to understand how the female majority in this field affects both compensation and prestige of the field. As men become an "endangered species," the field also risks sublimation to a related department. In addition, the feminization of public relations may lead to encroachment on the managerial function.

CONTENTS

By limiting our discussion of women in public relations to the relevant literature of public relations, organizational sociology, business management, and feminist theory—and by focusing on the large-scale survey research and focus groups commissioned by PRSA and on personal interviews—we can limit the length of this book to a manageable number of pages. But why have three busy faculty women collaborated to write such a book on women in public relations? After all, our rewards as educators come from fulfilling central, rather than what some people might consider marginal, responsibilities.

First, we are expected to teach—typically hordes of eager undergraduates enrolled in basic courses on public relations principles, techniques, and campaigns. We supervise internships and help sponsor student professional societies. We also work with a demanding coterie of graduate students whose experience may challenge our assumptions in the advanced-level management and research seminars.

We must contribute service to the university, to the community, and to the profession. This expectation results in countless hours of faculty and committee meetings, guest lectures, and consulting—often pro bono but always underpaid.

Finally, and perhaps most challenging of all, we must do research to "publish or perish." Where and what we publish, of course, is carefully prescribed to help ensure merit raises, tenure, and promotion. This means that we shoot for publication of our scholarly articles in prestigious (typically mainstream) academic journals.

Rarely do you find public relations educators who are employed in research universities devoting their time to a project of this nature. We introduce our book, then, with an explanation of our purposes. Our initial chapter talks about the need for research and writing about women in public relations. That need, responsive to students and practitioners alike, suggests that we write for a dual audience of scholars and professionals.

To do all this, we begin with a discussion of one of the major professional associations in the field, the PRSA. In 1989, PRSA established its Task Force on the Status of Women. The Task Force represents a response to growing concern about the opportunities for women in public relations and about the effects of the feminization of our field on women and men alike. In Chapter 1, we explore PRSA's Statement on Equality of Opportunity in Public Relations and, as a conclusion to our first chapter, we also work toward an understanding of gender and sex roles in the United States. In this introductory chapter readers will learn a great deal about the problem of sexism in the United States.

Chapter 2 introduces a definition of feminism and several feminist perspectives—Marxist, liberal, and radical—that have developed in response to gender bias. It helps readers understand the issues surrounding the feminization of public relations. These concerns include declining compensation and limited advancement for women in most professional careers, focusing of course on public relations. Here we contrast women's actual salaries with their salary expectations. We learn that the salary gap persists across occupations and over time. We go on to explore the broader picture of occupational segregation, integration, and ghettoization, including changes in the labor market, in demographics, and in occupational rewards. Here, too, we explain the "feminist fallacy," or the gap between modern women's expectations and the realities they may encounter in the work place. This chapter includes a discussion of the typical denial of gender bias in public relations. It concludes with a discussion of why the feminist fallacy and denial of sexism persist.

Chapter 3 compares the status of women in public relations with the status of women in other professions and near-professions. We look specifically at women in medicine, law, biology, higher education, scholarly publishing, trade and professional associations, and government and politics. We explore the similarities and differences between women in these white-collar fields with their counterparts in blue-collar or pink-collar work. Chapter 4 focuses on the concepts of management and entrepreneurship. Power, powerlessness, and empowerment are central to this discussion.

In Chapter 5, we discuss the promise of diversity for public relations. This chapter explores the question of multicultural inclusivity, in particular, juxtaposing the arguments of its proponents with the dire predictions of its detractors. Its companion chapter, Chapter 6, also compares the situation for women—this time between women of the dominant culture and those who are part of ethnic and racial minority groups. It highlights the roles and functions of three minority groups within public relations practice: Asian Americans, Hispanic Americans, and African Americans.

Chapter 7 is also concerned with comparisons and contrasts. It describes how the growing number of women who work outside the home may affect the prestige of the fields in which they labor. We describe three especially problematic areas here: the credibility or prestige of the field; encroachment on its management, in particular, by men in other fields; and the sublimation of the functional area to another, related function. All three issues are paramount concerns in public relations as it moves from a male to a female majority.

Chapter 8, the first to present our research results, exposes the discrepancy between men's and women's salaries. We explain the pay gap through factors such as age, experience, type of organization, public relations role, and—yes—discrimination. Chapter 9 describes public relations roles as predictors of salary and of advancement. It establishes the discrepancy between numbers and power. Chapter 10 presents our findings related to additional issues encompassed by the glass ceiling: hiring, promotion, notions of career success, organizational climate, job satisfaction, mentoring and networking, sexual harassment, and flexibility in the work place.

In Chapter 11, we attempt to explain the discrepancies we found between our female and male respondents over the 5-year period of the glass ceiling research. Our explanations for gender inequality at work include masculine value systems, women's exclusion from social and informational networks, women's timidity about salary negotiation, a dearth of female role models and mentors, faulty college curricula, socialization, negative attitudes among senior managers, the balancing act between office and home, stereotypes, tokenism, women's lack of self-esteem, sexual harassment and "lookism," ageism, marketplace factors, and the marginalization of public relations as an organizational function.

The next two chapters explore the implications of these research findings along with some solutions for helping overcome gender bias. Chapter 12, on liberal feminist strategies, explains "buying into" and working the system. These strategies include impression management, finding the right place to work, attracting men back into public relations, learning how to fight for salaries, women networking with men, gaining access to management decision making, denying the existence of discrimination, and making hard choices. It also promotes developing the skills and knowledge women need for public relations, for demonstrating professionalism, and for empowering themselves.

Chapter 13, on radical feminist strategies, works more at the societal and organizational levels than at the individual level. Here our (admittedly ambitious) recommendations begin with raising levels of awareness about sexism, electing women to high government posts, passing federal legislation that supports working parents, outlawing sexual harassment, recouping losses in affirmative action, mandating equal representation of women in government and organizations supported by government, eradicating sexism in education, breaking down gender stereotypes, and redefining feminism. Organizational-level changes would establish family-friendly policies; devise alternative career paths; rethink the masculine ethic and value the feminine; and make criteria for recruitment, hiring, retention, and promotion more fair. The transformation of public relations as elaborated in this chapter includes addressing the marginalization of the function and devising strategies for overcoming the problem, reassessing the mission of undergraduate education, incorporating women's perspectives into the curriculum, encouraging women to get advanced degrees, and women and men working together toward a politics of affiliation.

Our final thoughts, contained in Chapter 14, contrast women's oppression in public relations with their agency: women's ability to be effective in this critically important field. The chapter concludes with the directions we propose for further research on women and public relations: sexual harassment, globalization, and new communication technologies. The Appendix ends the book with a detailed look at how we conducted the glass ceiling studies.

Contents

WOMEN IN PUBLIC RELATIONS

Chapter One

The Purpose of This Book

The writing of this book began with a letter in 1989. That year the *Public Relations Journal*, one of the industry's premier trade publications, ran an article about female practitioners (Lukovitz, 1989). In those few pages, the man who was then president of the Public Relations Society of America (PRSA), John Paluszek, was quoted as saying that if there were a problem for women in public relations, he was not aware of it. Like many other public relations practitioners, he is now.

And like others who read that brief article, one of the authors of this book wrote a response. The letter began:

> Let me add my voice to what I am sure has been a chorus responding to your comments included in the article "Women Practitioners" in last month's *Public Relations Journal*. I hope the song we sing will encourage you, as the leader of a leading professional association, to act on the many issues brought up in that article on the feminization of our field.

Act Paluszek did. He established an ad hoc Task Force on Women in Public Relations. That group, forceful within PRSA since its inception, has become an integral part of PRSA's operations. Now called the Committee on Work, Life, and Gender Issues, it is working both from the top down at the national level and from the grass roots up at chapters throughout the country. In a way, this book chronicles its activities in its first 5 years of existence. In another way, this book goes well beyond a single commission within a single professional association. We hope it speaks to the lives of all women doing public relations.

We begin with the story of PRSA's Task Force on Women in Public Relations because that group's mission led in large part to the research that frames this book. Without those surveys and the focus group data that aug-

1

mented them, we would lack the solid foundation from which to interpret our own life experiences and those of the thousands of other women who practice, teach, and study public relations. Although we, the authors, do not consider ourselves victims of "methidolotry," we do appreciate the funding that made that research possible.

Statistics, then, tell part of this important story. The rest comes from the words of women throughout the United States who have found opportunity, frustration, discouragement, and success in public relations. You will find few famous women quoted here, however. One might argue that relatively few "big name" women in public relations exist. We do believe that the proportion of women who have achieved fame in public relations does not equal the prominence (or notoriety) of their male colleagues. That's one of the issues this book addresses.

However, even if the history books and the membership rosters of our professional societies were replete with the names of famous females who head major firms or serve as corporate vice presidents, we would want to go beyond those icons. We want to acknowledge the trials and the triumphs of the legions of women who work without fanfare as editors of employee publications, as account supervisors, as media spokespeople, as directors of community relations, as independent counselors, and as one-person departments "doing it all" in public relations.

Most of the women quoted here remain unnamed to protect both their own privacy and the identity of the organizations that employ them. Although we would like to be able to credit those companies, associations, governmental agencies, and nonprofits that have encouraged the aspirations of their female employees, we would almost by default be exposing the organizations that have discriminated against them.

Blaming the guilty and praising the enlightened is not our intent. Even if we had envisioned developing some sort of guide to the best and worst organizations for women in public relations, we know that would be impossible. Times change. Environments change. Bosses change. And the career plans and abilities of the women themselves who do public relations change. As a result, the list we would provide today might be altered radically in another year.

Perhaps more importantly, we do not presume to judge individual employers or organizations where female practitioners of public relations find themselves working. Instead, we are looking for more generic patterns and practices within organizations that lead to the empowerment of women. Unfortunately, we have uncovered a concomitant set of discriminatory organizational circumstances that should warn even the bravest, most ambitious, and best qualified women in our field.

Knowing, at the same time, that many women in public relations labor in organizations that devalue them—often subtly or inadvertently—we conclude our story of women in public relations with the best guesses we have on how to overcome the sexism that characterizes so many enterprises. When we're less honest, we call these guesses "recommendations," "suggestions," or "solutions." If anyone really knew how to solve the problem of discrimination in the work place, we are convinced it would have happened already.

You see, throughout the research reported in this book—our studies and those of countless others— we have discovered little overt bias against women in public relations. What we have found is that old habits die hard. Stereotypes persist. Family obligations overwhelm women. Women themselves doubt their own and their sisters' worth. Socialization undoes the best efforts of enlightened parents of both sexes. Role models for women are few and mentors overworked. Powerlessness begets powerlessness.

If knowledge truly is power, then the information contained here should help. We begin with this look at how one professional association, the PRSA, has begun to approach equity for the growing majority of women in the field. From this historical look at the PRSA Task Force on Women, we conclude this first chapter with a theoretical explanation of what we mean by "women." More specifically, this chapter ends with a brief review of the literature of sex and gender.

This book, then, integrates the theoretical literature of public relations and gender with the findings of the largest longitudinal study to date on women in the field. Through a series of lengthy interviews and focus groups, it also tells the stories of several dozen women in public relations. Because we have framed our research results in the context of the literature, we believe that our book should prove useful long after the survey, focus group, and interview data are eclipsed by findings of the subsequent studies that we consider inevitable. We began to write against a backdrop of recession in the United States, the wake of the polarizing Anita Hill–Clarence Thomas hearings, and an election characterized as "the year of the woman in politics." We believe, though, that our theoretical conceptualization helps transcend that historical contextualization.

RESEARCH QUESTIONS

More specifically, the book addresses the following questions:

- Is public relations more of a "velvet ghetto" for women than are other fields?
- How does gender affect salary in public relations?

- What is the relationship between gender and the glass ceiling?
- What factors contribute to sexual discrimination in public relations?
- How do women experience the fallout of discrimination in public relations?
- How are men in the field affected by discrimination against women?
- What solutions do the literature, the surveys, and the group and individual interviews suggest for overcoming gender bias?

The astute reader notices at this point that we are not asking whether sex discrimination *exists* in our field. As you will come to see from the exhaustive literature cited in the pages to come, the existence of bias against women has been established in both the professional and the academic journals of public relations. We reiterate much of the literature as a way of pulling it together coherently. We also grounded our own research in this literature to form a solid foundation for empirical study. Our main purpose in the book, though, was to begin moving public relations toward a solution to the problem. We used the "Noah principle" as an analogy: No more prizes for predicting rain; only prizes for building the ark.

Of the myriad concerns surrounding the feminization of public relations, then, we have selected these few key questions carefully. They provide the organizational scheme for the text that follows. They suggest that the book (1) is comparative, (2) goes beyond salary to include a consideration of women's ascension to the managerial ranks, and (3) concentrates on resolving the problem of sexual discrimination in public relations.

These same dimensions are reflected in the PRSA's Statement of Equality of Opportunity, which we will discuss at some length later in this chapter. First, however, we offer a snapshot of the background that led to our research and the subsequent publication of this book—among the first that focuses on women in public relations.

A SNAPSHOT OF WOMEN IN PUBLIC RELATIONS

The last 20 years has seen an influx of women into the practice of public relations. By their growing numbers alone, women have created opportunities for themselves beyond what fields traditionally considered "female," such as nursing and teaching, could have offered. On the other hand, any field suddenly shifting to a female majority—or even experiencing the hint of more women than men—faces the realities of dwindling salary, status, and influence within the organization. These consequences make the story of women in public relations an important one to tell.

This story of the burgeoning number of women in public relations should be understood in the context of the changing makeup of our work force. U.S. Department of Labor statistics for 1997 show that although women account for 58.7% of the U.S. labor force, 65.7% of public relations specialists are women (U.S. Bureau of the Census, 1998). Even in the late 1980s, Lukovitz (1989) put the figure at a majority: 58.6%—a dramatic change from 1970, when only 27% of all practitioners were women. This represents a faster rate of change than in many other fields that are moving from a male majority toward parity.

The work force is predicted to alter even more rapidly over the next decade because of the continuing influx of women and minorities. Studies of women entering other professions—including law, medicine, real estate, banking, and accounting—suggest that gender-based inequities similar to those facing public relations practitioners occur in these fields as well. Within this context, then, this book will dispel two myths about women and their careers. The first fiction is that when women move into a field, it is just a matter of time until they take over and have their way. The second is that the typical woman who aspires to a career in management is much better off today than she was a generation ago. The story will end with the conclusion that women do, indeed, add value to the field of public relations and that solutions to gender bias against them are possible.

The managerial emphasis of this text is especially relevant to any study of gender in public relations. The pattern of professional development over the last decade indicates that employees are shifting from the technician's role to that of the manager. (Chapter 9 explains the critical difference between these two roles.) This trend has significant gender-based implications. Students or beginning practitioners aspiring to managerial positions need to understand how feminization of the field will affect them, whether they are male or female. Also, women in public relations tend to see themselves in the technical rather than the managerial role to a greater degree than men do. So this book has special importance for the mushrooming enrollment of female students in journalism and communication courses and at the entry-level ranks of public relations practice.

Kosicki and Becker's (1998) studies of departments of journalism and mass communication place about 11,210 U.S. undergraduates in public relations alone; about 4,000 others are in sequences that combine public relations and advertising. They found the ratio of students in public relations versus the traditional area of news-editorial more than 2-to-1 in favor of public relations and advertising.

More significantly for this story, about 80% of all public relations students in the approximately 200 universities offering communication majors are women (Becker, 1990). Although about half of PRSA's members are women (Toth & Cline, 1989b), membership in the 6,000-strong Public Relations *Student* Society of America represents a 10-to-1 female majority (Hunt & Thompson, 1988).

When these students complete their undergraduate education, they may go on to join either the PRSA, with about 19,000 members, or the International Association of Business Communicators (IABC), with only slightly fewer members. Between 50 and 60% of the membership of these two major associations is female. In addition, a practitioner with professional orientation may belong to a specialized organization, such as the National Association of Government Communicators (NAGC), the Council for the Advancement and Support of Education (CASE), or the American Society of Association Executives (ASAE). Some of these professional societies, such as the National School Public Relations Association (NSPRA), may enroll as many as 70% women. Finally, female (and male) practitioners may become members of Women in Communication Inc. (WICI).

These professional associations are not the only groups to be concerned about the impact and treatment of women in public relations. Along with the feminization of the field and of the typical public relations classroom has come increasing interest in how educators can meet the needs of their female and minority students. Three articles in a single *Journalism Educator* explored the challenges and opportunities these changing demographics present (Becker, 1989; Creedon, 1989a; Kern-Foxworth, 1989c). Together these articles and, subsequently, a series of conference papers suggest that our understanding of public relations must be reconstructed by bringing gender and race fully into the center.

So far, however, the only substantial treatments of women in public relations have been published in trade journals or presented at academic conferences. Few books on public relations contain information about women or women's issues. Thus students relying on existing texts and coursework in public relations—whether their classes are taught in schools of journalism or departments of communication or mass communication, English, or business—learn little about the relationship between the glass ceiling and their own chances for a satisfying career in public relations.

Men and women alike—undergraduates, graduate students, and practitioners already working in the field—need to realize that the influx of women into public relations affects them all. On the one hand, the growing number of women studying and practicing public relations opens up a professional area once considered a male bastion. The new female majority also offers great potential for a field that some predict will be increasingly responsive to the publics that will make or break the organization over the long haul. It may result in a practice that is more professional, more ethical, and more effective than ever before.

On the other hand, the influx of women into a field traditionally dominated by men influences both the compensation paid in and the prestige of that field. As men become an "endangered species," the field also risks sublimation to a related discipline. In addition, the feminization of public relations may lead to encroachment on its managerial function by non-public relations people.

A FEW WORDS ABOUT "OBJECTIVITY"

By limiting our look at women in public relations to these key issues and to the relevant literature of only a few disciplines—primarily public relations, sociology, psychology, business management, and feminist theory—we have managed to limit the book's length to a manageable number of pages. Readers should be aware of what we have sacrificed in the process. We do not make the claim of being comprehensive. By necessity, we have been selective. We also do not claim to be objective.

The two concepts of selectivity and objectivity require some elaboration—especially given the controversial nature of any writing about women or feminist concerns. We anticipate a healthy skepticism about the ideas, the stances, and even the data we will be presenting here. Any challenge to the status quo is discomforting and may become divisive to a field. Promoting divisiveness, however, is not our intent. Quite the opposite. We are aiming at more inclusivity, wherein public relations as a vital societal function welcomes everyone whose capabilities as a practitioner or as a scholar stand to make a contribution.

Throughout this book—as we acknowledge and come to understand our shared predicament as students, researchers, and practitioners of a field increasingly changing—we will make our theoretical assumptions or presuppositions clear. We recognize that like everyone's, our ability to reason, to take new information into account, and to arrive at logical determinations is limited by our own frames of reference and, yes, bias. Thus we cannot and do not speak of an "objective" compilation of literature, collection of data, or analysis of findings.

Like the philosophers of science Stephen Jay Gould (1981) and Evelyn Fox Keller (1985), we consider objectivity a mythical norm in science. Gould explained that researchers are so embedded in their surrounding culture that they often fail to identify the assumptions of that culture. We are attempting to identify clearly both our strengths and our limitations—We are three white women whose gender helps explain why we consider our research questions so important yet who acknowledge that through our ignorance of other races and cultures, we may inadvertently distort or even omit issues of equal concern to other ethnicities.

Still, the impossibility of achieving total objectivity is not to say that "anything goes." Instead, like most scientists, we attempt to compensate for our acknowledged subjectivity. Our three-person team represents a strong integration of both the quantitative and the historical/critical research traditions. Our research design and the steps we have taken to help guard against the bias we freely acknowledge as human beings engaged in the research process are described in the Appendix. We further regard the notion of the external validation inherent in the funding process as important. As a result, we welcomed the oversight provided by the agency that helped fund this study, PRSA's research Foundation.

We also built safeguards into our research design through, for example, size and determination of sample in the case of the mail survey and through the process of biangulation, or the combined quantitative and qualitative methodology. The collaborative nature of the study, too, helped protect against individual partiality; after all, we were three, rather than one. Not only did this help to preclude excessive subjectivity, but one's methodological strengths could complement the other's.

Despite these cautionary measures, you may be asking whether we can "prove" all of what we contend here. The answer, of course, is "no." We cannot prove that our conclusions are correct—only that we believe we have made a strong case.

This approach to social science research prepares a fertile ground for further legitimate dialogue among scholars interested in solving the same intellectual and applied problems. We would welcome alternative accounts of the situation for women in public relations. Certainly, there is room for new points of view on this critically important subject—one that increasingly affects men as well as women in the field. PRSA, for example, has acknowledged formally the growing impact of female practitioners and has begun to question the reasons for and outgrowths of this contemporary phenomenon.

PRSA'S INITIATIVES ON WOMEN IN PUBLIC RELATIONS

On and off for decades, PRSA has been taking action to investigate the implications of women in public relations. At its 1971 Assembly, it established a committee on the Status of Women in Public Relations. The committee was charged with exploring what PRSA considered serious economic and advancement inequities for women (Gorney, 1975). The next year, it conducted its first research study in this area. In 1973, PRSA's Assembly called for a national affirmative action program to overcome the conditions its research revealed.

Throughout the decade of the 1970s, PRSA continued to keep tabs on how its female members were faring. By the 1980s, the question had shifted. Rather than exploring how public relations was treating women, PRSA began to ask how women were affecting public relations. An editorial in the *Public Relations Journal* may have articulated for the first time what has become a major concern:

> If women become a majority in public relations, the practice will be typecast as "women's work." It will lose what clout it now has as a management function and become a second-class occupation. In the process, gains made over 50 years to build and sustain the value of public relations will . . . disappear. (Bates, 1983, p. 6)

At the same time, the editorial acknowledged that women's academic backgrounds and writing skills seemed to be superior to men's. Joseph (1985), who surveyed PRSA members about the impact of the feminization of the field, found many who viewed the situation positively. Respondents talked about the likelihood of women raising the profession's level of performance, both ethically and in terms of bottom-line effectiveness.

By the late 1980s, PRSA combined its concern for the treatment of women in the field with its stake in the viability of public relations as an integral part of any organization. It continued to recognize the implications of the feminization of public relations for society at large.

More specifically, the mission of the ad hoc group for women reestablished by 1989 PRSA president John Paluszek developed out of the understanding that public relations is a counseling function. The job, in large part, entails advising management about the concerns of the organization's strategic publics. In fact, one of the most commonly cited definitions of public relations is "the management of communication between an organization and its publics" (J. Grunig & Hunt, 1984, p. 6). Strategic publics are the groups most important to an organization at any given time. They represent the constituencies most able to support or to thwart the organization.

Public relations people help the organization identify these publics, often called "stakeholders." Professionals in public relations go on to help their organizations deal with these employees, customers or clients, owners, communities, governmental regulators, and activists. Of course, they also communicate with the media that cover their organizations.

Charged with being responsive to each of these publics, public relations as an organizational function and as a professional field in turn must be responsive to the concerns of one of its own most strategic constituencies: women. The first chair of PRSA's contemporary Task Force on Women, Kathleen Larey Lewton, explained that this responsibility mandates practitioners to take the lead in addressing any inequities for women in their own profession. The task force agreed that all individuals should receive equitable rewards in terms of compensation and promotion for their work.

One of the major newsletters in the field, *pr reporter* ("Diversity in Action," 1991), focused on this very issue when it discussed work-place disparities between women and men. It asked its readers to question what message their department or organization was sending to its female employees, female customers, and female voters.

How, in turn, will PRSA and even corporate America benefit from equitable treatment of women in the field? In its statement of equality of opportunity in the field, PRSA speculated that the equal status of women would result in improved morale, less turnover, greater productivity, and higher quality of output—all important pluses for organizations. PRSA's statement also pointed out that these kinds of benefits are increasingly important as U.S. companies compete in an increasingly global economy. They need the participation of the most talented employees available, regardless of gender, race or ethnicity, sexual orientation, or age.

Eradicating sexism will mean that PRSA itself, and the profession at large, should be ensured that qualified, talented women will continue to work in this career. Without reversing what PRSA called the "downward salary spiral" that can occur when one segment of the profession consistently is undercompensated and denied advancement, surely such expertise will be lost to public relations.

In each of the years since its inception, the Task Force on Women has been a source of awareness and of change within PRSA. It began with the enthusiastic endorsement of PRSA's board of directors meeting in the fall of 1989. As Chair Lewton (1989) put it in an internal memo, "Our report was very well received . . . with nary a criticism or 'is this really needed?' " In fact, the board accepted all recommendations of the Task Force on Women, including the important yet hard-to-nail-down "making an issue of it" (sexism in public relations).

Since then, the group has become institutionalized within PRSA, as evidenced by two name changes. In 1992, it successfully petitioned to become the Committee on Women in Public Relations. The move up from task force to committee status is an important indicator of PRSA's affirmation of solid commitment to women's issues. The 1993 committee chair, Judith T. Phair, explained in a memo to members of her committee that the change also reflects women's key role in the future of the field. In 2000, the group became the Committee on Work, Life, and Gender Issues—a name change that signaled a broadening focus that encompasses men as well as women and the home issues that can affect the work we all do in public relations. Throughout the 1990s, the group could point to several major achievements.

Statement of Equality of Opportunity

The first significant product of this ad hoc group for women was its "Statement on Equality of Opportunity in Public Relations." The statement was adopted by PRSA's board of directors in January 1990.

PRSA Statement on Equality of Opportunity in Public Relations

Public relations professionals across the world are continually involved in counseling and advising organizations on the importance of equitable treatment of employees, customers and other publics. The Board of Directors of the Public Relations Society of America, speaking on behalf of the Society's 15,000 members, reaffirms PRSA's total commitment to equality of opportunity and compensation for women within the public relations profession.

Although many examples of the progress of women in public relations can be cited, the pace of progress has been painfully slow. Inequities in terms of salaries, advancement and acceptance continue to exist. As counselors to management and as leaders in helping organizations build effective relationships, and because an ever-growing number of those in our profession are women, we believe that public relations professionals must take a strong leadership position in addressing the need for equality for women.

Elimination of these inequities, by ensuring equality of opportunity and compensation for women in public relations, will benefit our organizations and clients, the overall American economic system and the public relations profession, as well as the women themselves.

- Equal treatment for women will benefit American companies and organizations, which are operating in an increasingly competitive global economy and which need the participation the most talented individuals available—regardless of their race, creed, religion, disability, sex, age, color, national origin, or any other characteristic protected by laws against discrimination.

- Equal treatment for women will benefit the public relations profession, by ensuring that qualified, talented women continue to pursue careers in public relations, and by preventing the downward salary spiral that can occur if a segment of professionals in the field is consistently undercompensated and denied advancement.
- Equal treatment for women will benefit the individuals who will receive equitable rewards of compensation and promotion for their work. This should result in improved morale, lowered turnover, increased productivity and higher quality of output.

There is ample evidence that public relations is not the only profession in which women are encountering inequities. During 1990, however, PRSA members at the national, regional and local levels will be developing research, education and communications programs to address the issue of ensuring equality of opportunity and compensation for women, similar to our efforts involving minorities. This will be a very high priority for the organization and will continue until our evaluations show that significant progress has been achieved.

January 20, 1990

We call your attention to three main aspects of the final paragraph in this declaration—issues that reach beyond this statement to frame our book. First, the paragraph emphasizes that public relations is not the only profession in which women are treated inequitably. Although one might be tempted to agree with this assertion on its face, we explore the contention here in Chapters 3 and 4. We look at how women in public relations fare by comparison with women in other fields—both white collar and blue collar. We are curious to know whether professions or vocations exist in which women are in a one-up rather than a one-down position.

More specifically, we want to know how salaries for women vis-à-vis men compare across the occupations. We want to know how history predicts the fate of women in different industries and different careers. In other words, is it more likely that women will succeed in fields traditionally male-dominated or in fields long recognized as pink-collar preserves? Has any of these occupational clusters managed to overcome any of the "isms"—such as sexism, racism, or ageism—that may characterize it? And how do the barriers to advancement for women in one profession, such as law or medicine, stack up against the obstacles facing women in another area, such as public relations?

Second, PRSA's statement on equality of opportunity goes beyond compensation to consider the question of women's ascension into the managerial ranks. In fact, the monograph that resulted from its major research project is titled *Under the Glass Ceiling: An Analysis of Gender Issues in American Public Relations* (Wright, L. Grunig, Springston, & Toth, 1991).

We add emphasis to the term "glass ceiling" because it figures so prominently in the literature on women in management. The phenomenon also may be called the "cement," the "iron," the "smoked," or the "sponge" ceiling. Women pursuing religious careers bump up against the "stained-glass ceiling" as they aspire to senior ministerial roles in mid- to large-sized Protestant congregations. Whatever we call it, we find that women in public relations do indeed work beneath this invisible but very real barrier to their advancement in the typical organization. The problem is considered so pervasive that the Civil Rights Act of 1991 created a Glass Ceiling Commission. Despite their qualifications, then, women often find themselves thus prevented from reaching their career potential in all kinds of organizations—corporations as well as nonprofits, governmental agencies, associations, and public relations firms.

Third, and finally, the PRSA statement focuses on developing strategies for overcoming sex discrimination in public relations. At this point, you may be asking how this professional society knew that such discrimination existed in its ranks—remembering, of course, that its affirmation of equality was written *before* its major research project was completed. The answer is that that research study, to be described in detail throughout this book, was not designed to determine the *existence* of bias against women in public relations. It was not conducted to expose the *extent* of such discrimination. Instead, its purpose was to explain *why* women and men experience their work lives in public relations so very differently.

Even in 1989 and before, there was more than enough research to substantiate significant differences in women's and men's pay and in their occupational roles. We had evidence that rates of promotion varied significantly by gender. We knew that even in the public relations classroom, female students were at a disadvantage. The question became, then, determining why these disparities persisted and what we could do about them.

The "Glass Ceiling" Study

The "glass ceiling" study was the second major contribution of the contemporary PRSA Task Force on Women. It developed out of the massive research project that is one of the key elements of this book. The two-stage, longitudinal study combined survey methodology with focus groups to address the pay question along with women's advancement opportunities and their satisfaction at work in public relations.

We on the research teams envisioned not only an initial study but an entire program of research. PRSA agreed that our investigation would begin in 1990 and be continued with longitudinal studies at 4- or 5-year intervals. We also agreed that as a first step, we needed to develop a salary survey of PRSA's members that would be both valid and reliable. That is, we needed a large enough sample, randomly selected, and a response rate high enough to help ensure the credibility and the generalizability of our findings.

We believe that this longitudinal study represents one of the most important contributions that scholars and practitioners together have made to the field of public relations. Its strengths lie, first, in the collaboration of seasoned researchers with activist professionals in the industry—people like Kathy Lewton, who chaired the Task Force on Women at the time; John Paluszek, who established the task force in the first place; H. J. (Jerry) Dalton Jr., who helped fund the first "glass ceiling" monograph in his role as past PRSA president and chair of PRSA's research Foundation; and John Beardsley, instrumental in funding the second stage of the research. The study is the product of both women and men, such as project director or codirector Donald K. Wright, who are concerned about the fate of women in public relations and of the profession itself.

The study also benefits from a combined methodology only rarely found in times of tight research dollars. The large sample size of the two surveys and the scientific way in which they were drawn both added to the accuracy of the research and the appropriateness of generalizing its findings at least to all members of PRSA. Of course, surveys are of limited value in examining the complex social relationships or the patterns of interaction involved in the question of equity for women. So we combined our quantitative data with qualitative data. We conducted two series of focus groups, some of women and others of men, among participants at the 1990 PRSA convention in New York and then, in 1995, across the country.

In our effort to systematically yet efficiently collect and analyze these data, we might have been tempted to confine our research within valid but insignificant parameters. We decided instead to be more than coding specialists—doing what had been done, say, with annual salary surveys in the past but with more accuracy and greater representativeness. Instead, we began with key concepts we knew were relevant: public relations roles, socialization, job satisfaction, and stereotyping. From these and other, related theoretical concepts, we developed research questions and what we considered an appropriate methodological design.

The first major result was a 42-page monograph, second only to an introductory issue that defines public relations in the PRSA Foundation series of research publications. Its release led to the following headline in *The Washington Times* (Rabin & Myles, 1991): "A battle of the sexes is brewing in public relations as the result of inequality between male and female practitioners, according to a survey by the Public Relations Society of

America Foundation" (p. B1). The *Times* columnists went on to quote from interviews with local public relations practitioners and one of the authors of this book. They concluded from these interviews that, surprisingly, neither Washington Women in Public Relations nor Women in Communication has "aggressively addressed the question of a gender gap in the workplace" (p. B1).

We intend to do just that. This book expands on the data presented and analyzed in the "glass ceiling" monograph. In addition, it incorporates the most recent research available on the status of women in public relations: the second stage in the longitudinal "glass ceiling" study. This second step, funded by the PRSA Foundation and directed by Elizabeth Lance Toth and Donald K. Wright, allows us to compare the women's situation at two points in time so that we can begin to understand whether, how, and why, if at all, that situation is changing. We combined all of those findings with a series of additional focus groups and long interviews with women who may not belong to PRSA.

To all of this, our own research, we add a discussion of a myriad other studies conducted over the last few decades to create a historical as well as contemporary picture of what it means to be a woman doing public relations. In these ways, we hope to broaden our understanding of the phenomenon beyond the members of a single professional group at discrete points in time.

Challenges for the Near Future

A summary (PRSA, n. d.) of the benchmark gender survey recommended several activities for local PRSA chapters to support efforts at the national level. Many of these action items resulted from a compilation of some 43 suggestions offered by members of the 1991 Task Force on Women. They included the following:

- Making members aware of the Statement on Equality of Opportunity in Public Relations.
- Seeking out women for board and leadership positions.
- Disseminating the full results of the national research study.
- Sponsoring programs for negotiating for salaries.
- Working with Public Relations *Student* Society of America chapters.
- Appointing local chapter task forces on women in public relations.

Not until 1993 did the first local chapters addressing women's concerns develop within the PRSA structure. However, shortly after publication of the "glass ceiling" monograph, leaders of PRSA did develop a list of "Ten Challenges to Public Relations during the Next Decade" (Warner, n. d.). This report grew out of the deliberations of a core group of nine committee members, led by president-elect Harland K. (Hal) Warner. Many of the challenges enunciated here are relevant to women in public relations, but one focuses especially on this question. Challenge 6 argues for the need for diversity in public relations. We reproduce it in its entirety:

> All recent studies reveal a massive shift away from diversity in public relations. Although women have made great strides and have entered the field in great numbers, much more needs to be done to achieve higher compensation for women and to encourage more men and minorities to enter the field. We must understand the different multicultural audiences—African-Americans, Asians, Hispanics and other subgroups.
>
> Although men make up a shrinking proportion of practitioners, they still hold most of the senior positions. Part of this is due to demographics. Women entered the field in large numbers only recently, and they are working their way up the ladder as the older leaders retire. Of course, talented women made it to the top even when males dominated the field, and many others would undoubtedly succeed whether older leaders retire or not.
>
> Public relations is predicated on building harmonious relationships between various publics. It is stultified when it reflects a limited slice of a diverse population. Steps should be taken to identify the factors responsible for the lack of minority participation and the declining number of males entering the field and to bring about a balance of practitioners that roughly reflects the makeup of our society.
>
> Another split shaping up in our society is age balance. Generational conflict can be expected to accelerate as the bulge of ambitious baby boomers pushes up against members of an older generation who control most of the senior jobs. Younger people no longer can look to an expanding economy to provide the ladder to the top. This will spark intense competition for existing positions that has not been seen since Social Security was established to encourage an older generation to make way for a [*sic*] younger men during the Great Depression. (pp. 2–3)

Analysis of this charge for diversity and the other nine challenges spelled out in the Warner report led to a description of what PRSA's leaders envisioned as the successful association of the 1990s. It would be an organization of strategists, of communicators, of learners, of risk takers, of philosophers, of leaders, of modest anxiety and high standards, and of *diversity*. The report's drafting committee explained that a variety of economic, political, social, demographic, and ethnic backgrounds would broaden PRSA's thinking and enrich its range of options.

Conceptualized in this way, diversity should enhance the future of PRSA or, in fact, of any organization. However, diversity comes with a price: the inevitable conflict that results from the "splits" alluded to in the litany of challenges. Exploring the implications of each of these potential "splits"—whether the divisions be based on gender, race, ethnicity, or age—is beyond the scope of this book or the expertise of its authors. However, we do try to articulate the parallels and divergences between the situation for women and that for racioethnic minorities whenever possible. We believe that to do less would mark our work as partial.

We also see very important points of convergence between the situation for women and the situation for other disadvantaged groups in the work force. Status as a minority, in our view, depends more on the existence and the perception of discrimination than on real numbers or proportion of a whole. This reasoning is consistent with that of Hacker (1951), who defined a minority as "any group of people who because of their physical or cultural characteristics, are singled out from others . . . for differential and unequal treatment, and who therefore regard themselves as objectives of collective discrimination" (p. 60). Accepting this definition leads to the conclusion that despite obvious and important differences between women and racial or ethnic minorities in public relations, the similarities should make research on any of these groups applicable to the other.

We hope readers will keep these parallels in mind. At the same time, we refer you beyond our limited treatment of racial and ethnic minorities in public relations to the first and most impressively comprehensive bibliography of references on diversity relevant to our field: *Multicultural Communications: A Bibliography*. This annotated list of more than 500 references was compiled by Debra A. Miller (1993), who chaired PRSA's Multicultural Affairs Committee and went on to become PRSA's first African American president.

Envisioning the Year 2000

By the time PRSA members met for their annual convention in 1992, the list of challenges facing the profession had developed into an action plan. President Warner unveiled his *Blueprint 2000* in Kansas City. This strategic plan grew out of the vision statement that included as one of seven key points the following reference to the special concerns of PRSA's female and minority members: "By the year 2000, the Public Relations Society of America will be: Composed of members representing the diversity in the profession and society at large."

Many of the goals of *Blueprint 2000* could be considered relevant to women and minorities. For example, the fourth goal referred to fostering and encouraging lifelong public relations education. One of the eight objectives supporting this goal was to "attract quality students to the field of public relations." We believe that women students represent quality—and we are not alone. Professor J. David Pincus of the University of Arkansas commented in the *Ragan Report* (as quoted in "What They're Saying," 1993) that "of our [more than 400] communication majors, about 80 percent are women . . . almost across the board, the strongest people have been the women. And this goes back eight or 10 years" (p. 4).

However, only a single objective designed to help achieve a single goal in PRSA's strategic planning and management document even alluded to diversity. As one way of meeting the goal of building understanding of and support for public relations among PRSA's constituencies, *Blueprint 2000* suggested making multicultural concerns an integral part of PRSA.

Still, PRSA's chief operating officer said he intends to address questions of diversity in the field. Ray Gaulke, quoted ("Q & A," 1993) in the same issue of the *Ragan Report* as Pincus, said: "Issues that PRSA is currently addressing include ethics and the reputation of the profession, multicultural diversity, and the status of women in the field. I plan to focus on those, and others as needed" (p. 3).

Some members of PRSA questioned Gaulke's commitment to women's concerns, however. In August 1994, he told a meeting of the National Capital Chapter that "there's not too much we can do about it," in response to a member's question about PRSA's role in helping close the pay gap between women and men. Although he acknowledged that the association cares about the problem of the glass ceiling, he said that the issue of salary equity is not on PRSA's agenda. He failed to mention that PRSA's Foundation had funded the second stage of the "glass ceiling" research and that the national conference programming would include, for the second year in a row, a special reception for women leaders.

In 1994, the committee adopted a new initiative: studying the problem of sexual harassment for women in the public relations work force. Also in 1994, plans for replicating the original "glass ceiling" study got underway. Although that research has been completed, PRSA's attention to the harassment issues continues. Finally, the committee is preparing a third stage in its longitudinal research on the "glass ceiling" as this book goes to press.

WHAT DO WE MEAN BY "WOMEN"?

The first few pages of this book have bandied about important yet everyday terms such as "women," "woman," "female," "sex," "gender," "feminine," "feminist," and "feminization." Are they synonymous? Do we use them almost interchangeably, to avoid boring the reader by repeating the same key words?

The answer to both questions, in part, is "yes." We read and hear about "sex discrimination" and "gender-based discrimination" in reports of court cases and in conversations. The distinction between these two phrases may have special meaning for feminist or legal scholars, yet everyday language suggests a common understanding of bias against someone because she is a woman. And, in a book that focuses on "women," an overly rigid reliance on nomenclature that allows for little or no substitution of close—if not exactly the same—terms surely would put most readers to sleep. Instead, we want our book to be widely read and understood. More importantly, we hope it spurs its readers to take action to eliminate any discrimination that may characterize public relations today—regardless of what words we use to describe the phenomenon.

The impetus for collective action may lie beneath women's willingness to be lumped together into a single category despite their understanding of the diversity among them. That is, there is enough commonality within the group to create what feminists consider a *standpoint,* or similar way of looking at the world. Such a standpoint does not deny the vast differences among women's experiences; it simply acknowledges that women have enough in common to unite around a set of issues. In this case, the issues involve the glass ceiling in public relations. Women may need to live with the tension between their individual identities and an affiliation with like others: women and men who are concerned about equity in hiring, pay, professional role, promotion, and balancing demands of home and work. Such an "alliance of convenience" is just that, rather than a genuine generalization of essential difference between the sexes.

We believe that a definition of terms makes sense at this point. We are especially interested in how scholars have distinguished between *sex* and *gender.* We even are interested in the distinction between *woman* and *women.* We also are concerned about words or concepts that are *associated with* certain sexes or genders. Thus we will belabor what it means to be (or perceived to be) *feminine* and to be *masculine.* This discussion, in turn, will lead us to the notion of *androgyny.* Androgenous management is much touted in the literature. We hope to clarify its relationship to the management of public relations, given the rapid feminization of our field.

Sex and Gender

One major problem in defining *gender* and *sex* and making a useful distinction between the two is that scholars disagree on exactly what the words mean. Few researchers proposed such concise definitions of *sex* and *gender* as has Wood (1997), in her *Gendered Lives*: "Sex is a designation based on biology, while gender is socially and psychologically constructed" (p. 23). To most other scholars, including the authors you're reading right now, any such precise differentiation between these two complex concepts is hard to come by. Some definitions actually contradict others—and these formulations come from theorists who have devoted their professional careers to this research. The definitions of still other scholars "essentialize," or suggest that all men are basically alike, as are all women, and that these two groups are inherently distinct from each other. Far be it from us to try to resolve this dilemma. Instead, we present these perspectives on the definitional question for your interest and, we hope, your thoughtful ruminations on the larger question: whether sex—or gender—is biologically or socially determined.

Socialization theorists believe that any behavioral differences between women and men are not biological but cultural. They hold that sex roles are a product of *socialization,* or learned behaviors consistent with one's society. Biodeterminists such as Bakan (1966), however, believe that gender dictates behavior. In this view, less widely held today than in the past, gender differentiation based on the reproductive system, secondary sex characteristics, and psychological makeup leads to predictable kinds of behavior on the part of women and men. This view, in turn, has led to women being told they are not competent to handle certain jobs (typically, the well-paid ones) because they are too right-brained, physically weak, poorly coordinated, or subject to pregnancy (Kleiman, 1991).

Gender

To sociologists such as Spence and Helmreich (1978), gender is a composite definition that refers to the biological/physiological characteristics determined by bodily structures, genes, and hormones. Thus superficial anatomical characteristics determine the biological classification of gender.

Kohlberg (1966), by contrast, looked at gender as a three-part product of sex-role acquisition. First, gender serves as an identity whereby we link ourselves to one of two groups: either men or women. Second, gender serves as an organizer whereby we develop a model for our own system of values and behavior, consistent with the reactions of that group. Third, gender is reinforced by imitating the behavior of the same-sex parent with concomitant rewards of attention and praise.

Bem (1976), who has done more research and theorizing in this area than perhaps any other scholar, contended that gender refers to biological functions determined at birth: genitalia, body build, reproductive system, and so forth. Her work led Powell (1988) to conclude that gender is a scheme for categorizing people based on biological differences. This scheme, in turn, becomes a basis for assigning social differences. (It also may determine income. As Benderly, 1987, put it: "Gender comes down to what life revolves around anyway: earning a living" [p. 65].)

For the purposes of this book, we have adopted Bem's notion. We equate gender with biology or physiology. We agree that "gender" involves predetermined physical traits.

Sex and Sex Roles

In contrast, "sex" involves such characteristics as masculinity and femininity—characteristics that lead to the "social differences" alluded to above. For example, certain traits tend to be associated with men and women, such as assertiveness and submissiveness, respectively (Spence & Helmreich, 1980). Sex is a matter of social rather than biological differentiation. We consider it a dependent, rather than an independent, variable. That is, sex is influenced by societal assumptions. We do not see sex as an independent variable, one that determines such factors as job aspirations, commitment to career, or managerial role.

An alternative view enjoying considerable media attention in the decade of the 1990s is held by management consultant Tear (as cited in "Gender Differences," 1990), whose work on gender dynamics has been published in the trade press of public relations. She considered the notion that differences between women and men can be explained by culture or socialization a "myth." Instead, she argued that differences between the sexes emanate from the physiology of the brain:

> One major difference is in the connective tissue between the left (linear, logical) & right (creative, visionary) parts of the brain. The tissue in the female brain is larger, develops earlier. Signals travel thru it faster & more easily. Women think in a synthesized way, blending logic & emotion. Men remain focused on one or the other. (p. 4)

Sex roles frequently are described as "feminine" or "masculine." However, the concept of *sex role* is hard to define (Spence & Helmreich, 1978). At once sex role refers to the positions that men and women should occupy, the relationship between women and men, and the characteristics that distinguish them (Angrist, 1969). These characteristics can describe behavior, personality, abilities, preferences, and so forth. Thus the notion of sex roles encompasses both psychological properties and situationally in-spired behavior.

The literature of sex roles in psychology paints a composite of women as more likely than men to possess characteristics or qualities ideally suited to the practice of public relations. These expressive traits should lead women to practice a model of public relations characterized by two-way communica-tion and an equal concern for both the organization's relevant publics and the organization itself. If supported, this hypothesis should lead us to conclude that women may be more socially responsible practitioners who would in-crease both the professionalism and the effectiveness of our field.

We could find only one study that actually measured masculinity and femininity in public relations and then correlated sex with preference for one approach to public relations over another. Wetherell (1989) found that femininity (whether possessed by women or by men) facilitates the practice of two-way, balanced public relations (a model to be described in greater detail later in this book). The association is a weak one, however.

In actuality, more men than women seem to practice this kind of sym-metrical public relations. Wetherell determined that far more men (and masculine people) than women (or feminine people) are in the managerial role—the role that correlates with the practice of symmetrical communica-tion. She further reasoned that if women even could *imagine* themselves in the managerial rather than the technical role, they would prefer this kind of dialogic communication. She concluded that to actually practice this effec-tive, sophisticated public relations, women must acquire more knowledge of public relations and move up into management. At that point, the whole field would benefit from a more effective and ethical practice.

One more study of public relations students does suggest ethical differ-ences based on respondents' gender. Wakefield (1993) found that 12 times as many female as male students recognized an overriding responsibility to society as a whole. Twice as many male as female students recognized spe-cific responsibilities to the general public. Nearly twice as many women as men recognized specific responsibilities to publics directly affected by a sit-uation. Nearly twice as many male as female students expressed a prefer-ence for situational ethics. From these data, Wakefield concluded that "For whatever reasons, men and women studying public relations look at ethics through different-colored glasses. And neither of them is ideal" (p. 4).

Femininity and Masculinity

At this point, we hope readers are thinking through their own understand-ing of sex and gender—perhaps with a growing realization that there is no *essential* gender or sex. Instead, social and biological influences are working together. To understand this concept, consider the drag queen: a man who dresses in ultrafeminine clothing. The drag queen establishes that gender and femininity are not necessarily linked.

Femininity and masculinity are defined as "attributes and behaviors that distinguish normatively between the sexes in a given society" (Spence & Helmreich, 1980, p. 147). What it means to be considered "feminine" or "masculine" undoubtedly varies by societal culture. The orientation toward femininity or masculinity one adopts is not necessarily what one prefers but what society expects. Concepts of femininity and masculinity may be considered stereotypes within each culture. So we look now at sex-role stereotypes in the United States. We will go on to consider whether these characterizations are helpful or harmful for women in public relations.

Stereotyping allows the brain to set expectations as a way of lending some predictability to life (Shepard, 1985). That's the helpful part. Stereotyping also tends to restrict the people being thus typed into a self-fulfilling mold. Sex-based stereotypes have worked against women in public relations in a number of ways.

At the outset, it seems obvious to us that any discussion based on a duality, such as female/male or men/women, is suspect. Such dualities pit one type against the other, assuming that they are opposites and that one is inherently superior. As Bryant (1984) described it, "There is women's work, and there is men's work—and men's is better" (p. 47). Stereotypes that speak to masculinity and femininity have assigned power and dominance to men and subordination to women. Traditional sex roles for women have cast them as caregivers and nurturers (Frieze, Parsons, Johnson, Ruble, & Zellman, 1978).

The trend toward more women working (including public relations work) from their homes may only reinforce this notion of women nurturing their families (Oakley, 1974; Zimmerman, 1986). However, as it happens, the actual traits of *entrepreneurial* men and women are strikingly similar. Self-confidence, risktaking, and internal locus of control are common to both. As Harvard psychoanalyst Abraham Zaleznik said of all entrepreneurs, "They don't have the normal fear or anxiety mechanisms" (as quoted in Cole, 1989, p. 63). This similarity may help explain why female entrepreneurs in public relations tend to be so successful (as we will see in Chapter 4).

As in the literature of entrepreneurship, the terms *masculinity* and *femininity* tend to be discussed in terms of *positive* traits and behaviors, such as self-confidence of willingness to take risks (Bem, 1976). However, not all feminine or masculine traits can be considered positive. The list associated with men and women is lengthy. Spence and Helmreich (1978) explored the following undesirable traits in their research. Characteristics associated with masculinity include boastful, egotistical, greedy, hostile, autocratic, opinionated, and opportunistic. Negative characteristics associated with femininity include weak, shy, submissive, fearful, high strung, inhibited, moody, whiny, complaining, fault finding, and nagging.

But what of the *positive* feminine traits that have special relevance to public relations? "Cooperative" figures prominently (e.g., J. B. Miller, 1976; Theobold, 1967; Bakan, 1966; Berryman-Fink, 1985; Sargent, 1981). Several corporate executives have cited sensitivity and perceptiveness; at least one alluded to high ethical behavior. The literature also contains references to women's intuition or instincts (Bates, 1983), and that, in turn, brings us back to sensitivity:

> Public relations is a highly intuitive business. The ability to recognize what sort of behavior brings about what kind of response is a talent inborn in little girls and developed to a high degree of sensitivity by the time they are through their teens. It's an invaluable asset in public relations. (Smith, 1968, p. 26)

Some scholars have suggested that the most effective public relations grows out of a worldview that is feminine (J. Grunig, 1992). That is, public relations that is practiced as balanced, two-way communication between an organization and its stakeholder groups stands to make the greatest contribution to organizational effectiveness. They see public relations that is practiced in a more persuasive, domineering, and unbalanced way as rooted in masculinity (Kanter, 1977; Kramarae, Schultz, & O'Barr, 1984). These practices may well be rooted in the values held by women and men (L. Grunig, Toth, & Hon, 1999).

Wetherell (1989) distilled a large body of knowledge from psychology, sociology, and anthropology and arrived at the understanding that the symmetrical and asymmetrical worldviews approximate the orientations attributed to men and women: "male agency/instrumentality (a self-centered orientation concerned with achieving one's ends) and female communion/expressiveness (an others-centered orientation that seeks the good of all and is characterized by cooperation)" (pp. 38–39).

Juxtaposing these two approaches to public relations—symmetrical, or the search for understanding and compromise, and asymmetrical, the more manipulative—may offer great promise for empowering public relations practitioners, whether they are men or women. Why?

One key element of the two-way symmetrical model of public relations is the value it places on resolving conflict between the organization and its publics. Negotiation often helps in the process of reconciling these competing demands. In their argument for the superiority of the feminine style of negotiation for groups that must maintain an ongoing relationship, Greenhalgh and Gilkey (1986) wrote:

> Negotiation skills are vital as organizations take new forms, such as matrix management, increasingly complex structures, team-centered work forces, and Japanese-style management. All these innovations emphasize agreement and coordination between people, which in turn call for effective negotiation skills. (p. 146)

Another key dimension associated with a feminine management style has to do with *relationship* building. According to Reif, Newstrom, and Monczka (1978), "The one difference that biologists, psychologists, social psychologists, and sociologists all seem to agree on is women's greater concern for relationships" (p. 13). Knowles and Moore (1970), too, concluded from their exhaustive review of the literature that "about the only testable difference between men and women seems to be women's greater ability in interpersonal relationships" (p. 72).

However, focusing solely on individual skills or traits—feminine or masculine—is unlikely to resolve many of the problems inherent in sexism in the work place. Hennig and Jardim (1977) took that approach in their landmark book, *The Managerial Woman*. In essence, they blamed gender inequality in the work place on attributes of individual workers that could be labeled "masculine" or "feminine." A decade later, Blum and Smith (1988) questioned the validity of this approach. They said the problem of discrimination exists within the structure of the organization. As a result, its solution is out of any individual's control.

Others question whether maleness—rather than either femaleness or the structure of contemporary corporations—is at the root of the problem for women who work outside the home. Shapiro (1990) put it this way: "Women, after all, are not a big problem. Our society does not suffer from burdensome amounts of empathy and altruism, or a plague of nurturance" (p. 62).

Still, a modest industry has grown up around the notion of women learning to recognize their own behavior that perpetuates negative sex stereotypes. One owner of a consulting firm in marketing and advertising regularly holds seminars that warn against body language and a mentality that shows ignorance of male culture. Stone (as cited in Humphrey, 1990) cautioned women against such behaviors as trying to be special, taking things personally, and acting timid.

Older women, in particular, may be convinced from having read the literature of the 1970s that they must accommodate the male model, as Lannon (1977) put it, to succeed. Early in that decade, Hennig (1971) studied 100 female executives who attributed their success to identifying with the masculine stereotype in their first managerial positions. Schein (1975) agreed that, given the existing climate in organizations, accepting stereotypical male characteristics would be necessary for ambitious women in management. Block (1973) expressed the same thought another way: "Among those women who do elect to enter the occupational arena, advancement in status is more likely to be achieved by women who diverge from the traditional feminine sex role stereotype" (p. 525). The result was the ubiquitous training course that taught women to think, act, and even dress like men (remember those floppy silk bow ties for women?).

Women's emulating the male model comes with a tremendous price. Scholars such as Block (1973) and Riger and Galligan (1980) described the costs of women suppressing their communal traits and exaggerating the aggressiveness inherent in what is considered masculine management. These women suffer physical and mental consequences. Moreover, women who adopt the male model experience no fewer negative consequences at work. In other words, this approach is fruitless for women anyway. Thus we would not be overstating the case to conclude that it is bad for women. By the end of the 1970s, Riger and Galligan also had determined that the efficacy of the traditional male model had come into question and that characteristics associated with the traditional female model actually might prove more effective at work. In other words, it's bad for business, too.

So we consider a different perspective. Must women adopt masculine characteristics (aggressiveness is mentioned most often) to succeed? As an alternative, Loden (1985) suggested accentuating the positive aspects of what is considered feminine in this country. What she called "feminine leadership" takes advantage of the range of women's talents and abilities. Among those traits she included maintaining close personal relationships; considering feelings in decision making; and putting the long-term health of the organization above one's own short-term, personal advancement.

Loden also considered women superior communicators. This belief is widely held (e.g., Frieze et al., 1978) but largely unsubstantiated in the scholarly literature. You may believe that the stereotype of women excelling at written and oral communication can benefit female public relations practitioners. However, Lott (1981) concluded that even labeling behaviors as "feminine" or "masculine" serves only to reinforce the gendering of behavior. We have to agree. A stereotype is a stereotype. As Yamashita (1992) found in her study of Asian American practitioners, even a positive stereotype tends to pigeonhole and dehumanizes the person being thus labeled.

We end this section of our discussion of masculinity and femininity with more musings than a true conclusion. We do believe that gender and sex-role orientation are not the same or interchangeable. As a result, much confusion surrounds any discussion of "women and public relations." When we think about women, are we really talking about gender, which we consider biological, or a constellation of socially determined sex roles, which encompass stereotypical qualities associated either with femininity or masculinity?

We know that not all people biologically classified as "women" act alike. People of either gender may have feminine characteristics. We value the traits associated with femininity, but of course not all women exhibit female characteristics or are "feminine." Not all men act "masculine," and not all traits considered masculine are antithetical to feminism. More important, we are not convinced that the literature establishes that women are better suited to managing public relations programs than are men.

We are encouraged to know, though, that writers in both the trade and the scholarly press acknowledge what may be women's unique attributes or abilities to help their organizations achieve their missions. This is increasingly important at a time of changing demographics in the work force and the concomitant requirements of our service economy and competition from abroad. More and more women are working outside the home, and the demands of the work place have changed right long with the characteristics of today's employee. As the prescient social psychologist Jessie Bernard (1976) explained years ago, "In the industrial age, the traits associated with maleness were called for; but in the post-industrial or cybernetic age, the traits associated with femaleness as we know it today will be" (p. 12). At the very least, we emphasize that women are not unqualified or underqualified to excel in public relations management by virtue of their gender or their sex-role socialization.

Perhaps most important, sifting through literally hundreds of studies on gender and sex roles has convinced us that there is more variation within one gender than there is between men and women. For just a glimpse of the depth of this research, see Bakan (1966), Jacklin and Maccoby (1976), Deaux (1976), Cox (1976), Bernard (1976), Spence and Helmreich (1978), Benderly (1987), and Wetherell (1989). These studies show that most hypothesized distinctions between masculinity and femininity are either unsupported or weakly supported. At most, the evidence is equivocal. Meta-analysis of the research also belies what may well be a false dichotomy between the cultural notions of masculinity and femininity.

Finally, differences that do exist between men and women tend to offset each other (Powell, 1988).

Thus we do not embrace a "no differences" approach wholeheartedly. Such a position is well intentioned but faulty. As Bernard (1976) explained it, denying any sex differences "implies that in order to prove themselves worthy, women must prove themselves no different from men. We're just like you, see?" (p. 13). We are more persuaded by Loden's (1986) and Garen's (1982) warning against confusing equality with sameness.

If anything, then, we concur with Yelsma and Brown (1985), who found that sex-role orientation is a more significant predictor of communication behavior than is biological sex or what we have agreed to call "gender." Matteson, J. F. McMahan, and M. McMahan (1974) came to a similar conclusion in their study of male and female supervisors: Because they found few significant differences in supervisory style, they theorized that female/male differences may result more from role than gender. Perhaps Camden and Witt (1983) said it best:

> Sex per se is not an effective variable in understanding sex-role behavior. . . . True insight into sex-role behavior requires a use of psychological sex rather than biological sex as an independent variable [because] socialization processes may be so varied that gender uniformity for social roles is no longer present. (p. 265)

Bear in mind that despite this rich body of relevant literature, many of the earliest studies of gender, sex orientation, and management or communication are methodologically flawed. We have concentrated on contemporary rather than classic references largely because research conducted before the 1960s made assertions about women but often failed to include women in the population studied (Caplan, 1985; Carlson, 1985).

The Promise of Androgyny

Androgenous management was touted as the style for the 1980s. Garen (1982) described it as a "male/female approach . . . attuned to the new worker, new environment, and new realities of the 1980s" (p. 42). Does this model continue to hold promise for public relations management as we approach the 21st century?

To answer, begin by recalling that we already have challenged the validity of any dichotomy or bipolar construct between femininity and masculinity. As early as 1973, Constantinople noted that this dualism had evolved from operationalizations with no theoretical foundation. The next year, Bem (1974) introduced a new stream of psychological research with her theory of psychological androgyny. She argued that masculinity and femininity are constructs that vary independently of each other rather than being opposite ends of a single construct, as had been believed earlier.

Psychological androgyny, according to Bem, is a state of interaction or of being both masculine and feminine. The androgynous manager could respond to a situation with great flexibility, presumably with high levels of either (masculine) independence or (feminine) nurturance, depending on what the situation calls for (Bem, 1977). Bem's analysis of androgyny, like most research on sex and gender, has been critiqued extensively on both operational and conceptual grounds (e.g., Spence & Helmreich, 1978; Locksley & Colten, 1979; Pedhazur & Tetenbaum, 1979). However, we see much potential for public relations in this program of research.

Our reasoning is based on two main factors. First, we know that numerous researchers (reviewed in Wetherell, 1989) have concluded that men and women tend to manage alike—that there is no real masculine or feminine management model. Second, effective management does not rely exclusively on traits associated with femininity or with masculinity. Instead, today's business environment requires both the task orientation associated with men and the others-centered, people-focused orientation associated with women. Such behavioral flexibility combines skills so that the organization can use the multifaceted potential of all of its members. As White, DeSanctis, and Crino (1981) put it, "The two sexes can function to complement each other without in any way modifying their basic behavioral style" (p. 551). Perhaps most important, androgyny goes beyond being "trendy" to reject any polarized masculine–feminine dichotomy.

Our final answer to why androgynous management offers potential for an increasingly feminized public relations comes from the work of Eisler (1987), who predicted that the social structures of the future will be based more on linking than on ranking. If Eisler is correct, then we will not be forcing a choice between the masculine and the feminine or between the managerial and the technical in our field. Instead, institutions Eisler called "heterarchic" (rather than hierarchical) will encourage diversity. As a consequence, Eisler concluded, "The roles of both men and women will be far less rigid, allowing the entire human species a maximum of developmental flexibility" (p. 200).

Women and Woman

The title of this book refers to "women" in public relations. We hesitate to use the plural word, however. The distinction between the singular and plural forms is not a specious one. Every time we write the word "women," we may be suggesting a single orientation or a false consensus. The styles, concerns, and experiences of individual women are as varied as the mind may imagine. We do not want to perpetuate the "alpha bias" inherent in much of the literature. *Alpha bias* occurs when research treats members of any minority group as more homogenous than members of the dominant group. As Hare-Mustin and Maracek (1988) pointed out, "Men are viewed as individuals, but women are viewed as women" (p. 459).

This is not to deny that general statements can be made about women's experiences in public relations. Instead, we hope that the patterns emerging from our original research and from our search of the relevant literature are true to our own feelings and experiences and those of the women we chronicle here. We trust the our readers, too, may see themselves in the stories these women tell.

One of the major goals of feminist scholarship is to distill from women's immensely varied experiences certain patterns that help to legitimate the existence of critical issues and to point toward a resolution of those issues. In other words, by describing and explaining what amounts to a social history of the lives of women practicing public relations, we are doing what PRSA's Task Force on Women suggested early on: We are making an issue out of sex discrimination in our field. Rather than getting hopelessly bogged down in anecdotal and statistical information that all indicates such gender bias, we also trust that we can point toward a transformation of our field for its growing number of women.

To do so, we try in this book to make meaning out of women's experiences in public relations—assuming diversity among their perspectives rather than universalizing those perspectives. As one author (L. Grunig, 1988), said before, there is no "we" of feminism—and thus no "master theory" of feminism. So, no solution—not even any single perspective on the problem—provides *the* answer to the "woman question(s)," as Tong (1989) reminded us.

Instead, we need to respect the preferences that become reflected in the postmodern career choices of individual women. Despite our emphasis on the importance of the management role for public relations, we do not denigrate or trivialize women who choose to remain technicians. In fact, we distrust this dichotomous concept of technician versus manager—acknowledging that although the roles typology helps us understand, describe, and then teach about public relations, the work women do in public relations actually transcends such facile categorization. We do not intend to devalue any of the strategies that women may adopt to help them succeed—or even to survive—at work.

In the next chapter you will be introduced to three feminist perspectives that suggest either working within the system for slow but steady progress or radically transforming that system. Once again, we seem to be dealing with a (false) dichotomy between the liberal and the radical feminist approaches. However, as Chapter 2 points out, what we find most useful is a synthesis of these two rather than a choice between them.

Based on what we have read and what our research results tell us, we have our own ideas on which perspective offers potential for most women in public relations. Once again, though, we celebrate the efforts of all women in the field who have entered what once was a masculine domain, who have practiced their craft so effectively there, and who in many cases have advanced despite the inordinate roadblocks they faced. It would be presumptuous to determine that only certain solutions would have worked for all these women or, for that matter, all practitioners of public relations.

Finally, the ontological and epistemological status of "women" has become a pivotal issue in the development of feminism. Feminist scholars such as Forsythe (1998) have argued that "women" represents a category of identity, a heuristic device for inquiring into the dimensions of power that characterize modern societies around the world. Working from the Rockefeller Institute's Center for Women in Government, Forsythe's historical analysis of so-called women's movements explored the shift in focus from "women's" subordination to "women's" knowledge and power. This standpoint, consistent with that of our book, offers a viable perspective from which to interpret the past and present and to imagine the future.

Chapter Two

Understanding the Issues

This book addresses the phenomenon of gender and the public relations industry. Although women are featured in the title of our book, we look at both women and men in public relations and their response to the increasing number of women entering public relations and organizational communication. In this chapter, we introduce a handful of problems women typically encounter as well as the accompanying denial of gender bias that persists. We concentrate on what we consider to be one of the most pervasive and insidious of these issues: the pay gap between men and women. We do not restrict our discussion to the field of public relations. However, in this chapter we also begin to explicate the promise that the feminization of any field may hold. We conclude with several perspectives on feminism that may enlighten this exploration of women's opportunities.

Steadily, women have entered the work force of the United States. The Bureau of Labor Statistics predicted that women would represent almost 48% of the work force by the year 2000, an increase of 8 percentage points since 1976. The white male share of the labor force would drop to 39.4% by 2000, with black, Hispanic, Asian, and other "minority" males completing the total (Solomon, 1990).

Women have entered many professions. Note that women have not become the majority in all professions—just the majority in terms of the three groups women, white men, and minority men. In 1986, women held the majority of all professional jobs in the United States. Naturally, women increasingly entered the public relations profession as well (Winkleman, 1986). So why should there be a book specifically about women in public relations?

What interested us was the short amount of time in which women have become the majority in public relations. Women accounted for more than half of all public relations practitioners in less than a generation, according to demographers Barbara Reskin and Patricia Roos (1990). Reskin and Roos listed public relations as one of the occupations in the 1970s to show a "disproportionate" increase in female workers, "during a decade in which their advancement into most male occupations was modest at best ... " (p. 6). As university professors, we have seen our classrooms attracting an equal number of men and women and then suddenly become more than 80% female in the 1990s (see also Becker, 1990). We believe that our students should understand what their gender will mean for them if they choose to do public relations work.

There were already explanations in print on why women have been welcomed into public relations. Donato (1990) provided seven reasons: the sex-specific demand for women, women as a "better buy," new publics, female-intensive industries, affirmative action, gender ideology, and women's attraction to public relations.

The *sex-specific demand* for women refers to the failure of the occupation of public relations to attract men after 1970. Employers increasingly turned to women to fill new jobs. Donato (1990) made the point that the real earnings of male public relations practitioners declined during the 1970–1980 decade: "In 1970, male public relations specialists averaged 40 percent more than the mean earnings for all male workers. In 1980, they averaged only 26 percent more" (p. 134).

Women as a *"better buy"* refers to the surplus of women in entry-level public relations jobs and their subsequent segregation into technical positions, whereas men were more likely to advance into higher paying managerial jobs (Broom & Dozier, 1986). Because there was an overrepresentation of women in technical positions, these women provided a cheaper labor supply than did men.

New publics refers to the need for public relations to address the emerging groups of women who now own a substantial portion of the country's wealth, do the majority of the shopping for the family, and have established voting strength. That is, women have come to represent a "commercial value" (Donato, 1990, p. 135) that they had not previously offered to business and society.

Female-intensive industries such as banks, hospitals, and educational institutions increased further the number of women in public relations, according to Donato (1990), because these fields were particularly receptive to employing women. They also were more attractive to women because they "offered flexible hours and fewer sexist barriers than the corporate world" (p. 135).

Repeating Donato's reasoning that female-intensive industries were more welcoming and attractive to women because of better-than-average pay, career adaptability, and fewer barriers, *Working Mother* recently selected public relations as among the 10 hottest careers. Andrea Pace, vice president of national media relations at Ketchum Public Relations in New York City, pictured on the cover of the April 1998 issue of *Working Mother*, said that the advantages of working in a public relations agency were "flexibility and no glass ceiling" (as quoted in Cheney, 1998, p. 28).

Affirmative action guidelines explain some of the hiring of women into public relations. In the 1970s, for the first time, employers faced federal government pressure to hire and promote women into professional and managerial jobs. In 1978, *Business Week* described public relations as "the velvet ghetto" of affirmative action:

> When is affirmative action not so affirmative? When companies load their public relations departments with women to compensate for their scarcity in other professional or managerial capacities that usually lead more directly to top management. . . . ("PR," p. 122)

Gender ideology refers to the view on the part of business and society that public relations is "emotional labor" and therefore suitable for women (Donato, 1990, p. 139). Public relations people are called on to explain the actions of their employers, to listen to complaints, and to raise money—all activities that require social skills that employers believe women are more likely than men to have. Art Buchwald (1992) made fun of this viewpoint in a column about women in public relations:

> Most ex's have not figured out how to correct course in a dismal economic era. But they have been smart enough to keep their distance from any bad news that could affect management. They are doing this by appointing women as their chief spokesperson. It sounds sexist to me, I said. Probably, according to one recruiter. But, when a woman is sent out in front of the cameras to announce that her firm just lost the farm, the audience thinks of her as their mother or girlfriend. Instead of focusing on the bad news, they're all asking, what's a nice girl like her doing with a company like this? (p. A10)

Finally, Donato (1990) reasoned that women increasingly are *attracted* to public relations because the field offers them good opportunities—competitive if not more competitive than other accessible occupations. Donato explained: "Although women in public relations earned only 60 percent of what men did in 1980, the occupation paid better than the average female job" (p. 141).

INTRODUCTION TO THE ISSUES

Taken together, these explanations suggest several issues for women and men in public relations. Two of the most obvious of these issues are the *salary disparity* that can be attributed to gender alone and the potentially *declining status* of the public relations field. We (Wright, L. Grunig, Springston, & Toth, 1991) found, based on a sample of more than 1,000 members of the PRSA, that a statistically significant degree of salary disparity between men and women appears after the fifth year at work. Lesly (1988) predicted that the increasing number of women in public relations would have consequences on the perceived value of the field itself:

> The impact of a largely feminine public relations field will have such consequences as creating the image of public relations as a "soft" rather than "heavy-hitting top" management function, lowering professional aspirations because women want functional (meaning technical) rather than policy-making roles and lowered income levels because fields that become "female" experience such a loss. (p. 5)

Our book substantiates Donato's (1990) explanations of why women have moved quickly and in disproportionate numbers into the public relations field. However, our primary focus is on what these women are experiencing as public relations professionals. Some of the other issues we'll discuss include the perceptions that women have created an image of public relations as a "soft" part of the management function (Lesly, 1988); that women have lower career aspirations than men (DeRosa & Wilcox, 1989); and that the growing presence of women has led to encroachment on the function of public relations by professionals in marketing, law, human resources, or engineering (Lauzen, 1990a, 1992). We also take up the issues of hiring, training, promotion, the glass ceiling, sexual harassment, breadth of public relations roles, and work-place restrictions. Finally, we'll discuss the challenge to the field itself by some who wish to integrate public relations and marketing and the gendered nature of this challenge. We begin, however, with an exploration of the differential in compensation women typically experience.

THE PAY GAP

The pay differential between men and women may have been mentioned first in the book of Leviticus (27:3–4). God told Moses that the work of women was worth three-fifths the pay of men, or 30 shekels of silver versus

50. Considerably more recently, Kaufman and Richardson (1982) concluded that women historically have held lower-status positions than have men. Paying lower wages to women was justified by assumptions that they were working for "pin money," as in the New England textile mills of the early 1800s. By the mid-19th century, women earned about half of men's pay for comparable work. Women's earnings were considered part of the larger family wage.

Whenever we discuss issues such as the salary relevant to women and public relations, we do so acknowledging that similar issues face most women working in the United States. Certainly, the problem of the pay gap is pervasive. So is the existence of the glass ceiling that prevents women's advancement into managerial positions in their organizations. However, there are dissimilarities between all women in the work force and women in public relations. For example, women entering public relations have earned a better average wage than women entering all-female occupations (Donato, 1990). Women coming into public relations have done so in such a dramatic fashion that they have resegregated the occupation from a male majority to a female majority (Reskin & Roos, 1990). In this chapter we provide a general description of findings on women and work—their placement, their educational preparation, their pay, their advancement opportunities, and theoretical explanations—before we examine the situation specifically for women in public relations in later chapters.

Mass media appraisals of women and work persist in discussing the traditional model of men in the labor force and women staying at home. They dwell on women who work outside the home—and the stress those women typically experience. But women succeed despite the odds. "Superwomen" can do it all. For example, The Wall Street Journal Marketplace section (Lublin, 1997) did a cover story on 44-year-old Janet M. Clarke, Cox Communications outside board director, titled "How One Woman Manages in World of Male Directors." Clarke was depicted as winning a chair in the boardroom, which remains for women "an arduous task" (p. B1). Her approach is "to try and act like one of the guys in Cox's otherwise all male boardroom" (p. B1). She "rebels against sex-role stereotyping," citing a lost directorship because she was flippant when asked if she planned to have children. She replied: "I'm going to be a stepgrandmother in the fall. Should I bring him or her to a board meeting?" (p. B1).

Clarke was described as a hoped-for appointee to assist with Cox's expansion into new technologies such as the Internet, as having sports knowhow from playing college ice hockey, and as a ruddy-faced fast talker with an athlete's lithe build (Lublin, 1997, p. B1). Her challenge, according to the reporter, was to "navigate the fine line between being a hardball businesswoman and a women's advocate" (p. B7).

Such portraits may sell newspapers. However, other issues that seem more important to us rarely get covered. These neglected stories concern why there is a gender gap in wages and why women work in sex-segregated occupations. We are especially interested in exploring the theories that have attempted to explain women's roles in the U.S. labor force. We have labeled these theories human capital, sex-segregation/systems analysis, organizational and social models of the work force, and discrimination. We will discuss each theory in turn. First, though, we will provide baseline data to set the stage.

Women in the Work Force: Findings from Diverse Studies

That substantial numbers of women are in the U.S. work force to stay should be of little news. Demographers have told us that by the year 2000, "81 percent of 'prime working age' women will be employed, compared with 93 percent of similar men" (Fullerton, 1987). Married women, especially those with children, have represented a major source of growth in women's labor-force participation; 51% of the women with children younger than age 3 were working by 1986 (Reskin & Roos, 1990). The U.S. Department of Labor, Women's Bureau, forecasted that by 2000 women's share of the work force would reach 47.3%, up from 40.5% of all workers in 1976 aged 16 and over (as cited in Miller, 1991, p. 8).

Although we hope employers are preparing for the eventual numerical parity of women and men in the work place, the facts about female workers today indicate that women exist and work in a society that devalues their talents and contributions. Two-thirds of all American women who work outside their homes for pay enter traditionally female fields (Sidel, 1986). To some, this statistic represents a disappointing result of our society's supposed interest in the status of women. At the same time, the number of women entering what many consider the more prestigious professions has increased.

Interestingly, women who hold white-collar jobs are educationally better qualified than are their male counterparts. Mason (1988) reported that barely half of all white males holding white-collar jobs in this country have completed 4 years of high school, whereas three-fourths of all women have done so. Even so, women who enter the traditionally male professions stand to earn about three-fifths of what men earn there. The wage gap between women and men is far greater for those in white-collar jobs than for hourly workers (Rigdon, 1993).

In 1997, the Bureau of Labor Statistics reported that the median weekly earnings of full-time working women were just under 75% of the men's median wage, down from 77% in 1993—the peak at which women made up ground against men's full-time wages (as cited in Lewin, 1997a). Lewin (1997a) reported that salaries of the youngest working women—those between the ages of 16 and 24—come closest to men's. These young women earn more than 90% of the wages of full-time male workers their own age. Midcareer women earn about 75% and women over 55 earn about 65% of the salary of their male peers.

How should one regard statistics like these? Is the glass half-full or half-empty? Karlyn Keene of the American Enterprise Institute, a conservative think tank, warned against negativity. She said: "If you continue to see yourself as a society that's not doing well by women, the implication is that it could become a self-fulfilling prophecy" (as quoted in Nasar, 1992b, p. G3).

However, many economists describe a complicated social and political landscape that works against wage parity. They suggest that a drop in wage parity may result from welfare overhaul (Lewin, 1997b, p. A12). Heidi Hartman, director of the Institute for Women's Policy Research in Washington, concluded that "women are losing out because more of them are moving into the losing category of lower skilled workers than into the winning categories of highly skilled workers" (as quoted in Lewin, 1997b, p. A12).

The Equal Pay Act, now more than 35 years old, was intended to equalize any such disparities between female and male workers. However, at least nine times since the act was passed in 1963, the salary gap actually has widened from one year to the next (Rigdon, 1993). Turk (1992), a public relations scholar and dean, agreed that the passage of equal employment legislation in general has not overcome discrimination in the work place. She cited data from the velvet ghetto studies (Cline et al., 1986; Toth & Cline, 1989a) in public relations as evidence confirming sex structuring in her field.

This kind of discrepancy makes a lie of headlines that suggest, for example that "women, blacks dominate work force" (Doig, 1992). The lead of that news story may be on target, "It's not your father's work force anymore" (p. D1), but the fact that more women and people of color than ever before have gone to work for pay in this country does not necessarily lead to their "domination" of the work force.

Although the gendered pay gap across an amalgam of jobs ranging from the lowest to the highest in status has decreased overall in recent years, this can be attributed primarily to the fact that men's wages have fallen, not to the fact that women's wages have risen. Rigdon (1993) reported that the Economic Policy Institute calculated that between 1979 and 1992 men's median hourly pay fell $1.84 an hour to $11.03—based on

1992 dollars. By contrast, women's median hourly wages increased 31 cents to $8.42, again based on 1992 dollars.

Women at Thirtysomething

A study conducted by the U.S. Department of Education (Adelman, 1991) found that U.S. women are among the best educated in the world. We have known for some time that women generally are better educated than men who hold similar jobs (Mason, 1988). Let's take a hard look at how this tremendous resource is being exploited—or squandered—in the job market.

Adelman (1991) initiated his report on "Women at Thirtysomething" with the revelation that women not only have achieved equality of education with men but have surpassed men in academic achievement all along the line. Shanker (1991–1992), then president of the American Federation of Teachers, reacted to this finding of the "Thirtysomething" study with shock. Why? Because, in his words, employers "continue to pay women less than men even when they are doing the same jobs and when the men are less qualified" (p. 5).

But do Adelman's findings, Shanker's outraged contentions, and even earlier scholarly studies (e.g., Mason, 1988) hold up across all occupations in which women find themselves laboring? The answer is a qualified yes. Yes, in almost every instance. In a few fields, such as chemistry and computer programming, women actually earn more than their male counterparts. Other occupations—including auto mechanics, data entry, and registered nursing—pay women and men roughly equivalent salaries. But, in most careers, men's pay surpasses women's—ranging on average from 15% more in pharmacy to 77% more in architecture (Shanker, 1991–1992).

Shanker (1991–1992) branded this system of differential rewards not only unjustified but stupid. He explained that employers, who complain about lagging productivity and the serious shortage of math and science graduates in the United States, still treat women—a class of workers who are in many cases better trained and more highly motivated—worse than their less-qualified male counterparts. Shanker concluded that "if employers wanted talented and dedicated workers, they'd better stop talking about it and start rewarding merit" (p. 5).

One talented woman, the graduate of an Eastern women's college who grew up believing that a self-confident, competent woman could accomplish whatever a man could, reviewed the history of women's entry into the paid labor force (Mason, 1988). Her goal was to understand the forces that shape women's lives in contemporary times, since she discovered early on that her childhood assumptions were largely ill founded. She concluded that the growing equality for women in the United States works well for our economy but not for women. The book that resulted is aptly titled *The Equality Trap: Why Working Women Shouldn't Be Treated like Men.*

Mason (1988) began her historical review with the metaphor of women as "the new immigrants," usurping the role of generations of aliens who in earlier years might have dug for iron ore and coal. In today's information age, they process paper. Since true new immigrants often lack the requisite language skills, they cannot compete with women for these jobs.

At the same time women are "lured," in Mason's (1988) terminology, into the work place at low wages. Why? This country's egalitarian ideal glorifies work even in its meanest forms, and it looks askance at those who expect special treatment. Thus Mason argued that it is advantageous for employers and the government to treat women as they treat men even though this egalitarian arrangement does not work well when women have children.

Mason (1988) further explained that mothers who work outside the home require costly programs that include maternity leave, children's sick leave, flexible hours, and child care. (Others might add elder care for the legions of women increasingly responsible for their aging parents or in-laws, regardless of whether they themselves are mothers.) Mason concluded that "it costs little or nothing to hire a woman rather than a man as long as the woman does the same job as a man and asks for no special consideration" (p. 16).

Of course, one might argue that women often earn less than men because they seek and accept jobs in the low-paying occupations that have attracted women in recent decades. We know, for example, that clerical work and library science have become female-intensive. However, in his "Thirty-something" study Adelman (1991) compared men and women with near-identical educational backgrounds and the same number of years on the job. He still found significant differences in their pay. Shanker (1991–1992) called this pay gap "disgraceful"—citing men who majored in foreign languages earning 54% more than women who did and (closer to home for the president of a teachers' union) men who majored in education earning 26% more than the women in that discipline.

The massive "Thirtysomething" study (Adelman, 1991), then, sets the stage well in this chapter for exploring women's issues at work. Key findings of this national research effort, which followed the work history of about 26,000 members of the high school class of 1972, include these:

- Young women in high school achieved at a higher level than young men, and not because they chose "easy" classes. Direct comparisons between male and female students studying math and science, for example, showed that women on average did significantly better.
- Parents had higher ambitions for their sons than for their daughters. Their expectations seemed to be reflected in the young women's expression of lower aspirations for themselves. Even so, in 1972 a higher percentage of women than men enrolled in college directly after high school. Women also received a higher percentage of scholarships.
- Regardless of their field, these women were more successful academically than their male colleagues in college. In fact, women in non-traditional fields for them (science, engineering, and business) fared especially well by comparison.
- Perhaps as a result of this academic success, the young women revised their educational aspirations upward. A greater proportion of female than male graduates looked forward to earning advanced degrees, and those women who actually enrolled in graduate school did significantly better (44% had a grade-point average of A– or higher, compared with 35% of the men).

Of course, for most people labor—not study—is life. The story of this thirtysomething generation does not end in graduate school but in the work force. Adelman's (1991) study found that a greater percentage of women than men became both unemployed and underemployed. Women's earnings were significantly lower. In 1985, women with a bachelor's degree who participated in the study earned on average $18,670; men with a comparable degree typically earned $27,606.

Predictably, such findings rarely are accepted with equanimity. They become controversial—fueling much reflection and debate among educators, government bureaucrats, politicians, parents, students, and workers (female and male alike). A single article in one of the nation's leading newspapers (Jordan, 1992) described the typical reactions to a series of educational reports that echoed the "Thirtysomething" research. The studies—all of which found gender bias in tests, textbooks, and teaching practices— were funded, conducted, or endorsed by agencies that included the U.S. Department of Education, the American Association of University Women (AAUW), the National Coalition of Girls' Schools, the U.S. Department of Labor, and Wellesley College's Center for Research on Women, as well as by university professors unaligned with any organized group.

Jordan (1992) sifted through reactions that ranged from disappoint-

ment to denial. She quoted the president of the association that commissioned the most comprehensive report, Sharon Schuster of the AAUW, as
saying that although bias in education is no longer blatant, "[girls] experience it on a daily basis" (p. Al). Jordan juxtaposed this quote with the remarks of Diane S. Ravitch, then assistant secretary for educational research
and improvement in the U.S. Department of Education: "You have to look
at the larger context, at all the great strides women have made" (p. Al).

The front-page article in *The Washington Post* continued with the
also-predictable "battle of the statistics." Ravitch, for example, countered
statistics on lagging pay for women compared with men and with women's
underrepresentation in certain professional fields with her department's
own numbers. She cited the rapidly increasing number of women who are
entering the fields of law and medicine. The article (Jordan, 1992) concluded with a telling quote from Susan McGee Bailey, who directed
Wellesley's research center:

> "I think you can look at any situation and see the progress or see the way we
> have to go. But I think it's dangerous to say that because one-third of our med-
> ical students are now women, the struggle for gender equality is over. There is
> a great deal more to be done." (p. A8)

Any distinctions we make among women in different career fields—
such as law, medicine, or public relations—obviously are arbitrary. They
provide for neat categorization but may, in fact, disguise other, more useful
taxonomies of women who work for pay. Mason (1988) suggested we consider the dichotomy between those who live to work and those who work
to live. The former, she explained, include women who tackle male-
dominated professions such as public relations management. The latter include the majority of women who are flooding the more traditionally pink-
collar ghettos of, say, elementary education or the secretarial pool. For
these women, work represents an economic necessity (Nieva & Gutek,
1981). In fact, for more than 15 years the sole household wage earner in
20% of all American families with children has been a woman (U.S. Department of Commerce, 1984).

Mason (1988) also distinguished between entry-level and older, or re-
entry, workers and between women who work part time and those who
work full time. Most comparisons for the earnings of women and men fail
to account for part-time workers. Since more women than men are part-
timers, and since part-time work usually pays less than full-time work, this
kind of comparison would accentuate the wage gap.

Less important than any one system of categorization of women workers we may choose is not lumping all women together. Working women in the groups described above, and more, undoubtedly experience very different problems and have equally different opportunities and rewards. As we pointed out in Chapter 1, their situations, in turn, demand different solutions.

EXPLAINING THE PROBLEMS

Mason's (1988) observation that it is advantageous to employers and the government to treat women as they treat men, even though this egalitarian arrangement does not work well when women have children, represents one theoretical explanation for the wage and advancement gender gaps experienced in our society. We turn now to other theoretical perspectives on pay and advancement that scholars and other authors have proposed. In this section, we discuss several types of theories, the points of agreement between them, and their points of distinction.

Human Capital

Human capital theorists have sought to explain the differences between men and women's wages and opportunities in the labor market on the basis of productivity variables. That is, if women earn less than men it is because women have invested less in on-the-job-training or educational preparation, or have less work continuity, and therefore have less human capital to invest in the labor market. Paglin and Rufolo (1990) described this approach as follows:

> The human capital model is based on the insight that investments in human beings produce an intangible form of capital that is significant in analyzing production. Differences in the amount of a person's human capital explain many of the commonly observed differences in both productivity and earnings. (p. 140)

Several assumptions fuel human capital research. First, the focus of human capital theories is on the variables of "demand" and "supply" in the marketplace. For example, industrial restructuring, which is moving our society from a goods-producing economy to a service economy, lessens the demand for blue-collar workers and increases the demand for white-collar workers. Supply-side factors include the maturing of the baby-boom generation and the rise in the number of women in the labor force (Ryscavage & Henle, 1990). The underlying assumption here is that workers and employers negotiate the value of wages and promotions based on productivity and the scarcity of skills.

Second, human capital scholars assume that the investment in human capital is equally available to men and women. Women and men can secure additional human capital by choosing specific college majors and obtaining advanced training, specific work experience, and on-the-job training experience. A third assumption is that the variables themselves are gender-neutral. How job opportunities, job training, job tenure, and educational preparation are experienced by men and women should be treated neutrally. This assumption gets argued as individual choice. If we choose well, we get rewarded—regardless of our gender.

Given that women have entered the labor force in greater and greater numbers, Wellington (1992) assumed that women's productivity-related characteristics, such as work experience, should be approaching the level of men's. Therefore, there should be an overall reduction in the wage gap as women invest more in their work.

Wellington (1992) studied the work history and training information collected directly for both men and women across all occupations using data from 1976 and 1985 questionnaires of the Panel Study of Income Dynamics (PSID). Given this advantage of studying specific work-history components contrasted with previous studies that had relied on potential work experience, Wellington sought to examine more closely the importance of work experience, tenure, and training in determining earnings. Using this longitudinal database, Wellington found over the 9 years (1976–1985) that the wage gap between women and men had narrowed to about 4%. In 1976, women earned 61¢ for every dollar earned by men. In 1985, women earned 65¢ for every dollar earned by men. Wellington also found that four variables significantly reduced the wage gap, and only one—years of work experience before present employer—significantly increased the wage gap.

Paglin and Rufolo (1990) sought to advance the research on human capital models by refining the focus to homogeneous stock of capital, measured by years of schooling and experience. They argued that individuals initially would have different attributes that led to types of human capital. They hypothesized that differences in earnings across occupations could be explained as a return on scarce quantitative ability: "If women differ from men in the kinds of educational capital they produce, then our theory should account for part of the observed differences in earnings" (p. 136).

To test their theory, Paglin and Rufolo examined the results of two large-scale tests, the Scholastic Aptitude Test (SAT) taken by high school seniors and the Graduate Record Exam (GRE) taken by college seniors in the 1981–1982 academic year. In both tests, men were more likely than women to score in the top intervals of the math portion of the exam. They concluded that men and women self-select into academic programs and occupations on the basis of abilities. Men, in turn, are more likely to choose higher paying occupations because of their higher math scores, rather than such rival explanations as sex segregation and discrimination. Paglin and Rufolo explained:

> Similarly, graduates in physical science and engineering are not paid more because of the high proportion of men in these fields but because the production of human capital in these areas requires a much higher than average level of mathematical ability. Males dominate in these fields because they are two to five times as numerous as females in the top three intervals of the SAT-M and GRE-Q distributions. (p. 137)

Gerhart (1990) also sought to explain gender differences in current and starting salaries on the basis of such human capital variables as performance, college major, and job title. He used a database of 4,617 employees hired between 1976 and 1986 by a large private firm that produced industrial and consumer products. Using the supply-and-demand analogy, Gerhart argued that several key factors in examining the wage disparity had been neglected. For instance, men and women are unequally distributed across fields of study that have different starting salaries. On the demand side, men and women may vary by their actual work content. Finally, men and women may vary by their performance in specific jobs and their performance may result in different pay decisions. He found that "even with a comprehensive group of control variables, women had significantly lower starting and current salaries than men" (p. 427). He determined that the current salary disadvantage largely resulted from a lower beginning salary.

This kind of research into wage and occupational differences between men and women has made a persistent argument that given time, women will choose the more potentially rewarding college majors and—subsequently—occupations. Women will have established similar years of experience and job continuity. Then, there will be no discernible difference between women's and men's earnings.

Sex Segregation: A Systems Analysis

Although the weight of this line of reasoning is substantial, one distinct area of human capital research argues that much of the wage and promotion difference should be tied to specific occupations. Several researchers have argued that women seemingly "crowd" specific occupations, bringing their wage value down because there is an "oversupply" of women to fill these positions (Field & Wolff, 1990; Gerhart & El Cheikh, 1991; Terrell, 1992; Orazem, Mattila, & Yu, 1990; Preston, 1990; Skvoretz & Smith, 1990). Reskin and Roos (1990) concluded that fully 30–45% of the pay gap between men and women can be attributed to occupational segregation.

Reskin and Roos (1990) proposed a model of occupational composition that accounts for the uneven distribution of men and women across occupations. Essentially, they introduced the notion of a dual-queuing process to explain occupational segregation, wherein "labor queues" order groups of workers in terms of their attractiveness to employers and "job queues" rank jobs in terms of their attractiveness to workers. Labor markets have these queues because employers tend to rank potential employees based on their preferences for certain kinds of workers. These preferences can be explained on the bases of custom, "the belief that women's lower productivity or other factors will offset their lower pay" (p. 36), and sex bias. Together these considerations have led employers to hire men over women even though they could employ women for less.

Reskin and Roos (1990) argued that labor queues have turned into gender queues on the basis of five factors. First, the force of custom has characterized jobs as "women's" or "men's" and therefore influenced employers' hiring decisions. Second, employers use such variables as educational attainment, experience, and group membership and their subsequent stereotypes because they cannot identify productive workers. Third, employers worry about male employees' negative response to women entering the work force, thereby reducing productivity. Fourth, some employers opt for more costly employees, even when they could be reducing wages (which occurs when hiring women). Fifth, employers have been willing to pay higher wages to retain men.

Workers themselves also rank occupations in the labor market, hence creating a job queue. Reskin and Roos (1990) were most interested in whether women and men value different job characteristics. They concluded that overall, they generally rank occupations similarly. They countered the notion that women's family roles lead them to choose different occupations or that men and women vary on whether they judge a job to be prestigious. Therefore, it is only when employers shift their preference from male workers that women make inroads into male occupations.

Reskin and Roos (1990) explained that the queuing perspective improves on the traditional economic explanations for occupational segregation and its resulting wage difference between men and women. They offered four reasons. First, they argued that queuing stresses the collective nature of sex segregation: "It sees segregation as not merely the sum of individual decisions but the result of socially structured rankings by groups in conflict" (p. 308). Second, they said that queuing takes seriously the noneconomic factors—preferences of employers and employees for working conditions, autonomy, prejudices, stereotypes, and custom. Third, Reskin and Roos contended that their perspective redirects us to look at the structural or systems aspects rather than individual characteristics of labor markets, which are shaped by employer preferences and male workers. They concluded that queuing explains why women have entered formerly male occupations, such as public relations, and become ghettoized within them.

Organizational and Social Models

Considerable support has developed for the Reskin and Roos (1990) position that we should look at structural or organizational characteristics rather than individual characteristics of labor markets. Scholars who have sought to explain the wage gap between men and women have examined organizational and social variables as well as productivity variables. For example, Haberfeld (1992) described previous research as splitting the observed wage gap between men and women into two portions: "the legitimate" portion, resulting from differences in characteristics known to affect workers' productivity, and the "illegitimate portion resulting from gender-based discrimination" (p. 161). To obtain the legitimate portion of the wage difference, human capital researchers held constant such organizational characteristics as job, hierarchical position, and department location—"or ignored them completely" (p. 161). Considering this approach a conventional model, Haberfeld hypothesized that wage discrimination occurs in part when people are assigned to organizational positions, thereby arguing for an organizational model.

Haberfeld (1992) obtained data on individual and organizational characteristics during 1987 from a large Israeli corporation that employed a heterogeneous work force of 5,087. He found that gender-based discrimination occurred in the determination of rank (the glass ceiling phenomenon). Taking into account this prior discrimination in rank, Haberfeld concluded that organizational rather than individual variables accounted for most of both portions of the wage differential, the discriminatory and the legitimate.

Canning (1991) also took the view that human capital variables focus too narrowly on the wage gap. She proposed that in addition to the typical individual productivity variables, we should examine such behavioral vari-

ables as attachment to the employer, use of informational networks to secure career choice, and span of control. We also should consider such organizational variables as department location and such family-commitment
variables as household duties, number of children, and two-career problems. Doing so should create a social model of earnings.

In her study of Canadian middle managers, Canning (1991) found that
a substantial amount of earnings difference could be explained by sex. She
concluded that women receive lower rates of return on their productivity
attributes than do men. She also concluded that to some extent women are
penalized by an unequal division of labor in the household. What is most
notable in Canning's work is the theoretical extension beyond human capital variables to ascertain an alternative explanation for the wage gap.

Hersch (1991) agreed that we should add more comprehensive information to our studies of the salary differential. She used a data set that examined
the wage effects of human capital, household responsibilities, working conditions, and on-the-job training. She collected original survey data from employees of 18 firms in the Eugene, Oregon, area in 1986. These companies
were selected because their workers and jobs in these industries were similar.
Using a regression analysis, like Canning (1991), Hersch found that "household responsibilities had a negative effect on women's earnings, but the unexplained difference between the earnings of men and women is not greatly reduced by the inclusion in the explanatory model of information on either
housework or working conditions" (p. 746).

Discrimination

Although the preceding studies are based on solid research, the efforts of
the researchers to go beyond human capital variables indicate a promising
new approach to explaining the wage gap. However, all these researchers
concluded that discrimination, defined as the illegitimate portion of the explanation, persists as an important factor.

This finding is echoed most dramatically in a comparison of female
and male managers' career progression when the women in the sample had
followed the traditional model. That is, they had done all the "right stuff."
In a study of male and female managers employed by 20 Fortune 500 corporations, Stroh (1992) found significant disparities in men's and women's
salary progression and geographical mobility even when the women had
gotten "a similar education as the men, maintained similar levels of family
power, worked in similar industries, [had] not moved in and out of the
work force, and [had] not removed their names from consideration for a
transfer more often" (p. 251).

THE FEMINIST FALLACY

Accompanying these issues and explanations have been two optimistic assumptions: As women become more visible in public relations work (or most other fields), they will achieve more prestigious positions and higher salaries, and women will experience similar successes and needs as have men who advance in public relations. Exemplifying this optimistic position was 1989 PRSA president John Paluszek, introduced in our first chapter as a prime mover in this book project. He said:

> I think it may be that we've gone beyond the point of feeling a need to address women's status in an industry-wide, organized manner . . . but I might be proven wrong. . . . As for women's roles in professional organizations, they have increasing visibility, and will soon inherit the land. (as quoted in Lukovitz, 1989, p. 16)

An all-male focus group we conducted seemed to agree. As one man said: "Roles change; women move up. They'll have similar needs as men have had" (Wright, L. Grunig, et al., 1991, p. 31).

Similarly optimistic headlines and article titles in public relations publications proposed: "Gender gap narrowing" (Wright & Springston, 1991); "Gaps are narrowing between female and male students" (DeRosa & Wilcox, 1989); "Breaking public relations' glass ceiling" (Dozier, 1988); and "Salary Growth Stalls, but Firms and Women Gain" ("Cover," 1993).

Ferguson (1990) called such assumptions "the feminist fallacy" in her writing on women's absence from media content and contemporary media organizations. Referring to the fallacious rhetoric of national leaders and headlines that mask a very different reality, Ferguson argued that media content, industry gender structures, public imaging, and the record on power and women all contradict the actual gains that have been made by women in social, legal, and political spheres. To illustrate, consider the headline attached to Ingraham's (1995) op-ed piece in *The New York Times*: "Enter, Women: What Glass Ceiling?" Ingraham argued against seeking systemic changes because women just need to be judged "fairly."

Some leaders in public relations, too, have pronounced that "the work" has been done and the gaps narrowed to insignificance. However, statistical data have contradicted their rhetoric. Women in public relations have continued to earn substantially less than men, as documented by such trade publications as *pr reporter* and the *Public Relations Journal* as early as 1988 and by the International Association of Business Communicators biannual trend studies between 1998 and 1997. (We will have more to say about these data in subsequent chapters.) PRSA reported that on average, female public relations practitioners make 45% less salary than men in the field ($41,110 vs. $59,460) (as cited in Simmons Market Research Bureau, 1996).

Although attractive salaries have brought women to the field of public relations, these women have found themselves segregated within the lower paying technical positions (Donato, 1990, p. 142). At least at the time of the gender switch from a male to female majority, men occupied the higher paying managerial positions. Also, women have been more likely than men to work in lower paying organizations within the field, such as the nonprofits, health care, transportation/hotel/resort/entertaining, religious/ charitable organizations, and associations (Jacobson & Tortorello, 1992). However, in the economic downturn of the early 1990s, men moved increasingly into these organizational types and women moved to "other" types (Simmons Market Research Bureau, 1996, p. 6).

Lesly (1988) argued that women actually seek out lower status positions. As we report later in this book, we tested this claim by determining whether such work-place constraints as the traditional work-day hours, skepticism about maternity and parental leave, no standardized child care, limited training for advancement, lack of promotions, and discriminatory attitudes might prevent women from seeking more senior management, policymaking positions. These positions have required professional commitments to take priority over personal or family matters in the past. Are women aware of the different sacrifices and choosing to define success differently than men do?

DENIAL OF THE PROBLEM

Coupled with the fallacy of increasing equality in the work place is the denial that gender-based inequities even exist. As with many fields, this is the case for public relations. In the same year that Paluszek stated that the profession had progressed beyond the problem of male–female differences, fellow professional Wilma Mathews (1989) reported a "flat, almost frightening denial that a problem exists" (p. 1).

Public relations professionals—both men and women—and students of public relations often discount the statistics showing bias in salary and promotion. We (Wright, L. Grunig, et al., 1991) reported from our focus group research that men in particular continue to refute the salary disparity even when assured that this disparity has been documented in several studies. In 1995, when we returned to discuss wages, men focused on pay equity. As one participant in this later focus group study said, "There's a difference between feeling like you're making enough money to get by on and how much money you feel you should be worth or you deserve to be making" (Serini, Toth, Wright, & Emig, 1997, p. 110). Men saw downsizing as a "boon to women."

We also found that male PRSA members believe that men are not more quickly promoted than women in most public relations employment situations and that it is not more difficult for women than men to reach the top in public relations. Jacobson and Tortorello (1992) reported that only one-third of the senior men they surveyed in public relations recognize any gender bias in reaching that executive level. In our most recent research, we learned that men believe women are advancing because men are leaving the field or have lost their jobs, to be replaced by lower salaried women (Serini et al., 1997).

Students of public relations, the practitioners of the future, also tend to deny the existence of gender bias in the field. Mathews (1989) hypothesized that students do not want to hear such bad news about the field they intend to pursue. Similarly, Jones (1991) found that college students who participated in her focus groups either were unaware of the problems women typically encounter or they did not believe such discrimination would pose a problem for them. She concluded that these undergraduates, particularly the female students, were unprepared for the challenges they inevitably would face in public relations.

Although, predictably, male public relations practitioners and male students of public relations might deny the statistical realities evidencing bias in salary and promotion, it was worse in Mathews's (1989) view that the refutation was pronounced among those most disadvantaged by discrimination: the women themselves. She found that although some female practitioners were candid about their situation when responding to an anonymous questionnaire, they seemed embarrassed to admit openly to their peers that they had experienced discrimination. In a 1992 *Public Relations Journal* survey, women only narrowly agreed that it was harder for women than men to reach top jobs, despite evidence that relatively few women are senior public relations pros (Jacobson & Tortorello, 1992). In both the 1990 and 1995 glass ceiling studies we conducted, we found only a slight shift in perceptions about the difficulty women face in reaching top positions in public relations. During that 5-year period, female respondents indicated uncertainty about their own organizations, whereas the men slightly disagreed with the statement about the existence of a glass ceiling for women.

WHY THE FEMINIST FALLACY AND
DENIAL OF GENDER BIAS PERSIST

Why do the feminist fallacy and denial of gender inequities in public relations persist, despite the statistical data from many sources confirming gender bias? Some people may consider the evidence insufficient. Another answer, heard occasionally in face-to-face talks with our female students,
concerns the association of women's issues with being a "feminist." Often,
feminism has been equated with any subject pertaining to women's issues.
Then too, students we interviewed have equated feminism with strident,
unladylike behavior. They cannot identify with women who discuss the issues of salary and status; yet they expect to have careers, marry, and raise
families. These students hold opinions not unlike a depiction of women under age 30, described in a *Time* cover story (Wallis, 1989), who would not
identify with the word "feminist" but who would demand the rights feminists have worked toward.

> Ask any woman under the age of 30 if she is a feminist, and chances are she
> will shoot back a decisive, and perhaps a derisive, no. But, in the very next
> breath, the same young woman will allow that while she does not identify with
> the angry aspects of the movements in the '60s and '70s or with its clamorous
> leaders, she certainly plans on a career as well as marriage and three kids. She
> definitely expects her husband—present or future—to do his share of the dust-
> ing, the diapering, the dinner and dishes. She would be outraged were she paid
> less than a male colleague for doing equal work. Call hers the "no but . . . "
> generation. No, they are not feminist, or so they say, but they do take certain
> rights for granted. (pp. 80–91)

If women perceive a relationship between unequal treatment in the
work place and unladylike behavior in society, they may subconsciously
adopt a set of assumptions, culturally learned, about the role and value of
women in our society. Rakow (1989) explained that women have been
thought to be biologically emotional, caregiving, and cooperative in their
behavior—and thereby devalued in comparison with men in this culture.
Men, according to our society, hold the more highly valued attributes of
aggressiveness, competitiveness, and rationality in thought.

Gender, then, has become something that we do rather than what we
are. Our identity is assigned and reinforced through societal interactions.
As Rakow (1989) explained:

> There is, in other words, no inner core or essential identity that is male or fe-
> male, something that would make us feel male or female if culture could be

stripped away. Rather, we are continuously "acting out" our own gender and assigning gender to others. (p. 289)

This societal identification and reinforcement of what it is to be "male" or "female" could be unproblematic—except that women are generally seen as deficient in relationship to men. Women who cannot identify with salary inequities and loss of career opportunities simply may be reflecting how they see themselves. Rakow (1989) described women who do not value themselves sufficiently to seek promotion: "These women get blamed for not being sufficiently committed to career: they're not assertive enough in setting career goals, or in negotiating salaries" (p. 288).

Feminism and feminist theory, rather than associating women's empowerment with unladylike behavior, have sought to look at women through a different lens. They value the feminine and the characteristics socially ascribed to women. Creedon (1989b) argued that we should "revision" the work of women in public relations. Rakow (1989) asked, rather than railing against women entering public relations, why not consider the "promise of feminism" to public relations?

THREE FEMINIST POSITIONS

Steeves (1987) provided three means of looking at some of the positions feminists have taken on the issue of unequal treatment in the work place. She labeled these positions "liberal," "Marxist" or "socialist," and "radical." We will explore these perspectives in depth later in the book. The discussion here merely serves as an introduction to different ways of regarding the issues we have presented in this chapter.

Liberal feminists, according to Steeves, "believe the inequity is simply a matter of irrational prejudice that can be solved through rational argument" (p. 100). They advocate working toward equity within the system. For example, the velvet ghetto research (Toth & Cline, 1989a) provided a liberal feminist approach to women in public relations. It encourages women to look to themselves for answers, thereby supporting the assumption that there are rational answers:

1. Accept that the velvet ghetto is real.
2. Learn to play the game.
3. Develop a career plan.
4. Define success.
5. Accept your limitations.
6. Celebrate your triumphs. (Cline, 1989, pp. 302–307)

Throughout this book, we'll explore and describe the substantial research that has developed about women in public relations. However, a brief appraisal suggests that much of this research assumes a liberal feminist approach like that of the velvet ghetto studies. Perhaps this should be expected from those women and men who have public relations industry experience and from whom we gathered information. They're part of an occupation that seeks accommodation, negotiation, and the resolution of conflict between organizations and the groups on which their employers depend. Therefore, they *should* be optimistic about working for change within organizations and themselves.

Research that speaks to the notions of liberal feminism typically assumes that the inequities women face result from their being denied jobs or promotions because they are deficient in their knowledge and preparation to work in organizations. For example, in a focus group discussion of successful female managers of public relations, one woman argued that "if you want to be a manager, you have to train to be a good manager" (Wright, L. Grunig, et al., 1991, p. 28). To this person, the responsibility for change is on the individual, to find his or her way through to the strategies, skills, and knowledge needed to succeed.

Marxist or socialist feminists do not believe that equal opportunity is possible within the existing capitalistic economic and social system (Steeves, 1987, p. 101). Socialist feminists stress collective benefit over individual gain. They believe the devaluation of women will not change unless our class and social structures reject capitalist ownership of goods and services and male-centered gender relations. An example of Marxist or socialist feminist thought is expressed in the notion of "an even playing field." This saying condemns games in which the rules are too oblique or are invoked inconsistently so that one side is more advantaged than the other. This position is reflected in the following letter to the editor.

> The glass ceiling has become the smoked ceiling. . . . In simple English: those of us who have worked long and hard with the carrot of a promotion to management dangling before us are not told carrots are no longer on the menu. The reward has been removed mid-game. We are encouraged to work as hard or harder . . . take on more responsibility . . . fulfill the functions of supervision and management . . . yet altruistically waive the rewards that went to our predecessor on the ladder. ("Glass Ceiling Update," 1992, p. 1)

Marxist and socialist researchers have argued that the organizational rules and structures for how public relations is carried out cause women to make a disproportionate amount of sacrifice. Women, more than men, seem to have questioned the impact of the work-place structure on their lives. In our survey of American public relations, we found that women favored flexible hours significantly more than did men. Women also advocated more flexible locations and parental leave policies, and they recognized more acutely than did men in the study that sexual harassment was an important issue in their work (Wright, L. Grunig, et al., 1991).

In our focus group research, we asked female and male participants whether they thought women were attracted to public relations because of its flexible work schedule. At least one man thought flexible structure would be very important to women: "Look at the average female—she would favor a flexible situation. Females are primary caretakers of young children. Males are more oriented toward a career path, a long work day" (Wright, L. Grunig, et al., 1991, p. 29).

Structural changes to accommodate employees already have met with strong resistance, according to our research in public relations. Those in power have chosen, rather, to devalue the public relations function—lowering salaries and limiting the role in such a way that men from other functions in the organization could take on added responsibilities without being called public relations professionals (Lauzen, 1990a, 1992). This organizational strategy has been termed *encroachment,* the adopting of public relations roles by others who have more credibility or organizational power.

Radical feminists, according to Steeves (1987), "all agree that women's oppression is widespread and that the problem is rooted too deeply to be removed by either individual action or social change" (p. 97). One radical feminist position is that women should live and work separately from men.

Although little research in public relations can be considered "radical" in terms of proposing solutions to the problems of gender bias, we have begun to describe such approaches. We have suggested eradicating sexism in education and other institutions, establishing family-friendly policies, outlawing sexual harassment, and rethinking the masculine ethic in organizations. Perhaps we believe we are radical in our intentions. More of this discussion of our radical intent appears in later chapters.

Because we are practicing public relations people as well as scholars and professors, we care deeply about the role public relations plays in organizational life and in the broader society. We believe that by describing women in public relations, we are focused on a most powerful predictor of the future of the field. In this book we describe what it means to public relations as an occupation to experience a gender switch in less than a generation. Despite the optimistic views reported by leaders and headlined in publications, we need to view women in public relations as they actually are instead of how we wish they could be. That women should be pivotal in the survival of an occupation seems unfair. However, if women are so perceived as to reduce the salary and status of occupations in which they are the majority, we have a responsibility to document this case of occupational resegregation as well.

Chapter Three

Parallels with Women in Diverse Fields

Carlyle told us in the 19th century that "labor is life." Indeed, work outside the home has meant existence for millions of U.S. women. Times have changed since the days in classical Rome when only slave or poor freeborn women worked at physically taxing jobs. Upper-class women stayed within the domestic realm. Little changed for women and work until the 18th century, when women of different social strata—black and white alike in this country—began to participate in cottage industries, producing goods and services from their homes. Today, throughout the globe, women are leaving the private sphere of their homes for the public sphere of paid employment.

Some feminists, such as Wood (1998), have argued against what they consider an artificial distinction between the public and private areas of life. Although many of us assume that those distinct domains exist, Wood believed they are only artifacts of discourse—and dangerous ones at that, because the dichotomy privileges the public sphere over the private. It is in the public arena where people typically find success, at least as measured by outward symbols.

Without settling this debate, we must acknowledge that by 2005 women are predicted to compose nearly half of the total U.S. labor force (U.S. Bureau of Labor Statistics, as cited in "Women in the Workplace," 1998). They are not only more likely to work for pay, but they also spend more time at work than did women in the past.

At the same time, women are moving beyond the traditional female occupations and into careers formerly dominated by men. The demands of those occupations—along with economic necessity—increasingly have led women to work full time and year-round. This chapter explores how women at work fare across specific occupations. In the chapter that follows, we search for parallels between the situation for women in public relations and those in management per se. In Chapter 4, we also examine the situation for female entrepreneurs in this country.

By making these comparisons, we may determine how U.S. women in public relations, in particular, are achieving and are being rewarded for their contributions to the work force. At the same time, this chapter does not claim to be a comprehensive study of women in every white-collar and blue-collar field. Nor do we claim to be experts in every field we attempt to describe. We have tried, though, to find and digest the scientific studies that are relevant. We also have tried to bring these findings to life through anecdotal evidence and the thoughtful commentary of women who work in those jobs.

The text in this chapter is interrupted more frequently than usual with citations to the literature of a number of career fields. We have been careful to document every statistic, every charge, every claim, even every story. We did this for two reasons. First, we wanted to reduce the risk of being charged with bias ourselves, that is, with the allegation that the abysmal figures and scenarios related here represent more our own subjectivity than the reality of the world for working women. Second, and more importantly, we wanted to give credit. We wanted to credit the scholars—men and women alike—who have staked even a part of their precious academic careers on doing research about or for women. We also wanted to credit the women from within each of the occupational realms discussed here who have spoken up to tell their tales in print.

Even so, this chapter barely scratches the surface of the constellation of issues facing women in diverse occupational fields. These concerns include (1) the opportunity for women to enter in substantial numbers, (2) their segregation in certain subspecialties or in support rather than in line functions, (3) advancement, (4) pay, and (5) the difference that women may or may not make in the way the work is done.

Sociologists have conducted countless studies of gender in different occupational clusters. However, to read, reflect on, and then synthesize all of this literature in the scholarly journals of sociology, women's studies, and public relations is beyond the scope of this book. Instead, we have selected professions and cases within fields we consider information-rich and especially appropriate for comparisons with U.S. women in public relations.

Within these carefully selected cases, we have taken the time and space to quote a large number of women who represent sometimes opposing perspectives on both the situation for women and the solutions to any sexual discrimination they may encounter at work. Simply by introducing these women from labor economics, a conservative think tank, an English faculty, the administration of a major business school, divorce law, scientific agencies, and so forth we hope you will be impressed with the array of professional fields in which women work today.

We believe it is important to quote women directly. In each chapter, this book gives voice to their personal concerns. The quotations come not only from public relations practitioners but from political wives, government bureaucrats, experts in human resources, administrators of trade and professional associations, biologists, corporate executives, politicians, surgeons, university deans, management consultants, journal editors, and research directors.

Listen to how these women describe their frustrations, their triumphs, their strategies. Hear their histories and those of the pioneering women before them. How do they explain the dilemmas that still face women in the work force? And what do they envision for the future in their field? Their points of view eloquently support the contemporary feminist contention that women are hardly a homogeneous group.

Interestingly, much of the information in this chapter comes to us from the popular press: newspapers, magazines, and books. This suggests that the problems and opportunities of working women are of concern not solely to scholars in sociology, in women's studies, or in the career fields affected.

Taken together with the academic literature, these articles and books should help answer the key question framing this chapter: How do U.S. women in public relations fare by comparison with their sisters in other occupations? In other words, are we better or worse off than, say, women who teach, who practice medicine, or who do construction work? In particular, we will explore how our salaries compare and, perhaps more important, what special barriers we all may face in our quest for advancement in the field.

We will begin with a look at the professions that the PRSA, in its 1991 conference planning, considered most relevant to women's issues in our field: law and medicine. At the same time, we acknowledge that public relations—a career that does not require the licensing of its practitioners—has not achieved professional status itself. So, from this discussion of female attorneys and doctors, we will proceed to a discussion of women in other professional and near-professional fields: higher education, publishing, association management, and government and politics. Then we will touch briefly on the situation for blue-collar and pink-collar women as well.

We approach the occupational sectors in this order not because of any hierarchical sense. Rather, more data are available on women in white-collar jobs and—more importantly—these data are the most relevant to the focus of this book on public relations. We certainly do not consider the few (super)women who have succeeded in these high-status professions as somehow a living rebuke to their sisters whose heads bump into the ubiquitous glass ceiling, whose feet stick to the floor, or who reel from the glass walls. At the same time, we recognize that of the nearly 58 million women who were employed in 1995, the largest proportion still worked in technical, sales, and clerical jobs ("Women in the Workplace," 1998).

WOMEN IN THE PROFESSIONS

Women in Law and the Biomedical Fields

Women are making great gains in the professions of law and medicine. As more and more women practice public relations, we stand to learn much from these two fields. For this reason, representatives of the American Bar Association (ABA) and the American Medical Association (AMA) were invited to address the 1992 annual convention of the PRSA. In the panel "Gender Gap Issues," we heard from Nancy Slonim, director of media services for the ABA, and from Claire V. Wolfe, former chair of the AMA's Women in Medicine Advisory Panel. Despite the cute titles attached to their remarks ("Disorder in Court" and "The Gender Gap: Is There a Cure?"), these women made substantial contributions to our understanding of how to achieve equity in our own field.

Both panelists began with statistics. We learned that from zero representation among the officers and trustees of the AMA in 1980, women had come to represent 21% of that leadership corps. By 1992, almost 25,000 women were in medical school. This accounts for about 38% of enrollment for the past decade, up from 9% in the 1969–1970 academic year. Contrast this with the times of Elizabeth Blackwell who, in 1849, graduated at the top of her class at Geneva College to become the first female physician in the United States; she had been rejected because of her gender by 29 other medical schools.

As early as 1979, the AMA recognized the importance of directing an ad hoc group to study and act on women's concerns. Between the time its Women in Medicine department was established in 1989 and the fall 1992 PRSA conference, the AMA had (1) adopted a policy on gender-neutral language, (2) recommended a policy on maternity leave, (3) conducted a survey on the gender implications of residency programs, (4) surveyed the availability of child care in hospitals, (5) developed grievance procedures and guidelines for preventing sexual harassment of members, and (6) advocated for women's health issues, even in that time of scarce research dollars.

Wolfe emphasized that with women approaching 30% of the field, the profile of the physician is changing. She also told us that female physicians operate differently from male physicians. Women in medicine are less likely to be self-employed, they work fewer hours per week, they see fewer patients, they are clustered in the lower paying medical specialties, and they earn less. Finally, we heard that the glass ceiling remains firmly in place in academia: Only one dean of a medical school was female at the time of Wolfe's presentation.

The status of women in law is similar. Slonim, however, described a "dual" glass ceiling. First, female attorneys have a harder time than male attorneys becoming partners in law firms. Men comprise almost 90% of the private partnerships in the nation's largest firms. Second, women rarely play the managerial role in their firms. Managers make critical decisions about how to distribute the income at the end of the year and about hiring practices.

Perhaps because of these kinds of problems, the ABA in 1986 adopted as a goal the full and equal participation of women and minority members. Those members are increasing. Although the first female lawyer came to the colonies in the 17th century (and tried 124 cases here!), only in the 1970s did women begin to enter law schools in significant numbers. By the end of the 20th century, women made up 43% of all law school students and about 22% of all practicing attorneys. Unfortunately, they may continue to face discrimination and harassment even from fellow students. For example, a flyer distributed at Yale's law school made news when it "rated" female students in sexual terms. Male students there routinely ignore women's comments and devalue their opinions on legal issues (Torry, 1995).

Schools of veterinary medicine increasingly enroll female students—to the point where women represent about three-quarters of the typical classroom (Gose, 1998). By contrast, men make up about 69% of professional practice. Women, their colleagues of the future, may be ideally suited to the field. One student, who acknowledged the danger of pigeonholing women into a caring role, nevertheless commented: "When I think of any kind of a medical profession, I think of people who are nurturers. . . . I do think women are by nature nurturers. Now that women have the opportunity in these fields, you're seeing them flood in" (as quoted in Gose, 1998, p. A55).

What accounts for the opportunity more and more women are finding in veterinary schools? Until the 1970s, admissions committees discriminated against female applicants because they considered women too physically weak to handle large animals. Today's restraining drugs have eliminated that concern. At the same time, men increasingly have been opting out of veterinary medicine. Salaries in the field have been stagnant. Money is a major factor, one that may cause ambitious men to reject vet schools when they understand that medical doctors earn two to four times as much. Loss of prestige, in this era of hospital TV shows such as *ER* and *Chicago Hope*, is a second factor discouraging men. A third explanation for the dearth of men in vet schools is their self-fulfilling perception. As the director of admissions at UC–Davis's school put it, "Men are saying, 'I don't want to be in a field that is predominantly women' " (as quoted in Gose, 1998, p. A56).

All of these reasons should sound familiar to the student of public relations, a field like veterinary medicine that is recently feminized and suffering the same salary doldrums, male flight, and perceived loss of status. Nevertheless, the marketplace suggests that women have a vital role to play in communicating with diverse publics—and in treating animals as well. As a former practicing vet explained her customer base, about three-fourths of the people who bring their pets to the vet are women; men typically show up on Saturdays or for emergencies only. Regular customers, overwhelmingly female, want to see other women: "What I hear from clients is that the bedside manner of women is better" (as quoted in Gose, 1998, p. A56).

Slonim, the attorney addressing public relations professionals, concluded that "clearly, women have made numerical progress—but numerical progress doesn't necessarily mean parity." At the highest levels, men continue to dominate. Only one of the U.S. Supreme Court justices was a woman at the time of Slonim's remarks. Women made up 12.3% of the federal court system.

The ABA's subcommittee on women and minorities (a joint venture of its Commission on Women and Commission on Minorities) is working to eradicate this kind of imbalance. Already it has discovered the importance of documenting and officially recognizing problems. (In much this same way, the PRSA set up its ad hoc Task Force on Women in part to establish the existence of any gender discrimination in the field.)

The bar association proceeded with a state-by-state process of establishing, over and over, that special problems exist for women lawyers. It also began issuing what became an annual report card to the ABA, measuring its progress in eliminating bias there. Slonim promised to "keep their feet to the fire." By 1998, women made up 46.1% of the enrollment in U.S. law schools; meanwhile, minority enrollment has increased to 20.1% ("Law School Diversity," 1999).

In 1992, the same year as the PRSA conference that picked the brains of these two women from different professional fields about how they were working to eradicate sexism in their disciplines, salary statistics from the U.S. Bureau of the Census showed median salaries for women in law and medicine failing to match men's salaries by approximately the same difference. Female lawyers earned about 78% of what their male counterparts took home; female doctors earned slightly over 72%. The AMA (as cited in Herman, 1993) offered even gloomier figures. The AMA found that female physicians earn less than two-thirds of what male physicians earn.

In both law and medicine women are congregated in certain subspecialties (Cohn & Vobejda, 1992). Women are more likely to be trust and estate lawyers than highly paid litigators. They are more likely to be pediatricians than surgeons. In veterinary medicine, they treat small rather than large animals; and more women than men are attracted to wildlife medicine, although the pay in that area is substantially less than for vets in private practice (Gose, 1998).

Segregation in these areas may not reflect true choice for women. For example, Baker (1996) found that female physicians opted for lower paying practices that allowed them to meet their family responsibilities. Female physicians who are black and who treat patients in poor neighborhoods may be ostracized from health maintenance organizations (HMOs) because those patients tend to be sicker and thus cost more (Sugg, 1995). From these instances, Benokraitis (1997) concluded that "having a family or being altruistic penalizes women in even the most respected and highest-paying occupations" (p. 25). Thus we have to wonder about the situation for women in public relations, rarely touted as a "most respected" and "highest paying" career.

We also question the situation for women who choose medical or legal fields that remain nontraditional for them, fields such as surgery or litigation. As with male nurses, female doctors rank lower in prestige than do their sex-role-congruent counterparts (Nilson, 1976). In fact, women in any male-dominated profession may be perceived (and thus treated) as deviant (Epstein, 1970; Patterson & Engleberg, 1978).

In 1992, only one-sixth of all doctors were women (Nasar, 1992b), although one-third of the new graduates of U.S. medical schools were female (Nasar, 1992a). Thus we see that doctors who are women continue to be considered at least an anomaly, if not deviant. So it was with physician Mary Walker in 1864 (Stephens, 1993). Dr. Walker was forced to crossdress in the service of her country. During the Civil War, only a special act of Congress allowed this first lieutenant to wear Navy pants and tunic while treating the wounded. (After the war, Walker continued to sport trousers while lecturing about the health hazards of wearing constricting corsets.)

A living example of female-physician-as-anomaly is surgeon Kathryn D. Anderson, profiled in *The Washington Post* (Herman, 1993). Anderson contended that she was unfairly denied a promotion to chair and chief of surgery at Children's National Medical Center after 10 years of distinguished service there as vice chair. In her lawsuit against Children's, she claimed that the search committee discriminated against her because of sex stereotyping. She alleged that members of the committee considered a strong personality, such as hers, laudable in a man but unacceptable in a woman. Anderson subsequently became chief of surgery at Children's Hospital in Los Angeles.

The case of *Kathryn D. Anderson v. Children's National Medical Center* is not atypical. According to a reporter who specializes in health issues (Herman, 1993), leaders in medicine are beginning to question why so few women have arrived at top-level positions in hospitals and medical schools. The answer, as in the Anderson case, seems to be sex stereotyping.

Neurosurgeon Frances Conley, who like Anderson considered herself a victim of sexism, wrote in an editorial in the *New England Journal of Medicine* (as quoted in Herman, 1993) that "role stereotyping has been instrumental in maintaining a 'glass ceiling' for women in medicine" (p. 7). The first female director of the National Institutes of Health, Bernadine Healy, seemed to agree. She explained that "the very elements that are essential to succeed in a stereotypically macho environment are considered unpleasant in a woman. . . . [If a woman is] gentle, sweet, compliant, soft . . . then everybody may like her, but she doesn't have the right stuff to succeed" (as quoted in Herman, 1993, p. 7).

Not only do the medical schools and hospitals stereotype female students and physicians, women may see themselves stereotypically. As Anderson (as quoted in Herman, 1993) put it: "Women are so socially programmed to take secondary roles that they almost apologize for being tops in their field. Women doubt themselves frequently" (p. 7).

In addition to the socialization that may cause women to feel like outsiders in their own field, they may doubt they belong because they see so few others like themselves there. Male scientists, in particular, may fail to appreciate the importance of their female counterparts being given visible roles at scientific meetings. Mary E. Clutter, who established an anti-sexism policy for the National Science Foundation (NSF), where she worked as assistant director of biological sciences, said: "Some of these guys don't get it" (as quoted in Rensberger, 1992, p. A21). In an effort to overcome this subtle form of discrimination, her directorate stopped funding meetings if too few women were among the main speakers.

Why do so few women appear at the podium? According to Clutter, the biologists she worked with argue that women give poor talks or lack stage presence. One scientist organizing a conference defended his all-male roster by claiming there were no women in his field. (Eva Barak, who heads NSF's cell biology division, subsequently offered him the names of several women she knew whose research in his field was outstanding.)

Even women may not go out of their way to include female colleagues on the dais. Barak (as quoted in Rensberger, 1992) told of a woman who justified overlooking female speakers for the meeting she was organizing by stating that she wanted "only the best."

Of course, not all professional women become socialized into doubting their own or other women's competence. To provide balance (if not in actual numbers), consider now the case of divorce attorney Marna Tucker, profiled in a *Washington Post* magazine article (Harrington, 1993). The subhead of the article described Tucker as seeming to have it all: "a rewarding career, idealism and a happy home life" (p. 9). The question that follows is how she pulled this off.

History provides the answer. According to her biographer (Harrington, 1993), Tucker happened along at the right moment. That point in time was the convergence of feminism, the opening of the professions to women, and the liberalization of American divorce laws. Tucker was among the few women in law school in the early 1960s. By the end of that decade, coincidental with the most recent women's liberation movement in this country, she had been profoundly affected by feminism. As one of the few female lawyers in the nation's capital, she worked to eliminate sex-biased laws. She helped set up the Women's Legal Defense Fund and the National Women's Law Center. By the 1970s, she was pioneering a new method of divorce law that came to be called "no fault." She was the first female president of the 60,000-member Washington, DC, bar association.

Harrington (1993) concluded that Tucker "is a window on the lives of women in her unique generation—a generation sandwiched between the stay-at-home, raise-the-kids, volunteer-at-school era of her mother and the I-can-be-anything-I-want-to-be era in which her 17-year-old daughter is now becoming a woman" (p. 10). He considered her a blend of "old and new ways, making the story of her life simultaneously a reminder of how poorly women were treated only two decades ago and a celebration of remarkable progress" (p. 11).

Maybe so. But despite her obvious successes, both as a lawyer and as a parent, Tucker herself lamented that "you can't have it all" (as quoted in

Harrington, 1993, p. 11). As she explained, "You can't say you can't meet with the president of Abu Dhabi because you're going to the farm with your kids this weekend" (p. 11). And her triumphs came at no small price: "I paid my dues to all the boys 10 times over" (p. 20). She worried about the younger women who believe in entitlement, rather than assuming that bias against them continues to exist and noted that they, too, must pay their dues. She said, "They will hit that glass ceiling and realize it's important to give something back" (p. 22).

One of the first female lawyers in this country, Clara Shortridge Foltz, was herself a divorcée (Stephens, 1993). Like her modern-day counterpart Tucker, Foltz fought for women's rights. During the previous century, she wrote and then argued successfully for passage (by a margin of two votes) of the "Woman Lawyer's Bill" in 1878. However, Foltz was kicked out of law school because she was considered a distraction. (By the last decade, women represented more than 40% of the new graduates of law schools in the United States [Nasar, 1992a].) Foltz remained self-taught. However, one of California's chief justices praised her as being "not only a good mother . . . [but] a good lawyer" (as quoted in Bird, 1987, p. 47).

Another 19th-century lawyer, Belva Lockwood, had to sue the U.S. government to allow her to practice before the Supreme Court and the Court of Claims. She went on to form a mother–daughter law partnership that ultimately won a $5 million settlement for her client, the Cherokee Nation, against the government (Stephens, 1993). Stephens (1993), who has developed biographies of more than 100 such rebellious women, explained that Lockwood and Foltz exemplify women in any field who behave first like human beings and second like ladies.

"Ladies," of course, never are mentioned in the Constitution. Rose Elizabeth Bird, a modern-day lawyer who was the first woman appointed to California's Supreme Court and who became its first female chief justice, believed that Thomas Jefferson voiced the popular sentiment of his time when he said: "Were our state a pure democracy, there would still be excluded from our deliberations . . . women, who, to prevent depravation of morals and ambiguity of issues, should not mix promiscuously in gatherings of men" (as quoted in Bird, 1987, p. 46). Bird also quoted the reaction of J. Elizabeth Jones, who in 1850 spoke at a women's rights convention in Ohio: "The very first act of this nation was to deprive a majority of those whom it claimed the right to govern, of any lot or part in the government— its very birth-cry was a denial of women's equality" (p. 46). More than a century and a quarter later, when in 1977 Rose Bird crashed the white-male membership that had characterized California's highest court, the press referred to the court as "Rosie and the Supremes." One trial judge later introduced her to a group of lawyers as the chief justice with the "cutest butt" (Bird, 1987, p. 45).

Despite such seeming devaluations, women on the bench undoubtedly will make a difference in the way our laws evolve. Ruth Bader Ginsburg said she expected significant changes when she joined Sandra Day O'Connor as the second woman on the U.S. Supreme Court—not because women look at law differently but because they look at life differently. She (as quoted in Reuters, 1993) explained: "There's so much Justice O'Connor and I will have in common because of our life's experience growing up as women in the United States at about the same time" (p. A7). In 1981, O'Connor was the first woman appointed to the U.S. Supreme Court.

Even as students, some women seem to look at the law differently from their male peers. One undergraduate women's studies major at the University of Maryland may not be atypical. Even as a college senior, Suzanne Jean Marcus put her education to use at a shelter for battered women in Washington, DC. Her plans beyond graduation included working at a legal clinic and then entering law school to focus on social law. Her motivation came from the inspirational work of lawyers helping women at My Sister's Place. She explained, "I'm seeing the kind of struggles the women have with the legal system" (as quoted in Burch, 1998, p. 29).

Already, Marcus's work at the shelter may have helped women heal in this feminist environment. She has contributed to the D.C. Clothesline Project, whose theme is "airing society's dirty laundry." She organizes displays of T-shirts at colleges and universities, places to draw attention to gender-related violence. Battered women tell their stories in words and pictures drawn on shirts whose colors indicate the kind of brutality they have experienced: Yellow represents domestic violence; red is for rape.

Women in Associations

The headline said it all: "National Trade Groups Pay Women Executives Much Less than Men" (Sugawara, 1992, p. D1). As in the biomedical and legal fields, gender-based discrimination seems to characterize associations. The wage gap between women and men there amounts to an average of $12,000 per year.

Encouragingly, women have made their numbers felt in the association world. They head about one-fourth of the 1,376 national associations in the United States, according to a survey by the American Research Co. (as cited by Sugawara, 1992). However, the study also found that men direct a full 92% of the country's largest, wealthiest, and most powerful associations. By contrast, women tend to head the small trade and individual membership groups. The wage gap exists, though, regardless of the size of the association. Even controlling for factors that include size, type of industry, and location of the main office, the median salary of a male association head is $85,638 versus $73,931 for his female counterpart.

At this point readers may wonder why, in the few pages of this book on women in public relations devoted to comparisons with other careers, we have chosen to discuss associations even briefly. The survey described above is the first to look at sex differences in this field. However, we believe that many of our students will find employment in this arena—especially in Washington, New York, and Chicago, where so many associations are headquartered.

Associations are, in essence, communication entities. Because they value communication—with members, with lawmakers, with the media— they tend to pay their heads of public relations well. A 1990 survey conducted by the Greater Washington Society of Association Executives reported an average salary for directors of public relations of $52,556 (and even higher—$66,012—in the large groups with annual budgets greater than $2.5 million) (Rabin, 1990). The American Society of Association Executives surveyed its members 2 years earlier. Even in 1988, public relations directors were earning on average $48,000, compared with the median salary for all association employees of $44,000 (Rabin, 1990).

We also predict that trade and professional associations increasingly will represent real opportunity for advancement for ambitious women in public relations. The women already employed there believe that two main factors bespeak that opportunity. First, as newcomers in what had been a "clubby, white male world" they have proven themselves on the legislative "battlefield" (Sugawara, 1992). The growing proportion of women in government has helped establish their legitimacy and their effectiveness as well.

Evidence to support these women's optimism can be found in the increasing number of women who hold next-to-the-top spots in associations. More and more women serve as general counsel and vice president. At least one woman believes her gender actually helped her get the job of chief executive officer. Denise A. Bode said she became president of the Independent Petroleum Association of America (IPAA) because the IPAA was trying to change its image from that of wheeling-dealing oil men (as quoted in Sugawara, 1992).

Women in Government and Politics

Women have become an overwhelming presence in federal service. Robert E. Griffiths of the Metropolitan Washington (DC) Council of Governments explained that during the 1980s, the government job market became increasingly top-heavy at the same time that professional women were entering the work force. A survey by the U.S. Merit Systems Protection Board confirmed that the number of women in government has mushroomed in the last 2 decades.

Legions of these women undoubtedly work in public affairs. Many more are press secretaries or their assistants in the press office. Still others handle constituent relations on Capitol Hill. Thus, once again, we see extraordinary opportunity for our female students in public relations.

However, women (and some minorities) in government bump into the same glass ceiling confronting their sisters in other fields. They may be unaware of how widespread sexual discrimination is, however, because at least one "glass ceiling" study never was published. The Federal Page of *The Washington Post* (Pincus, 1994) explained that a classified study from 1992 documented that half of the white, female case workers for the Central Intelligence Agency (CIA) reported experiencing sexual harassment. More than half of all black respondents reported racial harassment at the CIA. This information only came to light because of a court filing by a case officer who sued the CIA for discrimination. She claimed her agency's glass ceiling study established discrimination against women especially in the area of promotion. As of 1991, women comprised 40% of the CIA's work force but only 9% of the senior intelligence service positions (which are considered "career-making assignments"). *The Post* quoted one source familiar with the case as saying that there was "a significant difference in promotion between men and women and the chance it was caused by other than gender was less than 1 percent" (p. A25).

Other, similar studies do not remain classified. For example, the report "A Question of Equity: Women and the Glass Ceiling in the Federal Government" revealed that although women represent nearly half of the federal government's white-collar workers, few are executives or hold supervisory responsibility (McAllister, 1992). One in four federal supervisors is female; one in ten senior federal executives is female.

More disappointing, the rate of women being promoted is so slow that, according to the Merit Board study, women are unlikely to be represented in top government slots for another quarter century. Instead, women remain clustered in low-paying jobs that offer little chance of advancement. Women occupy 86% of all federal clerical jobs. Women account for almost two-thirds of the lowest rated positions, GS-1 to GS-8.

Some of this imbalance can be attributed to differences between men and women in terms of their education and length of service in the government. Another possible explanation for the disparity lies in denial or lack of awareness of the problem. As Shannon C. Roberts, a past president of Executive Women in Government explained, many managers in her agency (the National Aeronautics and Space Administration) are unaware of the extent to which women are passed over for promotion. She herself was not surprised, however: "I am aware of how unaware we are" (as quoted in McAllister, 1992, p. A4).

Stereotyping also blocks the careers of female civil servants. Commenting on the findings from the Merit Board report, the legislative director of Federally Employed Women (an organization of current and retired federal workers) said: "Women are facing both institutional and attitudinal barriers in the government. The federal government is not a panacea" (as quoted in McAllister, 1992, p. A1).

Neither is the 1978 Civil Service Reform Act, designed to eliminate the underrepresentation of both women and minorities in all levels of the federal government. Despite this legislative reform, the Merit Board study found "a resurgence of discrimination" in the 1980s (as cited in McAllister, 1992, p. A4)—the exact time period during which women were surging into the federal bureaucracy. Lynn Eppard, an officer of Federally Employed Women, explained that federal managers assumed that the government had become "even" and thus made no concerted effort to help minorities and women. Like many senior women in public relations in regard to their field (e.g., Mathews, 1988), she believed that the government was a better place for women in the decade of the 1970s than today.

However, Carol A. Bonosaro, former president of the Senior Executives Association, contended that government was doing more for women than was private industry. At the same time, she conceded that "it just hasn't done well enough" (as quoted in McAllister, 1992, p. A4). She and other spokespeople for federal employee groups were optimistic that significant numbers of retirements at the senior executive level would provide more opportunity for women over time.

Creating an equitable situation for women in government may require more than the inevitable retirements. In the Foreign Service, only a hard-fought lawsuit helped overcome the discrimination against women in hiring, assignments, and honors there between 1976 and 1985. As a result of *Palmer v. Baker*, about 600 women were entitled to court-ordered relief—including promotion to more senior positions. Presumably, many of those "stretch" assignments, or jobs above the individual's personal rank, encompassed communication responsibilities in missions overseas (L. Grunig, 1991). The importance of women doing this vital work in developing countries lies in the prediction that they may practice a more cooperative, negotiational style of public relations than would men. This is especially likely to happen when women see themselves in a managerial—rather than a technical—role (Wetherell, 1989). At that point, they may be able to influence the priorities of their missions and those of the indigenous groups with which they interact.

Similarly, the selection of Wilma Mankiller in 1985 as the first female principal chief of a major Native American tribe, the Oklahoma Cherokee, is significant in its potential for both Native American and women's rights. The year before, Democrat Geraldine Ferraro had become the first woman nominated as vice president by a major U.S. political party.

A significantly earlier milestone was Jeanette Rankin's 1916 victory in the House of Representatives. She became the first woman elected to Congress, in large part because of her platform of extending voting rights to women and banning liquor. She voted on legislation in the House, but she could not vote for herself (or anyone else) in the 1916 election because women were not enfranchised until the 19th Amendment passed in 1920.

However, the elections of 1992 stand out as an unprecedented opportunity for women, truly "the year of the woman in politics." That year saw several firsts for women: both of California's Senate seats were won by women, Barbara Boxer and Dianne Feinstein; the first Mexican American and Puerto Rican women were elected to the U.S. House of Representatives; and the first African American female senator, Carole Moseley Braun, was elected.

There seemed to be both a gender and an age gap in voting behavior in 1992. Women account for 54% of the U.S. electorate. In his first presidential election, they gave Bill Clinton 45% of their votes, contrasted with the 41% of male voters who supported Clinton. The chasm widened to 48% of women under age 30, versus 38% of men the same age. Playboy Enterprises CEO Christie Hefner, addressing the Brandeis University Women's Network in the spring of 1993, predicted that "the fact that younger, better educated and employed women were major contributors to the gender gap suggests that their influence will grow" (p. 50).

Novelist and New York Times columnist Anna Quindlen characterized the 1992 election as a "mini-revolution" at the polls. She explained that women's anger after the Clarence Thomas appointment resulted in their determination to "do something" about government (as quoted in O'Briant, 1992). The editor of Majority Rules! (Struck, 1992), a newsletter for and about women in U.S. politics, described this same election as "a crossroads in history." He explained that qualified, conscientious, accomplished women were "at the brink of becoming the mainstream political force in the United States" (p. 1). Perhaps the outcome of the 1992 election could best be described, as The Arizona Republic (1993) described it, as a case of hit-and-miss: The number of women in Congress had quadrupled since 1963 (hit), but women still made up just 10% of U.S. lawmakers (miss).

Working together, however, the Senate's five female Democrats managed to end a decade-long ban on abortion coverage in health plans for federal employees. Led by Senator Barbara Mikulski, the women outstrategized the anti-abortion forces. According to a newspaper account, "The Democratic women huddled in the well of the chamber as the roll was called, lobbying their male colleagues to the last vote. And the victory was so shaky that the women took turn as 'sentries' on the floor during debate on the rest of the bill to make sure they had enough votes in case antiabortion senators tried to reverse the vote" (Dewar, 1993, p. A4). A former lobbyist for the National Organization for Women pointed to additional issues where women are especially likely to play a prominent role: schools; day care for children, the elderly, and the disabled; and equitable treatment for minorities and women (Babington, 1993).

Despite this kind of potential for change, the 1998 election was called "Year of the Woman, The Sequel" by political analysts. Their analysis? "It's a very different year," according to media consultant Anita Dunn (as quoted in Harwood and Seib, 1997, p. A24). "The novelty of having women run doesn't generate the same excitement." Consider, too, how a political columnist at *The Washington Post* characterized, on balance, the aftermath of the November 1992 elections: "Stories boasted that there are 24 more women in Congress (up to a rousing 11 percent of the House of Representatives), four new women senators (that makes six) and, to boot—a ladies' bathroom built on the first floor of the Senate" (Mathias, 1993, p. B5).

As the elections for the year 2000 approached, women in Congress questioned whether they had as much influence as they had enjoyed in 1992. We see, then, that what political clout women do have can be a one-step-forward, two-steps-back phenomenon. Debra Dodson, senior research associate at the Center for the American Women in Politics at Rutgers University, explained that women are constrained from making much difference in the House because most *members* are Republicans at a time when most *women* are Democrats (as quoted in Eilperin, 1998). The highest ranking woman in the House at that time, Washington's Jennifer Dunn, believed women would bring "a softer side" to the conservative message. Fellow Republican Deborah Pryce, from Ohio, said much the same about the potential contributions of her female colleagues: "Perhaps we're more sensitive to how deeply troubling our harsh rhetoric is to some people, especially women" (as quoted in Eilperin, 1998, p. A19).

What is the situation for women who work as aides on Capitol Hill? In the wake of allegations of sexual harassment directed at Senator Bob

Packwood, *The Washington Post* surveyed 603 of these female legislative assistants (Morin, 1993). Respondents indicated that they regularly lose out on pay and promotions to men. One-third said they had been sexually harassed by coworkers, supervisors, lobbyists, and the legislators themselves. Most agreed that women who work for Congress are less respected and valued than their male colleagues. They blamed the male culture that continues to dominate the Hill. As a result, even senior staffers like Nancy Weist may be made to feel like intruders. She said: "You see it at meetings where women kind of vanish into the woodwork, even when their issues are discussed" (as quoted in Morin, 1993, p. A1). The bottom-line finding of the study was that working conditions for women on the Hill are strikingly similar to conditions for working women everywhere.

An innovative program that teams women in business with politics offers great potential for change. McDonnell Douglas joined with the National Women's Political Caucus to encourage and support its female employees interested in entering the political arena. Republicans and Democrats alike are optimistic that these candidates will succeed. They reason that both women and business leaders are viewed as fresh and untainted by voters who prefer outsiders on Capitol Hill. A 1991 survey found that a hypothetical female executive would outpoll a hypothetical male business leader by 10 percentage points (Times Mirror Center for the People & the Press, as cited in Dunham, 1993).

One local politician made a point of telling voters that she offered an alternative to the good-old-boys politics in her state. Speaking from her home, which doubles as her office, Maryland's former state senator Mary L. Boergers explained: "People are definitely looking for a different kind of leadership. They're dissatisfied with the field they know" (as quoted in Babington, 1993, p. B1). Boergers believed that stereotypes about women may help her in her political races because voters "want someone who really cares about them. Women are perceived as not being beholden to special interests, not being into back-room deals" (as quoted in Babington, 1993, p. B1).

However, Boergers seemed to be suffering from stereotyping during her state's 1994 gubernatorial primary. She complained that "a lot of times people will come up and say, 'You sure would be the prettiest governor'" (as quoted in Heath, 1994). One fellow candidate for the governorship said she took "the wrong way" his remark about how attractive she is and his suggestion that she drop her bid for governor and become his running mate for lieutenant governor. *The Washington Post* (Heath, 1994) reported that many of Boergers's female colleagues in the race for political office in 1994 had run into the same stereotypical stumbling blocks. The good news in this story is that an unprecedented number of women sought higher office in Maryland that year: three for the governorship alone. Their collective opinions, quoted in *The Post*, made a strong case for the charge that society still believes men grow wiser with age and women just grow older. *The Post* reported that one gubernatorial candidate, Representative Helen Delich Bentley, got "at least one facelift" because of the perceived importance of the "image thing" (p. B4).

Christie Hefner (1993), who manages the $215 million Playboy publishing and entertainment enterprises, credited much of her success in expanding the company's influence worldwide to forming strategic alliances with international partners. This networking mode, she contended, also has been key to women's political success. Speaking at her alma mater, Brandeis University, she explained that "qualities that many people want to see in the leaders of the future match characteristics typically associated with women's leadership style: openness, trust, compassion, understanding. Indeed, in a *U.S. News and World Report* poll . . . a stunning 61 percent of those surveyed thought the country would be governed better if more women held political office" (p. 50).

Megatrends for Women (Aburdene & Naisbitt, 1992) predicted that a woman will be elected president of the United States by early in the 21st century. (Virginia Woodhull was the nation's first female presidential candidate when in 1871 she ran from the Equal Rights Party.) In the meantime, feminists in 1997 were encouraged by President Bill Clinton's selection of Madeleine Albright as secretary of state and Janet Reno as U.S. attorney general. That year marked the first time that half of the high cabinet positions in this country were held by women. (The first woman named to a presidential cabinet was Frances Perkins, who became secretary of labor in 1933. Historians Hine and Thompson, 1998, reminded us that during that same administration, Mary McLeod Bethune organized the Federal Council on Negro Affairs—the so-called Black Cabinet—to advise Franklin Delano Roosevelt. Thus Bethune is often considered the most powerful black woman in U.S. government to date.)

We come back time and again to the question of whether simply having women in government (or in law or in medicine or in public relations) makes a difference in the way government (or any other field) operates. We have to believe that women's representation does indeed matter. Take the case of Albright. By her second month in office, she was acknowledged as a proponent of women's issues in this country and abroad (Lippman, 1997). Almost immediately after taking office, she instructed U.S. diplomats around the world to make women's rights a priority of our foreign policy. As a result, the State Department contributed funds to a school for Afghan refugee girls who otherwise would be without education; the U.S. Embassy in Namibia used its entire discretionary fund to help combat sexual violence against women there.

Did Albright push for this feminist agenda because she believes that if the world were run by women war would disappear? Not at all. Instead, she explained: "The history of this century tells us that democracy is a parent to peace. And common sense tells us that true democracy is not possible without the full participation of women" (as quoted in Lippman, 1997, p. A9).

As a result, Albright stated her commitment to U.S. participation (despite objection by Senator Jesse Helms) in the Convention on the Elimination of Discrimination against Women. This treaty, adopted by the United Nations General Assembly in 1979 and signed by the United States in the last year of President Jimmy Carter's administration, obliges signatories to condemn sexual discrimination and take measures to overcome it. A second domestic initiative in Albright's agenda is a joint State and Justice Department program to halt trafficking in Russian women duped into prostitution by organized crime.

Despite the optimism inherent in the work of high-level government figures such as Reno and Albright, women in political or civic work still must overcome a host of obstacles. To some, their efforts on women's behalf are merely cosmetic. As one State Department official put it, "We're upping the profile on this issue, but it's not going to start trumping other considerations" (as quoted in Lippman, 1997, p. A9). He explained that despite the Clinton administration's focus on women, the Foreign Service is not about to "beat up on the Saudis," for example, because of the status of women there (women who reputedly cannot drive or travel without the permission of their husbands or fathers).

Time is a second major factor. Because of working what amounts to a double shift at home and at the office, women have little opportunity for the outside activities that might boost their careers, whether in business or in politics. As Elizabeth B. Karabatsos, McDonnell Douglas Helicopter Company's ombudsman, put it: "The men only have seven-day weeks. Women have eight-day weeks" (as quoted in Dunham, 1993, p. 66). Both stereotypes and men's and women's attitudes contribute to the problem as well. When campaigning as the Republican candidate for governor of New Jersey, Christine Todd Whitman explained that women are used to thinking that "politics is dirty. We can't get involved" (as quoted in Dunham, 1993, p. 66).

Women who are ardent about their political ambitions may feel thwarted because they are not taken seriously. Like so many other women who work outside the home, they face a glass ceiling. Senator Boergers, in her bid for the governorship of Maryland, constantly combated the speculation that she actually aspired to be someone else's running mate for lieutenant governor. As a result, she wears a cracked-crystal pin to symbolize her determination to succeed in shattering that glass ceiling.

Even the working wives of political figures often experience discrimination. A *Washington Post* reporter (Grove, 1993) found that "because politics in America has always been a male-dominated profession, it's the working wife who almost always bears the burden of proof: Did she get her job and advance her career through her influential husband?" (p. C9). A Washington expert on political spouses (M. E. Miller, 1992) explained that women are thus scrutinized because society has yet to acknowledge that women can achieve professionally on their own.

Marilyn Quayle, wife of the former vice president and a member of the Indiana bar, was more optimistic about the situation for political wives: "All you have to do is keep doing the job, do everything the best you can, and things will work out for you. If the truth is there on your side, you're going to win" (as quoted in Grove, 1993, p. C9). As support for her contention, recall the life and career of perhaps the most influential first lady in history, Eleanor Roosevelt. Roosevelt's victories include great gains for women, people of color, and the poor—largely through her leadership of the United Nations Commission on Human Rights.

Women in Higher Education

Women in higher education have not been winning, at least in the decades since Bernard (1964) first studied gender differences in academia. She discovered then that female faculty's experiences differed significantly from men's. Her findings held in 1981 (although she did not restrict her research at that time to the academy). She concluded that women and men continue to labor in markedly different worlds.

Perhaps for this reason, a 1992 panel at the annual convention of journalism educators was titled "Old Issues Unresolved: Women Educators' Status in the Academy." Commenting on that working paper session, Ramona Rush (1993), professor of communications at the University of Kentucky, exclaimed: "Isn't that the godawful truth!" (p. 71). She went on to acknowledge the gains women educators have made over the last 20 years. However, she charged both the academy and the profession with falling short of resolving the issues that continue to plague women who teach. In her commentary, Rush listed a number of those concerns: sexual harassment, political power harassment, inadequate search and hiring procedures, dismal retention rates, academic and professional dirty tricks, salary inequities, and the fundamental lack of awareness that all of these problems persist.

Unless the academy makes a systemic commitment to overcome this kind of discrimination against the women who work there, we will remain stoop laborers. That's what we are. Women in academia—especially the untenured—have been called higher education's most dispensable of workers (McCarthy, 1991). One professor who attempted to organize the 300,000 nontenured teachers in this country asked:

> Could anyone capable of teaching in higher education—and whose capability has been proven, first by being hired and then by doing the job—actually "deserve" as little as $1,750 a course, without benefits, in 1991–92? . . . Either these people are professionally qualified, or they are not. If they are, they deserve to be treated as such. If they are not, then who hired them? (as quoted in McCarthy, 1991, p. A27)

Too often treated as "academic detritus," faculty women particularly in part-time positions are debased by the senior, tenured faculty who tend to be male. The result? As public relations educators Zoch and Russell (1991) put it, women in higher education are "overworked and overlooked" (p. 31).

We belabor this discussion of academic women primarily for the sake of students reading this text. We believe you need to understand the situation of your female professors, many of whom do not enjoy the rank, salary, or job satisfaction of their male counterparts in communication or journalism education. The greatest difference by gender and racial diversity seems to exist in the latter dimension: satisfaction at work. A recent survey by Riffe, Salomone, and Stempel (1998) found that "generally speaking, tenured, white, male full professors are happier than their [minority and female] counterparts" (p. 116). This satisfaction gap becomes increasingly important with the increasing number of women teaching in mass communication programs (the Riffe et al. study showed that growth in racial diversity in such schools is significantly slower than in gender diversity). Riffe and his colleagues concluded:

> Growth in the presence of both women and minorities is indeed progress. Institutions and colleagues must continue to work to help women and minority faculty develop and attain the levels of productivity that ensure comparable compensation. But until acts of discrimination are eliminated and the workplace climate is supportive of all faculty, celebration of that progress is premature. (p. 118)

Concerned with the implications of any hegemonic education on diverse student populations, the University of Maryland's 1998 Outstanding Woman of the Year has devoted a major program of research to what she called "discovering culture in education." Barbara Finkelstein (as cited in Hawes, 1998) tackled issues related to educational programs designed to address and foster understanding among diverse groups.

Women in higher education across the disciplines tend to suffer from the discriminatory gendered stereotype that they themselves are transgressing their traditional role designations. In this sense, they are like their sisters in law and medicine. As feminist and public relations scholar Lana Rakow (1991) explained, by their very gender women who teach at the university level violate the "natural order." In her remarks upon receiving her woman-of-the-year award, Finkelstein told this wrenching story:

> As a pregnant Ab.D. [in 1968], I was foolish enough to believe it was possible to sustain three absolute commitments simultaneously: the life of the mind, a professional academic career, and a career of devoted parent. . . . As a working mother I tried, without success, to dignify motherhood and teaching as social institutions and to seek, also without success, a level professional field at my workplace. One of a few female faculty on campus, I waited on line while six of my less published peers climbed the academic ladder more quickly and less problematically. (p. 3)

As a direct result of women like this not seeming to belong, they often are judged harshly by their students. Lueck, Endres, and Caplan (1993) reviewed the literature that explores the effects of gender on student evaluations. Some findings were equivocal. Others stood in direct contradiction with each other. However, their meta-analysis concluded that most studies have found that male professors are rated higher than female professors.

Small wonder, then, that junior female faculty suffer. They suffer attacks of anxiety even when their teaching evaluations are superior to those of their male colleagues. Untenured women, in particular, feel more pressured than junior men to do research. And they may experience conflict between their own orientation toward teaching and the priority attached to doing the research required for promotion (Locke, 1992).

Lumping together tenured and nontenured college faculty, we find an average pay gap of 23.3% between women and men. The average female professor in 1990 earned $32,240 compared with $42,016 for the typical male professor (Bureau of Labor statistics, as cited in Morris & Siegel, 1992). This places university teaching salaries just above the midpoint in terms of salary gap between the narrowest (registered nurse at 1.3%) and the widest (graphic designer, 38.1%) in that year. (In only one job classification did women outdistance men paywise in 1992: Female postal clerks on average earned 2.4% more than males.) The salary differential between women and men on campus has been described in numerous studies (e.g., McElrath, 1992; M. J. Clark & Centra, 1985; Etaugh, 1984; Evangelauf, 1984; Ferber, Loeb, & Lowry, 1978).

Other research has established that academic women tend to be excluded from informal networks (Fox, 1985; Simeone, 1987) and that they often are sexually harassed (Theodore, 1986). There is a pernicious disregard for gender-related research and this, in turn, may disadvantage women at tenure time (Theodore, 1986; S. M. Clark & Corcoran, 1986; Simeone, 1987). Women who interrupt their careers or change academic jobs also jeopardize their achievement of tenure. McElrath (1992) found no evidence that men are similarly disadvantaged.

Taken together, these problems result in what S. M. Clark and Corcoran (1986) called the "accumulative disadvantage" of faculty women. Given the pervasiveness of this devaluation of women in the academy, Annette Kolodny (1998) promoted a university code against what she considered anti-feminist intellectual harassment. While dean of humanities at the University of Arizona, she proposed a ban on policies, actions, or statements that discourage or thwart research and teaching pertaining to women or gender inequities.

Pay and all of the other issues described above undoubtedly discourage and demoralize faculty (and prospective faculty) women. These are the folks who teach the public relations practitioners of the future. We, the authors of this book, are *personally* concerned as well. In one way or another, we have suffered from gender discrimination in academia.

This kind of bias exists in community colleges as well as in the research universities where the three of us teach. An extensive review of the literature pertaining to gender and these postsecondary institutions (Twombly, 1993) showed them to be relatively hospitable to women at all levels: students, staff, administrators, and faculty. However, despite the significant number of women who have come to teach and learn in the community college, it remains—like so many other work places—inequitable. The inequalities persist primarily in recruitment, promotion, tenure, curriculum, and classroom climate. (This assessment results from Twombly's meta-analysis of 174 relevant articles published between 1970 and 1989.)

The National Women's Studies Association (NWSA) regularly monitors the status of women in higher education, whether they teach in 2- or 4-year universities. Its newsletter runs a section of "Success Stories," highlighting the cases of women who win academic discrimination suits.

The NWSA also offers advice to women who labor in the groves of academe. Tenured women must remain vigilant as they peruse the resumes and publications of colleagues they are reviewing. Alert junior women to what is in their personnel files. Be aware that students tend to rate their female professors lower than their male professors. Department chairs have been known to solicit these kinds of judgments from students known to dislike a woman professor. Departmental administrators also may assign women to teach classes of students known to be contrary. Understand that scholarly research by women may be devalued, especially if it deals with women or is developed from a feminist perspective (Pratt, 1990).

Even scholarly publishing seems to devalue women. A study of the status of women described the glass ceiling in university presses. Two-thirds of the employees there are women, yet women hold only 14% of the directorships. Almost 30% of the women surveyed attested to some form of discrimination. More than a quarter said they had been harassed, sexually or otherwise. In a comment more indicative of the climate for women in this field, one respondent characterized the problem as "more in the nature of a chronic disease than catastrophic illness" ("Women in the Workplace," 1992, p. A11).

One publisher passionate about women's issues, Miriam Daum Selby, established her own company dedicated to giving voice to women. The first title published by Sibyl Publications was *The Next Step: Women's Educational Issues in the Greater Portland Area, 1993–94*. Selby planned to update this guide each summer and, along the way, seek out the writings of other women interested in furthering the discussion of women's empowerment. As she explained it: "Average women are doing extraordinary things in all walks of life, and I want to share their stories. A friend has collected 30 rejection slips for a book on women in midlife. Publishers don't take our issues seriously enough" (as quoted in McDermott, 1993, p. E3).

Perhaps this kind of systematic devaluation helps explain women's declining interest in teaching as a career. Some 40 years ago, education was women's first choice as a college major. Today it is business management (Nasar, 1992a).

What of women at the managerial level in higher education? Kolodny (1998), former dean of the College of Humanities at the University of Arizona, painted a gloomy picture and speculated on an even bleaker future. She left a distinguished career as professor of literature at the Rensselaer Polytechnic Institute to test her contention that as a feminist administrator she could be instrumental in helping academia progress toward equity and educational excellence. She blamed contemporary management structures for constraining people like herself who seek ethical solutions to problems created in large part by the politicization of higher education. The situation is compounded, in her view, by the fact that university administrations remain "structurally male." Management emphasizes the public at the expense of the private and the personal.

A reviewer of Kolodny's latest book (Abrahams, 1998), himself an academic administrator, countered that "this is true no matter which gender the manager is, because the competitive environment for universities, no less than corporations, has become so demanding and unforgiving" (p. 23). Given the proportions of woman and men in managerial positions in academia, we are not convinced. Female administrators remain the exception. Kolodny was the first and only female academic dean at Arizona. But despite her pessimism over the fate of U.S. universities (and the fact that her administration coincided with what Abrahams considered arguably the worst years financially for higher education since World War II), she did in fact make progress during her tenure at Arizona. When she arrived in 1988, 30% of the faculty in the humanities were women; by 1992, that proportion had risen to half. Minority students enrolled in great numbers and, even according to critical reviewer Abrahams, "the University of Arizona has emerged as one of the top 10 public universities in the country" (p. 25).

WOMEN IN BLUE-COLLAR WORK

Although women have made significant gains in entering professional and managerial occupations, U.S. Bureau of the Census figures paint a gloomier picture for less-educated women. As a front-page headline put it, "For Women, Uneven Strides in Workplace: Census Data Reflect Decade of White-Collar Progress, Blue-Collar Resistance" (Cohn & Vobejda, 1992, p. A1).

Women's access to the minimum-wage labor market varies by occupation. Although women recently doubled their representation in the ranks of mail carriers and now comprise nearly half of all bus drivers and dispatchers, some other trades are more resistant. For example, women broke into construction, fire fighting, and auto repair a quarter-century ago yet they still hold only a tiny fraction of these high-paying blue-collar jobs. (Drivers of heavy trucks, typically male, earn on average twice the weekly pay of a child-care worker, typically female [Ingley, 1993].)

Trade unions may be partly accountable. They control access to apprenticeships and training jobs. Today, only 12.3% of women in the United States belong to unions—down from 14.6% in 1983 and contrasted with the 17.2% of men who are union workers (Grimsley, 1997). We point our finger at the media as well. Claire Moses, a historian who heads the

Women's Studies Department at the University of Maryland, challenged the popular notion that the women's movement of the 1970s was largely white and middle class. She explained that the history is significantly more complicated than journalists have reported: "The media was [sic] not interested in all the feminist work that was happening, in labor unions, for example" (as quoted in Burch, 1998, p. 28).

The recession of the 1990s also may be to blame. Women's advocates point out that as last-hired blue-collar workers, women are likely to be the first laid off (Cohn & Vobejda, 1992). Little has changed in some ways, then, since the days of Rosie the Riveter. In the early 1940s, she became an icon for women who replaced men in the work place leaving for World War II. In the later 1940s, women like Rosie were encouraged to forego their blue-collar jobs to make room for male veterans returning from the war.

Finally, some people charge that women shy away from work such as construction because it's a dirty job. However, as Cynthia Marano, executive director of Wider Opportunities for Women, pointed out, "Being a waitress and being a home health care aide are very dirty jobs" (as quoted in Cohn & Vobejda, 1992, p. A12). Girls' Inc., a national youth service group, also denies the validity of the "eek and yuck" factor. Its research on girls aged 9 to 14 showed that despite socialization to the contrary, girls do take risks and they do get their hands dirty.

One newspaper columnist commenting on the Girls' Inc. study called the notion of women avoiding dirty work "ludicrous." Kleiman (1991c) pointed out that "women change diapers more often than men, and anyone who has ever changed a diaper should be able to meet the 'eek and yuck' standard" (p. B1). She explained that "eek and yuck" is a stereotype that puts women down. As with so many sex-linked stereotypes, it blames the victim for the problem. (What's truly "eek and yuck," in Kleiman's view? The fact that although she considers women better educated, more enthusiastic, and more interested in developing their skills than are men, women remain underpaid, underemployed, and unable to move ahead.)

A pervasive male culture may do more than anything else to discourage women from entering certain spheres of the blue-collar world. Heidi Hartmann, who directed the Institute for Women's Policy Research in Washington, DC, speculated that the masculine culture that prevails in fields such as construction may result in hostility and harassment from the men there (as quoted in Cohn & Vobejda, 1992). Indeed, little about the construction industry seems to support women. An article in *Newsweek* (A. Miller, Springen, & Tsiantar, 1992) chronicled the trials of Marilu Meyer, president of the $7 million-per-year Castle Construction Co. Bankers she approached about a loan to start her business suggested she try opening, a stationery store or a T-shirt shop instead.

Other vocations, such as meter reading, are more receptive to women because people in those jobs tend to work alone. Hartmann concluded about women in blue-collar fields, as have so many scholars studying women in white-collar careers, that "there has been truly a tremendous amount of progress for women. . . . At the same time, it's true there are tremendous problems" (as quoted in Cohn & Vobejda, 1992, p. A1).

The earnings gap between men and women tends to be smaller in blue-collar than in white-collar jobs (Bureau of Labor Statistics, as cited in Rigdon, 1993). Significant exceptions exist, as in the case of machine operators, assemblers, and inspectors. In that line of work, women tend to earn less than 70% of what men earn—or about the same percentage as female versus male managers in public relations.

In most other hourly work, however, the distinction is less pronounced. Female cashiers and data-entry keyers, for example, make about 95% of what male cashiers and male data-entry keyers earn. (Contrast this 5% pay gap with the fact that female financial managers earn about 62¢ on the male dollar in that profession.) On average, though, women in the minimum-wage labor force earn less than 75% of what men earn (Cohn & Vobejda, 1992). This happens despite the fact that, according to at least one long-time laborer, "Women try 100 percent, and it makes men look bad" (Kifer, as quoted in Melton & Grimsley, 1998, p. A1). Louise Kifer, who worked for more than 4 decades in a Pennsylvania glass factory, realized by age 60 that "these damn men need an attitude adjustment" (p. A1).

Finally, we need to mention the "pink-collar" fields, or the low-level jobs from banking to beauty shops that employ tremendous numbers of women. Since the early 1980s, women's unemployment rates have been lower than men's because of this boom in service work (Nasar, 1992a). However, these low-paid women rarely manage to move up and out of their pink-collar ghettos. One notable exception, of course, is Madame C. J. Walker, who turned her talents as a hair stylist into a lucrative hair-straightening empire—thus allowing her to live in a sumptuous estate where she hosted anti-lynching fundraisers (Hine & Thompson, 1988).

We write the word "ghetto" cautiously, fearing that its racist or ethnic implications may offend readers. However, we have decided to use it here because it truly characterizes the situation for so many women who, as a kind of minority, find themselves relegated to certain occupations and because it is a term endemic to the literature about women and work. The situation for women who are typists, nurses' aides, and day-care workers also has been called a "sticky floor." They are "stuck" on the ground floor of relatively low-paying positions considered low status in this country.

CONCLUDING THOUGHTS

Opportunities for Entering Diverse Fields

Many women are working in jobs that would have been unthinkable to their great-grandmothers' generation. In the last century, women in law and medicine were distractions at best, moral threats at worst. Today, most fields we reviewed did not discriminate overtly against women. Associations and government offices, for example, welcome women. Only a few, such as the construction trades, continue to support a male culture actively hostile toward women.

Despite the growing number of women even in blue-collar work, women still represent only a tiny fraction of the total work force in some occupations, such as surgery and politics. In others, including public relations and scholarly publishing, women are the majority. However, in almost every occupation the proportion of women is increasing exponentially.

Where women remain an anomaly, they face incredible pressure to overcome stereotypes or sex-typed behavior. They often encounter animosity from their coworkers because they are refuting what may be considered the norm for their gender. When a field becomes female-intensive, such as the federal government and public relations, it may suffer from the loss of status we will describe in Chapter 7. Finally, we allude to a concern occasionally voiced about encouraging women to pioneer new careers. In so doing, they necessarily abandon the fields traditionally associated with women. A leader in education (as quoted in Smith, 1993) called this "one of my biggest gripes with the women's movements; they push women towards non-traditional careers or away from careers in education or child care" (p. 5).

Segregation Within a Field

Majority or not, women fail to "dominate" any career we've investigated. Directly or indirectly, many women are funneled away from the most high-status and lucrative fields to the less prestigious, poorer paying specialties.

In medicine, this may be pediatrics and in higher education, part-time or non-tenure-track slots.

Public relations itself has been considered a specialty within the broader field of communication—a specialty that invites women because it is a staff rather than a line function, such as advertising. Being a member of a support staff is consistent with society's expectations of the working woman. Nurturing, caregiving, being cooperative, and being concerned with relationships are all traits associated with femininity. As a result, many women find themselves in what have been called the "pink-collar ghettos" of service fields. Women are also more welcome in small than in large associations and in 2-year rather than 4-year universities.

Advancement and Pay

Top positions and top pay elude women in most of the careers we described here. As the old saying goes, "We can get in, but we can't get on." The floor is sticky and the glass ceiling is ubiquitous.

Despite all of the references to the glass ceiling, we have concentrated on wages rather than career advancement in this chapter. Why the seemingly inordinate emphasis on pay? We know that gender is the greatest determinant of salary (P. Edwards & S. Edwards, 1985). Our own research has shown that women in public relations are especially timid about the process of salary negotiation. Several of the practitioners we interviewed explained that women are more likely than men to take a smaller salary than they deserve. Humphrey (1990) found that women are demoralized not because they necessarily want higher salaries but because their pay may not be commensurate with their responsibilities at work. Even with less pay for at least comparable work, one female editor for a national trade association told us that women are "grateful."

We found a compensation gap in almost every occupational cluster we studied. That discrepancy in public relations is greater than in some, such as data entry, and smaller than in others, such as architecture. We remain concerned that salaries for everyone are in jeopardy, however, should a recession combine with sex discrimination and a growing female majority. In the professions, in particular, the wage gap actually is widening.

Do Women Make a Difference in the Work Force?

In law and in politics, we offered dramatic examples of women who are changing the nature of the work they do. Female judges, attorneys, and legislators have focused their attention on issues considered important primarily to women and minorities: wages and taxes for domestic workers, child and elder care, divorce law, rights of ethnic and racial groups, and abortion. In these ways and more, women truly seem to be making a difference as they move from the private into the public sphere. So, too, may the influence of women in public relations extend beyond their own organizations to enhance their communities around the world.

Chapter Four

Women in Management and Entrepreneurship

In this chapter, like the previous one, you will find many allusions to the glass ceiling. Both the business press and the mass media have referred to the special roadblocks women encounter toward advancement because of their gender. The glass ceiling speaks to the absence of women in positions of top management. Writing in *The Wall Street Journal*, for example, Hymowitz and Schellhardt (1996) described the glass ceiling for women aspiring to top corporate positions: These women can see where they want to be but unless they manage to break through the barrier, they will stay below the men in the corporation.

On any given day, major metropolitan dailies are likely to report on this dilemma for women as well. On one Sunday, *The Washington Post* alone dedicated two major stories to the phenomenon. A page-one article in the Metro section described the sexism confronting a woman running for governor (Babington, 1993). The first page of the Business section focused on discrimination against a female executive in a brokerage house (Mathews, 1993).

Management has been a male preserve (Kanter, 1977). This represents a concern not only for ambitious and capable women, but for others whose lives they would affect as managers who may bring a feminine orientation to their work. Nevertheless, studies by Baron (1977) and the U.S. Department of Labor showed that until the 1980s, the growth of women in management remained relatively constant.

That situation is changing. More and more women are filling managerial roles. Labor Department statistics (as cited in "Women in the Workplace," 1998) compared the situation for women in 1985 versus 1995. In

1985, women held a little over one-third of managerial and executive jobs. A decade later, they held 48% of those positions.

Thus we consider it vital to include a separate chapter in this book about women in public relations for an exploration of the opportunities and constraints that *any* female manager is likely to encounter. Of course, not all women in the field aspire to a managerial role, as a later chapter focusing on promotion in public relations makes clear. However, those who do see themselves as part of the management team also tend to perceive a transparent but very real barrier to achieving that status. For women of color in management, the barriers may be even more formidable.

As a result, this chapter concludes with a look at women who have opted out of the salaried labor force to manage their own businesses. This new breed of female entrepreneurs has been called "open collars" and "Mompreneurs" (Kim, 1991). However, we know that not only mothers—at least in public relations—work from their homes. Many women, both mothers and nonmothers, have chosen the autonomy of self-employment over the obstacles chronicled elsewhere in this book: low pay, sexual harassment, lack of flexibility, powerlessness, excessive family obligations, tokenism, gender stereotyping, and so forth. Thus we dedicate considerable space to exploring the circumstances of women who are self-employed in a variety of endeavors—including communication management.

WOMEN IN BUSINESS MANAGEMENT

The Miami Herald conducted a study of the American work force, looking at gender, race, and ethnicity of workers in 512 occupations in 325 metropolitan areas around the nation. It found a significant gain for women, especially in the executive and managerial ranks. Whereas in 1980 there were 29% fewer women in these roles than would be expected in terms of their share of the total work force, by 1990 that gender gap had shrunk to below 8% of the ideal.

Some parts of the country are more receptive than others to women at the highest ranks. In Washington, DC, for example women account for about 22% of all executive, administrative, and managerial positions (U.S. Bureau of Labor Statistics, as cited in Grimsley, 1997). Next highest is the Silicon Valley of California. Meanwhile, the percentage of women in areas such as Buffalo, New York, and Providence, Rhode Island, is only half that of the nation's capital.

Consider just one managerial environment in the Northeast: Wall Street. Catherine Kinney, executive vice president for equities at the New

York Stock Exchange, believes that the situation for women is looking up, even in very traditional male-dominated fields such as hers. She explained the lingering discrepancies between men's and women's salaries and positions there as a function of three factors: women's lack of experience, their need to find mentors, and their willingness to take risks. She concluded, "I think over time it will clearly improve" (as quoted in Mathews, 1993, p. H5).

In other fields, such as the media in general and broadcasting in particular, women remain dramatically underrepresented in the top ranks of management (Stone, 1987; Sohn, 1984). One notable exception was Nancy Woodhull, who at the time of her death in 1997 was senior vice president of communications at the Freedom Forum. Her 33-year-career encompassed the founding editorship of *USA Today*, presidency of Gannett News Services, and managing editorship of the Rochester, New York, *Democrat and Chronicle* and *Times-Union*. Woodhull brought if not a feminist perspective, a woman's view regarding issues of gender and diversity. To honor her career, Charles L. Overby (as quoted in "Tribute," 1997), chairman and CEO of the Freedom Forum, announced the establishment of an annual Forum on Diversity and the Media: "The forum will allow the impact that Nancy had on diversity to be renewed every year" (p. 76).

Woodhull had inserted herself into any number of organizations and initiatives aimed at enhancing women's visibility and their careers in the media. She was vice chair of the International Women's Media Foundation, chair of the Peabody Radio and Television Awards, and president of the National Women's Hall of Fame. She cofounded Women, Men and Media, an organization dedicated to monitoring women's coverage and presence in the media. Because she herself had risen to a position of prominence, her "Woodhullisms" were well known. They speak to the influence her work unquestionably had on women and the men who traditionally had dominated their work place. For example, to explain the bottom-line necessity of reporters' beginning to cover women and the issues that resonate with them, she said:

> Think of women as a suburb you don't cover very well. If your newspaper didn't cover a suburb well, it wouldn't surprise you that readership is not there. So, why are we surprised when women are buying [fewer and fewer newspapers]? (as quoted in "Tribute," 1997, p. 76)

In a related point, Mark Trahant (as quoted in "Tribute," 1997) spoke to Woodhull's influence on him as a former reporter:

... I would often hear Nancy's voice asking me if I had done enough reporting. If the story's voices were all male, I would hear her ask if that story was an accurate picture. And usually I would make one or two more calls. (p. 76)

Given the importance of women like Woodhull making a positive difference in the way journalism is done, not just in terms of ethics or fairness to women but in terms of its effect on the financial bottom line, we consider it unfortunate that so few women rise to her managerial level. Why is this? Stone (1987) attributed it to women being less likely than men to aspire to upper management. A spate of studies conducted in the 1970s (e.g., Hennig & Jardim, 1977; Kanter, 1977), too, has suggested that women's career goals are more conservative than men's and that women have less effective strategies for achieving their goals. The next sections of this chapter explore a host of other issues related to women in management and, at the same time, the explanations typically offered for the one-down position in which such women often find themselves.

Credentials and Competence

The question of women's credentials relative to men's comes up in nearly every discussion of women in management. A study conducted by a professor of economics at Eckerd College in Florida analyzed the salary and the qualifications of almost 200 corporate managers. He found that if the women in his study had been men with the same credentials, they would be earning about 18% more (Rigdon, 1993). This study, then, belies the commonly heard corporate argument that female managers are paid less than men because their credentials do not stack up against men's.

Similarly, a competency bias exists against women in many organizations. O'Leary and Hansen (1982) blamed stereotyping for the perception that men are more competent than women. They found that women are judged to be proficient only when they achieve success in occupations traditionally considered masculine or when their performance is deemed exceptional—based on standards of male culture. This problem may be exacerbated for women of color. As one African American professional explained: "You always have to portray an image of competency, more so than your white male and female counterparts. It doesn't matter that you're a female—it matters that you're black" (as quoted in Wise, 1997, p. 82).

We noticed a similar phenomenon related to the labeling attached to the question of credentials and competence. We've all heard about the company's search for "qualified minorities" and "qualified women." How many of us have heard the term "qualified whites" or "qualified men"? Because these labels are not reciprocal, they suggest that whites and men are inherently qualified for the position, whereas people of color and women must "measure up" to them.

Organizational Culture

Our own research (Hon, 1992) found that women in public relations are relegated to the technician role in large part because of the job segregation that results from a masculine organizational culture. Even powerful women in the institutional-development area of public relations may be precluded from senior management roles because of what some called the "history" of the universities. Two participants in Doonan's (1993) study of female fundraisers believed that because their institutions had been all male, the hiring and advancement policies there continued to affect women adversely. A third interviewee enjoyed what Doonan characterized as an "extremely friendly" work environment at a former women's college. Doonan concluded that "what this means for women fund raisers is that they must be very selective in choosing the organizations for which they work" (p. 119).

Organizational culture is a historically transmitted system of beliefs, symbols, and values (Eadie, 1997). As organizations change over time, their cultures too must shift to value non-traditional employees such as women in public relations.

The Pay and Promotion Gap

Employers may justify giving women lower salaries because of their belief that women are less loyal than men, quicker to leave the organization, largely because of family considerations (Powell, 1988; Nieva & Gutek, 1981; Toth & Cline, 1991). The pay differential between male and female managers is most pronounced at the executive level, and that gap even may be widening. A survey by a New York–based employment firm found that in 1989 average compensation for male executives was $86,134 compared with an average $63,339 for women. A year later, in 1990, executive men were earning an average of $88,796 whereas women earned $63,555. The chasm between men and women at the senior-most levels at that time reflected a difference of 40% (as cited in Swoboda, 1990a).

Not only do women in management tend to earn less than men, they rarely reach the top of the hierarchy (Raynolds, 1987; Dexter, 1985; Tsui & Gutek, 1984). Ragins and Sundstrom (1989) synthesized a series of studies and concluded that women represent 15% of entry-level managers, 5%

of middle managers, and 1% of top managers. Even when women are promoted, they tend to advance more slowly and, as shown above, only rarely
do they reach the same heights as men who are managers (Stewart &
Gudykunst, 1982). Three-fourths of the women responding to a survey
felt excluded from management ranks simply because of their gender
(Houghton, 1988).

The situation is no better in public relations. A recent study published
by PR Week ("Women on Top," 1999) showed that not one of the top-10
public relations firms in the country (ranked by fee income in 1997) was
headed by a woman. A single woman, Andy Cunningham, of Cunningham
Communications, was chief executive officer among the next 10 companies. To Dorothy Crenshaw, president of Stanton Crenshaw Communications, this represents "an embarrassment" because the field is filled with
talented women (as quoted in "Women on Top," 1998, p. 17).

Slowly, the gap between women and men in positions of corporate
leadership may be closing. A recent study by Catalyst, the nonprofit group
working to advance women in business, reported that women are landing
more high-level jobs than ever before. In 1998, they accounted for 11.2%
of all Fortune 500's corporate officers—up from 10.6% the year before (as
cited in Gonzalez, 1998). They earned on average 68¢ for every $1 in sal-
ary and bonus paid to their male counterparts. Median compensation for
these highest paid executives was $765,000 for men, compared with
$518,596 for women. At the time of the Catalyst survey, the Fortune 500
included only two female chief executive officers.

Although the top spot eludes most women, more and more are making
it into line-officer roles. Line management has responsibility for profit and
loss. Men hold 94% of all line positions in this country. Female vice presidents are more likely found in staff functions such as legal services, human
resources, and public relations. Because of the gradual increase in the percentage of women in the executive ranks, Catalyst's president, Sheila
Wellington, said: "The question isn't, 'Is there progress?' It's, 'What would
it take to speed up the rate of progress?'" (as quoted in Gonzalez, 1998,
p. E9).

Backlash against women, which Rosen (1982) defined as men's resentment toward groups given access to managerial positions (typically
through affirmative action), represents an important barrier. Faludi
(1991), author of Backlash, explained that many sources have contended
women have achieved equality in this country. Why, then, she asked, do
U.S. women "face the worse gender-based pay gap in the developed
world?" (p. xiii).

Public and Private Roles

One situation facing women who do make it to the managerial decision-making table is friction between their roles at home and their roles at work. Of course, some women facing these double or triple demands rise to the nearly impossible situation. One such manager, Nancy Woodhull, put it this way: "Women are like tea bags. They never know how strong they are until they're in hot water" (as quoted in "Tribute," 1997, p. 76). In fact (and typical of many women we know), she attributed much of her career success to the very family that must have created role conflicts for her: "How good I am has a lot to do with my husband and daughter" (as quoted in "Tribute," 1997, p. 76).

This struggle between competing responsibilities and opportunities is similar to the gap between sex role and professional role. Thus we discuss these two related conflicts in the same section of our discussion of women in management.

Nieva and Gutek (1981) may have done more to explicate this complex conundrum than any other researchers. They wrote extensively about women's search for a compromise between their sex- and work-related roles. They explained that women's traditional female role often spills over into the office; women continue to fill helping and service roles rather than the independent, command roles more typically associated with their male colleagues. They also pointed out a catch-22: Women are ignored if too passive, but considered alienating if too aggressive. Nieva and Gutek concluded that when sex and work roles conflict, the sex role dominates and the occupational role recedes.

A growing concern is providing medical or residential care for aging parents as well as nurturing spouses and children. According to Brody, Litvin, Albert, and Hoffman (1994), many adult children *but mainly daughters* are taking on this responsibility. Undoubtedly, the obligation to care for the elderly or disabled can adversely affect women's career potential. It also affects the corporate bottom line. According to a 1997 MetLife Study of Employer Costs, lost productivity from employees caring for elderly relatives costs U.S. business $11 billion yearly. Interruptions during the work day for employees taking on this responsibility cost another $4 billion annually in lost productivity. Worker absenteeism to attend to these and other personal problems costs more than $1.7 billion ("Odd Jobs: How Work-Life Programs Help," 1998b).

In public relations, even the *perception* that women are willing to sacrifice work to family demands often bars them from the managerial ranks

(Toth & Cline, 1991). Jo Weiss, a vice president of Advisory Services for Catalyst, talked about this problem for women anxious to break the glass ceiling in public relations. She described what she considered a "paternalistic" dynamic wherein bosses who think they are acting in women's best interests deny women the opportunity to relocate for a promotion. Her solution was to develop a new communication model, wherein employees and their managers actually talk about issues such as relocation and promotion as a way of customizing the career path for both women and men ("Helping Women Rise," 1998).

Women may sabotage their *own* ambitions if, as Johnson (1976) found, they fear success because of what they perceive as its negative consequences on their personal (as well as professional) relationships. Of course there remains the ever-present problem of men's relatively low level of participation in household tasks and child care. As we have known for some time, "Family concerns may impede some women because women continue to do more than their share of home maintenance activities in addition to pursuing careers" (Hon, L. Grunig, & Dozier, 1992, p. 427).

Doonan (1993), who came to similar conclusions after interviewing female fund raisers in academia, offered this poignant and intensely personal comment:

> As a professional who is facing the prospect of having family responsibilities that have not been a factor in my career to this point, these issues are of great concern to me. The optimist in me wants to believe that I can have a successful career, raise children and keep a home with the aid of my husband. The pragmatist in me questions whether this rosey [sic] scenario is truly an option. (p. 121)

Youthful readers may find themselves counterarguing at this point, contending that their contemporary personal relationships are more balanced in terms of sharing the work load at home than was the case when the authors of this text were first married. However, shared parenting and other home-maintenance activities remains more rhetoric than reality. Studies too numerous to cite here (e.g., Sommer, 1994; Bianchi, 1990; DeStefano & Colasanto, 1990) compare factors such as amount of parental contact with young children, care of sick children, interest in flexible work schedules to accommodate family concerns, and taking advantage of parental leave for birth or adoption. They conclude that there are significant gender differences.

The good news is that public relations may be more welcoming than other management fields for women who are mothers. Andrea Pace, vice president of national media relations at Ketchum Public Relations, recently adorned the cover of *Working Mother*. She was interviewed as part of a cover story on 1998's "10 hottest careers" for working moms, telling of her promotion to vice president upon returning from maternity leave. Pace, however, later cautioned women to establish themselves and their credibility before they decided to have a child ("Advice for Soon-to-Be Working Mothers," 1998). Other female practitioners interviewed for the *Working Mother* article alluded to the all-important flexibility the field affords: opportunities for hourly work; variety of the work itself; and options of working for a firm, a corporation, or on your own.

Management Style

We chose to introduce our discussion of personal and professional roles with a quotation from a woman who viewed the two not as competing but as complementary. Like Woodhull, we believe that just as private roles can enhance work-related roles, so too can any feminine traits associated with nurturing one's family enhance the way that all managers—men and women alike—do their jobs. Perhaps Barbara Finkelstein, the University of Maryland's woman of the year for 1998, expressed it best. In her acceptance speech, she described herself as a product of her generation. Married for 39 years, she continues to believe in the value of domesticity. She also believes families, schools, governments, and even universities share special obligations to children—and that those obligations supersede all others. Toward the end of her lengthy and distinguished career in academia, she has "learned to believe that compassion, sympathy, empathy, sociability and cooperative behaviors were women's things—to be exported to men if possible" (as quoted in Hawes, 1998, p. 3).

Does gender make a difference in the way that people "manage"? It may, although the evidence suggests otherwise. You may want to reread the portion of Chapter 1 that talks about socialization—a process that leads us to play traditional sex roles. With that understanding of early gender-based "programming," you may arrive at the conclusion that men and women cannot help but adopt different managerial styles. Aldoory (1998) did, after interviewing 10 female public relations professionals and educators at length. As one practitioner explained to her, "Among the things that we learn very early in our life that we are good at is the bringing together of disparate points of view. Creating some kind of harmony so that we can move forward" (p. 95). Perhaps this helps explain why the women she talked with considered the goals of their communication to be the building of relationships, cooperation, and consideration (see also

Henzl and Turner, 1987, and Statham, 1987). In addition to their communication style, these women's management style was consistent with the
transformational or interactive style typically associated with female gender
(Rosener, 1994).

Futurist Patricia Aburdene (1990) told a conference of public relations
professionals that what she considered women's preference for nurturance
and developing relationships, in particular, may be exactly what the next
century's managers will need. Perhaps the chair and CEO of Playboy Enterprises expressed it best:

> While I have seen highly autocratic women managers and very nurturing men
> managers, women managers are *considered, generally*, to be more humanistic
> and involving, and what are considered traditional female personality traits,
> such as the ability to build a consensus and encourage participation, are now
> much in demand. *I personally believe* that these traits are as much genera-
> tional as they are gender-related. *Regardless*, these characteristics will have an
> impact on how organizations manage an increasingly diverse workplace,
> which must allow opportunities for women and also people of different ethnic
> backgrounds, cultures and family relationships. (Hefner, 1993, p. 50; empha-
> sis added.)

We have added emphasis to several key concepts in those remarks of
Christie Hefner. We first italicized "considered, generally," to suggest that
these notions of women as especially participatory are based more on assumptions or public perceptions than based firmly on any empirical data.
Second, we highlighted "I personally believe" to indicate that Hefner, like
many CEOs of multimillion-dollar operations in this country, operated on
the basis more of personal beliefs than empirically generated data. Finally,
we underscored "regardless," again to suggest that the force of perceptions,
beliefs, values, or assumptions about women being ideal at contemporary
management may matter as much as any "proof" that their gender determines their suitability or even potential for top slots in organizations.

We can point to many studies that both affirm and deny the existence
of difference in the ways in which women and men manage. A number of
scholars (e.g., Bartol, 1973; Jacobson & Effertz, 1974; Feild & Caldwell,
1979; Sanders & Schmidt, 1980; Dobbins & Platz, 1986) consider management a gender-neutral endeavor. Loden (1986) may be the most widely
read of the proponents supporting the existence of gender-based management. She contrasted what she considered the male and female models of
leadership (a concept she used interchangeably with management). She
found both approaches equally effective. The feminist style of management,
in her opinion, favors cooperation over competition. Female leaders prefer

working in groups, rely heavily both on intuition and rational thinking to solve problems, focus more on long- than short-term goals, and tend to approach conflict resolution from a win–win rather than win–lose perspective.

However, one of the most comprehensive meta-analyses of dozens of studies of gender and management concluded that gender has no significant effect at least on the communication behaviors of male and female managers. Wilkins and Andersen (1991) explained that socialization and stereotyping, rather than innate difference, account for any *perceived* differences. They also found that inculcation processes such as professional orientation and mentoring lead both men and women to adopt masculine characteristics at work. M. A. Baker (1991) concurred but added that androgynous traits, as well as the masculine, may be instrumental for both male and female managers.

An extensive literature on women in management (e.g., Stead, 1985; Moore, 1986b) suggests, at the same time, that women and men do bring a different orientation to the management table. Philosopher Carol Gilligan (1982), too, believed that gender affects one's orientation toward the world and work. In one of the few empirical studies of gender and public relations management, J. B. Christensen (1993) found that female respondents rated themselves at a significantly higher level than did male respondents on three traits associated with male management: self-sufficiency, independence, and self-reliance. He acknowledged that one explanation may be that women public relations managers are indeed significantly more self-sufficient, independent, and self-reliant than their male counterparts. He preferred the following explanation:

> In the realm of organizational management (which has been dominated by males in the past), women managers may be under greater scrutiny than men managers to demonstrate such traits, especially if they work for bosses who are male chauvinists. Therefore, such women may feel an exaggerated need, and even an expectation, to prove that they are capable of handling the job of management without having to depend on others. (p. 86)

In the same vein, J. Grunig and White (1992) were unwilling to say that gender determines management style or competence; but they did talk about important gender differences in worldview, or one's assumptions about the world. One's fundamental beliefs about the way the world works—or should work—are especially important in public relations: As J. Grunig and White explained, practitioners are responsible for trying to understand and explain the behavior of people.

At this point we interject a study of college students that surprised us, because of the conventional wisdom holding that this group is more critical of traditional norms and values than are other age cohorts. I. K. Broverman, Vogel, D. M. Broverman, Clarkson, and Rosenkrantz (1972) found that subjects asked to list characteristics on which men and women differ valued masculine traits more highly than feminine traits. Female characteristics were perceived as less competent, less independent, and less logical. We can only hope that the intervening years have seen a halt to this devaluing of what is perceived to be feminine.

Some evidence suggests that this is so. Researchers at the National Education Center for Women in Business believe that the curricula of business schools need to be transformed to capitalize on what they consider women's distinctive talent in nurturing people. Harvard University echoed this concern for the education of both men and women about management. Future case studies, centerpiece of the school's curriculum and integral to many other business programs, will feature more female executives. Matching funds to develop the new cases came from the Committee of 200, female executives and business owners from throughout the country. Kim B. Clark, dean of Harvard's business school, explained that, although his university is searching for instances that include executive women as central: "That the decision makers happen to be women is a sub-text. A case about marketing will still be about marketing" (as quoted in "Footnotes," 1997, p. A12).

In addition, the National Educational Center conducted a study to document women's special skills and strategies. The Center's director explained: "Women's natural abilities in business have been squelched. . . . We want to encourage women to use their natural abilities, and men to recognize these abilities" (Iannarelli, as quoted in Lively, 1994, p. A5). She counted women's proclivity to encourage employee participation in managerial decisions as one such facility. Empowering employees in the decision-making process would be especially relevant for managers of public relations, who often are involved with human resources.

One final note on different abilities of female and male managers comes from a field many people consider a part of public relations: fundraising, or development. As early as 1982, Turk studied the membership of the Council for the Advancement and Support of Education to develop a profile of development as a profession. She found that women held lower level positions than men; their mean salary was more than $8,000 less than that of men's.

Ten years later, a survey by the Association for Healthcare Philanthropy (Joseph, 1992) also found a significant disparity between salaries of female and male fundraisers in hospitals. Even more significant was the finding that regardless of position held, men earned more than women in this setting. The largest gap existed between men and women with the highest positions. In fact, female foundation executives had a lower average salary than men at the next level down, that of head of development.

How can this be, short of overt sex discrimination? Donato (1990) characterized fundraising as emotional work that is personally satisfying for those who do it well. She further explained that because successful fundraising depends on personal interaction during social gatherings, employers may consider women better suited than men at these traditionally "female" social skills. However, Donato was careful to point out that this attitude—which she attributed primarily to male employers—is based on stereotypical thinking. (For more on the devastating effects of gendered stereotyping in fundraising, see B. W. Miller and Schroeder, 1983, and Rosen, 1982.)

Nowhere in the literature did we read about "love" and "respect" as sources of power and legitimacy for managers, whether female or male. However, we would do well to consider these traits as we try to determine the characteristics of an ideal manager. Frances Conley (1998), Stanford's professor of neurosurgery whom readers met in Chapter 3, pointed out that these qualities—along with emotion, warmth, and demonstrable humanity—frequently are equated with weakness and also with femininity. She questioned, though, why these should be used as criteria when choosing a leader in what she considered this masculine-dominated culture.

Communication Style

Much has been written about the ways in which men and women talk and how their conversational approaches affect the way they are perceived at work. Deborah Tannen is a leading scholar in this domain. Her (1990) work on women's *rapport* talk and men's *report* talk helps us understand that although neither style is superior, they do have implications for public relations management. For men, she explained, "talk is primarily a means to preserve independence and negotiate and maintain status in a hierarchical social order" (p. 77). Thus men communicate to demonstrate their knowledge and skill—typically in a public setting. In a related study, Leet-Pellegrini (as cited in Tannen, 1990) established that although people with expertise on a subject under discussion talk more than do nonexperts, male experts talk more than do female experts.

Women, by contrast with many men, prefer private speaking. Tannen (1990) found that women tend to use conversation to help establish connections with others and to negotiate relationships. They do not use speech to the extent that men do to jockey for position or to set the agenda. Instead, women typically react—agreeing or disagreeing (Aries, as cited in Tannen, 1990). These differences in communication style, then, may reinforce the stereotype of women as most comfortable in a supportive role, such as that of the technician. Men, because of their comfort level in expressing opinions and speaking authoritatively in a large group, may seem more suited for a leadership or managerial role.

In her later work, Tannen (1998) offered additional support to these notions of gender-based language. However, she was able to tease out a subtle, intricate complex of biological and cultural factors that make different conversational styles so deeply ingrained in women and men.

Tannen's later work has equally important implications for public relations—and the women and men alike who practice this challenging field. Tannen contrasted what she considered Americans' addiction to adversarialism with cooperation, or seeking a larger, more complicated truth. She decried the "argument culture" endemic in our systems of law, politics, and journalism. She proposed, instead, the kind of dialogue more likely to bring people together than to bifurcate them. We see obvious parallels with asymmetrical public relations—using sophisticated arguments to persuade publics to our side—and symmetrical public relations, the dialogical approach aimed at enhancing public discourse and leading to win–win solutions.

The Experience Gap

Despite the critically important proclivities some women bring to their work, relatively few women ascend to positions of power in organizations. One frequent explanation for women's underrepresentation in top management is that too few qualified women are available to fill those spots. According to Ragins and Sundstrom (1989), this undersupply of women could reflect two possibilities: "a shortage of women who enter the labor market or deliberate choices made by women that lead them into less powerful positions" (p. 54). Of the two possible explanations, they favored the latter as more plausible. They cited a number of statistical studies attesting to the fact that women enter the labor force in large numbers.

More recent research by *The Washington Post*, the Kaiser Foundation, and Harvard University went a long way toward dispelling the notion that women simply have not been in the pipeline long enough to quality for high-level managerial positions. One of the surveys, conducted as part of a study called "Reality Check: The Gender Revolution," profiled female

MBAs. It established that although thousands of women had received master's degrees in business administration and arrived in the work place during the 1970s, today they hold only 3% of the top six executive positions at large Fortune 500 companies (Grimsley, 1998).

The study went on to explore, through long interviews, the reasons why women's ascent has been slower than their education and middle-management experience would promise. It found the 20 interviewees—graduates of elite business schools at Harvard, Stanford, and the University of Pennsylvania—to be unusually committed to their career tracks. Despite their willingness to pursue good jobs by moving cross-country and investing thousands in career development, the women considered themselves largely neglected. As Myra Strober, professor of education at Stanford University, explained it: "If you think about discrimination as doing something 'bad' to women, that's not what happened so much . . . [as] men are being favored, and women are being ignored" (p. A1). To illustrate, *The Washington Post* (which ran a lengthy series detailing the findings of the project), quoted Lillian Lincoln, who in 1969 became the first African American female MBA to graduate from Harvard. She learned "women need to fight for air time," or risk being ignored in meetings with men. She found that "you get to a certain level, and you know that you'll never get to the positions men do, so you start your own company" (Grimsley, 1998, p. A8).

So, perhaps Ragins and Sundstrom (1989) justifiably speculated on the self-selection hypothesis that women may be more likely than men to choose jobs unlikely to result in powerful positions later on in their careers. Beyond such conjecture, however, they pointed out that in fact self-selection into gender-typed specialties may reflect societal forces beyond any woman's individual control.

Keep in mind that public relations itself may be one of those specialties. We found that just being in this field ranks right up with gender discrimination as a barrier to advancement. Further evidence comes from a survey of executives in 2,900 high-tech companies. In that industry, a discrete category representing "public relations" does not even exist at the highest levels. Instead, the data were reported for jobs including chairman; CEO; and vice presidents of marketing, sales, international, finance, information systems, personnel, administration, purchasing, R & D, manufacturing, engineering, technology transfer, corporate development, and strategic planning. Across these vice presidencies, women account for 5.1% of the total (CorpTech study, as cited in "Tech's Faded Promise," 1990).

We agree with professor of linguistics Tannen (1994): "The 'pipeline' argument has simply not panned out. Years after women entered the pipeline, they just aren't coming through the other end in proportion to their numbers going in" (p. 130). In fact, as experience and seniority increase, salary gaps between women and men may increase as well. Benokraitis (1997) adapted figures from an American Association of University Professors survey to show that male faculty fare better than do female faculty at all ranks. Most significantly, the wage differential between them increases as rank increases.

Similarly, C. L. Baker (1996) found that in a survey of doctors under 45 years of age with 2 to 9 years of experience, men's mean hourly earnings were $56 compared to $49 for women's. After controlling for additional relevant factors such as personal characteristics, specialty, and site of the practice, Baker determined that men with more than 9 years of experience earned on average 17% more than did female physicians.

POWER AND POWERLESSNESS

What explains this chasm between women and men in management? In a word, "power." More precisely, the answer may lie in *perceptions of power*.

To understand the power differential, real or perceived, begin with the extant scholarly literature on gender differences in organizations. Ragins and Sundstrom (1989) reviewed this extensive body of knowledge and arrived at three major conclusions. First, they determined that power increases over time as people advance in their careers. However, women and men traverse different paths to power as they develop professionally. They characterized the path for women as more of an "obstacle course" (p. 81; see also Kanter, 1977, and Harragan, 1977), fraught with many impediments and barriers. Further, they found that women who manage to master the obstacle course differ significantly from the population of women and, in fact, of men as well. If nothing else, these supersuccessful women, according to Ragins and Sundstrom, represent the hardiest survivors.

Second, the Ragins and Sundstrom (1989) review concluded that power derives from multiple resources. They include formal position in the organization, interpersonal relationships, and individual characteristics. These differences compound over time. At each career stage women tend to be less likely than men to gain access to the organizational and interpersonal resources available to men. Obviously, women are less likely to benefit from having them. Disappointingly, too, Ragins and Sundstrom found that "even when women obtain [these organizational assets], their value as resources for power appears to be less than that for men holding the same assets" (p. 81). Further, Ghiloni (1987) found that women in the public affairs department she studied were playing an increasingly important role in maintaining corporate power but they themselves were unlikely to gain power.

Finally, Ragins and Sundstrom (1989) determined that power begets power. Its development is synergistic. Thus, over time the attainment of power—relatively more difficult for women than for men—perpetuates and even enlarges the existing differences between the two.

Taken together, these three factors result in a cycle of powerlessness for women in management. They suggest a complex situation wherein power is both actual and perceived (Kaplowitz, 1978). As Ragins and Sundstrom (1989) explained, "A person can have objective control over organizational resources or rewards, which may or may not be perceived by self or by others" (p. 51). The significance of this statement lies in the understanding that sex-role stereotyping leads some people to perceive women as less empowered than they actually are (I. K. Broverman, Vogel, D. M. Broverman, Clarkson, & Rosenkrantz, 1972). Johnson (1976, 1978) contended that gendered stereotypes even may contribute to a distortion of women's self-perceptions related to power.

Finally, in a modification of the Ragins and Sundstrom (1989) explanation of the role of controlling resources, consider the theorizing of Powell (1988). He believed that power comes primarily from providing one sought-after resource: expertise. He advised developing an area of expertise that is vital to the organization. Public relations is just such an area, especially in times of crisis. The boundary-spanning role of communication management provides for a deep understanding of the organization's environment, both internal and external. Being the eyes and ears of the organization makes the public relations professional especially valuable during times of turbulence in its environment. Thus expertise in such functions as environmental scanning, formative and evaluative research, and crisis management can add to the power base of women and men alike. It also increases and may demonstrate one's self-confidence.

In addition to crisis communication, successful fundraising may bring considerable power to public relations practitioners. Doonan (1993), in her qualitative study of female fundraisers in higher education, established that the women she interviewed at length did enjoy power by virtue of their positive impact on the financial health of their institutions.

Interestingly, however, Doonan (1993) also found that having power may not equate with having a powerful position. The participants in her thesis research considered their prospects for reaching senior management slim. They offered such explanations as a husband's career moves dictating their own, other family concerns, no aspiration to a higher level job, poor relationship with the president, age (being 50), reluctance on the part of a male alumni body to accept a female vice president, sex discrimination within the university, and contentment with the current position. The preponderance of evidence suggested that family responsibilities and discrimination represent the two primary barriers to advancement for the women within her sample—all of whom she knew well and considered bright, aggressive, motivated, and forward thinking.

What all of this simply may mean is that female managers are only as powerful as they, and others, think they are. Without being considered powerful, women are unlikely to be promoted to senior positions within organizations. This gendered perception may account for the dearth of women in the highest ranks of corporate management (Brown, 1979; Dipboye, 1987; Raynolds, 1987; Dexter, 1985; Wallace, 1982) and their concentration, instead, in lower ranks (U.S. Department of Labor, 1979, 1984; Blau & Ferber, 1987).

Networking and Mentoring

Networking, often suggested as a technique for enhancing women's power base in organizations or in their professions, takes many forms. Some of those models may be influenced by gender. For instance, Halberg (1987) found that women use their network of relationships for help in solving problems and for protection. She called such behavior "interdependent," rather than dependent, and she considered it a viable style of leadership. To put this in applied, rather than theoretical, terms, consider the role of Nancy Woodhull in mentoring other women in journalism. Mindi Keirnan, vice president of Knight Ridder News Service, said of her: "Nancy would always say, 'Every day, every woman must reach out and help another woman.' She didn't just preach it, she practiced it" (as quoted in "Tribute," 1997, p. 76).

Leaders like Woodhull typically make good mentors. Mentors, in turn, can provide role models who have a positive influence on career attitudes. Savenye (1990) found that a lack of female role models may prevent women from envisioning themselves in high-level positions. On the other hand, Kremgold-Barnett (1986) established that early identification with a role model demonstrates the importance and use of personal power—which we deem more important for women than men in many organizational contexts. For all these reasons, Novarra (1980) concluded that women mentoring other women is vital to increase the number of women in managerial positions.

Lack of female role models contributes to the lack of female leaders in a setting with which we're very familiar: the college campus. Our own research (L. Grunig, 1989a) documented few opportunities for women in academia to share resources and information, to network, and to build coalitions.

A number of additional studies in public relations and other fields has established the role of mentoring, or pairing a senior with a junior staffer for guidance and skills development, in career advancement (Turk, 1986b; Ervin, B. J. Thomas, Zey-Ferrell, 1984). Taken together, these studies provide a taxonomy of roles that mentors assume. Turk, for example, identified the mentor as personal supporter, teacher, and "bestower of legitimacy." This last role seems especially critical in public relations, a field that an ensuing chapter will characterize as facing loss of legitimacy along with the feminization of the field.

Mentors also serve as role models (Nieva & Gutek, 1981), helping the newcomer bypass the hierarchy through informal interaction. Again, this is vital to public relations. Recent research has established how rarely the function is situated at the top of the hierarchy (Dozier, L. Grunig, & J. Grunig, 1995). Thus, learning to shortcut passage through the layers of the typical organization is a critical skill for many women in the field. Unfortunately, Nieva and Gutek found, men rarely mentor female subordinates in this way because they underestimate or question women's commitment and skills. Thus Turk's (1986b) suggestion that women borrow a chapter from the "male playbook" and seek out a powerful mentor may not be viable. We believe this significantly disadvantages women in public relations, at least in the area of fundraising. Doonan (1993) found that six of the seven women she interviewed at length credited role models and mentors as critical to their advancement in the field.

Kaufman and Richardson (1982) cited limited access to the power center of organizations as one of the three major barriers facing ambitious women. The other factors were exclusion from male-dominated networks in organizations and lack of role models and mentors.

Cheng (1988), too, noted a lack of mentors as an impediment to women's progress at work. She cited the additional contributing factors she considered internal to women themselves: sex-role stereotyping, fear of success, and a perceived loss of femininity associated with their success. However, Cheng pointed most directly to the external factor that inhibits women on their way to top management: male dominance of the uppermost levels of the typical organization.

Kanter (1977) had a somewhat different take on the situation. She wrote about women's exclusion from powerful networks or mentoring relationships as a function of tokenism. *Tokens,* she explained, are treated as representatives of their category rather than as individuals. Because women and minorities so often represent small proportions of their organization's total work force, they may be tokens. Tokenism, in turn, leads to further segregation and stereotyping. It may lead, as well, to the token person's either overachieving or hiding her successes. Because there are so few women at high levels of U.S. organizations, Kanter found that the token females who do ascend to those levels also experience isolation—both from other women at lower levels of the organization and from the dominant male coalition.

We noted, however, that Kanter's research predated our book by a good 2 decades. So, in an effort to explore any change in top management's willingness to support women in management, we turn now to a discussion of contemporary literature in this area.

Top Management Support

Unsupportive bosses continue to figure prominently and directly in holding women back. A top executive who managed human resource development for a high-tech firm in California described her former "boss from hell": "He fostered an environment where a lot of subtle, negative things happened to women" (as quoted in Kleiman, 1992, p. B1). He also sexually harassed female employees. He may not be atypical. Women members of Exec-U-Net, a national networking organization, reported that most—a whopping 91%—had worked for "doozies" in their career. Cynthia Buzzetta, the president of a management consulting firm who conducted the study, called these bosses "hinderers." She described them as insecure, threatened, secretive, egomaniacal, incompetent, psychotic, abusive, exploitive, unbalanced, racist, and sexist.

About 86% of the female executives surveyed also reported that they had had good bosses at some point in the past. Buzzetta described these "helpers" as good communicators who are empowering, risk-takers, skilled, delegators, bright, honest, and open.

What kind of boss do you work for, a hinderer or a helper? This is not an idle question. Buzzetta believed that bosses are a critical factor in explaining why women are where they are. But why is the nature of the boss especially important for women? According to Buzzetta (as quoted in Kleiman, 1992):

> Managers influence not only the work performance, career growth and confidence of subordinates, but also the ability of the work unit to do its job well. The work force has changed in complexity and diversity and will continue to

do so in this decade. A good boss allows you to grow, and when the board-room is made up of only 55-year-old white men, we have to start addressing this for what it is, a bottom-line issue—not a sociological one. (p. B1)

One major finding of Doonan's (1993) study of women in institutional advancement was that simply telling their supervisor they wanted to get ahead could aid in their promotion. She considered this a "relatively simple tactic" (p. 119). She added, however, that interview data suggested how few women know how to approach their bosses about getting ahead. Fur-ther, she explained, "If their supervisor is not responsive to their request, and does not give them the chance to take on additional responsibilities, they must be prepared to make a move in order to achieve their career goals" (p. 120). The problem here, of course, is that moving may not be an option for women who face the pressures of multiple roles pertaining to work and family. Doonan considered it unfortunate that this circumstance has not changed even after the rapid growth of dual-income families.

Racial and Ethnic Diversity

The foregoing quotation brings up the issue of race as well as gender among important managerial considerations. One study of women of color in management established that race makes little difference in earning par-ity with men. Catalyst, the New York-based research organization we in-troduced earlier in this book, studied "Women of Color in Corporate Man-agement" in 1997 (Wynter, 1997). It compared managerial salaries by race and gender. It found that for every dollar white male managers earn, mi-nority males earn 73 cents, white females earn 59 cents, and minority fe-males 57 cents. Despite the small disparity between white and nonwhite women's salaries, the Catalyst survey exposed a large gap in employment potential: White women hold 86% of all management positions occupied by women even though white females make up only 77% of the female work force.

Among minority women, African Americans make up the largest share of the managerial work force with 6.6% of the positions held. They are fol-lowed by Hispanic Americans at 5.2% and Asian Americans at 2.5%. However, Asian American women earn the highest median weekly pay at $593, contrasted with the lowest average salary, Hispanic women at $423. Black women earn slightly less than white women in management roles: $514 versus $528. So far, Catalyst has offered no explanation for this find-ing—which is curious when considering that on average, African American female managers have more years of education (35% compared with

33.6% of Caucasian women with an advanced degree). Also, black women who are managers are significantly more likely to be single mothers than are Hispanic, Asian, or white women. The study, precursor to a larger project Catalyst planned on women of color in the corporate world, merely concluded that "Being a female and a minority can . . . be two minuses" (Wynter, 1997, p. B1).

Despite the conclusion of the Catalyst research, we try to avoid the "social problems approach" to our study of gender and public relations. Like the editors of a major anthology on race, class, and gender (Andersen & Collins, 1992), we hope to study groups of people—Asian American managers or female entrepreneurs, for two examples—in their own right. We look for relationships between those groups and structures within the larger society. In this way, we also hope to avoid a portrayal of these groups as victims—a portrayal too often skewed, in our opinion, by the perspective of the more privileged groups. At the same time, like Anderson and Collins, we acknowledge that although race, class, and gender are separate axes of social structure, individuals can and do experience them simultaneously. We have more to say about how race, ethnicity, class, and gender intersect in public relations practice in the next chapter. These discussions—of race and management and of race and public relations practice—are aimed at transforming our understanding of the way our world works by making it more inclusive.

Oppression brought about by racial or sexual discrimination is likely to generate resistance, according to experts in women's studies, African American studies, and sociology (Anderson & Collins, 1992). The last 2 decades of this century may well mark the most volatile period in shifting relationships between black women and black men and also between black women and white women. Thus we turn to a look at how the oppression of women in diverse career fields has led them to take action. The form of activism we explore here is entrepreneurship: leaving the salaried work force to go into business for oneself.

WOMEN MANAGING THEIR OWN ENTERPRISES

Women and men, majority and minority alike, often opt out of the salaried work force, in public relations and in other fields, to go into business for themselves. However, the number of *female* entrepreneurs increased dramatically during the last couple of decades, according to the National Foundation of Business Owners (NFBO) (Nelton, 1992).

The explanation for this phenomenon may be hard to pinpoint, but sex discrimination may play an important part. As Tannen (1994) put it, "A lot of women are seeking alternatives simply because they tire of feeling like strangers in a strange land when they go to work each day" (p. 130). For one anecdotal example, consider Joanne Flynn, who was fired from her executive position at one of the premier investment banks in the world. She filed a sex-discrimination lawsuit against Goldman Sachs & Co. in 1991. Ultimately she established a successful firm of her own, but her 8-year-old daughter continued to refer to her old office in Manhattan as "the place that didn't want Mommy anymore" (as quoted in Mathews, 1993, p. H5). (Fortunate, indeed, to have been wanted was Maggie Lena Walker, who became the first African American woman to serve as a bank president [Hine & Thompson, 1998].)

Racial discrimination may play a part as well. Of the 13 public relations practitioners of color Len-Rios (1998) interviewed, one had left the field and two were considering leaving because they were dissatisfied and wanted to pursue other interests. One told of his female friend who was turned off by a public relations firm because a client would not be "comfortable" being represented by a black executive. The firm, in turn, feared it would lose business.

One survey (Scott, 1986) determined that the reason for so many women choosing self-employment was the combination of increased compatibility with family obligations and the chance to overcome the lack of opportunity they had experienced while working for others. Other reasons include the challenge of being their own boss and the possibility of making more money. Men and women alike cited the advantages of freedom from office politics and no more hassles with commuting (Wolfgram, 1984).

By contrast, Paige Eversole McMahon (as quoted in Fishman, 1998), former president of the National Capital Chapter of PRSA and owner of a home-based public relations firm, explained two of what she considered the *worst* reasons to go it alone: the notion that you would have more time for yourself and your family and shorter working hours. Instead, she said, "You'll never work harder in your life" (p. 1).

The NFBO published a conservative estimate of 5.4 million American women who, for whatever reasons, do own their own businesses. The editor of *Entrepreneur* magazine put the number at 7 million (as cited in A. Miller, Springen, & Tsiantar, 1992). These independent women generated up to $500 billion in annual revenue by the early 1990s, which represented more than a 500% increase over the previous 10 years.

Bureau of the Census figures for 1992 suggested an even greater contribution from female entrepreneurs. Their data (as cited in "Women in the Workplace," 1998) showed women owning more than 6.4% of all American businesses, employing more than 13 million people, and generating about $1.6 trillion in revenues. As with women in management across the board, the numbers vary by region of the country. According to the National Foundation for Women Business Owners, in the Washington, DC, area women own 40% of all businesses (as cited in Grimsley, 1997).

As we move from an industrial society and through the decades of this information- and service-based society, the trend seems likely to intensify. The U.S. Small Business Administration predicted that women would own 40% of all business in this country by 2000 (Lively, 1994). Female entrepreneurs create jobs for millions of employees each year.

But how about the women who work alone and from their homes? They number about 9.8 million, according to the market research firm Link Resources (Kim, 1991). They are called "open collars," a term coined by Paul Edwards, a home office consultant. He (personal communication with Humphrey, 1990) reasoned that this label would convey the comfortable, laid-back dress of the typical home-based worker. The work appeals in large part because women typically lack sufficient funds to start up a business outside of their home. Bankers are leery about lending women start-up capital for fear that they are less serious than men about their enterprises and that they may drop out to have a baby (Cole, 1989).

About 90% of women who work outside the home either have children or are projected to have children during their lifetime. The fastest growing segment of the labor market is women with children under age 6 (Nollen, 1989). No wonder, then, that about half of the female open collars in the United States are mothers. P. Edwards and S. Edwards (1985) hailed the trend toward home-based work as good news because it offers women who work the chance to spend more time with their families. It also saves money: Child care, even if available, is rarely affordable. Although badly dated, the most recent statistics we could find on costs showed a range from $3,500 for nursery school to $8,000 for in-home supervision (Fierman, 1988).

The United States is the only major industrialized nation without a federally supported child-care system (Braddy, 1989). Pulitzer Prize-winning author Anna Quindlen, whose novels and newspaper columns focus on the family, called for the creation of government- or community-based programs to deal with children of working parents. She also held organizations responsible. As she explained:

> We have been held back by [the] reactionary "Let's go back to the old days." Instead of bemoaning the old days, we have to figure out how we can organize

the new days. Corporate culture has got to change and make the workplace more family-friendly. (as quoted in O'Briant, 1992, p. 1)

Mothers who work from home have been called "mom-preneurs." Men still run most home-based businesses, but the number of home-based working mothers mushroomed by 9% in 1990 alone. The Mothers Home Business Network attributes this leap to three major factors (Kim, 1991). First is family focus, or the ability of home-based moms to balance the needs of corporate accounts and children. More than half of all open collars have children under age 18 at home (Micheli, 1988). Half of the women responding to a U.S. Bureau of Labor Statistics survey said they became open collars to spend more time with their families (as cited in K. Christensen, 1988). A study of women in marketing and public relations (Chadwell, 1993) found that more time with the family and choosing their own clients both figured prominently in the decision to go freelance. However, in her own study of home-based workers, Christensen found that although mothers did get to spend more time with their children, they still needed some type of additional care so they could devote enough attention to their jobs.

As important as flexibility for family duties may be, then, work-place woes provide the second explanation for women with kids shifting from office to home. The recession undoubtedly accounted for some women (and men) losing their salaried positions. This is especially likely at the executive level, according to a survey by Drake Beam Morin (DBM), one of the nation's largest employment firms (as cited in Swoboda, 1990). The DBM study concluded that the trend toward women going into business for themselves may result in large part from the fact that it takes executive women who are unemployed increasingly longer (on average 6.4 months in 1990) to find a new job.

We belabor this dissection of the reasons why women leave the paid work force to go it alone for one main reason: Research has established that colleagues and bosses typically misunderstand why women quit. Another study conducted by Catalyst and reported in *The Wall Street Journal* (Hymowitz, 1997) exposed the gender divide between why women really leave their salaried positions to start their own businesses and the reasons former coworkers assume. The "pernicious myth" cited in *The Journal* column is that women's personal lifestyle choices dictate career moves. The myth exists in large part because women are less than candid when they leave a job—often creating the impression that they are quitting the career entirely, rather than just the current position. They do this, the Catalyst research established, because of their eagerness to avoid conflict or the perception of disloyalty.

But sadly, by failing to mention or even by playing down the better opportunity they are going to, these women contribute to some men's conclusion that the risk they took grooming women as managers has not paid off. A young female law clerk found herself ostracized from just such a superior when she revealed her plans to move to a larger firm. She said to one partner, "You're acting like jilted lovers, like I left you at the altar" (as quoted in Hymowitz, 1997, p. B1). A second piece of relevant research, cited in the same *Wall Street Journal* column and conducted by the Employee Benefit Research Institute of Washington, DC, showed that in actuality women are more loyal than men: They tend to stay with one employer longer, on average. The question for the most driven among women, then, becomes not why they could leave the stability of working for a company over time but why they had chosen to survive in that often-oppressive environment for so long.

We return now to the previous question of the role of family responsibilities vis-à-vis entrepreneurship for women. We know that the glass ceiling for mothers also is a key in the "work-place woes" factor. By 1997, the cost to U.S. businesses for replacing employees who resign because of work and family conflicts reached $4.9 billion yearly (as cited in "Odd Jobs: How Work-Life Programs Help," 1998). As Dana Friedman, copresident of the Families and Work Institute, explained, "You're not promoted or don't get that choice assignment because you're seen as someone who won't stay the extra hour" (as quoted in Kim, 1991, p. 4B). Apparently female executives in the high-tech industry are especially disadvantaged. Ella D. Williams (as quoted in Rebello, 1990) found that the only way for her to move up was to start her own firm, Aegir Systems Inc.

The third factor explaining why women increasingly strike out on their own points to technology. High-tech, low-cost home-office products make going to the office unnecessary for many women. Judith Wunderlich can even operate her freelance employment service from the bathroom, thanks to equipment such as modem, cordless phone, and fax machine. Through them, she is so linked to the world that she acknowledges, "I've conducted business from the bathtub many times" (as quoted in Kim, 1991, p. 4B). She considers her situation "ideal."

Other mom-preneurs complain about problems such as isolation. Chadwell (1993) found that many freelancers in public relations and marketing miss having someone to discuss their ideas with. Scholars have worried that this link between women and the domestic sphere also will create a "woman's boutique" image (Olerup, Schneider, & Monod, 1985). Others believe that such dual responsibility reinforces the stereotype of woman as nurturer. Further, it implies that neither job—family nor office—is full time and thus neither is valuable (Zimmerman, 1986).

The majority of home-based working mothers, however, seem to value the opportunity to be with their children when it matters most. Like Lillian Vernon, who began her catalog-accessories business on the kitchen table, they may go back to an office outside the home when the children are grown. In the meantime, resources have developed to help women start and maintain their own companies. The 5,00-member Mothers Home Business Network doubled its rolls in a single year. The Mothers Entrepreneurial Association, too, doubled its membership between 1990 and 1991 and expects to do so annually.

In 1988, the federal government entered the scene with its Women's Business Ownership Act. Not limited to helping mom-preneurs or even salaried women who work at home, this program funds demonstration projects to train female business owners. It also established the National Women's Business Council, which advises the White House and Congress. It created incentives to encourage banks to provide women with loans guaranteed by the Small Business Administration (Nelton, 1992).

The National Education Center for Women in Business (NECWB), located on the campus of Seton Hill College in Pennsylvania, is dedicated to shaking up business education. Its main purpose is to teach women and girls about business ownership. A second major focus of the NECWB is educating others about the contributions of entrepreneurial women. Such special emphasis on the needs and values of female business owners undoubtedly grows out of the understanding that even in the 1990s girls were less likely than boys to aspire to own their own enterprise. As a result, the NECWB sponsors programs for teenaged girls. It also coordinates research from other institutions about the history of female entrepreneurs in this country. Finally, it works with disabled women, who find a forum for discussing their special experiences as owners of businesses.

The director of this educational institution for female entrepreneurs has emphasized that *most* women who decide to strike out on their own face more obstacles than do men—especially in the critical area of financing (Iannarelli, as quoted in Lively, 1994, p. A5). Financing typically is a significant problem for women who start their own firms. In public relations, as in most other home-based ventures, adequate funding is a necessary first step. In her talk to a PRSA chapter, Katherine Hutt, owner of Nautilus Communication, emphasized the importance of stockpiling at least 3 months' worth of living and business expenses at the outset. Lou Walls, owner of Walls Communications, speaking on that same panel, echoed the importance of what he called the "3 Cs formula" for start-up success: credibility, contacts, and cash (as cited in Fishman, 1998).

Once again, however, determined women like Hutt too often encounter the glass ceiling. According to Felice Schwartz and her women's advocacy group Catalyst (as quoted in A. Miller, Springen, and Tsiantar, 1992), when women leave the corporation, they often bump their heads again. Like all entrepreneurs, they lose perks and worry about meeting a payroll. However, women have unequal access to credit and to lucrative government contracts (receiving only 1% in 1992).

Hear the story of Ella D. Williams, who called her industry—high tech—"vicious," one that is still "tough for women." For the first 2 years after she started her own company that analyzes the reliability and safety of defense equipment, she could not land a contract. She had taken out a second mortgage on her house, but even so she had to collect cans for recycling to feed her two children and herself. Then she thought back to her mother's advice about the way to a man's heart being through his stomach. *USA Today* (Rebello, 1990) reported that "she baked banana, pumpkin and zucchini breads and dropped them off with clients each time she visited. Finally, the clients relented. They began to listen to her, and the contracts came in" (p. 7B).

Why is it so difficult for many women to land those contracts or to obtain that financing? One female entrepreneur actually considered her gender a plus at times. Cristi Lyn Cristich (as quoted in Rebello, 1990), whose firm makes electronic connectors, explained that "there are people who are initially resistant about working with you, but you just have to prepare more. But it [being a woman] can be an advantage. When I go out to see vendors, they remember me" (p. 7B). More often, as independent investment manager Adela Cepeda discovered, in this male world "men associate their wives and daughters with *spending* money, not making it" (as quoted in A. Miller, Springen, and Tsiantar, 1992, p. 54, emphasis in original). Construction company president Meyer, whom you met in Chapter 3, added the insight that "women are not perceived as having a small business; we're perceived as having a *little* business" (as quoted in A. Miller, Springen, and Tsiantar, 1993, p. 55, emphasis in original). Once again perceptions. And once again, stereotypes.

The law, of course, plays a role in what female entrepreneurs can and cannot achieve. Taking the same industry, construction, we explored an affirmative action program that ended up financing some women's new ventures. At the same time, it divided women and African American men vying for highway jobs. Janet Schutt, who founded her own construction company, applied to enter a federal program aimed at female entrepreneurs.

However, many considered her a "front" for white male engineers who were suspected of using women or blacks to win Department of Transportation contracts. One African American owner of a trucking business, Vechel Rhodes, went so far as to claim that 95% of white women are fronts. As a result, he considered himself "socially handicapped." As a result, too, Schutt's application ultimately was rejected (Sharpe, 1997).

Despite the difficulties of finding seed money, more and more women are rejecting the often-discriminatory rules of the big leagues and, as an article in *Newsweek* put it, they vow to create a league of their own (A. Miller et al., 1992). In so doing, they may be able to act on their ethics to a greater extent than when they were employees of a larger organization. For Ellen Bonnin-Bilbrey, the advantage of her solo operation Eco-Logical Marketing is having clients she ethically and morally wants to represent (Chadwell, 1993). For Carey Sweet, the benefit of her Voices in Ink is the ability to work directly with principals in the small companies she targets (Chadwell, 1993).

Women in public relations may be no different from these entrepreneurs in other fields. However, it is hard to pinpoint the number of female entrepreneurs in our field. Definitional questions, in particular, perplex those of us interested in a count. Do we include moonlighters and volunteers in our tally? How about women who work fewer than 8 hours a week in their electronic cottages? We do know that 89% of all women-owned businesses are one-woman shops (Cole, 1989), and so we consider it reasonable to speculate that public relations figures prominently among these enterprises.

In her in-depth study of a dozen open collars in public relations, Humphrey (1990) found that a home-based career in this field was generally a rewarding experience. The women she interviewed at length were operating successful businesses. Several had major clients. Their biographies were filled with impressive qualifications and experience. Even with small offices, no staff, and limited budgets, these women were doing a superlative job. Their defection from office to home meant a loss of talented employees for the organizations where they had worked previously.

At home, several women described the positive balance they had found between family and career. They also talked about the value of proving to themselves that they had the independence and self-discipline necessary to succeed in business. Thus Humphrey concluded that "with a little experience, ingenuity, motivation, equipment and room in the house, a woman can control her own career and still include time to dedicate to the things in her life outside work that are most important" (p. 144).

The most common factors leading to women's work from home were gaining autonomy and flexibility, caring for children, and escaping a perceived glass ceiling. However, the importance of the gap in salary and promotion opportunities that women perceived was not so strong as some of the earlier literature in public relations might suggest (e.g., Toth & Cline, 1989b; Broom & Dozier, 1985). In fact, only one woman in Humphrey's (1990) study attributed her entrepreneurial move directly to sex discrimination. At the same time, all the other participants in the research said that bias in advancement opportunities figured into their decision. Also, once they had their own business, they felt great relief from such problems.

This study of entrepreneurial women in public relations offers important insights into the negative stereotypes about working women. For example, contrary to studies by Fernandez (1988) and Shepard (1985) that found women typically regarded as less efficient and less job-oriented, the Humphrey (1990) study looked at women who were held in high regard by their previous employer. As she said, "Ironically for the companies, it was this efficiency and professionalism that helped their former employee become an open-collar success after breaking away" (p. 135).

Sexual harassment did not figure prominently in women's decisions to open their own businesses in public relations. However, Terpstra (1989) found sexual harassment to be a widespread, pervasive problem in corporate America. Houghton (1988) reported that two-thirds of 17,000 female and male employees surveyed in the country's largest corporations cited evidence of sexual harassment. In 1995, claims of sexual harassment at work began to grow exponentially. At this point, insurance against such claims is the fastest growing sales area for at least one insurance company ("Odd Jobs: Harassment Insurance," 1998a). We know this is a problem for women in public relations, even for senior women in the field ("Sexual Harassment," 1993). In Humphrey's (1990) study, however, only one woman said she left her company to escape sexual harassment. Several other interviewees described the sexual harassment they encountered as mildly offensive, merely an irritating factor.

We can conclude, then, that home-based work in public relations becomes an attractive option for extraordinarily capable women who are tired of fighting inflexible structures for inadequate pay. These independent women are motivated less by a desire to avoid or escape from sexual harassment than they are to spend time with their children.

CONCLUDING THOUGHTS

Public relations has been considered a specialty within the broader field of communication—a specialty that invites women because it is a staff rather than a line function, such as finance, that has direct responsibility for corporate profits. Being a member of a support staff is consistent with society's expectations of the working woman: Nurturing, care-giving, being cooperative, and being concerned with relationships are all traits associated with femininity. As a result, many women find themselves in what have been called the "pink-collar ghettos" of service fields. Women are also more welcome in small than in large associations and in 2-year rather than in 4-year universities.

We have prolonged this discussion about women in management and those who manage their own enterprises because the managerial role for public relations professionals is taking on increasing importance. A recently completed 10-year, $400,000+ study of public relations in three countries (J. Grunig et al., 1991) concluded that the strategic management of this function is one of a handful of key characteristics that predict excellence in public relations. Only when the public relations department is managed strategically can it contribute substantially to the overall effectiveness of the organization. Of course, without a manager (rather than a technician) heading the public relations department, strategic management is highly unlikely to occur.

Readers will learn more about the importance of women attaining the role of public relations manager in subsequent chapters of this book. For now, understand that high-level positions and high pay elude women in *most* of the careers we describe here. Today's woman can get into management at the entry level and then move into middle ranks, but she continues to find it difficult to get on—much less arriving at the executive suite or the CEO's office. The glass ceiling in particular thwarts the ambition of highly educated women from the trades to the professions, from hourly workers to senior executives. It remains a fact of life for the managerial woman in public relations and across the fields.

One final vignette may capture the essence of much that has come before in this chapter. It is the story of Muriel Siebert, a former state superintendent of banks who now owns her own brokerage firm. In 1968 she was the first woman allowed to buy a seat on the New York Stock Exchange (NYSE). She assumed that other women quickly would follow. Instead, after 10 years, she was joined by only one woman among 1,300 men. When we began writing this book, 40 members or 3% of the NYSE were women. Siebert explained that despite the growing number of women on Wall Street: "Women are not in the executive offices. A man will make partner in a brokerage firm in seven or eight years, whereas a woman will not" (as quoted in Mathews, 1993, p. H5).

We arrive, then, at the same conclusion as did former Labor Secretary

Lynn Martin. In one of her final press conferences during the Bush administration, she released a departmental report called "Pipeline of Progress: A
Status Report on the Glass Ceiling." She told reporters that although
"much is being done in corporate America to eliminate barriers . . . much
. . . —too much—remains to be done. We continue to find a general absence of minorities and women at the highest levels in the corporate work
force" (as quoted in Rudavsky, 1992, p. A19). This chapter attests to the
scores of women who have entered into management—once considered a
male bastion—but who continue to feel that they are not getting a fair deal
when it comes to the top jobs and compensation.

We belabor the issue of the wage gap between women and men in
management in part to compensate for the fact that some women make
light of financial issues. Take even radical and outspoken feminist Phyllis
Chesler. Writing as recently as 1998, she devoted only a half-page to the
necessity of economic independence for women in her *Letters to a Young
Feminist*. However, Chesler did acknowledge one theme of this chapter:
that despite career gains, too many women are still stuck making the coffee.

By contrast, in Chapter 3, on medicine, law, and politics, we offered
dramatic instances of women who are changing the nature of the work they
do. Along the way, they have the potential to change the larger world for
the better. In management, too, we see the potential for more negotiation
and less domination. In these ways and more, women truly seem to be
making a difference as they move from the private into the public sphere.
The influence of women in public relations management, in particular, may
reach well beyond the organizations that employ them to benefit the larger
society and even the world.

This "essential difference" argument is a risky one to make, of course.
We continue to believe that there is more variance among women, say, than
there is between men and women. Biology does not program women to be
more supportive and men to be more aggressive. At the same time, we cannot ignore women's socialization into roles that emphasize the value of cooperation and men's socialization into roles that promote autonomy. Also,
we know from the "Thirtysomething" study described in greater detail in
Chapter 2 that women are generally better educated and often more motivated than their male counterparts in similar jobs.

So, in spite of juggling home and office responsibilities, U.S. women
are finding rewarding careers in nontraditional areas. Public relations management is one of those areas. However, success in public relations, as in
the other careers discussed here, comes with an inordinately high price tag
for most women. And the positive changes for many women in management we have described here seem to come excruciatingly slowly.

In an effort to escape the frustrations of that kind of gender-based discrimination, unprecedented numbers of women are striking out on their own. They may work from home or from their own shop. However, even these female entrepreneurs who risk the loss of benefits for job autonomy end up reeling and rubbing their heads bruised from the jolt of invisible yet very real barriers: the glass walls and glass ceiling.

Chapter Five

The Promise of Diversity for Public Relations

Anthropologists recently have taken a real interest in describing the lives of working women in different cultures and from different racial and ethnic backgrounds. Just as Chapter 3 asked how U.S. women in public relations fare by comparison with their sisters in other professions and occupations, this chapter looks for parallels between white women of European descent and women of other races and ethnicities.

We would expect significant differences. Although culture is not static, in large part these differences are attributable to the cultural roots from whence the women came. Geert Hofstede (1980), whose work on culture may be cited more than any other in business and communication management, defined one of four predictive elements of culture as "masculinity/femininity." Adler (1997) subsequently renamed this factor "career success/quality of life." Whatever we call it, we know that some societies place greater emphasis on traits associated with masculinity than those associated with femininity. For example, societies that emphasize career success value assertiveness and material wealth. Thus work is central to people's lives; they prefer greater salary to shorter working hours. Few women work in high-paying jobs. By contrast, societies oriented toward quality of life place higher value on relationships and concern for others.

WHY STUDY RACIOETHNICITY IN PUBLIC RELATIONS?

To provide less than what is admittedly the abbreviated analysis of diversity in this chapter would be a disservice to our readers. As Cox (1990) explained, "As the composition of work groups becomes increasingly ethnically diverse, the assumption that knowledge about organizational issues compiled almost exclusively by white men using white subjects applies equally well to nonwhites is increasingly inappropriate" (p. 5). In fact, most theories of both management and communication have been developed by Western scholars—especially U.S. academics.

Limaye and Victor (1991), noting that culture often has been ignored in the development of these paradigms, explained that "for years, the conventional scholarly and practical wisdom has been that concepts and precepts of communication and management are universal and hence can be applied across countries or cultures" (p. 280). We do *not* assume that the theories and models developed in this society are effective or even applicable in every society—or even within every organization in this society. That kind of linear thinking becomes less and less viable as the demographics of organizational environments and of employees become more and more culturally diverse.

So, we are trying to break through what Myrdal (1944) described as the "cultural fog" enveloping Western scientists. More than a half-century ago he pointed out that cultural factors determine the questions we ask, the interpretation we ascribe to the answers they generate, and the conclusions we reach at the end of our inquiry. Unless or until we manage to pierce the fog, Myrdal predicted that we would make countless errors. Perhaps more damning, we probably would be oblivious to those omissions and misinterpretations. Perhaps most important, we agree with Ang and Hermes (1991), who explained that "since a subject is always multiply positioned in relation to a whole range of discourses, many of which do not concern gender, women do not always live in the prison house of gender" (p. 320).

We begin this chapter, then, with an explanation of the growing importance of diversity—both gender and ethnic—to the U.S. economy in general and to the public relations industry in particular. We continue with an overview of how public relations can contribute to organizational effectiveness at a time of growing heterogeneity within and around organizations. We conclude the chapter by reiterating the question of whether this nascent attention to multiculturalism is mere "political correctness." In our answer, we explore the role that the reptilian brain may play in defending the status quo and thus opposing the recruiting, hiring, or promoting of more racioethnic minorities to positions of top management in our field.

WHAT DO WE MEAN BY "MINORITY"?

Throughout this chapter, we attempt to describe both the situation for "minority" employees and any special impact they may be having on the organizations that employ them. We place the word "minority" in quotation marks here because in a sense we are all members of a minority group at different times and places in our lives (Gross, 1985). We also understand that a minority is any part of the population that differs from others in some characteristics and as a result is subjected to differential treatment (*Webster's New Collegiate Dictionary*, 1987, p. 757).

Thus, although minority may suggest less than the number necessary for control, it actually refers more to perception and bias than it does to any percentage. One major contention of Gould's (1981) classic work *The Mismeasure of Man* is that although racists and sexists may confine their bigotry to the one disadvantaged group such as African Americans or women, race, sex, and class go hand in hand. Each acts as a surrogate for the others. As Gould argued so compellingly, hierarchies of advantage and disadvantage affect both women and racial minorities. Further, we believe that cultural identity results in large part from the intersection of all these aspects of an individual's identity.

This understanding becomes critical with the knowledge that the non-white population of the United States is growing faster than the country's white citizenry. African Americans are projected to become the majority of the population in many of our largest cities by the turn of this century. Williams (1990) pointed out that blacks or Hispanics already have the advantage in terms of numbers in Atlanta, El Paso, San Antonio, Los Angeles, San Francisco, and Washington, DC.

At the same time, we acknowledge important differences between the United States and other countries from which our immigrant populations are coming. These distinctions make direct, one-on-one comparisons difficult if not inherently flawed. For just one example, we cite the explosion of new jobs in the United States during the 1980s—a decade characterized by declining employment in most other industrial countries. (Economists and business journalists tend to attribute this phenomenon to the influx of women into the U.S. job market.) The assumption of comparability where none may exist is a persistent weakness of the research on international management in general and, according to Limaye and Victor (1991), of business communication in particular.

Finally, it could be argued that women themselves represent a separate culture, largely unknown to university scholars much less society at large (Acker, Barry, & Esseveld, 1983). Perhaps more importantly, women and minorities—any group that does not fit the norms of the dominant culture—often face extraordinary challenges at work.

Limitations to This Discussion

Despite our best intentions in this chapter to report faithfully on the situation for diverse people, then, we must acknowledge at least two important limitations. First, we three white women authors do not represent the diversity that undoubtedly would enhance both the perspectives and the credibility of this book. One professor of business administration who has studied race and ethnicity extensively concluded that whenever possible, research teams should be what he (Cox, 1990) called "multi-racioethnic." That is, they should include representatives of all racial and ethnic groups included in the research. Cox considered this racial and ethnic mix, or inclusion of insiders and outsiders, not only desirable but crucial in reducing bias in research involving racioethnicity.

Before we go on to our second major caveat, we need to introduce a few words on words. Scholars have tended to use "race" to refer to biological differences among groups; "ethnicity" traditionally has referred to cultural differences (Alba & Chamblin, 1983). Cox (1990), however, disavowed the belief that a group is either biologically or culturally distinct from another rather than both. Thus he introduced the term "racioethnic" to refer to biologically or culturally distinct groups—or both.

Our second main limitation at this point is that relatively little research that is relevant to our purposes has been published. The extant knowledge of how race and ethnicity are related to the work place has been called "appallingly limited" (Cox, 1990, p. 5). For example, despite the established need for information about the effects of racioethnicity in organizations (Ilgen & Youtz, 1986), few such reports have been published in U.S. management journals (Cox, 1990).

Why So Little Research on This Topic?

The lack of scholarship on this key issue can be attributed to two main factors. One is that the publication of racioethnic research in the academic press is problematic. The rate of publication in leading management journals of articles related to racioethnicity actually has fallen over the last 2 decades, from 11.7 per year in the 1970s to fewer than 4 per year in the 1980s (Cox, 1990). Reasons include journal reviewers' unfamiliarity with the relevant literature, editors' and reviewers' insistence on research designs that compare men with women or whites with nonwhites, incompatible ideologies between those media gatekeepers and scholars who do research on racioethnicity, and low submission rates of such research (Cox, 1990).

Thus we see that the second, perhaps more disturbing, explanation for the dearth of knowledge on racioethnicity in the organizational setting is that little of this research is being done in the first place. Given its significance, one has to wonder why. To discover the answer, Cox (1990) queried 75 scholars who have written about race or ethnicity. He also reviewed relevant literature on research methods and the journal reviewing process. Through this combined methodology, he concluded that white Americans generally do not consider racioethnicity a topic of universal importance. Instead, they deem it a "minority issue," important only to members of the minority group.

Cox also found that scholars from both majority and (especially) minority groups often are pressured against conducting such research. Even those who believe that racioethnic topics should be the exclusive domain of minority scholars also caution against their being "pigeonholed" as "the minority researcher" on a faculty. Further, Cox discovered the paradox that, as one white female participant in his study expressed it, "If one is a minority researcher, one is assumed to be biased, but if one is a non-minority, one's legitimacy is questioned" (p. 10). We know this damned-if-you-do, damned-if-you-don't situation quite well.

Further obstacles to the conduct of research that would be relevant for a comprehensive chapter of this nature include a lack of cooperation in the field for such a "hot topic" (Cox, 1990) and the fact that research on nonwhites in organizations often results in disappointingly small sample sizes. This last problem was expressed by an author whose work was criticized by a journal reviewer: "Yes the sample size for the minority managers is small. However, it represents the proportion of the minority managers in the company and of the larger population. Obtaining a sample of minority managers at this management level is difficult" (as quoted in Cox, 1990, p. 12).

Small sample size also is a problem highlighted specifically in the modest body of research on minorities in public relations. Zerbinos and Clanton (1993) cited the difficulty of locating Asian American and Hispanic American practitioners for their study of job satisfaction, career influences, and discrimination in the field. Graduate theses reviewed in these pages are almost entirely based on smaller samples than their authors would have liked to employ. (What they lack in breadth they typically make up for in depth, in our view, because most of these studies are triangulations of qualitative and quantitative methodology.)

Another contributing factor may be the unwillingness of practitioners to participate in such research. For example, PR News and the public relations firm Ketchum (PR News/Ketchum, 1994) jointly sponsored a study of diversity in the work place. They distributed their survey instrument to more than 2,000 regular recipients of PR News. Only 257 of those public relations professionals responded. Zaharna, Diggs-Brown, and Yamauchi (1994) conducted a third study measuring attitudes toward diversity in public relations and found what they considered to be actual *resistance* to diversity within the industry.

One final explanation for the lack of substantial research on racioethnic issues in business management is the fact that such intercultural investigation is inordinately time-consuming and expensive (Limaye & Victor, 1991). Perhaps as a result, our understanding is limited by the fact that anecdotal treatment dominates the literature (Chesanow, 1985; Kennedy, 1985; Snowden, 1986; Harris & Moran, 1987). One important aim of this book is to enrich the discussion of multiculturalism in public relations by contributing our rigorous empirical research and grounding that research, in the first place, in a solid theoretical conceptualization.

A FEW WORDS ABOUT ANOTHER UNDERRESEARCHED AREA: SEXUAL ORIENTATION AND PUBLIC RELATIONS

We have established, then, that the published research on racioethnicity and communication management is minimal. However, by comparison with literature that deals with sexual orientation and management, it seems extensive. Despite this lack of theoretical knowledge about the impact of gay and lesbian issues on public relations, in particular, we are convinced that these concerns are becoming increasingly important to managers of public relations. Three trends support this contention.

First, we believe that public relations professionals will encounter such issues related to heterosexism as they work with activist groups representing either heterosexist or gay and lesbian concerns. For just one example, consider the special interests pressuring organizations to provide equitable benefits for gay and lesbian employees and their partners. Second, we know that employee populations today include more gays and lesbians who have "outed," or revealed their sexual orientation. Along with this openness comes the need both to provide benefits—such as bereavement leave or health insurance that covers same-sex partners—and to work with employees who may have markedly different appearances, values, or concerns than their heterosexual bosses.

Third, and finally, in *The Corporate Closet*, Woods and Lucas (1993) described the ghettoization of gays into support functions that include human resources and public relations (p. 230). Public relations may be attracting a disproportionate percentage of employees from the gay work force. Woods and Lucas, however, studied only gay men. Hall (1986, 1989) described comparable discrimination against lesbians in the corporation. In addition, though, lesbians face discrimination because they are women. Given the growing feminization of public relations, we should be aware of this double burden that lesbians may face. Unfortunately, this chapter on diversity is flawed by the paucity of evidence that we can bring to bear on this critical concern for management in the 1990s.

CULTURAL DIVERSITY IN THE U.S. WORK FORCE

In 1990, the year when the proposal for this book was being developed, the U.S. Department of Labor announced that ethnic minorities represented 22% of our work force. Scholars from a variety of fields have studied how African Americans, Hispanic Americans, Asian Americans, Native Americans, and other such groups have challenged the status quo in U.S. organizations (Awanohara, 1990; Balchen, 1987; Boowie, 1988). Other research has questioned the roles and status of minority workers (e.g., Kern-Foxworth, 1989b).

A number of studies focus on the question of promotion for people of color. One survey conducted by UCLA's Graduate School of Management produced what management experts called an "astonishing" revelation: Despite at least a decade of social change growing out of awareness about the values of multiculturalism, women and minorities have made little progress in being promoted to management positions (Silver, 1990). Almost 700 top executives participated in the longitudinal research. Their responses, compared with responses from a similar survey conducted 10 years earlier, supported the notion that an invisible ceiling for people of color and for women persists. The numbers for race were virtually identical: 99% of the executives said they were white. Women made a slight gain, up from 0.5% in 1979 to 3% a decade later. The lack of progress may be attributed to the fact that these groups only recently made inroads into positions of middle management; time may provide them with the experience necessary to secure jobs in top management. At least one executive woman, however, blamed subtle discrimination (Franklin, as cited in Silver, 1990, p. D1).

The dean of the graduate school at UCLA, commenting on the study, warned that "corporations are learning that it's bad business to ignore women and minorities, both because they wield growing economic clout and because they represent a rich pool of managerial talent" (LaForce, as quoted in Silver, 1990, p. D1). Despite the discouraging statistics from his own survey, we certainly agree.

So, too, do outsiders looking at the United States. Michael Morley (1998), a distinguished international counselor in public relations, pointed out the need for skilled internal relations experts to communicate with diverse employee publics. He explained his reasoning, in part, by the attendant legal issues: "In the USA particularly the need is accentuated by the epidemic of law suits brought by employees who claim they have suffered discrimination in hiring practices or have not had opportunity for promotion" (p. 65).

Thomas and the Influential American Institute for Managing Diversity

We also believe that most scholars and managers would agree with R. Roosevelt Thomas Jr. (1991) that managing diversity is an idea whose time has come. Thomas, founding director of the American Institute for Managing Diversity at Morehouse College, went from relative obscurity to prominence in boardrooms throughout the country. Visionary leaders increasingly seek his counsel.

Thomas's message begins with the notion that diversity includes everyone; it does not depend solely on race or gender. It continues with the understanding that the successful management of diversity hinges on *valuing*—rather than *tolerating*—difference. Diversity consultants such as Thomas have found concrete ways of doing just this. Communication plays a large part. Through dialogue, employees can confront their stereotypes. For example, the Anti-Defamation League conducts a workshop on the "Workplace of Difference" that includes several communication exercises designed to explore participants' attitudes toward those unlike themselves (Solomon, 1992). The goal is to promote the value of diversity.

Through his talks and his writings, Thomas relied on the metaphor of the diverse American work force not as a melting pot but as a mosaic. A special issue of *Time* magazine chronicled this departure from the assimilation model of the United States as the first "universal" nation ("The New Face of America," 1993). Thomas's bottom line is that building and maintaining a diverse organizational culture also builds long-term competitive advantage.

In arriving at these conclusions, Thomas discovered that the extant literature rarely focused on the experience of blacks or women from a managerial perspective—the perspective so central to this book on women in public relations. Instead, most of the relevant writings dealt with legal or moral responsibility, civil rights, affirmative action, or interpersonal relationships. The value of his contribution of the *managerial perspective* to this body of literature cannot be underestimated. It moved us away from the historical assumption that the solution to diversity is assimilation:

> *Management.* Here, managers place priority on the interests of their corporations. The principal questions are, "What do I as a manager need to do to ensure the effective and efficient utilization of employees in pursuit of the corporate mission?" and "What are the implications of diversity for how I manage?" (Thomas, 1991, p. 17)

Thomas also reviewed a number of influential writings that described how-to approaches for women or nonwhites to become successful at assimilation into the traditional organization. In what he called "the end of assimilation" (p. 7), he described two major flaws in newcomers' attempts to fit into the business world (much less society at large). First, Thomas and others had long determined that we are in a seller's market for work-force skills. Thus minority workers' unwillingness to conform to the existing corporate culture makes assimilation simply unattainable today.

Second, Thomas contended that even if diverse employees were willing to submerge their minority identity, this would be bad for business. Forcing everyone to conform leaves untapped potential, and thus leads to lackluster performance. Here the Center for Creative Leadership would agree. It found that homogeneity leads to a narrow view of the world, thus limiting any consideration of alternative perspectives and actions. It termed this myopia "perilous" for our tumultuous world ("Organizations Want Diversity," 1994, p. 1).

To capitalize on diverse employees' personal strengths and innovative ideas, initially Thomas set out to research the relationship between black employees and their (typically) white male managers. Along the way, he found that the key issues of racioethnicity applied to minorities in general, rather than to African Americans alone. He also found that women, regardless of their numbers in the work force, were often treated as minorities. Thus he broadened his scope to include all minorities and women. Likewise, he learned that all managers—not just white men—eventually would be managing employees unlike themselves and so he aimed for an understanding of all managers. Finally, Thomas expanded the traditional understanding of "diversity" beyond race, ethnicity, and gender to encompass other factors he considered relevant to the work place. These dimensions include age, functional and educational background, tenure with the organization, lifestyle, and geographic origin.

Thus the picture Thomas had painted by the beginning of the 1990s was a complex but critically important one. He argued that managing an increasingly heterogeneous work force has profound strategic implications both for organizations and for society.

The Growing Importance of Empowering Diverse Workers

Tapping the potential of an organization's diverse human resources—no longer as homogenous as that employee population once was—is what Thomas (1991) called a "tough reality" of the decade of the '90s. He considered diversity a new issue, increasingly important because of three main trends.

First, the global marketplace has become intensely competitive. By

1990, the value of import–export trade for this country surpassed $857 billion (*Direction of Trade Statistics Yearbook*, 1990). Likewise, international trade accounts for more than one-quarter of the economic activity in most European countries (Limaye & Victor, 1991). Thomas (1991) predicted that this trend is only going to increase. To remain competitive, he projected, U.S. business would have to scramble for the most lucrative markets and the best workers. As he put it, "To thrive in an increasingly unfriendly marketplace, companies must make it a priority to create the kind of environment that will attract the best new talent and will make it possible for employees to make their fullest contribution" (p. 4).

Understanding racioethnic aspects of managing the global enterprise also has domestic implications. Thomas (1991) pointed out that the makeup of the U.S. work force has become dramatically more diverse. As a result, even the manager who does not engage directly in international business needs to appreciate the principles of multicultural communication in this age of rapidly shifting demographics. By the year 2000, one in three Americans would be nonwhite. This country is becoming increasingly pluralistic in its ethnic makeup (Miller, 1991; Ward & Anthony, 1992; "The New Face of America," 1993).

The third major trend that Thomas highlighted has to do with individuals more than with groups of workers or the organizations that employ them. He discovered that people increasingly choose to celebrate their differences rather than struggle to fit into the mainstream. This unwillingness to assimilate or to compromise what makes each worker unique may represent the greatest departure from previous decades.

To this list of three major factors Jack O'Dwyer, publisher of a public relations trade magazine, may have wished to add a fourth. Speaking at a PRSA convention, he blamed *media exploitation* for "whipping up ethnic and racial feelings which America was created to calm down" (as quoted in "Presentation by Multicultural Panel Member Jack O'Dwyer," 1994, p. 12). As a result, O'Dwyer said, the business world has become "hysterical" over the topic of multiculturalism because "it sees ethnic groups as markets. If the groups want special programs, they'll provide them" (p. 12). O'Dwyer was opposed to any business approach that magnifies the differences among Americans—people whom he claimed created a society aimed at forgetting ethnic differences.

This view was called "panicky" and "reactionary" by one of public relations' leading black professionals, A. Bruce Crawley (as quoted in "Presentation by Multicultural Panel Member A. Bruce Crawley," 1994, p. 13). The research literature, too, supports the notion that universalist views such as O'Dwyer's are parochial and dysfunctional—especially in this global era. Business professors Limaye and Victor (1991) argued that both scholars and practitioners increasingly appreciate cultural factors as appropriate determinants of managerial practice. Similar sensitization seems to be occurring in the more specific practice of business communication (Kilpatrick, 1984; Haworth & Savage, 1989).

The business community and communication professionals in the related fields of advertising, marketing, and public relations must come to recognize the importance of understanding the needs of what Sheldon (1990) called our "increasingly diverse cultural fabric" (p. 21). That fabric is woven of different languages, suggesting that communication professionals must be fluent in those languages and the cultures that spawned them (Sheldon, 1990; McIntyre, 1991). Perhaps one participant in a study of African American practitioners put it best:

> A lot of professional organizations miss the boat when they talk about diversifying and wanting more African Americans in the field. The education process must occur inside public relations as well as within the different business communities we [public relations practitioners] work with to ease existing tensions and anxieties many white practitioners have of African Americans, largely due to a lack of cultural understanding. As a public relations counselor, your role is to be the consultant and tell people how to manage their businesses, crises, etc. To do this effectively, the client must be at ease with the consultant. (as quoted in Mallette, 1995, n. p.)

Distilling all of these concepts and trends resulted in the following definition of managing diversity: "A comprehensive managerial process for developing an environment that works for all employees" (Thomas, 1991, p. 10). Notice that managing diversity is a *process*, rather than a *program* or a *product*. Thomas also underscored the importance of the word "all," for he did not choose to exclude the white male. We applaud this inclusion because as AT&T's former (white male) public relations director put it, "White men, especially white, Anglo-Saxon, Protestant men, have been feeling left out of the multicultural movement" (Wann, 1993, p. 23). We know that the perception of reverse discrimination in an increasingly heterogeneous (and competitive) labor market may lead to feelings of frustration and threat.

An important word missing from Thomas's definition but inherent in all of his work on managing diversity is the notion of enabling, or "empowerment." Trendy as the word "empowerment" may be, this *concept* is likely to persist in business management. It may go by the alternative notions of "total quality management" (TQM) or "pushing decision-making down." Whatever the initiative is called, it gets at the heart of this book:

creating an environment wherein the full potential of each employee—male or female, gay or straight, white or nonwhite, young or old—is tapped. (Because this concept of empowering everyone, rather than having power over others, is so central to our work here, we will be saying much more about it in Chapter 7.)

Empowerment suggests that women and minorities must participate fully in the rewards and responsibilities of all sectors of U.S. life—economic, social, and political—if this country is to sustain its economic and political viability (Cantor, 1989). Thus empowerment rejects any duality or binary opposition between business issues and people issues. A tangential advantage here, as Thomas (1991) pointed out, is that in this approach managers spend less time doing the work and more of their time enabling their employees to do the work. Any diversity effort, Anderson (1993) argued, requires such a process that fosters equity, consensus, and *empowerment*.

Empowerment also speaks to the two-way street so relevant to any discussion of public relations. Adaptation and empowerment, to Thomas, are *mutual* processes between the organization and the employee. He pointed out the change from the traditional approach, where the burden of adapting rests on the individual employee who is different and the burden of decision making rests on the manager.

Barriers to Managing Diversity

As appealing and strategic as this contemporary approach may seem to our readers, we know also that change does not come easily—to the manager, to the organization, or to society. The field of public relations is no exception. This book began with a history of the involvement of one professional association, PRSA, to cope with the dramatic demographic shifts in its ranks. At the 1993 PRSA conference, a panel on multiculturalism exposed the strong feelings held by those who attended the annual meeting.

On the one hand, Panelist Crawley said that "I can't understand for the life of me how anyone can question the need for multicultural communications" ("Presentation by Multicultural Panel Member A. Bruce Crawley," 1994, p. 10). On the other hand, Panelist O'Dwyer, frequent critic of PRSA and editor of *O'Dwyer's PR Services Report*, was called a "Neanderthal" three times for asserting that "the surest route to success in the U.S. for anyone remains full assimilation into its Eurocentric culture" ("Multiculturalism Is Debated," 1994, p. 1). His own publication reported that one woman walked out in the middle of his remarks.

Those who would label someone of O'Dwyer's opinions a "Neanderthal" may know more than they realize. Wann, addressing not the PRSA but the IABC annual meeting in 1993, alluded to Carl Sagan's notion that within each of us lurks a prehistoric instinct to be territorial and combative. In explaining why so many people are threatened by the move toward multiculturalism, which he equated with diversity, Wann said: "Deep down, we are all frightened animals. And when put into new and fearsome situations, those animal instincts take command of our actions and thoughts. That is, unless we have the self-confidence to cope and self-esteem to believe we can gain from every situation" (1993, p. 24). Wann added that he is amazed by how many people in the Western hemisphere lack self-esteem. Thus people like O'Dwyer may be in the majority when it comes to valuing the familiar assimilation over the implications of the realities of our changing business environment. In his seminal book *Beyond Race and Gender*, Thomas (1991) made much of the fact that despite a trend toward participatory management, most managers still practice a top-down, directive style.

The Center for Creative Leadership, working together with the University of Maryland, has been studying the long-term effectiveness of these organizations that remain homogeneous—especially at the level of top management. It determined that organizations often fail to achieve diversity, even when they acknowledge its growing importance, because of the "ASA cycle." First comes the *attraction* effect, wherein employees are attracted to organizations based on the people who already work there. The *selection* effect explains that organizations only can hire new employees from the pool of applicants they attract. Finally, the *attrition* effect suggests that because attraction and selection are imperfect, some workers fit in better than others. Those who do not fit in ultimately leave (as cited in "Organizations Want Diversity," 1994). Thus, without dramatic intervention, over time the proportion of people who are similar in an organization increases.

Using Thomas's words to elaborate on this counterproductive ASA cycle, such organizations' " 'best' employees are those who come the closest to being clones of the boss" (1991, p. 46). As a psychologist who studies management issues explained, "There're barriers imposed if you don't share the same interests or follow the same football teams" (as quoted in Silver, 1990, p. D1).

Consider now the implications for those who, no matter how they might try, cannot come close to being "clones of the boss" by virtue of their skin color, cultural roots, age, or physical configuration. Because most U.S. managers remain white men of European extraction, women and people of color—regardless of their capabilities or motivations—are unlikely to approximate these managers. Thus we can set aside the tired assumption that "cream rises to the top," for it ignores the reality of mentoring or informal grooming for advancement in the typical organization today. As Thomas (1991) explained, an increasing proportion of employees with needs and preferences different from their bosses' will require management to create a new, more facilitative environment.

Even in public relations, an organizational function where the importance of multiculturalism at least with the internal public seems obvious, resistance to diversification persists. *PR News* and Ketchum Public Relations (*PR News/Ketchum,* 1991) distributed questionnaires on diversity to more than 2,000 *PR News* subscribers across the country. Recall that only 257 responded. One graduate student, herself an African American experienced in theater promotions, considered this "a strong indication that the public relations industry is not interested in workplace diversity" (Pendelton, 1996, p. 5).

DIVERSITY IN PUBLIC RELATIONS

Public relations may be the most critical department in which to establish such an environment. Valuing diversity within the organization and also its environment offers real payoffs. Public relations contributes to this effort at least in part through its emphasis on what Crawley (as quoted in "Presentation by Multicultural Panel Member A. Bruce Crawley," 1994) called "targeting": understanding the target audience, tailoring the message to that audience, and then reaching the audience through a medium it uses and trusts. As he said, "The marketing and advertising agencies have understood this for years and have successfully utilized such targeting for breaking America's 250 million consumers down into bite-sized subgroups with common demographics and psychographic characteristics" (p. 10). As a result, Crawley, president of his own public relations firm, decried the trade press and industry leaders who condemn the practice or goals of multicultural communication as divisive or somehow destructive.

By contrast, "ethnic marketing" is projected to become one of the top five areas of growth in our field ("Top 5 Factors," 1993). It has spawned a number of articles in the trade press that explore ways in which organizations can communicate with, say, the Hispanic population in this country. Some focus directly on corporate marketing efforts (Fry, 1991; Kern-Foxworth, 1991; Powers & Oliver, 1992), others on firms that target the Hispanic community (Westerbeck, 1992), and still others on philanthropic efforts or public service to Hispanic Americans (Fry, 1991).

Crawley and these authors all speak from the perspective of expert practitioners. Their insights, rooted in their experience and that of their professional colleagues, add to our so-far limited understanding of the need for communication programs that acknowledge and appreciate heterogeneity within internal and external publics. Their illustrations become even more credible, in our view, when supplemented by the rich conceptual work of theorists in sociology and psychology. We turn now to one such scholar, Karl Weick (1979), and his theory of requisite variety. In this way, we go beyond individual instances or experiences to look for patterns of behavior across hundreds of organizations. Perhaps more importantly, social psychologist Weick's theory of requisite variety explains *why* a multicultural and gender-inclusive appreciation is so vitally important to business management today.

Weick's (1979) work also broadens the discussion from a somewhat narrow marketing perspective. The articles in the trade press discussed above fail to distinguish between a "public" and a "market." Many of their authors use the terms interchangeably—and they are writing for the public relations, rather than marketing, industry! The marketing view looks at what we consider publics as consumers—even if they happen to be employees of the organization. Thus we often see affirmative action programs linked to bottom-line concerns, such as productivity. As just one example, Wagonheim (as quoted in "Changing American Workforce," 1993), director of the Center for the New American Workforce at Queens College, pointed to Toys R Us. Its most diverse departments outdistanced all others in productivity. Rather than this singular concern with the bottom line, whether it be called "productivity" or "profitability," the theory of requisite variety brings us to acknowledge the legitimacy of all strategic publics, internal and external alike, *on their own terms.*

Some practitioners may be particularly well equipped to function in a diverse environment. African Americans, in particular, have learned to exist in two cultures in this country: one of African and one of European extraction. Thus they have developed what nearly a century ago DuBois (1903) termed a "double consciousness." Double consciousness is the sense of seeing one's self through the eyes of others, always sensing one's twoness. African Americans' two-ness with both prevalent cultures provides them with a career advantage in many cases; it inevitably benefits their organizations as well. As Mallette (1995) explained the significance of double consciousness for our field, "The potential for greater cross-cultural insight exists and an environment is created promoting symmetrical communication and enhancing negotiated agreements" (p. 69).

In a move consistent with these assumptions of requisite variety, some organizations have established "diversity task forces" made up of representatives of all levels of the hierarchy, both genders, and all ethnicities. Their task is to use feedback from throughout the operation to help plan and implement diversity initiatives (Baytos, 1992). Ideally, they emphasize the interdependency of such programs with the long-term, strategic goals of the organization (Thomas, 1991). Such task forces, however, are rare. More often, the public relations function becomes responsible for importing the variety of perspectives necessary to keep the organization viable during this time of cultural upheaval.

The Implications of Requisite Variety for Public Relations

Weick (1979) developed the principle that there must be at least as much variety, or diversity, inside the organization as outside it. After all, we cannot rely on what he called the "reduction of variety," given the increasing pluralism in this country. So this correspondence between diversity within and without the organization (even if it is not one to one) is necessary or required to build strong, credible relationships with all critical aspects of the organization's environment. That is, even if the public relations department does not include a representative of every relevant ethnic culture, some diversity there is likely to result in the department's perceiving and subsequently dealing with its environment more effectively.

Why? Strategic parts of the environment—those publics that can most help or hinder the organization—are not so obvious as they might seem. Weick and other scholars have discovered that the environment is *enacted* rather than *objective*. That is, the environment will not be understood in the same way by everyone who considers it. So, for example, the organization whose strategic publics, such as consumers, include minorities still may not acknowledge the importance of those key stakeholders if all of its public relations practitioners are white. The concerns of another key stakeholder, the employee public, may go unnoticed if managers in the human resources department are male and most of the workers are female. As one practitioner of color expressed it, "I don't understand a company that doesn't kind of look like the population unless they are discriminating or at least not trying" (as quoted in Len-Rios, 1998, p. 547).

Even if a predominantly white male management acknowledges the existence of diverse publics, it may not consider those publics legitimate. Surely we all know business leaders who say (and probably believe) they "embrace" diversity, yet they act in ways that betray their bigotry toward groups that are different. Yet legitimacy, we believe, is one key attribute of an effective relationship.

The effective organization, we also believe, is one that manages its interdependence with all of its stakeholders: employees, stockholders, neighbors, governmental regulators, customers or clients, the media that cover it, and—especially—any activist groups that may oppose it. Although organizations would like to operate autonomously, without interference from these groups, the reality is that no organization exists in a vacuum—apart or independent from external and internal influences. So, organizations must adapt to (Katz & Kahn, 1978), cooperate with (Hage, 1980), or interact with (Buchholz, 1989) all of these groups that limit their independence.

This necessity for managed interdependence is perhaps greater now than ever before because of a scarcity of resources and the conflict that that scarcity engenders, the erosion of public confidence in most organizations and even institutions, growing public sentiment for corporate accountability and social responsibility, and *our increasingly heterogeneous society* (Pfeffer, 1981). All of this contributes to what Galbraith (1967) called the "countervailing power" of stakeholders.

Public Relations Practitioners as Boundary Spanners

As a boundary-spanning function, public relations can contribute in significant ways to organizational effectiveness (in some cases, even survival) in dealing with today's powerful publics. Boundary spanners are employees of the organization who interact frequently with members of its external constituencies. They gather, analyze, select, and relay the information gained in this interaction to the organization's decision makers within the dominant coalition. Managers of communication or public relations typically are among the organization's formally designated boundary spanners (Aldrich & Herker, 1977).

In their boundary-spanning role, practitioners not only enact the environment for top management; but they then design and implement communication programs tailored to the diverse strategic publics identified through that environmental scan. These programs go well beyond, say, learning the significance of exchanging business cards with their Asian counterparts. They are based on a true understanding of and appreciation for the uniqueness of other cultures. Thus diversity in public relations not only enhances the career potential of minority practitioners but enhances the effectiveness of their organizations.

In addition to acting as boundary spanners, public relations practitioners serve as change agents in the process of managing cultural diversity. Whereas boundary spanning deals primarily with external publics, this role is more internal to the organization. The role of the change agent in this context is to promote cultural transformation—a most difficult (and some would claim impossible) task. It often is approached through advising management on the value of such change, creating strategies to implement the process of change, communicating the new worldview to all employees, and helping foster understanding among them ("Public Relations Must Pave the Way," 1992). Public relations, in essence, becomes responsible for ensuring that everyone in the organization shares the same vision of valuing difference (Williams, 1991).

We would argue against the efficacy of what sounds like a top-down, largely one-way approach. However, we do believe that managers of public relations can encourage communication about issues of race and ethnicity that affect both the organization and its employees. As Williams (1991) pointed out, of course, listening is part of any effective communication effort. Thus we project that the public relations efforts likely to contribute the most to managing diversity will be two-way and symmetrical.

The multiyear, multicountry study of public relations, sponsored by the IABC Research Foundation and mentioned throughout this book (J. Grunig, 1992), highlights the importance of two additional characteristics of excellent public relations departments that are relevant to this discussion: sensitivity to societal culture and actual support of diversity. The first, quantitative, phase of the Excellence study, as it has come to be called, did not consider the ethnic diversity of publics within a single societal culture. However, it did emphasize the value of hiring and promoting women and minorities if public relations is to contribute the most to overall effectiveness in organizations.

Despite these understandings and best efforts, however, too few organizations actually achieve the requisite diversity. Why not? A study by the Conference Board (as cited in "Organizations Want Diversity," 1994) pinpointed three main explanations: (1) competition with other issues; (2) management's (mistaken) belief that demographic shifts will not affect its ability to attract good employees; and (3) confusion among the concepts of diversity, affirmative action, and equal opportunity.

One public relations expert on multiculturalism emphasized that cost is *not* a factor in organizations' failure to capitalize on the opportunities inherent in cultural diversity (Kern-Foxworth, as cited in "Organizations Want Diversity," 1994). But the consequences for remaining competitive may be dire. As the vice president of a major chemical corporation explained in a long interview conducted for the Excellence study (Dozier, L. Grunig, & J. Grunig, 1995), hiring out of some fraction of the population means that the quality of his company's work force—relative to those of its competitors—would diminish.

Even if the principles of requisite variety were widely adopted, however, the problems of communicating effectively across cultures may not be solved. Sha (1993), a student of intercultural communication, exposed two weaknesses in trying to apply Weick's (1979) tenets quickly and easily to public relations. The first relates to correspondence. She reasoned that organizations rarely find it feasible to hire a public relations practitioner to serve as cultural interpreter for each ethnic public that is strategic to the organization. Second, and more compelling in our view, is her argument related to the concept of power and top management: "The theory fails to consider that most communication decisions are made by dominant coalitions, which in most organizations across the country, are still dominated by Caucasian men" (p. 23). We agree, and thus we come back to our overarching premise that public relations professionals—whether they are women or men—must be included within that power elite.

The Contributions of Marilyn Kern-Foxworth

One of the first scholars to articulate both the necessity and the value of hiring minority practitioners of public relations was Marilyn Kern-Foxworth. Her work has focused on African Americans in public relations, but she has acknowledged the importance of studying practitioners of other races as well (Kern-Foxworth, 1991, 1993; Kern-Foxworth & Miller, 1992). She frequently fused the combination of the different groups of people of color into the acronym ALANA or AHANA, for Asians/Latinos/African Americans/Native Americans or Asians/Hispanics/African Americans/Native Americans.

Kern-Foxworth is one of a few educators—and the only African American woman to date—to win the coveted Pathfinder Award for research in public relations. Remarkably, she received this tribute (sponsored by the foundation that was then part of PRSA) primarily for work that was not published at the time yet considered so vital to the field that it deserved recognition. That research explored what Kern-Foxworth called the "acrylic vault" for practitioners of color. She explained that they often found themselves not only facing a transparent barrier to promotion but walls constraining them from communicating with audiences other than their own. In other words, she found that minority practitioners were being hired primarily as boundary spanners to publics of similar racioethnic heritage. They were, in essence, pigeonholed.

Later research suggested that practitioners of color accepted pigeonholing "as a typical part of their job and good business practice" (Len-Rios, 1998, p. 542). The African American, Asian American, and Hispanic professionals Len-Rios interviewed at length considered the expectation they would interact primarily with others of their race consistent with relationship building. They also considered this a logical responsibility to accept.

However, Kern-Foxworth's continuing concern for minority representation in this field was echoed by Williams (1991), who pointed out that although 22% of U.S. workers are minorities, only 7% of the 150,000 in public relations are members of a racial or ethnic minority. These figures, of course, are problematic. They are based on government statistics; however, the U.S. Bureau of Labor Statistics may not have the best "fix" on a definition of public relations. As we pointed out earlier (Toth, 1988), many people who practice in this field do not call themselves "public relations practitioners."

However we count practitioners of public relations, Williams (1991) contended that the small percentage who are people of color continues to encounter racial prejudice that impedes their advancement in the typical firm or department. In an effort to overcome such bias, some minority groups are establishing their own professional societies.

Recall that O'Dwyer questioned the need for special groups for black practitioners of public relations. In response, during a panel discussion on multiculturalism at the 1993 PRSA convention, Helen J. Goss explained that she had cofounded the Black Public Relations Society (BPRS) to provide a nurturing environment ("Rationale for Black PR Groups," 1994). The BPRS also serves to recruit blacks to the field of public relations and to help them develop leadership skills that should result in promotion. According to Goss, groups like the BPRS do not—as O'Dwyer contended—perpetuate separatism. In fact, one coalition of racially diverse practitioners, the Interassociation Council for Public Relations (IAC), serves as a bridge for the gap between minority and nonminority groups (Kern-Foxworth, 1989a; Williams, 1991). It represents an alliance among IABC, PRSA, and BPRS chapters in Atlanta, Georgia.

One immediate and positive result of groups such as the "Beepers," as BPRS often is called, is the publication of a directory of multicultural professionals and firms (Hines, 1994). This directory identifies the largest group of minority practitioners to date—about 800 individuals and 170 minority-owned companies. It was published by PRSA but funded by BPRS, the Asian American Advertising and Public Relations Alliance, and the Hispanic Public Relations Society. Proceeds from its sale help fund minority scholarships.

The previous year, PRSA had published a bibliography on multiculturalism and public relations (Miller, 1993). Regardless of the best efforts of organizations such as PRSA and BPRS, minorities remain underrepresented in public relations. Kern-Foxworth (1989b) suggested three explanations. First is racism or prejudice. Second, minorities are unaware of the profession of public relations. African American scholars (e.g., Clanton, 1990) and scholar/practitioners (e.g., Singletary, 1993) have suggested working through high school guidance counselors and teachers as the avenue toward increasing awareness.

We might also transform future editions of the textbooks students read in university public relations courses. Kern-Foxworth (1990) conducted a content analysis of books published from 1979 through 1988, comparing the total number of pages in each year to the number of pages that mentioned minorities in public relations. For all 9 years and 21,841 pages, she found 152 pages with some reference to minorities. Of these, only 21 pages referred to Hispanic Americans and only two referred to Asian Americans. Some of the books she examined, even the ones that were newest at that time, included no mention of racial minorities. She concluded that these vital resources for students presented a distorted view of the world of public relations in the United States.

Almost 10 years later, Hannon (1998) replicated Kern-Foxworth's (1990) study, comparing findings over time to determine whether the end of this decade showed greater ethnic representation in public relations textbooks. She found no "remarkable difference" between the 20-year-old texts and the contemporary ones she analyzed in terms of information provided about ethnic groups in communication management.

Third, and related to this problem of texts that fail to reflect the diversity of the field, minorities often do not have access to the training necessary to prepare them for jobs in the field. Even those who manage to enter the field encounter problems in mentoring, retention, and advancement. A survey conducted by the Minority Affairs Committee of the IABC found that 60 of the 85 nonwhite practitioners polled said they had experienced such barriers (Williams, 1991). They also cited a scarcity of role models. As one professional put it, "The first Black face I ever saw in public relations was in the mirror" (Lundy, as quoted in "The White Face," 1993, p. 25).

Of course, a lack of public relations professionals of color may be more perceived than real. Bovet (1994) pointed out that a full 85% of employees in minority firms are themselves minorities. Crawley (as quoted in Bovet, 1994), president of his own firm, asked the rhetorical question of why, since minority enterprises like his find qualified people, mainstream firms cannot?

Lack of opportunity to network is another real problem for people of color in public relations. Sharing experiences socially and informally on the job may lead to promotion. Here theory, rather than the life stories of practitioners, may provide a useful explanation for why networking and advancement go hand in hand. Ibarra (1993) theorized that limited access to informal networks precludes knowledge of how the organization actually works, the development of personal friendships, and social support—three factors that facilitate advancement. *Homophily,* the interaction of people of the same gender or racioethnicity, is one basis for networking. Perhaps through programs of cultural diversity, described earlier in this chapter, the makeup of the typical high-level network will change. Right now, though, most networks that could lead to professional advancement lack minorities. Thus homophilous networks that are influential do not serve minority practitioners—or women—well.

Perhaps for this reason, PRSA has elevated its committee on multicultural affairs to sectional status. The Multicultural Communications Section is one of the society's newest. Although its newsletter (via a "Dear Colleague" letter from Chair Norma F. Stanley) positions itself as a resource for marketing (rather than public relations) communication professionals, it offers members the following: networking opportunities, national conference activities, scholarships, an information clearinghouse, quarterly newsletters, a directory of multicultural practitioners, and professional development seminars and workshops ("Multi-Connections," 1997).

To this list of networking, role modeling, mentoring, education, and awareness, Paluszek (as quoted in Kern-Foxworth, 1989b), the PRSA president who inadvertently spurred this book project, added four more contributing factors to constraints facing people of color in public relations. These influences are stereotyping, cultural differences that are not valued or are mismanaged by supervisors in public relations, the white male club—real or perceived—that has controlled the field, and unwritten rules or criteria for success that minorities may not know. These factors emerged from a 1988 study by the Atlanta Inter-Association Council (as cited in Diggs-Brown & Zaharna, 1995).

Denise Gray, who worked in public relations for AT&T and served on PRSA's Minority Affairs Committee, explained it this way: "Much of the real business of public relations is done during social events to which minorities either aren't invited or are not made to feel comfortable attending. We often don't travel in the same social circles" (as quoted in Kern-Foxworth, 1989a, p. 18). Ruby Miller, the first black woman elected to PRSA's board of directors, hypothesized that because minority professionals are concentrated in big cities like New York and Los Angeles, too few whites have had the opportunity to work with them and get to know their strengths (as quoted in Kern-Foxworth, 1989a). We may conclude from all of this that, as one Asian American practitioner put it, our field has yet to become color blind (Uyeda, as quoted in Kern-Foxworth, 1989b).

When women are blocked from advancing, the phenomenon is called the "glass ceiling." With minorities, the term is "premature plateauing." By whatever name, we know that minorities and women—for all the reasons listed above—remain clustered at the lower levels of the typical organization (Thomas, 1991). Minority women fare even worse than their white sisters pay-wise as well.

WOMEN AROUND THE WORLD

Do working women around the world experience this kind of discrimination, or is it a uniquely U.S. phenomenon? Despite the United States being considered a land of opportunity and equality for all, women's pay equity here actually lags behind that of women in other industrialized countries such as Italy, Denmark, France, Sweden, and western Germany.

However, we consider the question largely rhetorical. We agree with First Lady Hillary Clinton, who joined this country's first female secretary of state, Madeleine Albright, on the platform of the 1997 U.N. Women's Conference in Beijing. She explained the significance to the Unites States of discrimination against women wherever they live:

> If half the world's citizens are undervalued, underpaid, undereducated, under-represented, fed less, fed worse, not heard, put down, we cannot sustain the democratic values and way of life we have come to cherish. (as quoted in Lippman, 1997, p. A9)

The most cursory look at the literature establishes that even professional women typically are disadvantaged around the globe. For example, a study (Cindoglu & Onkal, 1993) of female academicians in the Turkish medical education system established that women are concentrated in certain areas of specialization. These less prestigious, lower paying specialties include pediatrics, pharmacology, and physical rehabilitation. Turkish women are underrepresented on the more prestigious, higher paying faculties of surgery, nuclear medicine, and urology. Likewise, in China, nursing remains a female preserve; few Chinese women are physicians (Scanlan, 1993).

Rather than proceeding with this litany country by country, however, we prefer to cite a report from the U.N. Economic Commission for Europe ("Digest," 1994). It determined that women throughout Europe and North

America face a bleak outlook in terms of lower pay and rising unemployment, coupled with ongoing barriers to their entry into top jobs. It concluded that women are emerging as a special "underclass" in the paid work force. Women will become increasingly poorly paid, part-time, and temporary workers.

For a collection of papers and presentations on the global status of women, we also recommend the far-ranging volume edited by public relations and advertising scholars Newsom and Carrell (1995). There we learn that women in some countries have been able to enhance economic development, effect political change, and improve the lives of all. In other settings, the traditional cultural, social, economic, and political forces continue to silence women's voices.

Given the Asian philosophy of dual cosmic forces, one positive and one negative, we believe that Chinese women and their sisters in Korea, Taiwan, Japan, and other Far Eastern Asian cultures inspired by the yin–yang (or um–yang, in Korean) concept are at a similar disadvantage. You see, the positive force encompasses spring, day, and *male*; the negative force includes night, fall, and *female* (C. S. Chang & N. J. Chang, 1994).

Because of the influence of this philosophy on Eastern management, in particular, we fear for women's opportunities throughout Asia. However, establishing this to be the case is beyond the scope of this book—and also our understanding, as Western scholars. We find it especially difficult to reconcile the negativity associated with femaleness and the difference–complement dichotomy essential to yin and yang. Philosophers consider yin–yang a value-free concept. They consider positive and negative more in the mathematical than in the affective sense. Thus we see the cultural baggage we necessarily bring to our limited understanding of this duality. As C. S. Chang and N. J. Chang (1994) explained, the relationship between male and female is complementary: "Each element in a positive/negative pair needs the other to become a complete substance: A male needs a female. . . . " (p. 16). Thus we prefer to concentrate on the status and roles of female practitioners of color in this country, regardless of where their ancestors lived. The next chapter explores their opportunities and activities in depth.

CONCLUDING THOUGHTS

In concluding this chapter, we find ourselves thinking of words and phrases such as "empowerment," "celebrating diversity," "multiculturalism," and "racioethnicity." Sounds like political correctness, or PC, doesn't it? Like the many people who objected to or at least laughed at *The Los Angeles Times*'s "Guidelines on Ethnic and Racial Identification," you may be thinking that *words* do not create the racism or sexism most of us abhor. You also may be objecting to the very notion of "political correctness," seeing it as fairness to one through unfairness to another. You may be regarding us as the PC police, disguised as authors.

A leading newsletter for public relations professionals, *pr reporter*, took on the question of "mere" political correctness versus substance in its first-of-the-year issue in 1994 ("Public Participation," 1994). It began with the humorous reference to a holiday card from a public relations and advertising firm that rejected "a big HI from Santa" because it sounded "too pompous, too male-oriented & the ASPCA will have a problem with the way Santa treats the reindeer" (p. 1).

pr reporter used the greeting card as an illustration of the growing phenomenon of political correctness—one it believed could negatively affect how organizations build relationships. Why? PC may be a placebo, but one that feeds anger and disempowerment. This first issue of 1994 asked a series of troubling questions that juxtaposed McCarthyism against empowerment and accountability at work. Two paradoxes emerged. First, *pr reporter* asserted that a society moving toward egalitarianism (giving everyone an equal chance) may be impinging on the personal freedoms and privacy it has long held dear. Second, the office—which it called "the enslaver of us all"—may offer a "glimmer of hope" for restoring the balance between rights and responsibilities within a society that seems to embrace only rights of late (p. 3).

This growing sense of favoritism toward women and people of color may be the kind of social experiment to which a reader of the *American Journalism Review* alluded. Lomenzo (1993) argued against enforced diversity, which he contended was the approach that the typical newsroom was taking in an effort to increase its multiculturalism. In his letter to the editor, he wrote that "when certain entrenched (read: safe) white senior managers can play the P.C. game and suggest their desires to address the 'ills of past abuses' by 'favoring' or 'tilting' toward minorities and women, then the American pursuit of social equality takes a beating" (p. 5). The result of preferential treatment of targeted groups, he predicted, would be alienation of the "not guilty." He added that the sotto voce kind of resentment he foresaw is perhaps the worst kind because, as an undercurrent, it breeds estrangement.

The newsletter *pr reporter* attributed the PC movement to this underlying issue of people's sense of powerlessness. It questioned whether empowering people, such as consumers or employees, would diminish our concern for mere terminology and take us beyond political correctness to substantial and fair change.

What role can public relations play in overcoming the perception that PC poses a new totalitarianism? First, *pr reporter* recommended that we get serious about rejecting one-way communication in favor of truly participative dialogue. We have much more to say about the relative advantage of two-way over one-way models of public relations in Chapter 7. At this point, we simply reiterate the *pr reporter* suggestion that rather than paying lip service to the value of two-way communication, we should foster activities such as face-to-face talks between supervisors and their staffs, meetings in supporters' homes, ambassador programs, and advisory boards of opinion leaders. In so doing, we would make our public relations what Harrison (as quoted in "Public Participation," 1994, p. 4) called "transparent." Transparency goes beyond open communication because it shows the reasoning behind statements and decision. In this way, people affected by those decisions can participate.

Finally, the 1994 inaugural issue of *pr reporter* suggested that organizations establish policies on what is politically correct for themselves. Through a participatory process, the organization would come to state its support of inclusion, respect for individuals, and anti-discrimination. The key, according to *pr reporter*, is to define what diversity means *in that organization*.

To illustrate, consider AT&T's set of corporate values, called "Our Common Bond." First on the list is "respect for individuals." The AT&T credo goes on to spell out what that means: "We must treat each other with respect and dignity, valuing individuals and cultural differences . . . recognizing that exceptional quality begins with people." Thus AT&T, according to its former director of public relations Wann (1993), saw diversity not as a moral imperative but as a business strategy. (The astute reader undoubtedly has come to understand that we, the authors, see it as both.)

pr reporter concluded that diversity may be situational. It offered the example of obesity, which it considered the latest condition to have advocacy groups. It asked: "If you're a healthcare provider, or have a wellness policy, doesn't having obese people in the organization amount to not walking the talk? Isn't it like the doctor who urges patients to quit smoking while puffing away?" ("Public Participation," 1994, p. 4).

We relate this example not to divert readers from our central concern with women and racioethnic minorities to take up the cudgel for the overweight. Instead, we offer it as a way of illustrating the complexity and the emotional issues that often accompany any discussion of the nascent field of multiculturalism in public relations.

We acknowledge the anguish that accompanies these inescapable ambiguities and tensions. At the same time, we hope we have established the necessity of developing and implementing programs of diversity that have value for minority employees and for their employers alike. We believe this is so not only because multiculturalism is politically and morally correct. It is; and morality certainly matters. But diversity in the office, and especially in the public relations department, also works. Perhaps more compelling than any scholars' theories about why diversity is so valuable are the words taken from a speech reprinted in its entirety in IABC's *Communication World*—highly unusual in the trade press that typically condenses everything. Wann (1993), speaking at a multicultural reception held during the 1993 IABC conference, explained the essence of diversity applied to business this way:

> It is the differences that result in progressive, evolutionary change. Inbreeding, in business and people, ultimately produces idiots. In business, if everybody thought the same and acted the same, and believed the same things, the business would die a certain, boring death. Many did and many will. (pp. 23–24)

Chapter Six

African Americans, Asian Americans, and Hispanic Americans in U.S. Public Relations

T wenty years ago public relations was accused of being "the last of the lily-white professions" (Layton, 1980, p. 64). Does the label fit today? We explore this question here in Chapter 6.

The 1990 census was the first to find white males less than a majority of all workers in this country. An analysis of those census data showed that working women had made significant progress during the 1980s in narrowing the gender gap. However, an investigation by *The Miami Herald* newspaper (Doig, 1992) also established that the occupational situation for blacks had improved only marginally and for Hispanics hardly at all. And even at a time of high employment in this country, at the end of the 20th century, U.S. Department of Labor statistics showed unemployment rates significantly higher for women of color than for white women (as cited in "Women in the Workplace," 1998).

The growing heterogeneity of the population within this country makes such discussion of diversity or multiculturalism a hot topic in many fields—including public relations. It pertains to the increasing number of men as well as women who come to public relations from other than the traditional white, Anglo-Saxon background. However, the relevant literature in the scholarly journals of anthropology, of sociology, and of women in development is beyond the scope of this book. So, we do not pretend to explore the situation for practitioners in every racial

147

and ethnic group. Instead, we have selected cases we consider information-rich and especially appropriate for comparisons with Caucasian women in public relations.

In this chapter, we try to focus on what little is known about the practice of racial and ethnic minorities in public relations in this country. Taken together, these few studies—primarily of African Americans, Hispanic Americans, and Asian Americans—show that minorities are underrepresented in public relations practice. Often, although not always, both their status and salaries are low relative to their white colleagues. They typically play markedly different roles in the work place, which may account for the limited career advancement they experience. The discrimination they face is more often subtle than overt.

We found some evidence that gender played a part in both perceived and actual discrimination. For example, Len-Rios (1998) discovered that men recalled more instances of overt racism than did women in her sample of 13 African American, Asian American, and Hispanic American practitioners. She figured that managers may not feel so threatened by women in the workplace, and thus they may be less likely to openly discriminate against them. She also surmised that women of color perceive less discrimination than do men of color because they are used to accommodating to and rationalizing others' behavior. Her third explanation was that women may feel more disadvantaged by their gender than by their race.

The women Len-Rios (1998) talked with at length had noticed that they were viewed as practitioners of color, but they did not consider that a hindrance either in being hired or in their daily work. One woman commented that her gender and age were better explanations than her race for the discrimination she encountered. Another woman believed she was hired under an affirmative action policy *because of* her race: "They really didn't say it was 'affirmative action.' They said they were trying to increase diversity among the employees" (as quoted in Len-Rios, 1998, p. 547).

Perhaps because of affirmative action and quotas, mistrust and tension may characterize the hiring process for minority practitioners in public relations. Len-Rios (1998) cited the work of Haseley (1993) to explain why that process is too often missing the "comfort level" people of the same racioethnic heritage may share.

In fact, the history of the racial groups we explore here is one of exploitation, because in most cases people of color were brought to this country to work (Higginbotham, 1992). Rather than belaboring the past, however, our intent in this chapter is to go beyond the statistics to explore what inclusivity means for today and for the future of public relations.

AFRICAN AMERICAN PRACTITIONERS
OF PUBLIC RELATIONS

In 1980, it was estimated that 4,000 of the 70,000 public relations practitioners in this country were minorities (Layton, 1980). Despite the tiny percentage they represented and the racism they had encountered, the future looked bright. Words like "optimistic about career opportunities," "promising," "hopeful," and "most confident" characterized the writing about black professionals in particular.

Today, we read the words "atrocious" and "horrible" to describe the underrepresentation of African Americans in public relations (Unger, 1992; Zerbinos & Clanton, 1993). The percentage of blacks in public relations actually has declined from 7% to 6% during the same time period when the number of practitioners more than doubled, to at least 150,000 by the decade of the 1990s.

In many other areas of the labor market, representation of African Americans is increasing. Although the growing employment rate of blacks in this country is not so dramatic as that of other nonwhite groups, it still outstrips the growth rate of working whites. Between 1979 and 1986, the U.S. Labor Department reported that the African American labor force grew at a rate of almost 19%, compared with the white work force that grew by almost 11%. Projections (as cited in Thomas, 1991) called for an average increase in the black work force of nearly 29% by 2000, contrasted with 15% for whites.

We use the terms "African American" and "black" interchangeably to avoid excessive repetition of the same word. We acknowledge that the former refers only to Americans of African descent and the latter includes dark-skinned immigrants from other parts of the world as well. Although we are influenced by one African American scholar's preference for African American as the politically correct term at this time (Wise, 1997), we also appreciate that "black" reflects the key term in the name "Black Public Relations Society."

As is true for the population of Hispanic American and Asian American workers, the rate of growth will be significantly greater for African American females (33.2%) than for African American males (24.4%). Median pay for blacks continues to lag behind that of whites, and the wage disparity is greater for black women than for black men (U.S. Department of Labor, 1992b). Despite a near-doubling of the number of African Americans at the executive level during the last 10 years, they are still underrepresented in this top echelon by some 40%. Encouragingly, the underrepresentation of black *women* in top jobs narrowed from 55% to 36% in that same decade (Doig, 1992). Even so, law school professor Emma Coleman Jordan (1998) has characterized the situation for black women this way: "In the cultural cauldron of American identity politics, the images of African American women have been stubbornly stuck to the bottom of the pot" (p. B9).

The typical minority professional in public relations at the end of the decade of the 1980s was a black female (Kern-Foxworth, 1989a). She had worked in the field for 9 years and had reached a midlevel position, earning $38,337 annually. The question that occurs to us at this point is whether that typical African American woman tended to experience the field of public relations differently from her white sisters. To answer, we begin with a glimpse of black women at work in other fields, primarily government and politics. This choice may reflect our location—close to the nation's capital—but we also believe the focus on Washington is appropriate because of the many women who practice public relations around the Beltway and because of the many practitioners who do government relations. Further, Washington, DC, is the home of many African American professionals in public relations.

In the election year 1992, black women more than doubled their representation on the Hill: from four to ten. This was the largest group of black women ever elected to Congress. Although political analysts (Merida, 1993) doubt that they form a large enough bloc of votes to be feared, they do play key roles in two caucuses: the 48-member Congressional Caucus for Women's Issues and the 40-member Congressional Black Caucus. Their determination also may help them overcome their small numbers. As Representative Cynthia A. McKinney put it, "We're shaking up the place" (as quoted in Merida, 1993, p. A1). And since Shirley Chisholm served as the first black woman in Congress in 1968, women like McKinney, Carole Moseley Braun, and Carrie P. Meek have been adding a much-needed perspective to legislative deliberations.

A *Washington Post* reporter (Merida, 1993) covering the impact that these pioneering black women already have had on Congress explained how Meek's experience as a woman and as an African American has influenced legislation:

Rep. Carrie P. Meek (D-Fla.), 67, a granddaughter of slaves and a mother of three, once worked as a domestic, cooking and cleaning in other folks' homes. Hers is a different voice in the debate over overhauling the Social Security laws. The House has voted to require employers of domestic help to pay Social Security taxes on employees they pay at least $1,800 in 1994. (p. A10)

The influence of African American women may be felt in the judiciary as well as in the legislature. In earlier years, as Mary Francis Berry (former member of the U.S. Civil Rights Commission) pointed out, "The clear message [from the Supreme Court] is that they oppose the implementation of plans for women and minorities if it works to the disadvantage of some white male" (as quoted in Raspberry, 1989, p. A23). Berry contended that the conservative majority seemed unfamiliar with the realities of racism and sexism.

To explain segregation in public relations, we turn now to theorist Burlew (1992), who identified six factors that influence both the educational and career choices and their outcomes for black women, in particular. These determinants are the mother's employment history, attitudes about women's roles, perceptions of the attitudes of significant others about sex-role appropriateness, sense of self-efficacy, and knowledge of and exposure to the field of employment. This final factor is most telling for public relations. Because there are few African American women working in the field, and because the typical high school guidance counselor or teacher knows little of public relations, few black role models emerge for girls. The profession remains an unknown.

As a result, we only can speculate on how the black presence might transform public relations if more African Americans were to enter the field. Once again, we turn to theory. This time, the work of Hofstede (1980) on culture is most relevant. Wise (1993) used Hofstede's cultural dimensions to predict how the integration of black women into the field would enhance the management of public relations. She focused on the dimension of collectivism versus individualism. Individualism, Hofstede found, is the single greatest hallmark of U.S. culture. By contrast, the black community stresses collectivity. As a result, Wise reasoned:

> Many of the organizations within the African-American society are community service-oriented, such as fraternities and sororities, and were founded on the premise of uplifting the African-American community. Therefore, according to Hofstede's collective mental program theory, members of the African-American society share the ideals of collectivity and community. African-American women, specifically, have always taken on the responsibility of stressing the importance of community. (pp. 29–30)

Because of their appreciation for community, Wise further speculated, African American women would be especially likely to practice two-way symmetrical public relations. In her view, through an employment history rooted in slavery and continuing through this century as domestics and teachers, they are predisposed to monitor and cater to the needs of all in order to sustain the vitality of their own culture within mainstream white society. She likened this to the responsibility of the public relations professional in general, which is to serve the organization by attempting to maintain its identity and vitality in relation to its strategic publics. Wise concluded that the African American woman in public relations brings with her this crucial sense of community.

Pigeonholing

This kind of contribution only is possible if blacks—or Latinos or Asians—are not "pigeonholed" in nonprofit or government jobs, as Helen Goss ("Rationale for Black PR Groups," 1994) suggested was the case. Pigeonholing encompasses a second way in which minority practitioners may be disadvantaged: They may be hired only to fill quotas or for "show positions" with little real input into policymaking. Relegated to low-level, often stereotypical, positions, with little chance for access to upward mobility or the high-paying jobs the corporate world offers, minority practitioners may look to our associations for encouragement and professional development opportunities. PRSA has its National Minority Affairs Committee, IABC has a Minority Affairs Committee, and the Public Relations Division of the Association for Education in Journalism and Mass Communication has a People of Color Committee.

We have known for at least a decade that minority practitioners are pigeonholed in a third way as well. They may be hired primarily to communicate with minority audiences ("Minority Entrepreneurs," 1989). Ken Carter, president of a public relations firm in Texas, considered the belief that all minority agencies can do is communicate with minorities the major obstacle for black practitioners (as quoted in Kern-Foxworth, 1989a). About one-third of black practitioners surveyed indicated that they do direct their efforts to minority "markets" (Kern-Foxworth, 1993).

There may be times when this is both appropriate and necessary. In the aftermath of the Los Angeles riots in 1992, for example, several organizations sought the guidance of communication professionals with special expertise in, understanding of, and ties to the Asian American, Hispanic American, and African American communities. To ignore the counsel of minority public relations practitioners under such circumstances would be folly. At least some practitioners of color consider this responsibility a logical one for them to undertake in their work as relationship builders (Len-Rios, 1998).

With a strictly limited range of clients, however, we have to question whether the full potential of African American professionals in public relations is being tapped. For years, minority practitioners in the nation's capital have been considered experts in the black community. Some, such as Ofield Dukes, have tremendous local and national visibility. Dukes helped found the Washington, DC, chapter of the Black Public Relations Society out of frustration stemming from the isolation of his colleagues.

Many of these so-called black image makers have struggled for a larger share of the mainstream market. They are hired for projects aimed at African American publics; they fail to get other work because they are seen as lacking influence (G. Lee, 1993a). Lon Walls, owner of a DC-based firm, explained that public relations as a field remains dependent on the old-boy network; and blacks are not considered part of that network (as quoted in G. Lee, 1993b).

On the other hand, there may be prejudice against hiring minority firms even to do public relations for black clients. Herbert (1990) interviewed practitioners in the entertainment industry and found that most African American superstars are represented by white firms. However, Terrie Williams, a black woman who represents celebrities such as Eddie Murphy, a black entertainer, said that this may change. Black agencies such as hers are becoming more visible, thus highlighting the fact that there are "minorities out here doing PR, and doing it in a big way" (as quoted in Herbert, 1990, p. 38).

Williams owns her own bicoastal firm. She herself has achieved "superstar" status in the field of public relations—and, we would hope, the billings to match. On average, however, black practitioners are not earning on a par with their white counterparts. At $38,337, Kern-Foxworth's (1989b) "typical" minority in public relations earned on average $15,983 less than the majority practitioner at the same level. More than 60% of her survey respondents (77% of whom were African American) indicated that race had hindered their advancement in public relations (despite any affirmative action programs that may have existed in their organizations).

One of the most recent, comprehensive, and theoretically grounded studies of pigeonholing in public relations added the related issues of cultural interpretation and race representation to the equation. Mallette (1995) explored the burden that African American practitioners bear when racism and prejudice constrain them to communicating with racially or culturally defined publics within an increasingly heterogeneous U.S. society.

Mallette built on the work of Lyra (1991), who first identified the public relations model of *cultural interpretation* in her home country of Greece. In this approach, local communicators interpret or translate their culture to outsiders determined to do business in that locale. Subsequent research by

Sriramesh (1992) in southern India established that multinational corporations tend to hire local citizens for their public relations departments in each country. Mallette likened this practice to the way minority public relations firms and practitioners in the United States are sought after to work with minority publics in this country.

When minority practitioners handle only minority issues, they may also experience the burden of the *race representative*. Like women who are tokens in their organizations and thus responsible for representing "womanhood," race representatives cannot possibly represent the diverse ideologies and viewpoints of their collective ethnicity. However, often black practitioners in mainstream organizations find themselves the only member of their race in the public relations department. If consulted at all, it is only regarding issues related to African American publics (Mallette, 1995). As a result, they have had to interpret—directly or indirectly—their culture for Americans of European descent.

Frustration and other effects of discrimination ensue. Cose (1993) interviewed many African Americans around the country who were successful professionals. He described their encounters with racism, prejudice, and painful insensitivity at the hands of white colleagues and documented the effects that such treatment had on their careers, their lives, and even their children's lives. Most were frustrated at being pigeonholed into "black jobs" and treated as if they were drug addicts, thieves, or thugs. Cose added pigeonholing to his list of the "dozen demons" plaguing middle-class blacks.

This litany also includes the inability to fit in, exclusion from the club, low expectations, shattered hopes, faint praise, presumption of failure, coping fatigue, identity troubles, self-censorship and silence, mendacity, and guilt by association. These last two may not be obvious, so we add a word of explanation. "Mendacity" refers to the lies corporate executives tell when they claim their companies are color-blind. African Americans often find themselves "guilty by association" with the negative stereotypes other races have of them. For all of these reasons, Cose (1993) concluded that for many black professionals, race remains their most salient feature.

The Mallette Study

Mallette's (1995) thesis research led him to a similar conclusion. Although none of the African Americans he studied in depth was definitively pigeonholed, most communicated predominantly with African American publics. They tended to enact the *role* of cultural interpreter (which Mallette differentiated from the *model* Lyra, 1991, described because his interviewees performed many additional functions) as part of their overall work in public relations. When their organizations needed expertise on African American publics, practitioners in the technician's role had the opportunity to step outside their typical function to serve as counselors. In this sense, race worked to their professional advantage. However, the role of cultural interpreter was more likely to be enacted by managers than technicians because management positions lend themselves to counseling.

Most participants in Mallette's study considered themselves race representatives—that is, they were viewed first as African Americans and only then as public relations professionals. Mallette deemed this a problem, because "any preconceived notions non-African American practitioners have of African Americans have the potential to (and often do) interfere with fair and accurate recognition of the African American practitioners' abilities" (p. 123). The departments where they worked were dominated by white men and women. Often, the black practitioner was the only African American in the professional ranks. Thus Mallette concluded that too many public relations departments and firms fail to mirror America's racially diverse population.

A study exploring similar questions with African American as well as Hispanic and Asian American practitioners found that diversity within a race can confound any potential value of pigeonholing as relationship building. Len-Rios (1998) established through her long interviews that factors such as educational level, culture, and socioeconomic status all affect the professional's ability to identify with publics of seemingly similar racioethnic backgrounds.

The Importance of Diversity in Management

Let us now juxtapose the Kern-Foxworth (1989b) figures—which grouped together all minorities—with the research of Clanton (1990). In the Kern-Foxworth study, Asian American practitioners comprised 3% of the sample and Hispanic Americans 20%. Clanton separated out responses from different minority groups. Results show that African Americans believed they had experienced labor market discrimination to a greater extent than other people of color. Encouragingly, however, only half of the participants in the Clanton thesis reported that they experienced such discrimination.

Still, we remain concerned about the declining percentage of African Americans who earn their doctorate—down 22% between 1978 and 1988 ("Doctoral Recipients," 1990). This decrease is especially stark when contrasted with the rising percentage of other minorities who receive the terminal degree. Further, there are very few college professors of public relations in any minority group (Kern-Foxworth, 1989a). Professors represent both a mentoring and role-modeling factor for minority students. Few texts that students read in the public relations curriculum include any mention of minorities (Kern-Foxworth, 1990). Moreover, education and management skills are inextricably linked. So, we look next at the roles that black practitioners typically play.

Kern-Foxworth (1989b) found that 70% of the African Americans she surveyed considered themselves to be managers and 30% considered themselves to be technicians. However, their self-perceptions of role differed markedly from actual performance. She determined that her survey respondents spent on average 42% of their time in the technician role, 23% in communication facilitation, 22% as expert prescribers, and 16% as problem solvers. She found that they were less likely than their "majority" colleagues to participate in organizational planning and decision making.

Promotion from the technician's role into the management role is confounded both by race and by gender. Kern-Foxworth (1993) certainly found support for this contention in her survey of African American practitioners. So, too, did a study conducted with colleagues Gandy, Hines, and Miller (1994). Their results suggested the following profile of the typical female African American practitioner: She is a 33-year-old college graduate with at least 6 years of experience, working in a consumer service firm, and spending most of her time counseling clients. Kern-Foxworth and her colleagues, assessing not salary but managerial roles, concluded that black women see themselves occupying meaningful roles within the profession. Most considered themselves managers with problem-solving capability.

Diversity in management is critically important to the careers of individual practitioners of color, as well as to the function of public relations itself. Recall the discussion of requisite variety in earlier chapters. Organizations need boundary-spanning managers who reflect the heterogeneity of their environments. As the first African American woman to head PRSA put it, "The field is not so diverse as it should be given the kind of work that we do" (Miller, as quoted in Lilienthal, 1999, p. 18).

The same article that quoted Debra Miller in the trade press cited the fact that only 3% of PRSA's membership is African American, even though 13% of the U.S. population is black. Its analysis of the situation for top-ranking African American professionals showed (1) only a slowly growing appreciation for the value of diversity at the highest levels of public relations practice, (2) a concomitant growth in opportunity for African Americans in public relations, and (3) the need for earlier outreach to attract college students to the field—perhaps even at the junior-high level (Lilienthal, 1999).

The Wise Study

Wise (1997) came to similar conclusions in her thesis research. Although she found that women who participated in her study were, for the most part, emerging as managers, many believed that their competence was measured more by their race than by their gender or their ability.

Wise predicated her combination of qualitative and quantitative research on an assumption of the Velvet Ghetto study (Cline et al., 1986), that is, socialization causes women to self-select the technician's role. She realized that this assumption reflected inferences from white women being applicable to all women. She also realized the fallacy in that supposition. As Burgess (1994) pointed out, not all women come to this country under the same circumstances; as a result, "the social positions assigned to the various categories of women immigrants suggests different expectations for marital, familial, and work roles" (p. 393).

Wise (1997) emphasized that contrary to popular belief, the African American woman's place has not been in the home. Her sociohistorical discussion of these women established that since slavery days, many have elected nontraditional careers. Along the way, black women evolved differently than their white sisters, both professionally and personally. Wise's explanation lies primarily in differential socialization. (In a consistent argument, but one that considerably predates slavery in the United States, the anthropologist Helen E. Fisher, 1999, pointed out that the two-income family is far from unique in human evolution. She saw the country's trend toward gender equality as a return to the egalitarian relationship women and men enjoyed on the grasslands of Africa millions of years ago. Then both sexes had nearly equal responsibility for gathering resources for the family.)

We know that socialization affects both gender roles and work roles; we also know that black and white women are socialized differently (Burgess, 1994; Burlew, 1982, 1992; Davis, 1981; Epstein, 1973; Giddings, 1984; Sanders-Thompson, 1994). Consider just the notion of women's roles. Burlew (1992) explained that like white women, black women feel obliged to act in stereotypical ways to avoid threatening their men. However, African American women exhibit fewer stereotypical attitudes toward employment and other behaviors they consider sex-appropriate. More specifically, they have grown up with the expectation that as women they will work outside the home, they will keep working while they raise their children, and they are as capable of establishing strong relationships with their offspring as are nonworking mothers.

Thus, Burlew (1992) concluded, African American women are less likely than white women to believe that career or educational pursuits interfere with fulfilling their roles as wives and mothers. Contrast this belief with the perceptions of two prominent white women in public relations management. Wilma Mathews (1988) said that at least some women believe that to be active participants in their children's lives, they have to turn down significant job opportunities. Linda Stewart (1988) argued that wives and mothers who work in the public sphere will not be taken seriously unless they juggle their priorities and plan a schedule to accommodate theirs and their husband's careers.

What did Wise (1997) learn about the socialization of the African American women she surveyed and interviewed around the country? Using a modified version (Wood et al., as cited in McAdams, 1981) of the Bem Sex Role Inventory (Bem, 1974), she assessed her participants' personal characteristics as masculine or feminine (or both). First, she found that those who had achieved senior-level managerial positions in majority or minority organizations exhibited a combination of masculine and feminine sex-role characteristics. Second, many of those women attributed their success to their ability to balance. They spoke of balance between masculine and feminine traits as well as balance between family and career. However, they considered family the priority—and they included providing parents with medical, financial, or residential assistance as part of their family responsibility. One professional in Wise's study surmised, "There can be a brother and three sisters, and it is almost guaranteed that the one who takes care of mom is going to be one of the sisters" (p. 121). To avoid neglecting the job, then, these women stressed the necessity of skill, organization, patience, and hard work. They had grown up expecting that they would do all of this.

So, Wise's main finding was that socialization does indeed affect the advancement of African American women in public relations. Most of the women she interviewed were at the director level of their public relations department or owned their own consulting firm. She attributed their enacting this nontraditional role for women to expectations developed through childhood and a history dating back significantly longer.

Despite their managerial role, many of the women believed they were under scrutiny primarily because of their gender. As a result, they commented on the need to assert and promote themselves more aggressively than their white male and female counterparts. One woman put it this way: "The perception is that there are always people looking over your shoulder, wondering if you can cut it. You have no doubts, but they do" (Wise, 1997, p. 81).

ASIAN AMERICAN PRACTITIONERS OF PUBLIC RELATIONS

We continue our discussion of the status of minority women in the United States who work in public relations by focusing on Asian Americans. In the following discussion, we will allude to "Asians" repeatedly. However, just as we said in our first chapter that by writing "women" we did not mean to suggest homogeneity among all women, we do not consider the many different Asian ethnic groups synonymous with each other.

Thus we emphasize that although an ethnic group may seem homogeneous to those outside of it, significant differences exist among the Chinese, Japanese, Filipino, Korean, Vietnamese, and Asian Indian immigrants living and working in this country. In fact, these distinctions mean that a public relations message that is "targeted" or "tailored" toward one group of Asians, such as the Japanese, actually may offend another, such as the Koreans (Burton, 1993). However, because of the small sample-size problem we mentioned earlier in the previous chapter, our exploration of Asian Americans in public relations, in particular, almost demands the grouping together of all practitioners of Asian descent.

According to 1990 census data, Asians are the fastest growing minority in the United States. Female Asian Americans are entering the labor force at an even greater rate than their male counterparts. The frequency is 83.3% for women versus 61.3% for men. This pace is up from an average of 41.3% for all Asian Americans between 1979 and 1986.

Some ethnic groups within the Asian American population have excelled economically and socially. Asian Americans in general have a higher level of education than that of other nonwhite groups in this country. Perhaps for this reason, Asians working in the United States are considered the "model minority" (Woo, 1992). However, Asian Americans as a group remain in lower levels of the corporate pyramid than white workers (Hirschman & Wong, 1981). They are underrepresented in positions of political influence as well (Awanohara, 1990).

Even the largest public relations firms may not employ a single Asian American professional at any level of the hierarchy. Uyeda posed the question that "they may have an Asian receptionist, or an Asian CPA, or an Asian who sits in the back of the room. But do they have Asian PR people?" (as quoted in "Presentation by Multicultural Panel Member Lynn Choy Uyeda," 1994, p. 14). Fortunately both for Asian Americans and for business, she said, this situation is changing.

The first comprehensive study of Asian American practitioners of public relations was conducted as recently as 1992. At that time, Yamashita examined the status of these practitioners and compared her results with the status of female and African American practitioners. She focused on issues that seemed unique to Asian practitioners in the United States, beginning with a brief history of Asian immigration to this country.

The Gold Rush in California and construction of the transcontinental railroad brought the first Asians, who were Chinese, in significant numbers to the United States in the mid-1800s. Significant immigration of Japanese people began in the late 1800s, primarily to the sugar plantations of Hawaii and then on to California. Both Chinese and Japanese immigrants encountered discrimination, in large part because they worked for lower wages and were presumed to labor longer and harder than whites (Hirschman & Wong, 1981; S. M. Lee, 1989). This bias was expressed in the Immigration Act of 1924, which favored immigrants from northwestern Europe. Not until the Immigration Act of 1965 did such discrimination based on national origin end. This act emphasized scarce occupational skills and family reunification. As a result, the Asian population living in the United States has increased dramatically—from 250,000 in 1940 to 5.1 million by 1985 (Kitano & Daniels, 1988).

Just as the percentage of Asian workers is increasing in this country, so too is the number of Asian consumers. Especially in the large cities, where most immigrants live, Asian American public relations professionals would seem to be necessary to help their organizations communicate. They would add the all-important "requisite variety," helping their organizations enact an increasingly Asian environment of customers and clients. Perhaps this is why veteran practitioner Wann (1993) joked that he is tempted to tell people who hear his last name but do not know him that he is, in fact, Chinese.

However, Asian American practitioners are a recent phenomenon in public relations. Lynne Choy Uyeda, president of an advertising and public relations firm and founder of the Asian American Advertising and Public Alliance, explained at a panel on multiculturalism held during the 1993 PRSA conference that Asian culture is in large part responsible. As she put it: "[We] stay on the wall. Don't rock the boat. Asians are uncomfortable doing the PR thing" (as quoted in "Presentation by Multicultural Panel Member Lynn Choy Uyeda," 1994, p. 14).

On the other hand, a non-Western orientation to public relations may be exactly what both our increasingly diverse work force and the country itself needs. Along with the dwindling numerical dominance of the white male at work comes a shift from what Limaye and Victor (1991) called this country's "John Wayne type" of masculine, individualistic, and aggressive nature. They suggested that we are moving toward Asian patterns of communication behavior, modeled after the success of rapidly industrializing countries such as Japan and Korea.

S. M. Lee's Theory of Intergroup Relations

Still, calling attention to oneself is discouraged in Asian culture. As the Japanese saying goes, "The nail standing out will be hammered down." Framing this explanation in the scholarly literature rather than in proverbs or anecdotal information, we are led to S. M. Lee's (1989) theory of Asian–white intergroup relations. She developed this model specific to the Asian minority because most previous theorizing had been dominated by black–white relations.

S. M. Lee's (1989) model consists of three often interrelated factors that help us understand the typical relationship between Asians and white Americans living and working together in this country: economic competition, cultural racism, and American nativism. *Economic competition* helps explain the racioethnic antagonism that results from a large differential in the price of labor for the same occupation (Bonacich, 1972). When a split labor market develops along color lines, the dominant group typically limits the cheaper labor force's participation. Thus migrant or immigrant workers, such as the Chinese during the Gold Rush and construction of the transcontinental railroad, find their career options severely curtailed. *Cultural racism* results in a stratification of broad cultural categories—white and nonwhite, in this country (Daniels & Kitano, 1970). S. M. Lee explained that since Asians are defined as nonwhite, they experience the consequences of being considered inferior. *American nativism* equates being American with having an Anglo-Saxon heritage. People who are not of Anglo-Saxon descent are not considered "true" Americans and thus cannot participate fully in U.S. society.

The Yamashita Study

Yamashita (1992) explored the extent to which Asian American practitioners participate fully in the field of public relations. She surveyed and then interviewed at length 16 professionals in the Washington, DC, and New York areas. These practitioners came from four ethnic groups: 11 Chinese Americans, two Japanese Americans, two Korean Americans, and one Vietnamese American.

From among these practitioners Yamashita could identify two distinct types. One group, which she called the "government type," worked for government, government-related, and nonprofit organizations. These practitioners often communicated with Asian or Asian American publics, they were interested in Asian issues, and they considered themselves responsible for getting Asians involved in U.S. society. They were fluent in both English and an Asian language. The "firm-type" practitioners, who typically worked for for-profit organizations and in public relations agencies, tended to be younger (28 years old vs. 33 years old), earned more money ($47,000 vs. $38,000), and only rarely could speak an Asian language. The median salary for all participants was $44,258.

Only one practitioner from either type believed he had been hired specifically to communicate with Asians or Asian Americans. He considered this a serious limitation, although he had never protested. As he said: "I've been promoted in my salary because they feel that I did a good job in my capacity. But they have not thought of my ability beyond the Asian category. . . . I need to make them know that I'm also good at something else" (as quoted in Yamashita, 1992, p. 81).

A single participant in Yamashita's study engaged exclusively in the managerial role. The other 15 practiced both the technical and—to a lesser degree—some aspects of the managerial role. Yamashita speculated that Asian Americans could enhance their managerial responsibilities if they overcame the stereotype of being good at detail but not necessarily at management.

Yamashita also suggested more education in public relations as a way of learning strategic management skills. Although their level of education was impressive, none of her participants had studied public relations per se. Because of this higher education, she speculated that Asian Americans might have a better chance of getting ahead in public relations than do other minorities, such as blacks or Hispanics. The fact that Asian Americans are receiving doctorates at a dramatically increasing rate (up 55% in the decade between 1978 and 1988) is encouraging as well (National Research Council figures as cited in "Doctoral Recipients," 1990). Presumably some of these new PhDs will teach public relations, thus serving as mentors or role models for Asian American students considering a career in this field.

Women in Yamashita's study played the technician's role to a greater extent than did men. Yamashita characterized these (typically young) female practitioners as "very enthusiastic and self-assertive," "eager to gain experience . . . and to advance in their organizations" (p. 117). She believed their positive attitude would help them achieve professional goals, although she also warned that as women and as Asian Americans they may face a glass ceiling when they have been in the field for 5 years. In fact, as one of her participants expressed it, "Being Asian and female, I have two glass ceilings" (as quoted on p. 92).

Even in the culture from which her family immigrated, this woman and others like her may have been disadvantaged. Hung (1998), a Taiwanese doctoral student studying public relations at a U.S. university at the time of this writing, explained:

> Traditionally, women were thought to be a possession of their husbands or sons. Except for some extraordinary famous women in history, typically they were recognized by only their family names in the family books, while [their] first names were ignored. (pp. 14-15)

Seven of the 16 participants in this study were women. As Yamashita pointed out, this number is too small to draw conclusions about the status of female Asian American practitioners. Her sense, though, was that gender discrimination played a greater role in the work life of her participants than did racial or ethnic bias. Although the women in her sample were reluctant to discuss prejudice at all, one did volunteer that:

> I've never felt [discrimination as an Asian]. . . . Even when I was in [southern state]. I think this is probably because I was able to integrate pretty well in different environments and with different people. But I do feel that [discrimination] as a woman. This is a very conservative company, and you are also in a very conservative business community where you still have an "old boys' network." (as quoted on p. 98)

A single interviewee said he felt discriminated against at work because of his skin color. However, most participants indicated they were conscious of being Asian American and also inspired by the accomplishments of Asian American colleagues. (This shared difference did not lead to the networks among Asian practitioners that Yamashita had expected to find, however.) At least two described advantages of their ethnicity, primarily because of the positive stereotypes associated with being Asian. Employers often assumed they were hard workers and bright; clients often remembered them because they stood out from other practitioners.

This difference may extend well beyond physical appearance. The Asian Americans who took part in this cultural study tended to practice the most sophisticated models of public relations. They deemed a two-way approach vitally important in developing mutual understanding between their organization and its strategic publics. From her findings, however, Yamashita identified two new models of public relations. The first she called "gap-filling," which is similar to Lyra's (1991) cultural translation model for Greek practitioners. That is, the public relations practitioner—who is familiar with both cultures—works to fill in any gaps between the U.S. organization and its Asian clients or publics. In the "mission-oriented" model, practitioners whose identity as Asians is strong feel responsible for making their Asian publics aware of social issues and getting them involved in the mainstream of U.S. society.

Yamashita examined these findings in light of S. M. Lee's (1989) model of Asian–white intergroup relations. She discounted the economic-competition component as a significant factor in public relations. She reasoned that as an emerging profession, employers in this field are unlikely to hire people as "cheap labor." American nativism, the second factor, begs further study. On the one hand, Asian Americans tend to retain their "alien" character and thus lower their chances for acceptance in the dominant culture. On the other hand, most practitioners in Yamashita's study said they had not experienced discrimination at work—perhaps because of the positive stereotypes associated with their own culture. Cultural racism, on the other hand, did seem to be a significant factor because of physical differences between Asian Americans and those of European descent. Several participants in her thesis research acknowledged that they were looked on as "different," for better or worse.

Perhaps the high degree of job satisfaction exposed in this study can be attributed to the high salaries typically earned. However, Yamashita explained the fact that firm-type practitioners, in particular, worked in metropolitan areas where wages tend to be highest. She also speculated that her participants, who have used the positive ethnic stereotype associated with Asians to their advantage, still may not realize that *any* stereotype indicates prejudice. She attributed their lack of pigeonholing, or working strictly with Asian publics or issues, to the fact that Asians are so culturally and linguistically diverse from each other. As a result, it would be difficult for any one practitioner to speak all the necessary Asian languages and to appreciate all cultural idiosyncracies. However, Yamashita did conclude that the practice of both her gap-filling and mission models would help organizations understand and value their Asian publics—and vice versa. Undoubtedly their preference for a two-way, dialogic approach already is contributing to effective relationships between their organization and its publics, Asian or non-Asian.

HISPANIC AMERICAN PRACTITIONERS
OF PUBLIC RELATIONS

Although we know that the Hudson Institute's *Workforce 2000* report (Johnston & Packer, 1987) projected the highest rate of increase in the U.S.

labor market for both Asian Americans and Hispanic Americans, Asians are growing from a much smaller base. Thus, in terms of numbers, Hispanics are a more significant presence in the work force. They are projected to overtake African Americans as the largest minority group in the United States by early in the 21st century (McKay, 1982; Powers & Oliver, 1992; Braus, 1993; Exter, 1993; "Latinos on the Rise," 1993). Already, Hispanics are the country's second-largest racial minority, exceeded only by African Americans (Cuban American National Council, 1989).

Perhaps as a result, at least one major public relations firm has developed a viable Hispanic marketing operation: Ketchum Asociados. Perhaps this, too, explains why our friend Al Wann (1993) proposed that he may be Puerto Rican—in reality Al "Juan." We prefer to think of him as he described himself: a SNAG, or "sensitive new age guy."

The numbers, though, are serious. The U.S. Bureau of Labor Statistics (as cited in Thomas, 1991) predicted that the rate of growth between the late 1980s and 2000 for Latina females would be almost 85%, compared with close to 68% for Hispanic males. Like the escalating rate for Asian Americans, this pace is up from an average of 54.9% between 1979 and 1986.

In short, the Hispanic minority is one of the nation's fastest growing ethnic groups (Rocha & Frase-Blunt, 1992). Studies conducted over the last 35 years have documented discrimination against Hispanics in employment, housing, and education (National Council of La Raza, 1991; Verdugo, 1982). This discrimination has been found to be based primarily on racism, or the belief than one race—the Caucasian—is innately superior over other races (Daniels & Kitano, 1970).

Concern for Hispanic American Women in Managerial Roles

We are particularly concerned about the prospects for Latina women in the work force because of the cultural factors associated with "machismo." According to Marin and VanOss (1991), Hispanic men are considered the strong ones, fully in control and responsible for providing for their families. Their wives are expected to remain in the private realm of the home, with little power or influence even there, and to be submissive.

David Garcia (as quoted in Kern-Foxworth, 1989a), vice president of public relations for a bank in Los Angeles, spoke of another perception: that minorities are not so well educated as the white majority, and thus they do not know how to write. He also talked about the perception that minorities cannot play an important role in management.

Only one in ten of all Hispanics in this country, compared with more than one in five non-Hispanics, has completed 4 years of college (National Council of La Raza, 1991). Thus Raul Yzaguirre (1990), president and CEO of the National Council of La Raza, considered Hispanics' low level of educational attainment one important barrier to their success at work. He identified improving the educational status of his constituency as a national imperative. Already, Hispanics' rate of receiving doctorates is rising dramatically, up 26% between 1978 and 1988 ("Doctoral Recipients," 1990). Nevertheless, Hispanic Americans across the occupations earn less, on average, than both blacks and whites.

Many Hispanic immigrants arrived in this country with relatively less education and fewer job skills. Perhaps as a result, the Latino work force showed no measurable gain in white-collar jobs here during the 1980s. There are about 44% fewer Hispanic Americans in executive positions than should be expected by their share of the labor force. During the 1980s, Latino men actually lost ground in their share of top jobs, whereas Latina women narrowed their gap in job class somewhat (Doig, 1992). According to Gomez (1992), although diversity is the "buzzword du jour" in corporate America, Hispanics have yet to break through the glass ceiling and become part of the dominant coalition. He called them "grossly underrepresented in the upper echelons of management" (p. 16).

A blurb in a weekly newsmagazine highlighted the irony for the growing number of Hispanic Americans working in one U.S. governmental agency, the Labor Department. A departmental survey showed that its own house was not in order. Despite its charge to help create a "level playing field" in the private sector and despite progress toward equality within the department itself for blacks and women, Hispanics in Labor are underrepresented in senior posts (Fenyvesi, 1992).

The same undoubtedly is true for Hispanic Americans in public relations management. At this point we digress briefly to mention that we use the word "Hispanic" more frequently than "Latino," although to many scholars the two are interchangeable. "Hispanic" is the more common term because it refers to those of Iberian (Spanish and Portuguese) descent. It comes from the Latin word for Spain, "Hispania." Hispanic was the ethnic label of choice for the 1978 Office of Management and Budget to identify people of Spanish, Mexican, Puerto Rican, Cuban, and Central and South American culture or origin—regardless of race (Marin & VanOss, 1991). "Latino" refers only to immigrants from Latin America (itself an offensive term to some indigenous peoples of that area).

Also, as with the umbrella term "Asian American" that encompassed several nationalities, "Hispanic American" may suggest more homogeneity than is reasonable to expect. We know that immigrants included under this rubric come from Puerto Rico, Cuba, Mexico, Central and South America, the Dominican Republic, and so forth. We do not assume that these people of divergent cultures and regions think or act alike. As Cole (1992) explained:

> Certainly there is a language, or the heritage of a language, a general historical experience, and certain cultural traditions and practices which are shared by these [Latina] women. But a great deal of harm can be done by sweeping away differences in the interest of an imposed homogeneity. (p. 130)

Similarly, we understand that because of the different ways in which Latino immigrants organize themselves after crossing the border, even those of Mexican descent may live markedly different lives in Chicano East L.A. and Mexican South Central. Cubans arriving in Miami immediately after the 1959 revolution have resisted sharing their Florida neighborhoods with the more recent boat-lift Cubans (Suro, 1998).

The Ferreira Study

We are aware of only one major study of Hispanic public relations practitioners. Ferreira (1993) developed a profile of the typical Hispanic American doing public relations: She is a 39-year-old female with a bachelor's degree in communication or journalism who has worked in the field for about 11 years and earns between $50,000 and $60,000. Her job title is manager or director, and she works in a large governmental agency near the southwestern coast of the United States. She has been with her current employer for about 6 years. She was born in this country, but one or both of her parents came from Mexico. She is bilingual in Spanish and English.

Ferreira's thesis research is significant for several reasons, extending well beyond the fact that it is the first of its kind. She combined qualitative and quantitative methodologies to explore the status and roles of 42 Hispanic professionals across the country. Her findings showed considerable difference between this population of practitioners and their white colleagues. Those differences included preference for public relations model, level of education, reliance on research, role, level in the organization, and discrimination. Let's take each one at a time.

Hispanic practitioners, Ferreira found, preferred the press agentry, or publicity, model over the other three. They were least likely to adopt the two-way asymmetrical model. Ferreira did not isolate any other models that might be unique to practitioners from Spanish-speaking countries, nor were her respondents hired to communicate primarily with Hispanic publics. Thus they were not practicing a model or role of cultural interpretation or the gap-filling model first identified by Yamashita (1992). Ferreira did point out that the majority of her interviewees worked in Southern California, where the large Hispanic community had become critical for all communication managers—not just those who are themselves Hispanic. Still, they were the ones responsible for dealing with Hispanic issues or when Spanish language was involved.

Although practitioners in this study were most likely to practice the one-way model of press agentry, they indicated an awareness of the importance of two-way public relations for developing a mutual understanding with publics. Without expertise in research, however, they could not implement the two-way approach they acknowledged as effective. Research, which is an integral part of both two-way models of public relations, was not a common activity for the practitioners Ferreira studied. She found this regrettable, speculating that if Hispanic practitioners conducted more research both before and after their communication programs they would be better equipped to manage conflict and develop relationships between their organization and its strategic publics. At the same time, their behavior would professionalize their practice of the field.

Hispanic practitioners were more likely to enact the managerial than the technician's role. However, participants in this study also tended to fulfill the dual role of manager and technician, which is similar only to white *women* in public relations. Unlike white women, however, they tended to head their communication department and they were included in the dominant coalition of the organization they worked for. They had attained this level despite having less formal education in the field than non-Hispanics.

Recall that Hispanics in general have a lower level of educational attainment than the white population of this country. Thus Ferreira anticipated that the participants in her research would lack the necessary background to practice along the professional (J. Grunig & L. Grunig, 1992) continuum in public relations. This assumption was supported by her research. Ferreira further reasoned that these practitioners did not rely on the body of knowledge in public relations, nor did they conduct formative or evaluative research. In short, their approach was more craftlike than professional.

Finally, participants in Ferreira's study did not believe they had experienced either a salary gap or a glass ceiling. They were earning on average in the $50,000 range at a time when the median public relations salary was $46,556 (Jacobson & Tortorello, 1992). As one interviewee pointed out, of course, most respondents worked in California, where the cost of living is very high. Ferreira posited a similar explanation for the lack of perceived barriers to her participants' upward mobility: in Southern California, she figured, there may be a greater awareness of and appreciation for Hispanics. To that explanation, she added a consideration of the relatively high level of education overall (but not in public relations). Most interviewees had at least a bachelor's degree and several a master's degree. A third possible explanation was interviewees' unwillingness to admit to facing the glass ceiling. Many said they would not stay in an office where they lacked the opportunity they deserved to advance in their careers. As Ferreira summarized their comments in this area, "They worked hard to perform their best and demonstrate their capabilities, not as Hispanic public relations practitioners but as public relations practitioners who happened to be Hispanic" (pp. 151–152).

The majority of practitioners Ferreira surveyed headed their department and were part of the dominant coalition. She explained this anomalous finding in part by their tenure in the field (more than 11 years, on average). She also reasoned that members of the power elite recognized the need to have Hispanic decision makers included in the process because they could bring the issues and perspectives of the organization's Hispanic publics to the table. However, most participants in Ferreira's study agreed they had faced racial discrimination throughout their careers in public relations. Some mentioned sexism as well. This bottom-line finding, although explored extensively in the thesis, remains unexplained.

CONCLUDING THOUGHTS

At this point in our book, we have established that American women—minority and majority alike—are disadvantaged in most career fields where they work. Discrimination may take the form of glass walls that restrict them to certain specialties or "ghettos" within a discipline. Only now, early into the decade of the 2000s, are we coming to an understanding of how discrimination affects different minority groups in different ways. For this insight, we owe an enormous debt to graduate students such as Clanton, Ferreira, Mallette, Wise, and Yamashita. These young men and women of color probed deeply, often with smaller samples than they would have chosen in an ideal world, to explicate the existence of public relations professionals like themselves.

Even if they are not trapped in the acrylic vault affecting so many minority practitioners, all women may encounter a glass ceiling or a premature plateau that impedes their promotion. In the next chapter, we explain how the effects of racism and sexism may disadvantage *all* practitioners of public relations in this era of feminization.

Chapter Seven

Credibility, Encroachment, Power, and Sublimation

Gender is the greatest determinant of salary (P. Edwards & S. Edwards, 1985). This should concern both men and women. Researchers such as Pfeffer and Davis-Blake (1987) have documented an inverse relationship between the proportion of women in a given field and the salaries of both men and women in that field. Employers rarely offer to pay more than they have to get the job done. So, if women entering fields that had been dominated by men end up working for less money, we can expect that wages for everyone in those fields eventually will decline. At the very least, salaries will fail to increase at the rate at which they had in the past. We have discussed this financial concern at considerable length in Chapter 2.

Along with problems in pay, male and female practitioners of public relations face additional concerns with the feminization of the field. We do not intend to be naysayers or prophets of doom. We celebrate the mushrooming numbers of women entering public relations practice and the public relations classroom. We also take great pride and encouragement from the fact that these women are ambitious, competent, highly motivated, and professional. Throughout this book we have focused on the contributions that their expertise and their character offer to the field—contributions that go well beyond their predominance in the work force.

At this point, however, we feel compelled to discuss three major concerns—beyond compensation—that accompany the growing number of women in public relations. The first concern may be an issue for any field that moves from a male to a female majority. We call it the "credibility factor." Throughout this chapter, we refer to it alternatively as prestige, legitimacy, clout, marginalization, and status. We do not belabor this concept because we are status-hungry or power-mad. Instead, all of these terms speak to the relative *empowerment* of the public relations practitioner. Concern for the field being downgraded in terms of both status and pay characterizes the situation in Canada as well as in the United States (Scrimger, 1989).

Unless practitioners—whether they are women or men—are empowered to fulfill the managerial role, we risk losing any hard-earned gains we have made in professionalism. Employers, too, fail to tap the full potential of their workers and U.S. business may lose its competitive edge worldwide. For these reasons, the introductory chapter in this book belabored the involvement of the country's largest professional association, PRSA. We know from comparable worth theory that for "women's work" to be valued equally with men's, labor union action is often required (Blum, 1987). Comparable worth strategies often deal with discrimination that goes beyond hiring or pay to encompass systematic undervaluation of what women do.

The next two factors explored in this chapter are more directly tied to public relations. Perhaps as a result of the predicted decline in prestige that will accompany the growing proportion of women in our field, we are at risk of *encroachment*. Encroachment occurs when someone without training or experience in public relations is assigned to the top position in that department (Lindenmann & Lapetina, 1981; Dozier, 1988; Lesly, 1988). The impact of gender on encroachment is more indirect than direct, as we will see.

Finally, we are concerned about *sublimation* of the public relations function. That is, along with increasing number of women comes the very real possibility that public relations will be sublimated under another, related organizational function such as marketing.

CREDIBILITY, STATUS, AND PRESTIGE

The literature of anthropology suggests that women in most, if not all, cultures have lower status than men (e.g., Rosaldo & Lamphere, 1974; Friedl, 1975; Lamphere, 1977; Rosaldo, 1980). As Sherif (1982) put it, "The one clear generalization from anthropological research on gender is the asymmetry between men and women in social power in communal affairs. . . . Women have been subordinated to men in all known societies. . . . " (p. 379). From this analysis, public relations scholar Wetherell (1989) concluded that even when women's roles are vital economically, they are still valued less than men's.

Touhey (1974) determined that the status of an occupation declines when people even *think* more women than men would enter that field. At least one replication of Touhey's work (Johnson, as cited in "Feminization of the New Profession," 1987) has questioned his conclusions about the prestige and desirability of professions dominated by men and women. A scholar from Arkansas State University found that many respondents no longer consider male-dominated professions superior. In fact, they may not view specific professions as female *or* male.

However, we typically point to feminized occupations such as teaching, library science, and nursing as examples of the credibility problem. These fields are notorious for low pay and low status in this country.

Like elementary education and nursing, public relations employs significantly more women than men. We have known for more than 10 years now that the pattern of feminization in the field of public relations is likely to continue (Cline et al., 1986). One obvious risk inherent in the feminization of any field is that its credibility will diminish.

The explanation for this lack of status, or what Rosaldo (1974) called the "universal asymmetry of the sexes," may lie in social structures, rather than in any innate qualities of men and women. Traditionally women have been assigned domestic responsibilities and men public responsibilities. As this changes, women and men alike experience the fallout of women entering the public domain. Women are perceived to be usurping men's roles. As Wetherell (1989) summarized the situation so eloquently, "This stepping out of role and domain also could account for the near-universal view that women are ill-equipped to function in this domain because they are equipped instead with traits that are necessary for success in the other domain, and these domains are mutually exclusive" (p. 83).

Moviemakers struggling with the portrayal of women at work in their new roles often miss the mark and end up focusing on eroticism and objectification. In a fascinating feminist analysis of women as communicators in films, Kovacs (1992) found that films such as *Network*, *Broadcast News*, and *Working Girl* perpetuate the stereotype of the successful organizational woman as "a bullish, abrasive, devious and shrill communicator" (p. 13). These Hollywood productions also suggest that the woman must have a miserably unfilled personal life. Their portrayal of women, Kovacs argued, does not create the stereotype. It simply reflects the predicament shared by top-level male managers with an increasingly female work force: "Threatened, they take the path of least resistance—that is, they may resort to denigrating the image of those who threaten them" (p. 14). That denigration can be seen at work in such phenomena as diminishing the status of a field that becomes predominantly female or in limiting women to subfields that traditionally have lacked prestige.

Like the entertainment media, the news media have been accused of impeding the progress of women and minorities through their distortions. The National Association of Black Journalists (NABJ) reminded us of the conclusion of the 1968 *Kerner Commission Report*: This nation is moving not toward integration but toward two separate and unequal societies, one white and one black. The media, panelists at the NABJ meeting said, report and write from the white male perspective. As a result, news coverage does not begin to mirror the diversity of our population (French, 1992).

In a previous chapter, we explored the effects of a growing number of women in higher education, law, medicine, and other professional fields akin to journalism and public relations. Among the effects, of course, was either diminished credibility or the relegation of women to subspecialties that already had less status than others in that field.

We find, for example, that women are underrepresented in one of the most prestigious aspects of public relations: government relations, or lobbying. A Conference Board study compared public relations departments that encompassed governmental relations with departments that did not. Lusterman (1987) found that heads of the two kinds of departments differed significantly. Although age differences were insignificant, the head of a department with responsibility for governmental relations was more often a man and less often a woman than the head of a department without governmental relations responsibility (93% men vs. 7% women compared with 86% men vs. 14% women). Jaatinen (1998), who has studied extensively the relationship between lobbying and communication management, explained this finding as a function of the level of management. The head of the public relations department that includes governmental relations was a senior executive who reported to a top corporate officer (typically the CEO).

Earlier studies established that women and people of color were even less likely in the 1960s and 1970s to participate in lobbying than they are today. Respondents in Milbrath's (1963) profile of Washington representatives were 84% male and only 16% female. Almost all were white. One respondent was Asian American; none was African American. A decade later, L. R. King's (1973) study of lobbyists in higher education echoed Milbrath's findings. Most representatives were middle-aged white men. Minorities and women were assigned lower status: They often worked part time and failed to reach executive positions.

So, too, with the related area of institutional advancement, fundraising, or development. Analysts predict the familiar good news/bad news scenario there. More and more women are going into fundraising because they appear to be well suited for development work. Their growing majority, however, may well depress both salaries and prestige in this occupation (Goss, 1989).

Predictably, then, the influx of women into fundraising has raised concerns about the future of that function. According to Goss (as quoted in Creedon, 1991), female and male development personnel alike believe that feminization will have positive and negative impacts on their career. Goss explained:

> Women are enjoying tremendous success in a vocation for which they appear to be especially well suited. But at the same time . . . if women come to dominate the field, their presence could depress the salary levels and prestige of this traditionally male career. (p. 2)

However, Doonan (1993) countered that at least in higher education, fundraising just "may represent a niche in which female practitioners finally may have an opportunity to gain the power and professional prestige they deserve" (pp. 46–47). To support this contention, she cited Hon's (1992) finding that women's segregation might be more pronounced in the corporate than in the relatively open-minded university setting.

Prestige or credibility represents a major challenge in the work lives of boundary spanners in all functional areas of the organization—but especially of boundary spanners who are women. Several scholars (e.g., Keller, Szilagyi, & Holland, 1976; Schwab, Ungson, & Brown, 1985) have suggested that people who serve a boundary-spanning role may be more influential than other employees. As one moves up the organizational hierarchy, one's boundary-spanning activity typically increases. If women are relegated to lower levels, they undoubtedly will do less boundary spanning. So their influence within the organization is similarly limited.

Then, too, the incumbent in a boundary role, whether doing public relations or any other function that links the organization to external groups, in essence leads a double life. He or she represents the organization to the environment and vice versa. As a result, the boundary spanner experiences the occupational hazard of lack of trust and credibility from both sides. It goes with the public relations territory (Bales, 1984). It also may lead to job dissatisfaction (Miles, 1977).

Diminished credibility for public relations as a field undoubtedly diminishes the likelihood of practitioners achieving a role in top management. Why? If feminization is equated with "soft," then public relations may not be perceived as what Lesly (1988) called a "heavy-hitting top management function" (p. 5). This, in turn, becomes a major concern; because, as Dozier (1988) pointed out, the "fate of women in public relations—particularly their participation in management decision-making—is inexorably linked to the survival and growth of public relations as a profession" (p. 6).

Even women's communication style, as contrasted with men's, may disadvantage them and the future of their field as a management function. Tannen (1990), whose work on the difference between men's "report talk" and women's "rapport talk" was introduced in Chapter 4, explained that different goals explain the difference in those conversational styles. She said, "The game women play is 'Do you like me?' whereas the men play 'Do you respect me?' " (p. 129). It seems a small jump, then, to question whether the respect men traditionally demand through their talk at work may erode as women—with their more nurturing and submissive communicative style—outnumber men in public relations.

We want to emphasize here that feminization is hardly the only factor that affects the status of the field. Women themselves suggest other reasons for why public relations may not enjoy the respect it deserves. One woman interviewed for a study of female practitioners in Canada, for example, said that narrow vision adversely affects the status of public relations. In her words:

> I've seen people win prizes that are stunning pieces of art that don't communicate with their audience. I've seen editors who thought the publication was their own—not the organization's. We still have to be boundary spanners . . . but we also have to have a clear stake in the business. (as quoted in Scrimger, 1989, p. 239)

However, many women in public relations enjoy what Laura Cottone (1992), a former chair of the Speech Communication Association's Commission on Public Relations, called "dubious" status. She cited a number of studies that support her contention that female educators and practitioners alike fail to receive the acknowledgment they deserve. These studies all point to the underutilization of women's potential and talent. Cottone warned that "we can no longer afford to be painfully 'aware' of this 'problem' " (p. 2).

One final unfortunate offshoot of the seemingly low status of our field may be the fact that it discourages minorities from joining our ranks. In the previous chapter, we talked about the real need for more people of color to practice public relations. We also described how few ALANAs have been recruited and promoted within the field.

Perhaps our recruiting within the Filipino or Mexican or Sioux or Bahamian community actually would be irresponsible, if AT&T's former director of public relations, Al Wann (1993), is to be taken seriously. With his tongue in cheek, we are convinced, he told IABC members attending a multicultural reception that we may not be doing them any favors by encouraging talented young minorities to enter this business. He said public relations is where neither the money nor the power is. Instead, he suggested engineering, science, information systems, finance, politics, or law as career tracks that lead to the executive suite.

Just at the point where members of his audience may have been gasping, Wann added that people of color should be encouraged to go into communication if they are also encouraged to make changes in this field from within: "To become a person who counsels on what and how to communicate in order to bring about the human and behavioral changes business needs to make" (Wann, 1993, p. 26). Such counsel does not emanate from the bottom of the corporate pyramid. It takes someone at the level of management to advise the dominant coalition on real change. But we are concerned that with a growing female majority in a formerly white male preserve, any gains we may have made in elevating public relations to a managerial role may be curtailed.

Acknowledging the gravity of this concern, at least one female graduate student dedicated her thesis research to empowering public relations and the women who practice it. Brosco Christian (1996), who worked full time as a public relations officer at a community college, positioned herself in the study like this:

> As a practitioner in a technical public relations role, working for an organization that is often asymmetrically oriented, I have made many attempts to have issues raised to, and then considered by, members of the dominant coalition. As I have become better educated in both public relations management and organizational behavior, my success rate in management from below has increased. But what chance do other female practitioners in the manager or technician roles, who are excluded from the dominant coalition, have to bring important ideas to the table and have those ideas listened to and acted upon? (pp. 5–6)

Few studies of management from below, also called "upward influence," have focused on gender as a critical independent variable. However, Brosco Christian reasoned that studying gender is vital to public relations as it becomes more female. Thus she interviewed at length eight women in community college public relations. Her goal was to develop a taxonomy of female practitioners' techniques for managing from below.

Of course, scholars and practitioners debate whether women want to be part of the decision-making process, the dominant coalition, or management (e.g., McGoon, 1993; Creedon, 1991; Hon, L. Grunig, & Dozier, 1992; Lodahl & Kejner, 1965; Reitz & Jewell, 1979). However, most of the participants in Brosco Christian's study clearly were interested in being included in their college's top-level decision-making process. Many were frustrated at their exclusion. Regardless, the thrust of Brosco Christian's research was that management from below may be *necessary* for practitioners who are in nonmanagerial, technical positions—women's most typical roles in this field. She pointed out, for example, that many organizations employ a single public relations practitioner who must do it all.

Unfortunately, much of Brosco Christian's work had to be grounded in the asymmetrical literature—dating from the 1950s—of upward influence. Most studies she reviewed reflected the way in which management traditionally has been described in this country: middle managers clawing their way to the top by selling their agenda to the dominant coalition. Today's management world, however, advises executives to listen to their employees and treat everyone with respect. So, Brosco Christian hypothesized, "there is a need to look not at influence but at communicating ideas upward in a flexible way with a win–win goal—clearly a symmetrical view" (p. 17).

Two previous studies of upward influence focused specifically on women. Mainiero (1986) tried to understand the underlying conditions, social or structural, that explain gender differences in power. She found limited support for the socialization-process explanation. That is, early learning socializes men to expect women to be passive or ingratiating and not to emphasize logic when seeking to influence. As a result, men may perceive women who use little upward influence or who try to ingratiate themselves as performing their roles effectively.

Similarly, Kipnis and Schmidt (1988) found that women who fit categories aptly named "ingratiator" and "bystander" received high performance evaluations. *Ingratiators* use friendliness to influence their superiors; *bystanders* use the least influence of any of the tactical personality types Kipnis and Schmidt identified. The most highly evaluated men used the "tactician" style of upward influence. *Tacticians* rely on an average amount of influence and emphasize reason. The fact that women using the tactician style did not, like men, receive the most favorable performance ratings suggests that gender influences the relationship between subordinates' style of upward influence and their superiors' evaluation of their performance.

Brosco Christian (1996) found that supervisors' gender has little impact on the type of management-from-below techniques practitioners adopt. However, the boss's leadership style—participatory versus authoritarian—and his or her worldview for public relations either hindered or fostered management from below. Most important was the supervisor's understanding of public relations. The administration's understanding of the potential of public relations encouraged even midlevel communicators to counsel from below.

The practitioners Brosco Christian interviewed described these typical management-from-below techniques, in descending order of frequency, as rational presentation of ideas, consultation, formation of coalitions, persistence or assertiveness, inspirational appeal, and upward appeal (circumventing the chain of command and appealing to someone in a higher position than the immediate supervisor). In addition, interviewees alluded to three concepts rarely if ever defined in the literature of upward influence: strategizing, consensus building, and proper timing.

Strategizing with the supervisor or others in the organization is similar to consultation. Its essence is captured in this quote from one participant in the study: "I chatted with my boss every day. I would run ideas by her in a very informal way. We often strategized for months or years. We would have all our ducks in a row so that when the gate opens we can get as many ducks through before it closes again" (pp. 98–99). Consensus building is similar to forming coalitions, in which the aid of others is sought to build support for an idea or to add salience to an issue. However, consensus building represents more general agreement or accord. Timing is close to the tactic of persistence or assertiveness, but participants alluded more to realizing that their supervisors were very busy and thus certain times were most conducive to approaching them with new ideas.

Brosco Christian (1996) considered the most important aspect of her findings the fact that all three new concepts are positive. They suggest win–win ways in which women in technical roles can be effective in serving their organizations, their myriad publics, and their own careers. These techniques match closely with the two-way symmetrical model of public relations. In our view, they also suggest ways in which all practitioners may be empowered at a time when their field is risking devaluation.

Inevitably, then, the question of power surfaces. The head of the Center for the New American Workforce has urged women to make the attainment of power their most important personal goal. Her argument, made to a gathering of the Women Executives in Public Relations, is that power enables women to build coalitions and overcome the "comfort factor." She explained the dearth of women in influential positions in our field as follows:

> Every person brings a filter to every social interaction and they will make decisions based on comfort. The comfort factor is very powerful to combat because we don't have control over it. It threatens the social and economic viability of women. (Sylvia Wagonheim, as quoted in "Changing American Workforce," 1993, p. 1)

Wagonheim concluded that the best affirmative action to take is power. Achieving power, in her view, hinges on women's developing networks, setting clear goals, enhancing their communication skills, and demanding recognition for success on the job.

In the previous chapter, we described the obstacles that prevent minorities in public relations from networking to gain the advancement often denied them. Many of those same problems face who women would benefit from these support structures. Ibarra (1992) studied the effects of gender in networking in an advertising agency. Findings were similar to those for racioethnicity. That is, *homophily*, or preference for the same sex (just as preference for the same race or ethnicity), predicted networking among the dominant group: men. Women, on the other hand, participated in more heterophilic networks.

Ibarra did not find that women's exclusion from men's networks inhibited their advancement in the agency; however, women's own, more heterogeneous networks did not help them progress, either. We consider it significant that there was only one woman out of 11 senior managers in the agency. Nine of the 22 midlevel managers were female. None of the entry-level professionals was male. If this were a department of public relations rather than a firm, we have to question—given the increasing feminization of the field—whether the future would bring a woman to head that department or whether a male outsider would be brought in.

Professionals in public relations—men and women alike—are concerned about the problem of devaluation of their field. They believe a professional association such as PRSA should be able to help. Participants in our 1995 focus group discussions related to gender believed that the most important thing PRSA could do to improve the situation for women in the field was to elevate the perception of public relations. As one man put it, "It doesn't matter if a man's doing it; it doesn't matter if a woman's doing it. It's the profession [of] public relations." He argued for the importance of top management's understanding the value public relations contributes to bottom-line organizational success. To him, such appreciation was more critical than the APR designation PRSA offers or even professional licensing. In urging PRSA to take on this challenge of perception, he said: "Practitioner, heal thyself."

ENCROACHMENT

Encroachment, the management of public relations by non-public relations professionals, has been the subject of much scholarly interest (Lindenmann & Lapetina, 1981; Dozier, 1988; Scrimger, 1989; Lauzen, 1992; Lauzen & Dozier, 1992) as well as industry interest (Lesly, 1988; "Must Busy Professionals," 1984). The encroaching culprits have been said to come from engineering, marketing, sales management, finance, accounting, human resources, fundraising, law, economics, advertising, and so forth—almost any field outside of public relations.

Some women in public relations consider encroachment as a positive thing if the individual in question is a strong administrator and has the confidence of top management. In a study of Canadian public relations professionals, however, most women cited examples of the negative impact of encroachment on both their organization and on the field of public relations. They alluded to problems such as the "encroacher's" short tenure and lack of long-term interest in developing the organization's communication function; intolerance for the "fuzz," or ambiguity, that often characterizes the practice of public relations; lack of the knowledge, experience, or qualifications necessary to pitch ideas to senior management; and giving up too easily because he or she cannot defend the ideas that emanate from lower down in the public relations department (Scrimger, 1989).

The most significant aspect of the problem of encroachment, in our view, is that public relations is and must remain a *management function*. As the field becomes female-intensive, it is reasonable to speculate about the organization that discriminates against women. We are thinking not so much about overt discrimination as a pattern of systematically devaluing female employees. We have seen that such subtle discrimination often takes the form of pigeonholing women into dealing with women's issues; of paying women less than their male colleagues on the assumption that they are less experienced or capable; of relegating women to low-pay, low-prestige subspecialties; of failing to groom women for managerial roles in the first place; and of maintaining inflexible structures that preclude women's balancing work and family responsibilities.

For all of these reasons and more, women cite their gender (and unequal treatment because of it) as their foremost career obstacle. This finding comes to us from a survey of 300 women who managed to achieve the status of senior management: vice presidential level or above (University of California and Korn/Ferry survey as cited in Taylor, 1986). A second study, conducted at about the same time, found that half of the 128 female directors surveyed reported discrimination from male colleagues, employers, or both. About 91% of the women said that as a result of this discrimination, they had to try harder to get ahead because of their gender (Clutterbuck & Devine, 1987).

Such discriminatory patterns and practices often result from *stereotyping* women. In both Chapters 1 and 4, we showed that resistance against women moving up the corporate ladder results in large part from these preconceptions or from management's expectations or assumptions about female managers. Women are perceived to be almost captives of their families and thus unavailable for transfers to more responsible (and more lucrative) positions in top management. Women are seen as nurturers—ideally suited for support staff but hardly equipped for the rigors of line management. Women are regarded as less serious about their careers and thus not so ambitious (or driven) as men at work.

What happens when the organization with this system of beliefs finds itself with a female majority—perhaps even a totality—in its public relations department? Is such an organization likely to promote a woman to head that department? Our answer is no, not likely. It seems far more reasonable to predict that a manager from some other, related discipline would be brought in to direct the public relations function. And there is evidence to support our prediction. The chain of evidence is complex and intertwined. We begin more than a decade ago.

As early as 1985, two eminent scholars of public relations from San Diego State University, Glen M. Broom and David M. Dozier, postulated that encroachment may result from feminization. They predicted that the dominant coalition of organizations would turn to fields such as marketing, advertising, and law to fulfill the managerial role in public relations. Later, Dozier (1988) explained that encroachment was aggravated by feminine stereotypes, which help keep women out of decision making in organizations and, more specifically, the managerial role. That role is critically important, especially if public relations is to be practiced strategically and symmetrically.

Beyond stereotyping, Martha Lauzen (1990a), a colleague of Dozier and Broom's at San Diego State University, proposed a second, related reason for gender being a factor in encroachment. She reasoned that the professional *experience* of the top public relations practitioner in an organization is an important attribute leading to the possession of managerial competencies. Women may have been precluded from gaining those competencies. The glass ceiling, entering the profession later than men did, and career interruptions for family obligations all contribute to women's lack of professional experience. Johnson and Acharya (1982), too, found that both gender and longevity in the job predict public relations role. So, despite the large numbers of women in the classroom and in entry-level jobs, few senior women practice public relations. As Lauzen (1990a) explained: "While there are few men in the younger age category, males dominate the older category. As a result, male practitioners tend to have more professional experience than female practitioners" (p. 4).

Lauzen's (1990a) survey of 300 public relations managers throughout the country confirmed that gender of the practitioner, years of experience, management competencies, and dominant role enacted all contribute to encroachment. The female top practitioner is likely to possess fewer managerial skills and is less likely to behave predominantly in the managerial role than is a male. As a result, Lauzen argued, encroachment is more likely to occur. She was careful to point out that her model, which tested all other possible relationships suggested by the relevant literature, successfully decomposes the causal path of impact of gender on encroachment. She concluded that the result is a bad news/good news scenario:

> The good news is that as female public relations practitioners gain more years of experience, they may acquire more manager competencies and may assume the manager role, thus blocking encroachment in their organizations. The bad news is that organizations today, in which the top public relations practitioner is a woman, are likely to experience higher levels of encroachment than organizations where the top practitioner is male. Thus, being female does not lead to encroachment; however, technician competencies do. These findings should inspire female practitioners to find ways to acquire manager competencies. (p. 12)

This conclusion, that women somehow must develop managerial competencies, could lead to the intriguing question: Should women—often considered victims of sexism—themselves be responsible for overcoming the fallout of that discrimination? Or should the organizations that offer them too few opportunities to gain valuable management expertise or the society that expects them to nurture families at the expense of careers be charged with restructuring to equalize the situation between women and men?

Before answering, consider the serious consequences of encroachment when the organization's power elite brings in men from other departments who have general management credentials to direct the public relations efforts. This happens regardless of whether those "generic" managers are experts in communication. We decry this outgrowth of discrimination for three main reasons. First, it disadvantages the women who deserve promotion and all of the benefits that come with directing an operation. Second, it marginalizes public relations as a strategic function.

Third, and perhaps most important, society or at least the most significant elements of the organization's environment lose their voice in the organization. You see, public relations managers who are included within the dominant coalition relay the views of those strategic constituencies to top management. In so doing, their responsibility extends well beyond that of spokesperson for the organization or supervisor of an internal department.

They are no longer what the Dutch would call "his master's voice" or what Turk (1986a) referred to as "the chairman's boys or girls" (p. 13).

True managers of public relations act as boundary spanners. They develop relationships with all of the groups inside and outside of the organization that are important to it. Employees, members of the community, the press, stockholders, government regulators, and especially activist publics all have the potential either to support or to constrain the organization. Dealing with each of these publics requires more of a public relations manager than merely one-way communicative efforts.

At this point, a few definitions are in order. We need to review exactly what we mean by *managerial role* and models of public relations, whether asymmetrical or symmetrical. We will introduce the concept of *dominant coalition* and how that elite group influences both the model of public relations practiced and the role that practitioners are empowered to fulfill. We will conclude this section of the chapter with a discussion of two related concepts: power and empowerment.

Public Relations Roles

Many different roles have been described for people who practice public relations. As we will see in greater detail in Chapter 9, these sets of activities reasonably can be reduced to a two-part typology, that of the technician and the manager. We acknowledge, of course, that such a binary opposition is inherently false because, as Rakow (1989) pointed out years ago, this dichotomy tends to "homogenize and flatten" the work that public relations people do. Culbertson (1991), too, suggested taking apart the concept of roles categories.

At the same time, we contend that our notion of public relations must be broadened beyond its typical characterization as a technical operation to include its crucial managerial aspects as well. In other words, we suggest an integration of the technical and the managerial in each public relations program. We are not promoting a split, either/or, between the two.

We have said throughout this book that we conceive of public relations as a management function. We do not mean by this that everyone who practices public relations is or should be a manager. To do so would devalue the legions of women who work as technicians, whether by their own choice or because they are relegated to this role by superiors. We also acknowledge the validity of Creedon's (1991) concern that the roles research has led to the perception of a ranking between the roles. This hierarchical assumption devalues the technician's role, where women are clustered, and emphasizes the value of the manager's role, where male models predominate.

Likewise, we do not mean to imply that everyone in public relations should aspire to the managerial role. We understand that many practitioners are deeply attached to their craft. This may not be the case with students, who have not had the chance to develop that attachment. Parsons (1989) found that many of the public relations students he surveyed (80% of whom were women) rejected all forms of creative work in public relations. He reasoned that this may reflect students' rush to join the managerial ranks without understanding that they first must pay their dues, typically by practicing employee communication.

Creedon (1991) took this finding as evidence of students' naivete about abilities required by those who would hire them. She cited studies by Wakefield and Cottone (1987) and Baxter (1986) that both pointed to writing skill as fundamental to entry-level jobs in public relations. However, we believe that the Wakefield and Cottone survey of heads of public relations firms and of corporate and nonprofit public relations departments also speaks to the importance of management skills. Respondents, as Creedon acknowledged, ranked skills in decision making/problem solving and relations with clients or customers as most valued. Skills in writing, editing, and layout or design rated below these managerial competencies.

Despite these preferences by employers and in contrast with some students' inclinations, a large number of practitioners has reported a preference for remaining at the level of tactician—whether they be writers, photographers, editors, publication designers, or artists (McGoon, 1993). Many of these communicators who responded to IABC's informal fax poll eschewed promotion into senior management for what one called the "down and dirty" stuff (p. 14). More than half opted for writing, editing, producing publications, and so forth. Perhaps most surprisingly, only four of the 170 respondents said that working with top management was their favorite part of the job.

In a smaller yet more scientific study, Lauzen (1990b) also found that not all practitioners covet the managerial role. Her data confirm our assumption that practitioners' aspirations differ, whether they are women or men. As one respondent told her, "Let's face it, it's a lot more fun to try to crank out a feature query or press release or be quoted in the newspaper, than to try to figure out how in the heck to help build and promote a new program against stiff competition and to be accountable for that against some financial measures" (p. 6).

Undoubtedly, aspirations play a role in ascension to the management ranks. Recall that Lauzen (1990b) found that competencies figure prominently as well. She (1992) explained that a public relations practitioner must possess the behavioral skills, born of education and experience, required to engage in the activities that constitute the managerial role. Not all practitioners can be expected to aspire to or to have the expertise to be managers.

Related to job aspiration is the question of one's perception of self and of the job itself. Straughan (1990) characterized a career in public relations for woman as a "not-so-tender trap." Despite opportunities abounding for women to enter the field and then to attain midlevel positions, top management of public relations seems to elude them. In her survey of about 200 practitioners, Straughan found that fewer women than men looked at themselves as managers. Women, who acknowledged that they lacked adequate power for boundary-spanning or environmental-scanning activities, further reported that others in the organization did not consider them management-oriented either.

We believe that the department of public relations must be led by a person with managerial expertise and authority. Someone at the top of that department must have the ability to do strategic planning. That person must enjoy the confidence of higher management and have credibility within the circle of the organization's top managers. Thus, in this section of the chapter on encroachment, we have belabored the discussion of public relations roles.

One final reason may justify our lengthy treatment of the roles research, despite very solid reasons for questioning the prudence of this two-part typology. We know that the level of job satisfaction in public relations, which our research shows to be lower for women than men on average, escalates with a shift from the technical to the managerial role. Job satisfaction rises despite accompanying responsibility for the success or failure of decisions made and implemented, which often is cited as a negative consequence of achieving managerial status (Dozier, 1981). Perhaps most important, even staffs in public relations—including those who remain at the technical level—experience more job satisfaction as their superiors become increasingly influential (Jablin, 1980).

We close this section of the chapter, then, with a final word on job *dis*satisfaction. A study by Northwestern National Life (NWNL) concluded that job stress has reached critical proportions in the work force. Stress results from high levels of job demands and little control over one's work. *pr reporter* ("New Job Burnout Research," 1992) believed this characterizes the situation in many departments of public relations.

The article reporting on the NWNL research in the trade press highlighted two important implications of the study for our field. First, it urged supervisors to develop programs of teamwork, participatory decision making, and better communication. Second, it acknowledged that since women are more likely than men to suffer from job-related stress, managers of an increasingly feminized work force in public relations should learn to recognize burnout. Do you wonder about the reasons for women suffering more stress-related illnesses (41% vs. 26% for men), wanting to quit (44% vs. 36%), and burnout (36% vs. 28%)? Quoting from the NWNL study, *pr reporter* explained:

> Stress is compounded for women because they often earn low salaries even when they are college educated. Other factors may be related to organizations' failure to pay women & men equally for their work & to adopt policies that are responsive to family issues. (p. 3)

Unless we manage to empower workers in public relations, women as well as men, their demoralization and sense of hopelessness on the job will have both obvious and hidden costs for employers. Employee turnover, absenteeism, and disability claims resulting from stress-related illness are indisputable. However, lower productivity and diminished quality of customer service also may follow.

The Dominant Coalition

The *dominant coalition* is the group of senior managers who control the organization. They set goals and decide how those goals will be realized (Robbins, 1987). Broom and Dozier (1985) argued that the inclusion of public relations in the dominant coalition is one of the most important measures of professional growth in our field. J. Grunig and Hunt (1984) went further, in asserting that there is little justification for any practice of public relations unless practitioners are involved with the dominant coalition. There is good reason to support their argument. The IABC Excellence project (J. Grunig et al., 1991; Dozier, L. Grunig, & J. Grunig, 1995) determined that the most effective organizations in their international sample include the senior public relations executive as a member of the company's senior management team. Further, those outstanding organizations take steps to foster the careers of their female employees, especially female executives—thus making maximum use of all their human resources.

Without the support of the organization's power elite, public relations as a function is unlikely to be at the table when key decisions are being made. If not at the decision table, public relations is limited to the role of explaining and justifying others' decisions (Broom & Dozier, 1985).

Without the support of the dominant coalition, too, a woman is unlikely to head the public relations department—even if only female practitioners staff that department. Gender undoubtedly plays an important role in determining who joins the dominant coalition, as we will go on to demonstrate. Keep in mind along the way that a number of studies has documented and then looked at additional reasons for public relations being excluded from the inner circle (e.g., Anshen, 1974; Brown, 1980; Close, 1980; Greyser, 1981; Lesly, 1981; Lindenmann & Lapetina, 1981; Baxter, 1980; Burger, 1983; Newman, 1980; Strenski, 1980).

Broom and Dozier (1986) found in their panel study of PRSA members that being male is a powerful predictor of participation in management decision making. Studies of both PRSA and IABC members, however, determined that gender is still a weaker predictor than is the practitioner's predominant role (manager or technician) and the amount of environmental scanning he or she does. These findings held for a 1987 survey of IABC members (Dozier, 1990).

Thus Dozier (1988) concluded that formative research is an important tool for women trying to break the glass ceiling that often blocks their entry into the dominant coalition. Once again, then, we see the suggestion that women move to empower themselves. Whereas Lauzen (1990a) and Tear (as quoted in "Check Out Your Gender Dynamics," 1992), called a "gender specialist," advocated women's acquiring general managerial competencies, Dozier saw formative research such as environmental scanning as a useful means for women to be included in organizational decision making.

This well-intentioned suggestion nevertheless has its critics. Criticism comes largely from its grounding in liberal feminism. Radical feminists would prefer a restructuring of organizations so that employee empowerment, rather than power, characterizes effective management. We (Hon, 1993) explained it this way:

> Dozier's answer for female practitioners is to realign themselves with the masculine stereotype (power and control) through scanning research. By doing so, they will be more likely to "fit in" and be invited to participate in the deliberations of the powerful. (p. 6)

However, Dozier (1990) also pointed out that program research is related to the model of public relations practiced. Research characterizes both of the two-way models; it characterizes neither of the one-way models. We turn now to a discussion of these distinct approaches to the public relations function.

Models of Public Relations

Public relations professionals typically adopt one of four main approaches to their practice. Each of these four models grows out of different assumptions or worldviews about public relations. Each requires different types of expertise or education. And each can be expected to result in different degrees of effectiveness for the organization.

The scholar most responsible for research on these models has made the case for the *two-way symmetrical model* both pragmatically and philosophically. That is, James E. Grunig (1992b), colleague and spouse of one of this book's authors, determined that a dialogic, balanced approach to public relations characterizes departments considered most excellent. He also believed that the two-way symmetrical model is most ethical and socially responsible because it "manages conflict rather than wages war" (p. 10). It tends to be practiced in certain kinds of organizations, such as regulated monopolies, and by certain kinds of practitioners: those with education in public relations, those who are professional, and those whose CEOs value this interactive, adaptive style.

We agree with Rakow's (1989) speculation that the feminization of the field may signal a swing to this "ideology of cooperation and community" (p. 10). J. Grunig and his colleague White (1992, p. 50), too, agreed that the feminine worldview seems to be a symmetrical one. They considered the masculine worldview more asymmetrical, although they acknowledged that men also could practice a symmetrical model of public relations.

The two-way symmetrical model is a negotiational, cooperative approach to public relations. An equally two-way but persuasive, dominating model is the "asymmetrical" model. Both rely heavily on research, but for different purposes. The asymmetrical or imbalanced model uses scientific persuasion to identify the messages most likely to convince the publics without the organization having to change its own behavior. The two-way balanced or symmetrical model, on the other hand, uses research to help bring about symbiotic changes in the attitudes and behaviors of both the publics and the organization.

One-way concepts of public relations include the press agentry, or publicity, model and the public information model. Press agentry, as its name suggests, is a propagandistic approach that seeks media attention in almost any conceivable way (even disregarding the truth). Here the organization's goal is control or domination of its environment. Public relations contributes to this goal through advocacy or product promotion. It remains the most frequently practiced approach to public relations.

In the public information model, public relations practitioners serve as journalists-in-residence who provide truthful, accurate information. That information, however, may be incomplete because practitioners rarely volunteer negative information. This model can be traced to the turn of the century, when former reporters, such as Ivy Lee, were hired away from the newsroom to help organizations contend with the muckraking journalists who covered them. In this model, public relations helps the organization achieve its goals for coexistence with its environment through a one-way flow of factual information.

The four models, as J. Grunig conceived them, developed in a linear, historical progression that began in the late 19th century with practitioners such as P. T. Barnum, the quintessential press agent. Research has shown that the four models continue to reliably and accurately describe at least four typical ways in which public relations is practiced, although they have not explained well why organizations practice the models they do (J. Grunig & L. Grunig, 1989). They may function as discrete approaches to practicing public relations, as values held by the organization's dominant coalition, or in mixed forms that may be more situational than static.

Like the roles typology, this typology has limitations inherent in any dichotomous categorization. Its major architect has acknowledged the need to continue to refine our understanding of the four models (J. Grunig & L. Grunig, 1989). We (L. Grunig, 1991) have gone on specifically to question J. Grunig's assertion that the models developed sequentially. Olasky (1987), too, challenged the assumption that the models represent a historical progression of practice in the field. However, settling the question of linear evolution over the last century will be exceedingly difficult. We know too little of the history of public relations.

Little historical evidence of women's contributions to public relations, in particular, exists. It is as the Duke asked Viola in Shakespeare's *Twelfth Night*: "And what's her history?" She answered, "A blank, my lord" (2.4.111). What little *is* known, however, suggests that women in the last century practiced a model more closely paralleling the symmetrical than the asymmetrical (for a review of much of this speculation, see L. Grunig, 1989). This important aspect of the development of our field warrants much more investigation.

Women in public relations may stand to gain the most from an inclusive chronicle of the field. Feminist historians of various disciplines are replacing any single-sex view of development with the understanding that women not only have been present but have been active at each stage of the past (DuBois, Kelly, Kennedy, Korsmeyer, & Robinson, 1985). Along the way, of course, we will need to guard against idealizing women's roles in public relations. We know, for instance, that women worked as publicists for the Ku Klux Klan during the 1920s (Blee, 1991). We also need to avoid the pitfalls of "contribution history," or focusing almost exclusively on the "big names" of the field. As valuable as Henry's (1988) biography of Doris Fleischman is, we also need to highlight the activities of women less prominent than, say, the wife of Edward L. Bernays. One of our goals in this book, of course, is to relate the lives of "ordinary" women practicing public relations rather than dismissing female practitioners less visible than professional society presidents, CEOs of public relations firms, or vice presidents of corporate communication.

We will leave the writing of a historical record in public relations to other colleagues. We do look forward to the time when a comprehensive and integrated historical theory exists. We know that such a chronicle will bring together our personal, our professional, and our scholarly lives.

Working in a somewhat different direction than the historical, J. Grunig, along with a team of scholars and practitioners, subsequently has developed a theory of public relations that explores the *worldview* inherent in each of the four models. The team, working on a 10-year grant project sponsored by the Research Foundation of the International Association of Business Communicators, argued that the presuppositions about the role of public relations in society inherent in the two-way symmetrical model reflects more of a feminine than a masculine worldview. The theory concludes that excellent public relations embodies a worldview of the communication function as both symmetrical and managerial (J. Grunig, 1992b).

Without an expert in communication to manage the department, which model of public relations would you expect to see practiced there? Herein lies the crux of the problem of encroachment. We are not being territorial in warning about this outgrowth of sexism in the face of the increasing number of women in the field. True, the public relations manager who is shut out of the organization's top levels of decision making suffers, whether that manager is a man or a woman. However, we are reflecting the very real worry that neither the organization nor its key publics are well served when someone other than a professional who is a manager in public relations heads that function.

MBAs, attorneys, marketers, and experts in advertising or human resources may have impressive leadership and organizational skills. They simply lack the expertise in public relations that is required to practice the most sophisticated and the most effective approach. Two-way symmetrical public relations requires someone with management skill who is able to do research to scan the organization's environment. Conducting this kind of sophisticated public relations is a positive consequence of enacting the managerial role (Lauzen & Dozier, 1992).

Encroachment, on the other hand, is the negative consequence of powerlessness in public relations (Lauzen & Dozier, 1992). It is possible, as Lauzen (1992) acknowledged, that even the competent manager with high aspirations may be encroached on because of the glass ceiling. At this point, then, we turn to a brief discussion of power and a related term preferred by many feminists and others concerned with power's connotation of command or control: *empowerment.*

POWER AND EMPOWERMENT

The perception that public relations is a powerful organizational function decreases the likelihood of encroachment (Lauzen, 1992). Encroachment occurs not so much because of ambitious outsiders from engineering, say, or marketing who grab the turf of public relations. Instead, Lauzen found, it results from the glass ceiling and other structural factors within the organization, as well as from the low aspirations and competencies of some public relations practitioners.

The practitioner who views public relations as a low-level technical function acts accordingly. The leadership of the organization, in turn, looks to someone other than that practitioner for strategic management in public relations. As Lauzen (1992) put it, "The key consequence of this behavior and self-perception is encroachment" (p. 69). In other words, the vacuum in power is filled.

Thus we consider it imperative to define what we mean by both *power* and by *empowerment.* More important, we need to distinguish between these two related concepts. The need for the distinction will become clear with definitions of power, in particular. Taken together, they paint a picture of oppression or, at the least, the potential for abuse.

There may be as many definitions of power in the academic literature as there are scholars who study the concept. Common themes include the force necessary to change others' behavior (Emerson, 1962), an imbalance in the relationship between those with power and those without (Simon, 1953), and control over others (Morgenthau, 1960). Gaski (1984) considered the underlying element in all of these classic definitions the ability to change another's behavior.

The ability to force or influence a change in another's behavior does not have to be enacted for power to be a potent factor in organizational life (Katz & Kahn, 1966). Power has both potential and enacted components (Blau, 1964; Emerson, 1962, 1972; Cook, 1977; Provan, 1980). It also may be productive, rather than oppressive or manipulative (Kanter, 1979).

For example, *personal* power helps people control their own lives (Buffington, 1986).

This notion of productive rather than exploitive power brings us to the contemporary concept of empowerment. Empowerment is a logical outgrowth of the progression from schools of scientific management to participatory management on through to the trendy Total Quality Management (TQM) approach. For the last few decades, American organizations increasingly have emphasized the involvement or participation of their employees. In Chapter 5, we explored the relationship between the trend toward empowerment and the growing heterogeneity of U.S. workers.

We believe that public relations professionals, in particular, must be empowered to help shape the organization's ideology. If powerless, we cannot influence events, we cannot share in the decision-making process, and we cannot contribute the maximum to organizational effectiveness. Even if we are called managers but remain unempowered, we are less satisfied at work.

Employee satisfaction is correlated with empowerment. An analysis of a Fortune 500 manufacturing firm showed that satisfaction at work also is linked to management's commitment to empowerment (Popovich, 1992). The strongest link in that case study was between having the authority to do one's job and satisfaction with empowerment.

As Kanter (1979) showed, accountability without power leads to frustration or even failure. She advocated, instead, management that is team-oriented, participatory, and power sharing. Such a system enhances productivity, thus benefitting both the organization and the employees (in and out of public relations) who work there. Employees who have a sense of ownership in their work see themselves responsible for its quality.

Accountability is one hallmark of empowerment. It goes hand in hand with autonomy. We find an example in public relations with the concept of federated partnerships in GCI. When he was GCI's chief executive officer, Jack Bergen decentralized and deformalized the traditional hierarchical structure there. His aim was to open the communication channels and provide managers of GCI operations worldwide with more authority and responsibility. This, in turn, motivated superior performance (Skolnik, 1993a).

Other public relations firms—such as A. Brown-Olmstead Associates and Manning, Selvage, and Lee—similarly transformed their operations to empower employees through more teamwork, peer review, and interaction between top management and other levels (Bovet, 1993; Skolnik, 1993a). These new, more open, and enabling structures seem relatively effective as measured by profits, client base, and employee satisfaction. Firms such as GCI, Manning, Selvage, and Lee, and ABOA either have increased or maintained profits, held onto the same clients or expanded their client base, and kept employee turnover to a minimum (Bovet, 1993; Skolnik 1993a, 1993b, 1993c).

Wann, a former chairman of one of the leading professional associations in public relations, described the system of quality improvement through empowering employees as follows. Management begins by giving individuals the information and resources they need to do their job and then trusting them to do so. Managers praise employees for trying, not only for succeeding. More praise and greater rewards follow for success. Coaching follows when employees come up short. The toughest part, in Wann's view, is nurturing a diverse labor force to achieve all they are capable of on their own terms (1993).

This seasoned professional's description of empowerment seems right on the mark. As usual, we now turn to the theoretical literature for support or, possibly, for refutation.

Few scholarly studies have looked directly at empowerment or power and public relations. One extensive effort (L. Grunig, 1990a) did establish the many reasons for powerlessness in the field. Sexism was a major explanation frequently cited by participants in the research. Other reasons offered for the limited power practitioners experienced were newness to the organization, lack of education in public relations on the part of the dominant coalition, being in a regional office rather than at the headquarters, and restrictive government policy.

Women who teach public relations as well as those who practice it only rarely are empowered (L. Grunig, 1988). Unfortunately, actively seeking empowerment may not be adequate to overcome this problem. In fact, historical cases have shown that the more authority professional women seek, the more discrimination they experience (Abel, 1981; Epstein, 1970; Rothschild, 1978).

In looking for strategies that would help to empower women, feminist theoreticians such as Treichler and Wartella (1986) have pointed to knowledge. Knowledge at the very least should help women analyze the power relations in which we are all enmeshed. This book is one step in that direction. As we pointed out in our earlier work (Toth & L. Grunig, 1993), "If women's issues are not researched, women will risk continuing to reinforce the existing knowledge base that provided only one voice, the white male voice, of what is known of reality" (p. 158).

This kind of knowledge may be especially important in the international arena. Howe (1984) pointed to women's impact on public relations worldwide. She explained that in developing countries, "the need for more accurate information on which to base decisions that affect millions of persons, half of whom are inevitably women, makes . . . research on women—hardly a luxury" (p. 283). Even at this point, however, we understand that women are especially well suited to meet the global challenges of the next decade. In their study of North American women working as expatriate managers, Jelinek and Adler (1988) reported that traditional U.S. approaches to doing business abroad are risky today. As an alternative, they suggested that "alliances, cooperative efforts, joint ventures, and even business-as-usual carried out across cultural lines can be facilitated by skills traditionally thought of as 'female' " (p. 19). They explained that because relational capacities tend to be more highly developed among women than among men, women represent an underutilized resource. And, in fact, the women they studied emphasized that personal relationships are especially important in what they termed the "slow clock cultures" often found in developing countries. Thus Jelinek and Adler considered women "world-class managers."

If business in the 21st century becomes as heterogeneous as projected, then traits associated with women may come to be relied on more and more. Consider a single speculation. Bernard (1976) predicted that the basis of society in the cybernetic age will be an "information net," calling for an honest, cooperative society and greater acceptance of what many define as female characteristics. These are primarily the traits that define femininity in the psychological literature. In Chapter 1, we discussed these communal characteristics that, according to Bakan (1966) and others, focus on women's others-centered nature and their self-perception of being part of a larger collectivity of selves. Women, or anyone with these feminine traits, can maximize this potential when they are empowered to play the managerial role as head of their public relations department.

SUBLIMATION

Encroachment and sublimation are both examples of the *negative* consequences of not enacting the managerial role. If the public relations unit is headed by someone who is not a manager and who lacks power in the organization, that person will fail to maintain the department as its own domain. We saw in our discussion of management in Chapter 4 that women have a harder time than men obtaining power in the organizational setting. Thus the question of sublimation of public relations under another functional area becomes critical in any discussion of feminization in the field.

Sublimation, akin to "imperialism," has important negative consequences for public relations as a field as well as for female practitioners.

Sublimation of the public relations function typically happens under the marketing umbrella. Marketing imperialism, according to Dozier and Lauzen (1990), is most likely to occur when the top public relations practitioner is a woman.

What is the fallout of such sublimation? First, consider the consequences for the field of public relations. As with encroachment, sublimation tends to move the function back from any gains in professionalism made in recent years. Newman (1980) contended that public relations has evolved from its roots in the technical aspects of the field to a second phase of professional development. From here, he said, "We are ready to move inland, toward the command posts of corporate management" (p. 1). However, Hawver (as quoted in Baxter, 1980), a former president of PRSA, believed that we only will attain professional status when we regard ourselves as part of the managerial team rather than as craftspeople.

When public relations is sublimated to marketing, the public relations person is unlikely to become a top-level manager because the role of the practitioner typically is relegated to that of the technician. As B. King and Scrimger (1993) found in their study of Canadian hospitals, "There is potential for public relations to be restricted to the role of technical support in the areas of publicity and internal communications as fund raising moves from amateur to professional status and as hospital administrators investigate the revenue generating potential of marketing" (p. 40).

Confining public relations to a technical dimension also has important ramifications for establishing the field as a critically important part of any organization's overall operation. Ehling (1992) determined that public relations has had a particularly hard time demonstrating its contribution to the "bottom line" because of what he called "operational reducibility," or restricting it to low-level production functions such as copy preparation and distribution. A second contributing factor he called "goal displacement and functional subserviency." This relates more directly to sublimation or imperialism. It refers to making public relations subservient to other functions—such as marketing, finance, or human resources—without goals of its own.

In both of these cases—operational reducibility and functional subserviency—public relations is conceptualized as an end in itself or as a means of persuasion. In either case, measuring its worth is difficult. By contrast, Ehling argued that when public relations is conceived of as two-way symmetrical communication, quantifying its financial contribution to the organization is possible. In two-way public relations, of course, the goal is to reduce conflict between an organization and its publics. Thus public relations efforts can be measured in terms of their probability and cost as means of gaining cooperation or reducing conflict. Cooperation or reduced conflict, in turn, can be assessed in terms of maximizing monetary gain or minimizing monetary loss. Hoxie's (1992) empirical research did indeed find that utilities with excellent, two-way public relations programs tended to incur fewer of the costs associated with activism, regulation, and litigation than did the less-than-excellent utilities she studied.

Now, consider the consequences of sublimation on individual practitioners. Again, we cite the 1993 Canadian survey, which suggested that the roles of public relations practitioners in health care could be devalued—just as they had begun to become established in that industry. Marketing, on the other hand, more recently began to gain a toehold in Canadian hospitals. B. King and Scrimger predicted that the role of public relations in relation to marketing would depend on the level of public relations being practiced:

> If the public relations manager is already adept at environmental scanning, regularly uses research tools such as patient surveys, is an important resource for strategic planning advice, and is seen as the communications expert in the hospital, marketing will probably develop as a separate but complementary function. If the public relations staff act as communications technicians, they could become part of a research-oriented marketing department. (p. 44)

Finally, we know that sublimation is a precursor to encroachment (Dozier & Lauzen, 1990)—thus limiting the ability of the department to fulfill its potential within the organization.

Chapter Eight

The Gender Gap in Public Relations Salaries

W omen in public relations continue to make less money on average than do men in the field. This is the case regardless of age, experience, or type of organization where they work. Why this is so and whether we should be concerned about the gender gap in public relations have been the subjects of many articles, conference presentations, and public debates. Reasons offered for why the gendered salary gap exists include the following: (1) Women have less experience and tend to be younger than men because of their later entry into the field of public relations; (2) women cluster in lower paying kinds of organizations; and (3) women work in lower paying roles. Some researchers have argued that the salary statistics themselves are wrong. Others have acknowledged that things may have been bad, but "they're getting better."

If the debate were not so acrimonious, we would believe the participants were merely determined optimists. However, the kind of invective— almost argument for its own sake—we have experienced in more than a dozen years of research suggests more subconscious fears: that employers of women doing public relations know they can hire women for less money or perhaps that women in public relations really will devalue this field.

However, in 1995, Simmons Market Research concluded again what this chapter intends to illustrate: "There continue to be disparities between the salaries of men and women. These exist across age, experience and job title. On average, men's salaries are 45% higher than women's ($59,460 vs. $41,110)" (*Salary Survey of Public Relations Professionals,* 1995, p. 4).

Finally, after a 5-year gap in salary studies in public relations, Impulse Research for *PR Week* reported figures for 1999. The research found that despite outnumbering men by almost two to one, women earn 38% less (Leyland, 2000). The average salary for men was $81,920, whereas the average salary for women was $59,026. This salary divide is predicted to widen, rather than narrow, because men's pay increased by 8.3% in 1999, when women's pay went up by only 7.6% (Seideman & Leyland, 2000). The study concluded that the numbers show "a distinct discrimination" (Seideman & Leyland, 2000, p. 29).

This chapter explores the gap in compensation between public relations women and men. We begin by describing one of the most comprehensive studies done of the PRSA's members over a 5-year period. In addition, we look at the salary surveys of the U.S. Bureau of the Census and studies conducted by the International Association of Business Communicators, the *Public Relations Journal*, *pr reporter*, and others. Then, we discuss the explanations given for the gender gap in pay. We also explore our research participants' *perceptions* about the pay gap. We will conclude the chapter by challenging public relations professionals and our students, the future public relations professionals, to consider the causes and to seek solutions.

UNDER THE GLASS CEILING: AN ANALYSIS OF GENDER ISSUES IN U.S. PUBLIC RELATIONS

PRSA commissioned studies in 1990 and 1995 to assess the salaries and other demographics of its members. In the 1990 study, published as a monograph titled *Under the Glass Ceiling: An Analysis of Gender Issues in American Public Relations* (Wright, L. Grunig, Springston, & Toth, 1991), more than 1,000 PRSA members responded to a six-page questionnaire. In 1995, a very similar survey, sent to a smaller random sample, yielded 678 questionnaires, continuing to match expected rates of return for lengthy surveys of this kind. Results of the second phase appear as articles in a number of scholarly journals (e.g., Serini, Toth, Wright, & Emig, 1997; Toth, Serini, Wright, & Emig, 1998a; Serini, Toth, Wright, & Emig, 1998).

These two studies of PRSA members, which we refer to throughout this book as the glass ceiling research, represent the largest samples of public relations practitioners ever compiled. We described our method in greater detail in the Appendix. Now it's time to tell you what we found.

Demographics

Gender ratios of respondents in the 1990 and 1995 two-stage study reflect census data on the gender switch in public relations. In 1989, the census reported a 59% to 41% ratio of male to female public relations workers (as cited in Lukovitz, 1989). By 1994, there was a 37% to 63% ratio of male to female public relations specialists ("Statistical Abstract of the U.S.," 1995). The gender ratio in the glass ceiling study in 1990 was 58% male to 42% female. In the 1995 study, the ratio of male to female practitioners was 36.5% to 63.5%. Table 8.1 shows the demographic information from the glass ceiling research.

The median age of men and women in the 1990 and 1995 phases of the research remained the same: 45 for men and 35 for women. In both the 1990 and 1995 phases of the glass ceiling project, men reported earning median salaries of $55,000. In 1990, women's median salary was $37,000—$18,000 less on average than men's. That median salary for the 1995 sample of women increased by $3,000 to $40,000. The gap between women's and men's pay narrowed to $15,000.

The average number of years of professional experience for women in public relations increased from 8 years in 1990 to 11 years in 1995. However, the average number of years of professional experience stayed at 17 years for men over the 5-year period. These averages are consistent with the 1991 data reported by Dozier and Broom (1995), who found women possessing an average of 11 years in public relations and men 16 years of professional experience. Recent demographic data found the typical PRSA member had practiced for 15 years ("Special Report," 1997).

Data on the ethnicity of PRSA members, a demographic query added to the 1995 survey instrument, indicated that more than four out of every five men and women were of European descent. Other ethnic groups reported included African American, Mexican American, Asian American,

TABLE 8.1. Selected Demographic Characteristics of 1990 and 1995 "Glass Ceiling" Participants

	Men		Women	
Characteristics	1990	1995	1990	1995
Gender (%)	58	36.5	42	63.5
Average age in years	45	45	35	35
Median salary	$55,000	$55,000	$37,000	$40,000
Average years of experience	17	17	8	11
Ethnicity				
European American		83		88
Other reported (African American, Mexican American, Asian American, Native American)		3		6

and Native American. Of the total sample, 6% were self-identified as "other ethnic female" and 3% were self-identified as "other ethnic male."

In 1990 and again in 1995, the majority of PRSA members worked either in counseling firms or corporations. Table 8.2 shows a breakdown of type of organization and gender. Between 1990 and 1995 there was an important drop in the percentage of men and women working in corporations. In 1990, 35% of the men surveyed worked in corporations. By 1995, that percentage fell to 25%. The drop for women working in corporations was from 32% in 1990 to 25% in 1995. There was a fall in the percentage of men working in counseling firms of 5 percentage points. Three percent fewer women were working in counseling firms.

The respondents seemed to be headed toward work in education and nonprofit organizations. In 1990, 9% of the men reported working in education. In 1995, 13% of the men reported working in education. There were also significant percentage increases for both men and women reporting that they worked in types of organizations other than those listed. In 1990, 4% of the men reported working in other organizations; by 1995, this increased by 9 points to 13%. In 1990, 7% of the women reported working in other organizations; in 1995, 21% of the female respondents reported working in other organizations—an increase of 14 percentage points.

Experience and Salary

We have heard the argument that women will make the same salaries as men when they have had the same number of years of experience. However, Table 8.3 shows that women entering public relations make approxi-

TABLE 8.2. Gender and Type of Organization

Type of organization	% men 1990	% men 1995	% women 1990	% women 1995
Counseling firm	33	28	26	23
Corporation	35	25	32	25
Government/military	9	7	6	7
Health/welfare	6	7	13	15
Education	9	13	9	6
Trade/professional association	6	8	7	4
Other	4	13	7	21

Note. Percentages may add up to more than 100% because of rounding error.

mately the same salaries as do men but rarely do women achieve parity. This finding holds constant between the 1990 and 1995 studies. Keep in mind that the median salaries reported were—in some categories—for small numbers of respondents. When reading the table, also keep in mind that the data were collapsed into 10-year periods after the first few years of experience.

In only two instances after the first year on the job did women's pay supersede men's (in the seventh year for women in 1995 and in the 30–39-year range for the two female respondents in 1990). At some points, pay was virtually equal. However, we found that regardless of experience level, the earnings of women surveyed in the glass ceiling research more typically tended to lag behind men's in both our 1990 and 1995 studies. In one range of experience (20–29 years) in the more recent research, women actually reported earning $15,000 on average less than did men that year ($55,000 vs. $70,000, respectively). This finding is especially significant in light of the number of respondents contributing to this figure (45 women, 63 men).

Although these are not large numbers, neither are they so small as to be considered negligible (as with the two women with 30–39 years of experience whose median pay in 1990 was $103,000 compared with only $70,500 for the 48 men reporting in that same year and range of experi-

TABLE 8.3. Median Salaries by Gender and Years in Public Relations

Years in Public Relations	1990				1995			
	Men		Women		Men		Women	
	Salary	N	Salary	N	Salary	N	Salary	N
1	25,100	5	20,000	16	23,000	10	24,617	14
2	24,500	10	23,000	21	30,000	9	25,000	21
3	30,000	7	25,000	40	28,041	8	27,750	20
4	39,000	9	28,000	24	38,000	6	30,000	27
5	32,750	10	29,945	44	40,000	9	37,000	33
6	40,000	11	35,000	37	40,000	7	35,750	12
7	40,000	9	38,000	23	31,850	4	37,250	22
8	45,400	9	34,000	18	40,500	4	40,000	23
9	49,500	8	38,000	16	45,500	4	40,000	19
10–19	55,000	106	42,000	165	55,000	75	49,500	154
20–29	65,000	87	60,000	30	70,000	63	55,000	45
30–39	70,500	48	103,000	2	66,000	26	60,000	9
40–49	74,500	8	58,000	3	101,000	4	80,000	1

ence). When only two figures are used to calculate an average, that median can be misleading. For example, in 1990 the two women with 30–39 years of experience had significantly different salaries: $156,000 and $56,000. We regret that so many respondents of both genders in our survey research declined to answer questions about their pay. However, Table 8.3 shows that the bottom line is that women's salaries rarely seem to catch up.

WHERE ELSE CAN WE LEARN ABOUT THE SALARY GAP?

To either confirm or question our data, we turn next to other sources of information on the pay disparity between women and men in our field. These sources—to be discussed in turn—include the U.S. government, the trade press such as *pr reporter*, and the professional associations IABC and PRSA. In addition to the value of these diverse perspectives, we wanted to explore a longer time frame than the 5-year period of our own longitudinal research.

These salary figures for public relations should be considered in the context of the way they were gathered. Several of the salary surveys reported the pay of different groups of public relations people but not the entire population practicing public relations. For example, the U.S. Census reported on the income of practitioners who categorize themselves as public relations specialists, a job title that others in public relations might not identify with because they work in specialties of public relations such as media relations, public affairs, or employee relations. Also, public relations people who work in positions that have managerial or administrative titles may more likely identify themselves on such census counts as managers or administrators rather than as public relations specialists.

Professional associations, such as PRSA and IABC (each with fewer than 20,000 members), have reported salary information based on samples of their members. However, the U.S. Bureau of Labor reported that there were 159,000 public relations specialists (as cited in Wilcox, Ault, & Agee, 1992). Professor Robert Kendall of the University of Florida estimated that there are some 400,000 practicing public relations specialists (as cited in Wilcox et al., 1992). Thus we understand that members of the professional associations in public relations reporting their salaries undoubtedly represent less than 15% of all the people who may be practicing public relations. Certainly, then, caution should be used when looking at members of professional societies because they may not be representative of the entire population of public relations practitioners.

Surveying public relations people who have joined a professional association should suggest that we know most about people who care enough about their work to seek to develop themselves professionally. However, they also may be the practitioners who are earning the highest salaries, since membership costs about $200 per year for PRSA and IABC.

The PRSA and IABC surveys included public relations practitioners at all levels of practice. In addition to the PRSA and IABC surveys and the Bureau of Census statistics, a fourth source of salary information for public relations people has been *pr reporter*'s annual survey of the profession. A weekly trade publication for mostly upper-level public relations practitioners, *pr reporter* has surveyed the salaries of randomly sampled subscribers, members of PRSA, members of the Canadian Public Relations Society (CPRS), and many others. Although each of the four sources of salary information presented in this chapter has limited generalizability to all public relations professionals, taken together they provide a preponderance of evidence that a gender gap in compensation exists in public relations.

U.S. Bureau of the Census Statistics

According to the U.S. Bureau of the Census (as cited in Donato, 1990), in 1969 the mean earnings of female public relations specialists were $7,908 and of male specialists $13,420. In 1979, the mean earnings of female public relations specialists rose to $15,193 and of male specialists to $25,115. The ratio of female to male earnings for public relations specialists over the 10-year period barely changed. Women continued to earn about 60% of what men earned (see Table 8.4).

TABLE 8.4. Mean Earnings of Public Relations Specialists, 1969,[a] 1979,[a] and 1988[b]

	1969	1979	1988
Female public relations specialists	$7,908	$15,193	N/A
Male public relations specialists	$13,420	$25,115	N/A
Ratio of female to male earnings for public relations specialists	.60	.60	.58
Ratio of female to male earnings for managers in public relations, marketing, and advertising	N/A	N/A	.63

[a] *Source:* U.S. Bureau of the Census (1973a, Table 19; 1984c, Table 1) as cited in Donato (1990).
[b] Russell (1988).

In 1988, Russell pointed out that the Bureau of Labor Statistics had found that female public relations specialists earned 58% of what their male counterparts earned; female *managers* in public relations, marketing, and advertising earned 63% of what their male counterparts earned. Thus all three of the federal government surveys cited here have established a gender gap in public relations salaries that has held almost constant since 1969.

Public Relations Journal Surveys

Although the PRSA is more than 45 years old, only as recently as 1985 did the *Public Relations Journal*, the former trade magazine of the society, provide salary information on its members. The article on pay in public relations that appeared in 1985 used the results of a 1984 *pr reporter* survey and a survey from the PRSA Counselors' Academy. (The Counselors' Academy is a subgroup of PRSA. To join, a PRSA member must work in a public relations agency or firm.) The 1985 *Public Relations Journal* survey did not provide a median salary for the field of public relations or a comparison of salaries by sex.

Between 1986 and 1989, the *Public Relations Journal* surveyed its subscribers regularly, using an insert-poll technique. Respondents were self-selected readers—that is, those who chose to fill out and return the questionnaire. In his description of findings in 1986, Beyer still did not report a median salary for the industry. However, he did cite this comparison by gender: Men typically earned $11,000, or 39% more than women in the sample. There was no mention of what women earned (Beyer, 1986).

For the years 1986, 1988, and 1989, the *Public Relations Journal* reported median salaries for men and women in public relations (see Pollack & Winkleman, 1987; Russell, 1988; Tortorello & Barnes, 1989). Although these averages cannot be compared because they were not based on the random sampling of a population, the figures do illustrate the typical salary gap between men and women. In 1987, men earned a median salary of $48,000, while women earned a median salary of $31,000. The gap between them was $17,000. A year later, men earned a median salary of $50,300; women earned a median salary of $32,900. The gap between men and women had risen slightly to $17,400. In 1989, men earned a median salary of $51,716, and women earned a median salary of $31,993. The gap of $19,723 was even greater. These results are displayed in Table 8.5.

Beginning in 1990, the *Public Relations Journal* conducted its salary survey of subscribers with a systematically drawn random sample. Because

TABLE 8.5. *Public Relations Journal* Surveys of Subscribers

Year	Median salary		Gap
	Men	Women	
Self-selected readers (not representative of PRSA membership)			
1986	Not given	Not given	$11,000
1987	$48,000	$31,000	$17,000
1988	$50,300	$32,900	$17,400
1989	$51,716	$31,993	$19,723
Systematically sampled respondents (representative of PRSA membership)			
1990	$53,637	$35,933	$19,704
1991	$53,977	$37,621	$16,356
1992	$57,776	$39,207	$18,569
1993	$58,477	$39,542	$18,835

Note. The salaries reported here represent the median or midpoint score in a range of scores. That is, half of the salaries reported fall above the middle point and the other half below. Arithmetical averages, or mean scores, rarely are used to report wage information because a few high salaries could artificially inflate the average score.

of this change in sampling techniques, the figures for 1990, 1991, 1992, and 1993 can be compared. Thus, with greater confidence we can state that there was a salary gap between men and women in public relations.

In 1990, men in the sample of *Public Relations Journal* subscribers earned a median salary of $53,637. Women in the sample earned a median salary of $35,933. The gap in salary between them was $19,704 (Jacobson & Tortorello, 1990). In 1991, men in the *Public Relations Journal* survey sample earned a median salary of $53,977; women earned a median salary of $37,621. The gap between men and women shrank to $16,356 (Jacobson & Tortorello, 1991). In 1992, men in the *Public Relations Journal* survey sample earned a median salary of $57,776, while women earned a median salary of $39,207. The gap in their salaries rose to $18,569 (Jacobson & Tortorello, 1992). In 1993, men in the *Public Relations Journal* survey sample earned a median salary of $58,477 and women earned a median salary of $39,542. The gap between men and women in salary at that point was $18,835 (Tortorello & Wilhelm, 1993).

Fluctuations in specific age groups in the *Public Relations Journal* surveys did occur. Researchers were apt to point to these data as signs of narrowing the disparity in earnings. For example, in 1991 Jacobson and

Tortorello reported that the gender gap narrowed because the increase in median salary was higher for women than it was for men. However, in 1992 they reversed their conclusions, noting that the "gender gap widened" (p. 12). A year later, Tortorello and Wilhelm (1993) stated: "While the gender gap persists, there may be a trend toward male–female parity at lower executive levels" (p. 11). However, such a potential trend concerned 1992 and 1993 data only for men and women who worked as account executives in public relations firms—one of three types of organizations for which data were reported. (The other two organizational categories were corporations and government/healthcare/nonprofit.)

One explanation for a shifting gap in salary differences in the *Public Relations Journal* surveys is the change in the gender and age membership of the PRSA. That is, as the association's membership becomes younger and more female, the comparisons made in salaries with the older male members should tend to fluctuate.

In 1991, as members of the glass ceiling research team, we substantiated the gender gap in salaries between female and male PRSA members that has been reported since 1990 in the *Public Relations Journal*. Recall that our survey of nearly 2,785 PRSA members, representing 20% of PRSA's membership, showed a median salary for men in the sample of $55,000 and for women of $37,000. These data represent a gap of $18,000 (Toth & L. Grunig, 1993).

IABC Salary Profiles

Another source of annual salary information on the public relations field has been the International Association of Business Communicators (IABC). This professional association of public relations practitioners was the first of its kind to conduct membership profiles, based on probability samples of its international members. Profile data exist for the years 1985, 1987, and 1989. IABC did not continue this research regularly, but it did conduct a membership survey again in 1997.

IABC's four studies continue to confirm a salary disparity based on gender (see Table 8.6). The first, Profile/85 (as cited in Toth, 1989), reported that the average salary of male IABC members was $40,800 and of female members, $29,600. The gap in salaries between IABC's men and women in 1985 was $11,200. Profile/87 (as cited in Toth, 1989c) established that the average salary of male IABC members was $42,700 and of female members $32,200. The gap in salaries that year was $10,500. Profile/89 (as cited in Toth, 1989c) reported an average salary of $48,000 for men in the sample and $36,000 for women. The gender gap in salaries was

TABLE 8.6. IABC Salary Surveys

	Median Salary		
Year	Men	Women	Gap
Profile/85	$40,800	$29,600	$11,200
Profile/87	$42,700	$32,200	$10,500
Profile/89	$48,000	$36,000	$12,000
Profile/97	$58,261	$48,217	$10,044

$12,000. IABC reported in Profile/97 (*IABC Profile '97*, 1997) that male communicators continued to earn more than their female counterparts. The men's median salary was approximately $58,000. Women's median salary was approximately $48,000, for a gap of about $10,000. We should note that by 1997, IABC reported three women for every male IABC member.

pr reporter Salary Surveys

Yet another source of salary information for public relations professionals has been the annual research of *pr reporter*, a weekly newsletter. As shown in Table 8.7, over a 7-year period the gap in salaries between men and women persisted and gradually widened. In 1985, the median salary for men in the sample was $50,000 and for women $35,000. The gap was $15,000. In 1986, the median salary for men remained $50,000 and for women $35,500; the gap between them was $14,500. In 1987, the median

TABLE 8.7. *pr reporter* Salary Surveys

	Ratio	Median Salary		
Year	M/W	Men	Women	Gap
1985	60/40	$50,000	$35,000	$15,000
1986	56/43	$50,000	$35,500	$14,500
1987	54/45	$50,812	$35,500	$15,312
1988	52/48	$54,250	$37,000	$17,250
1989	51/49	$55,000	$39,000	$16,000
1990	44/56	$54,000	$40,000	$14,000
1991	51/48	$60,000	$42,000	$18,000

Note. Sources "Twenty-First Annual Survey" (1985), "Twenty-Second Annual Survey" (1986), "23rd Annual Survey" (1987), "24th Annual Survey" (1988), "25th Annual Survey" (1989), "26th Annual Survey" (1990), and "27th Annual Survey" (1991).

salary for men rose to $50,812 and stayed the same for women at $35,500. The gap between the sexes rose to $15,312.

In 1988, the median salary for both grew. Men earned, on average, $54,250 and women $37,000. The gap had grown to $17,250. In 1989, the median salary for men was $55,000, the median for women was $39,000, and the gap was $16,000. In 1990, the median salary for men was $54,000 and for women $40,000—a gap of $14,000. In 1991, the median salary for men was $60,000 and for women $42,000; the gap amounted to $18,000. Basically, then, we see a growing chasm between women's and men's average pay.

In 1992, *pr reporter* did not conduct its own salary survey but it did analyze other studies that used diverse measurements. Although its results cannot be compared with previous studies, *pr reporter* continued to find a salary interval between men and women. In an article that made clear that findings pertained to the entire field, *pr reporter* stated that men averaged an annual salary of $45,018 whereas women averaged an annual salary of $39,579. The pay gap was $5,439 ("Overall Salaries Remain Flat," 1992).

From 1985 on, the ratio of males to females shifted to roughly 50/50 for the samples reported. Although other reports on the increasing proportion of women in public relations are above 50%, again *pr reporter* surveyed primarily public relations people involved in supervisory or management activities. The salary disparities reported did not remain stable, with one bright year of a lessening gap in 1990. However, over time, the gap remained or grew, from $15,000 in 1985 to $18,000 in 1991.

The most recent *pr reporter* figures available paint a bleak picture indeed. We do not include the 1998 salary data ("30th survey," 1998) in Table 8.7 because of the significant break between 1991 and 1998. However, the numbers are startling. In 1998, the weekly newsletter reported that men's median salary of $72,000 was a whopping $16,000 greater than the average of $56,000 for women in public relations.

The 441 survey respondents, from Canada and the United States, were 44% male and 54% female. Women represented an even larger proportion of certain employment sectors: ad agencies, insurance, other financial institutions, hospitals and other healthcare operations, higher education, schools, trade and professional associations, not-for-profits, the travel and tourism industry, and high tech. Men were the majority in consultancies (other than advertising agencies), consumer products companies, the industrial sector, utilities, and the federal government.

The pay inequity between women and men was apparent at every age level and for nearly all titles or positions. As a result, *pr reporter* ("30th survey," 1998) concluded, "*It is no longer possible to deny a prejudice here. . . .*" (p. 1).

INTERPRETATIONS OF THE GENDER GAP IN SALARIES

In interpreting this survey information, we have noted several qualifications that have an important bearing on the gender gap in salaries. The most important qualification is that the survey research we presented here represents different populations of public relations practitioners. For example, the U.S. Census reports the salaries of practitioners who categorize themselves as public relations specialists and not others whose titles may have led them to report that their occupations were managerial or administrative—even though they may be responsible for carrying out the public relations function.

Nevertheless, researchers conducting the PRSA, IABC, and *pr reporter* salary surveys concluded most of their reports by suggesting explanations for the gender gap in compensation. Five of the most frequently mentioned explanations are age, years of experience, type of organization in which the practitioner works, roles carried out, and discrimination against women.

Age

The most recent salary statistics available show that women are typically more than 5 years younger than their male counterparts in public relations (Seideman & Leyland, 2000). Since 1985, *pr reporter* has commented on the composition of the public relations work force shifting toward younger, lower paid employees and more women ("23rd Annual Survey," 1987). In 1991, it pointed again to junior women entering the field: "Women predominate in the early years of practice, men at the senior levels" ("27th Annual Survey," 1991, p. 3). In 1998, *pr reporter* headlined an article "Wanted, a few good men—to keep the field reflecting society" ("30th survey," p. 1).

To understand the gender change by age, see Table 8.8. Over a 10-year period, the percentage of women entering public relations only has moved upward when compared with men entering the field. The shift comes in the 35- to 39-year age range, when women are still the majority at 55.5% of the sample. Then men become the majority from the 40- to 49-year age range on up.

With a few exceptions, men earned more money than did women at each age level reported. *pr reporter*'s data indicate exceptions in the 25- to 29-years-of-age group in 1985 (when women earned $2,300 more than men on average); in 1988 (women made $2,200 more than men on average); and in 1990 (women averaged $2,000 more than men). Although the *pr reporter* staff called the 1990 reversal a "small ray of hope" ("26th Annual Survey," 1990), for the upcoming generation of female practitioners

TABLE 8.8. Comparison of Age and Gender reported by *pr reporter*, 1981 and 1991

Age groups	% of total		% men		% women	
(years)	1981	1991	1981	1991	1981	1991
≤ 29	7.9	9	38	17.2	62	81.3
30–34	16	14	49.1	35	50.9	65
35–39	18.4	14	72.4	44.4	27.6	55.6
40–49	26.6	36	74.9	55.5	25.1	44.5
50–59	24.1	18	82.5	66.7	17.5	33.3
60–64	6.8	8	87.2	78.6	12.8	21.4

Note. Sources are "Twenty-First Annual Survey" (1985) and "27th Annual Survey" (1991).

that ray of hope faded. In 1991, women in the under-29 years age group typically made $5,000 less than did men.

Experience

Many researchers have explained the gender gap in salaries between men and women as a function of years of experience in the field rather than age. This explanation suggests that median salaries should rise with years of experience. However, this line of reasoning has not applied to women. A review of years of experience and median salary by gender for the years 1985 and 1991, as published in *pr reporter* and shown in Table 8.9, illustrates that women with the same experience as men continued to earn less. Also, the *Public Relations Journal* surveys from 1989 through 1993 reported a salary gap at every level of experience.

Indeed, men with little experience in public relations, but entering public relations jobs after working in other areas of the organization, actually may inflate the salaries for men with less than 3 years of experience. *pr reporter* ("27th Annual Survey," 1991) asked: "Is this because of the many cases of lawyers, strategic planners & others who are moved into top pr jobs—therefore, entry level because no prior pr experience—are mostly male, and thus skew the M/F ratio here" (p. 3). Finally, current figures from Impulse Research show salary bias even in the most junior positions, where skill and experience are less important (Seideman & Leyland, 2000).

Type of Organization

Another possible explanation for the sex-based salary difference in public relations is the type of organization for which a public relations person

TABLE 8.9. Years of Experience in Public Relations and Gender of *pr reporter* Sample, 1985, 1991

	Median Salary			
	1985		1991	
Years in Public Relations	Men	Women	Men	Women
≤ 3	$36,500	$29,000	$36,316	$27,000
4–5	$43,300	$34,500	$50,000	$33,000
6–9	$47,500	$38,050	$46,000	$39,000
10–14	$53,100	$44,100	$51,000	$44,875
15–19	$58,100	$34,850	$61,389	$50,000
20–29	$60,000	$41,000	$70,000	$58,000
≥ 30	$81,250	—	$75,000	$50,000

Source: "Twenty-First Annual Survey" (1985) and "27th Annual Survey" (1991).

works. Women were thought to choose to work in the kinds of organizations that are relatively low paying, such as religious or charitable organizations and the other nonprofits. Men outnumber women by 26% to 30% in what traditionally have been the best-paying jobs in public relations: corporate. Men also tend to work in the highest paying sectors: financial services, investor relations and mergers and acquisitions, industrial/ manufacturing, public affairs, and crisis communication (Seideman & Leyland, 2000).

This explanation was illustrated in the 1992 *Public Relations Journal* salary survey. As Table 8.10 shows, there was a correlation between the highest paying organizations and gender. Men were slightly more likely to be working in such high-paying spheres as industrial/manufacturing (61/39 ratio of men to women); utilities (57/43 men to women); and scientific/ technical (55/45 men to women). Women in the sample were more likely to be working in lower paying categories such as nonprofits/museums (81/19 ratio of women to men), religious/charitable (65/35 women to men), and miscellaneous services (81/19 women to men).

Consider the change during the next year, 1993. The higher percentage of women working in nonprofits and religious or charitable organizations continued to correlate with lower salaries in the *Public Relations Journal* survey (Tortorello & Wilhelm, 1993). Men continued to outpace women somewhat in the higher paying industrial and manufacturing positions (57/ 43 ratio of men to women there). However, by 1993 women and men were equally represented in public relations counseling firms and slightly ahead of males in utilities (51/49 ratio of women to men).

This reversal of gender and type of organization may reflect the in-

TABLE 8.10. Organizational Type, Median Salary, and Gender

Type of organization	Median salary	% men	% women
Industrial/manufacturing	$61,496	61	39
Utility	54,196	57	43
Scientific/technical	51,791	55	45
Public relations counseling firm	50,216	52	48
Media/communications	48,115	47	53
Financial/insurance	47,300	45	55
Government	43,420	49	51
Solo practitioner	42,845	50	50
Association/foundation	42,841	38	62
Health care	42,424	33	67
Transportation/hotels/resorts/ entertainment	42,136	35	65
Miscellaneous services	41,997	19	81
Education	41,927	54	46
Advertising agency	40,184	54	46
Miscellaneous non-profits/museums	34,409	19	81
Religious/charitable	34,150	35	65
Other	40,032	25	75

Source: Jacobson & Tortorello (1992). Sample of respondents totaled 2,019; of the sample, 47% were men and 53% were women.

creasing number of women across the board in public relations. Or it may be explained in terms of a decrease in the salaries of firms and utilities generally as well as the successful entry of women into formerly "male" jobs. Certainly, there needs to be more research to determine why some organizations continue to hire women primarily while others hire men and women in equal numbers.

Public Relations Roles

A major area of research in public relations has concerned the roles that people in public relations play. In fact, this concept is so central to the story of women and public relations that we devote all of the next chapter to roles. Here, we merely introduce enough of the roles research to help explain the salary gap.

Beginning in 1979 with the Broom and Smith depiction of a five-role typology, the question of what public relations people do has been developed through empirical tests that asked public relations practitioners to report how frequently they perform specific activities. In an initial study of 458 PRSA members, responding to 28 role items, Broom (1982) concluded that there were four main roles: expert prescriber, communication technician, communication facilitator, and problem-solving process facilitator. He found that men and women in public relations differ significantly in the extent to which they play these four roles. At that time, he concluded: "About half of the women see themselves operating primarily in the communication technician role, while more than half of the men report that the expert prescriber is their dominant role" (p. 21).

In 1986, Broom and Dozier published a longitudinal study of these same public relations practitioners. They continued to link gender and roles, finding a continuing pattern of women engaging in the technical activities with greater frequency than did men. Their roles also were linked to salary. Managers earned more than did technicians. Because women were more likely to be technicians, they were more likely to earn less.

> Women play the communication technician role with greater frequency than do men. As a result, segregation in the technician role couples with direct gender discrimination to depress women's salaries. However, women are paid less money than men in every dominant role at both points in time. (p. 54)

In 1995, Dozier and Broom queried 207 PRSA members and found that women increasingly were enacting the manager's role. They became more confident that gender-based salary discrimination and gendered role segregation existed in 1979 than that such discrimination and segregation no longer existed because of the small sample size of their later survey. They did believe that they detected progress and that "the patterns of gender salary discrimination and gender role segregation may be breaking down in public relations work" (p. 17).

Discrimination

There are many definitions of discrimination. We use the concept here to mean an employer's choice to pay women less because they are women. To test this notion—that women are less valued because of their gender alone—survey researchers have compared women and men who are similar in age, experience, type of organization where they work, region of the country, and so forth. Holding all factors equal, if women and men were of the same value to employers, they would earn the same salaries.

In fact, research has shown that when keeping these factors constant, men still make more money than do women in public relations. In the IABC "profile" studies, the gap based on gender alone persisted—although over the 6 years of analysis the gap decreased. Profile/83 reported a compensation gap due to gender alone of $8,100. This was the largest disparity in the 6 years of the series of surveys. Profile/85 reported that gap had shrunk to $6,000. Profile/87 reported a compensation gap attributable to gender of $5,500. Profile/89 showed the gender-based gap to be $5,600 (see Table 8.11). Thus, over time the pay differential based solely on gender does seem to be diminishing.

Current comparisons of salaries by gender show that even with direct comparisons, using specific job titles in specific positions, the numbers expose what *PR Week* called "a distinct discrimination" (Seideman & Leyland, 2000, p. 29). Others have provided a similar analysis of salary earned in public relations on the basis of gender alone (e.g., Dozier, Chapo, & Sullivan, 1983; Turk, 1986b). Childers (1986) found a statistically significant relationship between gender and salary "even after controlling for the effect of role, years in public relations, tenure in present job, participation in organizational decision-making, participation in evaluation research, and type of organization" (as quoted in Hon, L. Grunig, & Dozier, 1992, p. 421). In our 1991 simple random survey of PRSA members, we and our colleagues also concluded that "women are paid considerably less than men at all levels of the occupational role matrix, even after controlling for the influence of variables, such as age and years of experience" (Wright et al., 1991, p. 25).

However, recall that in 1995 Dozier and Broom reversed their previous position on the effects of discrimination. In their longitudinal study of the 207 PRSA members, they did not find a statistically significant relationship between gender and salary after controlling for the influences of professional experience, managerial role enactment, and participation in decision making. They found that "controlling for these influences, women averaged 95 cents for every dollar men make, up from 76 cents in 1979"

TABLE 8.11. Salary Gap Based on Gender Alone

IABC Profile Studies	Gap Based on Gender Alone
1983	$8,100
1985	$6,600
1987	$5,500
1989	$5,600

Source: As cited in Toth & Cline (1989b).

(p. 16). Future research on PRSA members should continue to assess whether this departure from previous findings persists.

In conclusion, then, even salary surveys looking at different groups of public relations practitioners and using different statistical methodology have exposed a compensation gap between women and men in public relations. Several explanations have been offered. They include the entry of women into the field of public relations later than men (thus women are younger and less experienced), the clustering of women in lower paying organizations, and women's work in less lucrative roles. With one exception, when these types of variables are held constant, the disparity in pay persists.

Of course, the numbers do not complete the picture. Beyond the conclusions that are drawn at the end of the quantitative reports, there is little research that has studied in depth why the gap exists in public relations. No studies, for example, have asked employers of public relations staffers why they might assign wages differently. No third-party surveys of public relations salary structures over time, such as in Gerhart's (1990) study of exempt employees' salaries and career tracks, have been conducted. These kinds of studies should be a starting point for determining the real causes of salary differences.

In the meantime, we need to go beyond the salary data and explore how our research participants *perceive* the pay gap. Recall from earlier in this chapter that regardless of which variable we correlated with earnings (type of organization, its location, experience in the field, and so forth), women's income typically remained lower than men's—and often by a significant margin. Here we use both focus group and survey data to flesh out the salary picture by adding our respondents' perceptions of equity and earnings.

In general, Table 8.12 shows, men disagreed and women agreed that women are paid less for doing comparable work in their organizations. However, they agreed that gender-based salary inequity is a problem throughout public relations. Women and men alike were fairly confident that any concerns they may have about pay would be dealt with fairly in their organization, although men were somewhat surer on this question. These perceptions did not change appreciably over the 5 years between the two stages of our longitudinal research.

Few men in our qualitative research challenged the findings related to wage discrepancy. However, one male participant did question the basis on which survey respondents answered. He considered salary discussions unreliable because, in his view, no one knows what anyone else is earning.

At least one man who participated in the focus group research had a

TABLE 8.12. Mean Scores of Salary Issues Broken Down by Gender

Issues	All	Men	Women
1. Generally women receive lower salaries than men for doing comparable public relations work.			
In your organization			
1990	3.74	3.09	4.24
$t = -9.06, p < .001$	(N = 812)	(n = 344)	(n = 460)
1995	3.85	3.08	4.29
$t = -8.41, p < .001$	(N = 661)	(n = 240)	(n = 418)
Throughout PR			
1990	5.39	4.67	5.93
$t = -14.42, p < .001$	(N = 812)	(n = 344)	(n = 460)
1995	5.05	4.36	5.44
$t = -10.38, p < .001$	(N = 661)	(n = 240)	(n = 418)
2. If I have concerns about pay, I know they will be dealt with fairly.			
In your organization			
1990	4.20	4.46	4.02
$t = 3.88, p < .001$	(N = 812)	(n = 344)	(n = 460)
1995	4.18	4.23	4.15
$t = .61, p = < .541$	(N = 661)	(n = 240)	(n = 418)
Throughout PR			
1990	3.79	3.90	3.71
$t = 2.64, p < .05$	(N = 812)	(n = 344)	(n = 460)
1995	3.84	3.96	3.77
$t = 2.51, p < .05$	(N = 661)	(n = 240)	(n = 418)

Note. Responses are coded as follows: 7 = agree very strongly, 6 = strongly agree, 5 = agree, 4 = uncertain/not sure/don't know, 3 = disagree, 2 = strongly disagree, 1 = disagree very strongly.

problem with the different perceptions espoused by male and female survey respondents: "All statistics just bear it out that men make more than women; how do men get off saying, 'Well, I disagree'?" He added that in every situation he has experienced, women make considerably less than their male counterparts—especially in the top tier. He speculated that men's skill in negotiation may account for their edge, "maybe ... because they're out there in the playing field playing hard ball." Another man offered this explanation for the perpetuation of the pattern of salary discrepancy: "I'm up for a job, and I come in asking for $50,000 a year because I'm coming from $45,000; and here's a women who's got the same experience and she's asking for $40,000 because she's coming from $35,000."

We heard a great deal about the relative strengths men and women bring to the salary bargaining table. One factor working against women, in particular, was guilt. One woman said, "They make you feel guilty and greedy and it works probably much better on women." One success factor for men was their willingness to walk if they don't get the raise they demand; another factor was top management's conviction that men indeed will jump ship if necessary. One man who is paid more than two female colleagues, including one partner who is at a higher level in the organization, attributed his success to aggressiveness, a trait he associated with masculinity:

> "I'm more aggressive about getting money, and these two women aren't; they're very passive. . . . performances are basically the same. And the other men in my organization are the same way. We're all pretty aggressive about making more money, and the women are less so."

When the moderator of this focus group asked other members what they thought, one quipped: "I think I need to take some lessons from him." However, most men in that group—albeit reluctantly—did agree that they believe men push harder than women.

These men also talked about what they considered the deeply rooted societal factors that somehow result in women earning less for comparable work. For instance, women either may be drawn to or constrained to work in small, nonprofit organizations (which participants considered the "softer side" of public relations) rather than "hard business and industries." Men believed these one-person or not-for-profit operations simply could not afford to pay more. They also reiterated the refrain that salary equity takes time—years and years, they acknowledged, before women can successfully compete for high pay. As it is, they believe bosses hire women because they are cheaper; women settle because they don't believe they have a choice. As another man expressed it, "They don't feel they can do a damn thing about it."

Another explanation posited for the pay gap was women's choice to become mothers at the expense of their career. Men talked a great deal about the role that family plays in the salary disparity. Some, like an agency executive, spoke from their own experience:

"My wife—different field, advertising—she's doing a job that she is woefully overqualified for; but it's convenient so she's close to home, being able to get her work done within the hours of 9 to 5, and nothing more is required of her."

Another man from the same focus group mentioned a female vice president for one of his city's top-10 agencies. The woman had taken a cut in pay to work 4 days a week so she could spend more time with her son. Others, such as a third man from the same area, spoke more speculatively:

"I wonder how many women leave the field for a while, 32, biological clock ticks, they want to have their children, they have them, they're at home 5 or 6 years 'til the children reach school age. They reenter the field. Now they've been in the business for 16 years but they haven't been at work in the environment for 6 of those 16, and they come in as supervisor, and their male counterpart who has stayed in there for the 6 years has reached some other level and . . . is paid considerably more and reaches VP."

(This scenario was challenged by another member of the group, who interjected that in his organization women more typically stay home with children for 12 weeks than for 6 years.)

Finally, men reasoned that women in public relations work for less in part because they want different things from their job than do men. For example, one man cited women's concern for a better health care package and a better work environment. He also figured women prefer what he called "nondestructive" organizations such as the American Red Cross. Of course, much of what we heard as part of this discussion was speculation since, as one man reminded his group, "salaries have been so confidential."

Then, too, these explanations resulted almost entirely from focus group moderators *probing*. The large and undeniable salary gap seemed to baffle most male participants in the group discussions. This was especially hard to understand in light of what some flagged as the profession's effort to ensure parity in pay scales. But, as one man said, "$55,000 [for men] and $44,000 for women is hard for me to believe." Whether or not they could explain it, most of his colleagues agreed when one said that a $15,000 disparity is "a shameful reality of our industry that needs to be addressed."

One major problem with the salary gap for women is the concomitant devaluation as people that they may feel. One woman characterized the large gift certificate she received in lieu of fair compensation as "throwing me a bone." She explained: "I don't feel that the company's saying, 'You're a valued employee,' so it's a mixed message."

WHY IS THE SALARY GAP SUCH A CRITICAL ISSUE?

One measure of the worth of an occupation, as well as the worth of its individual workers, is its salaries. Perhaps this should not be the case. Some would argue that teaching and the ministry are highly valued yet poorly paid. Nevertheless, it is an important feature of our culture. Because a lessening of worth can be tied to salaries, esteem or perceived value becomes an issue in salary discrepancies. But, if the gender gap can be explained, the occupation may remain valued.

Of additional importance to women in public relations are the explanations themselves. If age, experience, role, and type of organization are the arguments for less pay, these need to be tested against women's real opportunities to enter public relations at the same salary as men and ultimately to obtain experience and to enact the managerial role.

Our analysis of role enactment (Toth & L. Grunig, 1993) concluded that women who report carrying out managerial activities also continue to do technical activities—and still for less money. This finding calls for a clearer understanding of how employers of public relations people place a monetary value on what public relations people do.

A second, related study came to similar conclusions. For her graduate thesis, Kucera (1994) set out to answer what she called a "deceptively simple" (p. 155) question: why female managers of public relations tend to fulfill both the managerial and technical roles. Through focus group research and a subsequent survey of female PRSA members working in a host of different industries, Kucera reestablished that women do indeed fulfill this dual role. Almost all of the women she studied—a whopping 95%—were managers who regularly took on significant technical responsibilities at the same time.

Why? Participants in Kucera's (1994) research indicated that they "do it all" primarily to prove themselves equal to their male counterparts in the eyes of their superiors. This compulsion, they said, was based not on organizational demands made explicit but on implicit pressure to establish that women are capable to getting the job done—whatever it takes. They believed that if they worked only as hard as their male colleagues, they would be perceived as less valuable. Kucera figured that these women were given little choice: "Do the same thing as a man and get a great deal less for it, or do more than a man and get somewhat less for it" (p. 170). She concluded that women's individual behavior within their organizations was deeply and negatively affected by what they perceived as the climate of the organization. Thus we find support in this thesis for an approach we develop at some length later in the book: the need for *organizations* to change if they want to encourage excellence in public relations through the empowerment of their female staffers.

Discussing the gender gap will not lead to a lesser valued occupation. However, other fields that have become female-intensive or even female-dominated have experienced a drop in salaries. Rather than explain away the salary gap, it should be our task to expose it and to seek to clarify what the value of public relations is to society. Otherwise, the field faces what *PR Week* predicted as "potential for friction and decay" (Seideman & Leyland, 2000, p. 31). Commenting on salaries, Professor Clarke Caywood recommended that the industry focus on closing the gap. He called the pay discrepancy "unconscionable" and reminded us that "it's bad for all of us" (as quoted in Seideman & Leyland, 2000, p. 31).

Chapter Nine

Public Relations Roles

To understand the gender gap in communication management, we began by looking at the research on public relations roles. We introduced this important strain of inquiry in Chapters 4 and 7. Here, we go beyond our historical account of more than 20 years of scholarship to present relevant findings from the latest glass ceiling research. The study of roles helps to explain the salary gap, explored at considerable length in the previous chapter. In addition to determining what roles women and men typically enact in our field, this chapter delineates any differences in management style or ability that our research participants attributed to gender.

From its inception, roles research has chronicled what public relations people do, primarily based on a set of role categories. These categories were developed through an examination of secondary literature and empirical tests that asked public relations practitioners to report on how frequently they perform specific activities (Broom & Smith, 1979).

In a 1982 study of 458 PRSA members, who responded to 28 role items, Broom concluded that there were four major roles: expert prescriber, communication facilitator, problem-solving process facilitator, and communication technician. He defined these roles as follows:

> *Expert Prescriber*: In this role, the practitioner operates as the authority on both public relations problems and their solutions. The client, or management, is often content to leave public relations in the hands of the "expert" and to assume a relatively passive role. The practitioner researches and defines the problem, develops the program and takes major responsibility for its implementation.

Communication Facilitator: This role casts the practitioner as a sensitive "go-between" or information broker. The practitioner serves as a liaison, interpreter and mediator between the organization and its publics. The emphasis is on maintaining a continuous flow of two-way communication. Another concern is with removing barriers to the exchange of information to keep the channels of communication open.

Problem-Solving Process Facilitator: As members of the management team, practitioners operating in this role collaborate with others throughout the organization to define and solve problems. The public relations practitioner helps guide other managers and the organization through a rational problem-solving process that may involve all parts of the organization in the public relations planning and programming process. Likewise, the practitioner maintains a high level of management involvement in implementing all phases of the program.

Communication Technician: Practitioners operating in this role provide their organization or client with the specialized skills needed to carry out public relations programs. As their job description indicates, these practitioners are typically hired on the basis of their communication and journalistic skills— writing, editing and working with the media. Rather than being part of the management team, practitioners in this role are primarily concerned with preparing and producing communication material for the public relations effort. (p. 18)

At that time, Broom (1982) found that men and women differed significantly in terms of which roles they saw themselves performing. About half of the women saw themselves as communication technicians, whereas more than half of the men considered the expert prescriber their dominant role. Broom believed this difference could not be accounted for by variations in age or experience. Instead, he speculated:

It appears that even though both men and women are hired initially for their communication and journalistic skills, women tend to stay in the communication technician role to a greater extent than their male counterparts. Four out of five men in PRSA have expanded their roles to that of public relations experts and facilitators of communication and problem-solving. On the other hand, only half of the women participate in these management-level public relations counseling and problem-solving functions as part of their primary roles. (p. 21)

Most influential of the research that focused on the four-role typology was the longitudinal study by Broom and Dozier published in 1986. They prefaced their conclusions by stating that "a practitioner plays all four roles in varying degrees" (p. 39). However, they chose to report on the dominant role of each respondent, that is, the one role played with greatest frequency. Based on this choice they found that in the same group of PRSA members surveyed earlier, there was a continuing pattern of women engaging in technical activities with greater frequency than did men.

By 1992, Dozier was arguing for a reduction of the four roles into two major roles, "the manager–technician" typology, based on a series of studies that found these two to be empirically and conceptually distinct whereas the expert prescriber, communication liaison, and problem-solving process facilitator roles were not. He urged us to use the manager–technician typology because it provides "a parsimonious way to operationalize roles and test relations with antecedent and consequential constructs" (p. 334).

Although this argument for empirical parsimony helps link public relations roles to excellent public relations practice, it disadvantages our thinking about the complexity of public relations and how we view women in the field. Broom and Dozier's studies promoted a worldview of a two-tier career ladder in public relations wherein public relations practitioners ascend from the technician to the managerial role. Still, their research has contributed profoundly to our understanding of gender and the glass ceiling because they established that "changing from the technician role to the predominately managerial role is a transition biased in favor of male practitioners" (1986, p. 55).

EVOLUTION OR MORE COMPLEX PREDICTORS IN EVIDENCE?

In 1995, Dozier and Broom conducted a comparative analysis of PRSA members with Broom's (1982) 1979 sample. They used the same role activities. They reached slightly more than 200 PRSA members, for a response rate of 54%. They reported "an evolution of public relations practices away from systemic patterns of gender discrimination in roles and salaries documented in the 1979 study" (p. 14). Rather than finding a significant link between gender and role, they determined that professional experience explained better whether a public relations practitioner was a manager or a technician:

> Among men practitioners in 1991, 55% enact the manager role predominantly, virtually unchanged from the 57% of men enacting the manager role predominantly in 1979. Among women practitioners in 1991, 39% enact the manager role predominantly, up eleven points from 28% in 1979. Although men in the sample are more likely to enact the manager role predominantly

than women in the sample, the gender gap in role enactment has shrunk since 1979. (Dozier & Broom, 1995, p. 14)

Dozier and Broom (1995) qualified their evolutionary conclusion by noting the possibility of error because of small sample size. They also acknowledged that they were only able to generalize their findings to members of PRSA, an organization constituting a small fraction of the labor force in public relations. However, their study was significant in concluding that there was a crack in the glass ceiling in public relations because professional experience had become a more powerful predictor than gender of managerial role.

Although no research since 1995 has confirmed the Dozier and Broom conclusion that professional experience and not gender leads to managerial jobs in public relations, the first phase of the glass ceiling study (Wright et al., 1991) exposed more complex relationships between gender and roles than years of professional experience.

Our conclusion may be attributable in part to our using somewhat different items to measure public relations roles. Our analysis of this set of 17 role activities confirmed the existence of the same two dimensions— manager and technician—that Broom and Dozier had identified. However, we also found that the two major roles are not mutually exclusive. Significantly, we reported that gender predicts differences in eight of the 17 role measures. This is how we phrased our results:

> Findings indicate that women are more likely than men to plan public relations programs; write, edit, and produce public relations messages; implement new programs; and carry out decisions made by others. Men are significantly more likely than women to be involved in counseling management and somewhat more likely to make communication policy decisions and to conduct and analyze research. (Wright et al., 1991, p. 24)

At the same time, we (Wright et al., 1991) concluded that "gender appears to be considerably less significant in influencing a practitioner's occupational role. The number of years working in the field and whether or not a practitioner holds PRSA accreditation are more strongly associated with role than gender" (p. 25).

However, in a reanalysis of our original data set, we (Toth & L. Grunig, 1993) found that the failure to promote women derives not only from gender and years of professional experience, but from differences in their on-the-job experience in public relations. Although female managers in public relations perform managerial tasks, they continue to perform the technical tasks too. In a sense, women are "doing it all."

We based this conclusion on a factor analysis of the 17 role activities of the initial glass ceiling research. However, we did not stop at reporting only the highest factor loadings, as had Dozier and Broom (1995) and our own earlier studies (Wright et al., 1991). We set .20 as the point at which items no longer accounted for enough of the variance to warrant discussion. We based this position on Broom and Dozier's 1990 research textbook, *Using Research in Public Relations: Applications to Program Management*. With this statistical approach, we found that women are doing more activities associated with the managerial dimension than previously had been established.

We ended up speculating that organizations may be lowering the importance they place on women in management by adding on the technical activities as well. Alternatively, women might be choosing to retain their entry-level tasks even when permitted to advance into management because they lack the confidence to leave those duties behind. This reflects the "impostor syndrome." Women may not perceive themselves as fitting into the managerial role because that role was defined by and for men. Women who become managers yet feel like impostors at that level may counter the stress of being an outsider by holding onto the technical tasks they feel more psychologically secure in doing.

COUNTERPOINTS ON ROLES AND THE GLASS CEILING

In additional to Broom and Dozier's program of research on roles, other studies have provided alternative or complementary explanations for women's barriers to advancement in public relations. They include career longevity, shifting samples, roles in process, a false dichotomy, out-of-date categories, and encroachment.

Career Longevity

Few roles studies have questioned why women in public relations typically have fewer years of experience than men. In spite of the growing feminization of public relations, women and men in the field have not reported parallel increases in average years of professional experience. Dozier and Broom (1995) found that in 1979 and in 1991, men maintained on average about the same number of years of experience, 16.1 and 16.9 years, respectively. Women's experience increased on average from 9.9 to 11 years over that same 12-year span.

One key assumption has been that as years of experience increase, so too will job authority. However, over the period of the Dozier and Broom research, neither men nor women gained significantly in professional experience. So, we are forced to consider an alternative assumption: Men reach higher level managerial roles without investing more time in the field than do women.

Shifting Samples

There has been a gender shift in the membership of PRSA, the most widely sampled population of public relations practitioners in the United States. This switch from a male to a female majority could signal a concomitant change in the proportion of female to male managers. Dozier and Broom (1995) reported no gender breakdown of their 207 PRSA members. Broom's 1979 findings were based on a sample of 28% women and 72% men (1982). Our (Toth & L. Grunig, 1993) reanalysis of the initial Wright et al. (1991) data established a gender breakdown of PRSA members that was 58% female and 42% percent male. The glass ceiling study follow-up in 1995 identified 63.5% of the same population as female and 36.5% as male.

Roles in Process

Hugh M. Culbertson (1991) proposed taking apart the concept of role categories. He wanted to observe the interaction between public relations people and their environment, as opposed to asking for self-reported information, to describe what public relations people actually do. He argued for further research that focused on "role tightness or looseness and role-making" (p. 62). For example, with respect to the Broom and Dozier (1982) roles research, Culbertson hypothesized that "communication technician roles are highly codified and repetitive—hence tightly defined" (p. 54). He explained that communication managers must create more diverse roles because there are many functions of the organization that require what he called "role-making."

False Dichotomy

Pamela J. Creedon (1991) argued against what she considered a false dichotomy created by discussing the two dominant roles for public relations practitioners. She believed that the emphasis on two discrete roles has led to a "hierarchy of two seemingly dissimilar roles—the manager who decides policy and the technician who implements 'his' policies" (p. 79). She offered a counterperspective: "Some technicians process information, some produce creative products, and some manage the process as well as produce the product" (p. 78). She cited research (e.g., Johnson & Acharya, 1982) suggesting an overlap between roles: Women participate in decision making, considered a managerial activity, but at a lower level than do men. She also summarized research indicating that decision-making activity exists in other "apparently nonmanagerial categories, variously described as linking, liaison, or information-processor role" (p. 71).

Overlapping Roles

An overlap in public relations roles has been reported when researchers used role inventories other than those established by Broom (1982; Broom & Smith, 1979). For example, Mary Ann Ferguson (1987) developed a set of 45 public relations behaviors from secondary analyses of IABC data. She found through factor analysis four roles, representing problem-solving management activities, journalism/technical communication, research, and staff management. Later on, we (Toth & L. Grunig, 1993; Toth, Serini, Wright, & Emig, 1998a, 1998b) documented a different kind of overlap—this time between the managerial and technical profiles based on Wright et al.'s (1991) 17 role activities. We will explain this overlap in more detail later in this chapter.

Encroachment

Lauzen (1990a) reported that such variables as gender of the practitioner, years of experience, practitioner competencies, and role would influence the degree to which a non-public relations professional would come to manage the public relations function. She called this "professional encroachment," a concept we explored in depth in Chapter 7. Dozier (1988) noted that "encroachment is aggravated by feminine stereotypes, which work to keep women practitioners out of the manager role and management decision-making" (p. 9).

  Lauzen (1990a) relied on the public relations role items developed by Broom (1982) to examine managerial competencies and encroachment. She surveyed 166 public relations managers chosen from *O'Dwyer's Directory of Corporate Communicators*. She reported:

> When the top practitioner in an organization is a woman, she will have fewer years of experience than a male in the same position. As a result, the female top practitioner is likely to possess fewer manager competencies and is less

likely to enact the manager role predominantly. As a result, encroachment is more likely to occur. (p. 11)

Thus Lauzen's findings suggest that although women may want to advance to management positions in public relations, their way may be blocked by organizations filling these positions with others deemed more highly competent to do the job. That is, they encounter the ubiquitous glass ceiling.

THE GLASS CEILING RESEARCH

The glass ceiling study commissioned by PRSA reported trend data on its members between 1990 and 1995. The Appendix describes how we conceptualized and conducted the research. In Chapter 8, we compared our most recent salary data with results of previous studies of gender and pay. In this chapter, we report on the answers to additional questions related to the roles that speak to women's and men's experiences in public relations.

Demographic Trends

Both glass ceiling audits encompass some of the largest national samples of public relations practitioners ever collected. In 1990, 1,027 people participated in the survey; this represents a response rate of 37%. In 1995, there were 678 participants, for a response rate of 45%.

Between 1990 and 1995, the gender makeup of the samples grew increasingly female. In 1990, the percentage of female respondents sampled was 42%; in 1995, this had increased to 63.5%. (See Table 8.1 in Chapter 8, which shows these and other demographic data.) The percentages in general mirror U.S. Census data, which reported a 41/59 ratio of male to female workers in 1989 (Lukovitz, 1989) and a 37/63 ratio of male to female public relations specialists in 1994 (U.S. Bureau of the Census, 1995). The median age of men and women in the 1990 and 1995 samples stayed the same: Men averaged 45 years of age; women averaged 35 years of age.

Between 1990 and 1995, the average professional experience reported by women increased from 8 to 11 years. The average experience for men stayed at 17 years. These averages are comparable to the 1995 Dozier and Broom sample we discussed earlier in this chapter.

The ethnicity of the overwhelming majority of PRSA's members was white. Although we did not study ethnicity in the initial 1990 phase of the glass ceiling project, the 1995 sample yielded a mere 6% of respondents who identified themselves as an ethnicity other than white.

Between 1990 and 1995, there was no change in the $55,000 median salary for the men surveyed. For women over the 5-year span, median salary increased by $3,000 to $40,000. There was a $15,000 difference in median salaries between the men and women polled in 1995. (Refer to Chapter 8 for a more thorough discussion of this salary gap.)

The type of organizations employing these public relations professionals shifted. As indicated in Table 8.2 in Chapter 8, between 1990 and 1995, staffers of both genders left counseling firms and corporations. In 1995, 5% fewer men and 3% fewer women were working in firms. In 1995, 10% fewer male and 7% fewer female practitioners were working in corporations. There was an increase of 4% for men reporting jobs in educational institutions. The largest increases were in the "other" category. In 1995, 9% of the men checked the "other" category, while 14% of the women chose the "other" category. We speculate that these practitioners were now self-employed as consultants or freelancers.

Changes in Roles

Based on our review of the theoretical literature and previous empirical research by others, we hypothesized that roles would change over time and that professional experience as a predictor of managerial role enactment must be explained more definitively than by number of years of seasoning alone. By the second stage of this longitudinal project, the research questions guiding our study of public relations roles became the following:

- How have the reported roles of men and women in public relations changed between 1990 and 1995?
- Are women and men receiving professional experience on the job that prepares them for more advanced managerial assignments? (Toth et al., 1998a, p. 149)

In both our 1990 and 1995 factor analyses of the roles data, the results validated the manager and technician role profiles first proposed by Dozier in 1992. We also found that public relations practitioners tend to carry out both managerial and technical tasks. However, by 1995, a third role type emerged. We call it the "agency" type. Further, there were shifts in role activities over time for all respondents, as well as differences between women and men. We will discuss these shifts for each role and then discuss how they could affect the gender gap in promotion. We begin, however, with insights gleaned from focus groups around the country conducted in the mid-1990s.

In general, participants in our group discussions agreed on what it means to be a manager in public relations. They emphasized such qualities as challenging and motivating people, teaching them, mentoring, getting subordinates to stretch and become "all they can be," understanding others, rallying support, collaborating, having a vision, and being able to do it all: accounting, budgeting, technical designing, planning, strategic thinking, processing and synthesizing information, setting goals, and so forth. All of these traits and competencies should breed trust. Focus group members, male and female, agreed that "people skills" are paramount. The sense of most participants is echoed in these words of one man: "These attributes, good manager and bad manager, cut across the broad swath of men and women."

Diplomacy was a key skill mentioned by several participants— shuttling throughout the organization to bring people together and work toward the same vision. One man expressed the view of several of his colleagues of both sexes when he asserted: "I don't see gender issues. You either possess those qualities of vision and leadership, or you don't." The effective manager, to many of our group members, not only thinks about the public relations aspect of the job but looks beyond that to his or her impact on all corporate decisions.

Desire—rather than gender—is what separates the manager from the technician, at least in the opinion of one male respondent. Creativity is what keeps many technicians in that role, even when their organizations need them to become managers. We found it interesting that to members of one focus group, "creative" people were perceived as different from "idea" people, whom they considered management material. When the discussion turned to women making the transition from technician to manager, participants credited that promotion more to companies' recognizing the value of public relations than to either the managerial ability of the women or any advantage they enjoyed because of affirmative action. Several participants said they believed the field had gained significantly in credibility over the last 5 years, largely because public relations increasingly provides quantifiable, bottom-line results for clients, top managers, and CFOs.

Because our focus group participants largely agreed on the tasks that are common to public relations managers, they stressed the importance of what many considered "huge" differences in style. Most of the men we talked with perceived a discrepancy between male and female managerial styles. However, few were specific about those distinctions. More typical than a discussion of concrete contrasts was the following sentiment: "I just think there are differences in gender, period, end of story."

At the same time, of course, male participants in the focus groups acknowledged exceptions to the generalizations. One man, who had worked for two vice presidents of public relations—one male, one female—said that the woman was more competitive, cut-throat, and cavalier, and less team-oriented. The male manager embraced what he considered a very feminine managerial style. His ideal would be working for a manager who blended traditional male and female roles. Another man admitted that when "I run across a woman who is particularly successful, she would operate in what I would define as in a man's way." By contrast, to him the average female manager is likely to say, " 'Would you mind doing this for me?' when what she's really saying to you is, 'This needs to be done by the end of the day.' "

Patterns in men's comments about different managerial style accentuated women's perceived insecurity and weakness as decision makers. These problems mean that, in one participant's words, "I'm too often dealing with their egos and their personalities instead of . . . business decisions." He cited this scenario:

> "It's a very personal thing when you tear a newsletter up and say, 'Hey, let's do it again.' . . . it just freaks them out, and now they're angry at you, and they have an issue with you instead of going, 'Gee, he's a better writer than I am, and I can learn something from this experience.' Which is what I find happens with men more often; they're more secure."

Another man apologized for sounding sexist but went on to make the point that women he has worked for are more thin-skinned, "more alert to perceived slights or resistance." He attributed this to "their history." He also believed female managers have trouble compromising because they consider that "normal give and take" a challenge to their authority or their ability to run the operation. On the other hand, he preferred having women than men work for him: "In my experience, women who have worked for me, in general, have been in many ways harder working, easier to supervise, easier to convince that something needs to be done."

Men explained difficulties for women in terms of their being pushed into positions before they are ready. The sad result, to at least one participant, is that "now they're really all over the place, because they have more responsibilities than they can handle, because they haven't fully learned the gamut of all the technical things they need to know." At the same time, men acknowledged the pluses associated with what they consider women's managerial style: their "people orientation," sensitivity, intuitiveness, ethics, social responsibility, and willingness to communicate (which they emphasized as listening to others and building on what was said).

Other major differences in the way men perceive female versus male managers may be positive or negative. Several of our male participants agreed that women tend to see gray rather than the black and white of the bottom line in management. One man explained, "We're trying to establish that balance between bottom line versus social welfare." Men also credited women with being less aggressive and competitive than men. One man considered women successful as managers because they bring process to public relations, a field he considered "not a process kind of business." Men in his view are less process-oriented: "Men are fixers. They tend to jump in, get the tool box out, and do what they need to do." Despite his crediting women with managerial effectiveness, we have to question whether he really built a good argument for their qualifications.

Men who did not perceive gender-based differences in managerial style explained any differences that may exist in terms of the individual manager and his or her level of management. As one man pointed out, the top people in his hospital are men whereas 80% of the staff at the lower levels of management are women. He saw a distinct difference in managerial style between top and middle management, rather than between the sexes. One of the most thoughtful remarks about management style came from a man who said he hoped leadership manner is based more on individuals than on gender, but he remembered a time when his department was hiring: "I was really lobbying for another male and so now I start thinking about . . . why was I doing that if I didn't feel that there was some difference?"

As a result of perceived differences, several men we spoke with understood that men are more comfortable working with other men than with women in management positions—especially as public relations increasingly fills a counseling and strategic role. As one male participant put it, "Men will look for their own style of leadership to fit into the new role." When the moderator asked if the same would be true for women—that a woman at the decision-making table would be more comfortable promoting another woman for the same reason—participants offered an interesting reversal. At least one man believed that a female CEO, for example, would have enough authority not to have to "prove anything" and so she would not necessarily bring in another women. In fact, he said, "she might try and do just the opposite."

Finally, just as we have reiterated the concept of requisite variety throughout this book, so too did our focus group participants allude to a "male perspective" on management. In so doing, they underscored the importance of different perspectives as managers go about their work as strategic thinkers and decision makers.

The Managerial Profile

From the 1990 data, we (Toth & L. Grunig, 1993) reported that the activities loading highest on the managerial factor were roughly the same for women and men: counseling management, making communication policy decisions, evaluating program results, supervising the work of others, planning and managing budgets, planning public relations programs, and meeting clients and executives. The 1990 women's managerial factor included one additional activity, that of managing public relations programs. However, female managers did more technical tasks than did their male counterparts.

The 1995 data show a dramatic decline in the number of activities with high loadings on the managerial factor. For both men's and women's managerial profiles, only two role activities load at or above .60: planning and managing public relations programs. The managerial profile for men that year includes one additional activity: making communication policy decisions (see Tables 9.1 and 9.2).

Between 1990 and 1995, women in the managerial profile reported essentially the same role activities. However, the two activities loading below the .20 cutoff changed. In 1990, the women did not disseminate messages or write, edit, and produce messages to any extent. However, in 1995 the women reported a significant level of activity in these areas. The two items that dropped out are "meeting with peers" and "implementing the decisions of others."

The managerial activities reported by women in the 1995 sample were more sharply defined than those in the 1990 sample. That is, in 1990 women reported eight activities integral to their managerial profile: planning and managing budgets; making communication policy decisions; supervising the work of others; counseling management; managing public relations programs; planning public relations programs; meeting with clients/ executives; and evaluating program results.

By 1995, women's managerial profile included only two activities loading above .60: planning and managing public relations programs. At that point, a second tier of three management activities loaded between .53 and .43. They were implementing new programs, making communication policy decisions, and planning and managing budgets. Six activities were concentrated in the range of factor loadings between .30 and .39, indicating that these items were not central to the managerial profile. However, in this third tier were several of the senior-level activities with high factor scores in 1990: meeting with clients/executives, counseling management, supervising the work of others, and conducting and analyzing research.

TABLE 9.1. Trends in Women's Roles, 1990, 1995

Factor 1: Managerial activities for women[a]

1990

Planning and managing budgets	.76
Making communication policy decisions	.76
Supervising the work of others	.75
Counseling management	.72
Managing public relations programs	.71
Planning public relations programs	.69
Meeting with clients/executives	.67
Evaluating program results	.65
Implementing new programs	.50
Meeting peers	.45
Conducting or analyzing research	.43
Implementing event planning/logistics	.31
Making media contacts	.24
Handling correspondence/telephone calls	.21
Implementing the decisions of others	.21
Disseminating messages	.14
Writing, editing, producing messages	−.01

1995

Planning public relations programs	.81
Managing public relations programs	.80
Implementing new programs	.53
Making communication policy decisions	.46
Planning and managing budgets	.43
Making media contacts	.39
Meeting with clients/executives	.38
Evaluating program results	.37
Implementing event planning/logistics	.37
Counseling management	.36
Supervising the work of others	.35
Handling correspondence/telephone calls	.28
Disseminating messages	.24
Conducting or analyzing research	.21
Writing, editing, producing messages	.20
Meeting with peers	.19
Implementing the decisions of others	.10

Factor 2: Technical Activities for Women

1990

Implementing decisions made by others	.81
Writing, editing, producing messages	.80
Disseminating messages	.78
Handling correspondence/telephone calls	.69
Implementing event planning/logistics	.64

(*continued on next page*)

TABLE 9.1. *continued*

Making media contacts	.64
Implementing new programs	.63
Meeting with peers	.61
Planning public relations programs	.45
Evaluating program results	.40
Managing public relations programs	.36
Conducting or analyzing research	.32
Meeting with clients/executives	.26
Making communication policy decisions	.18
Planning and managing budgets	.16
Supervising the work of others	.02
Counseling management	−.10

<u>1995</u>

Disseminating messages	.81
Writing, editing, producing messages	.80
Implementing decisions made by others	.54
Making media contacts	.49
Implementing new programs	.45
Handling correspondence/telephone calls	.41
Implementing event planning/logistics	.35
Managing public relations programs	.30
Meeting with peers	.28
Planning public relations programs	.24
Making communication policy decisions	.24
Evaluating program results	.21
Conducting or analyzing research	.14
Meeting with clients/executives	.12
Planning and managing budgets	.11
Counseling management	.03
Supervising the work of others	.01

[a] Eigenvalues for the women's managerial profile in 1990 and 1995 were 7.37 and 7.11, respectively.
[b] Eigenvalues for the women's technical profile in 1990 and 1995 were 2.27 and 1.54, respectively.

For men in the 1995 audit, as Table 9.2 shows, the second tier of activities below the most significant level of .60—those between .53 and .47—was less robust than in 1990 but still held higher scores than those of the women's managerial profile. For men, these activities were counseling management, which had been the highest loading activity for men in the 1990 sample; implementing new programs; planning and managing budgets; and implementing event planning/logistics.

Overall, the managerial profile continued to show women carrying out all but two of the 17 activities to some degree. The activities to drop out

TABLE 9.2. Trends in Men's Roles, 1990, 1995

Factor 1: Managerial activities for men[a]

1990

Counseling management	.80
Making communication policy decisions	.77
Evaluating program results	.74
Supervising the work of others	.73
Planning and managing budgets	.73
Planning public relations programs	.70
Meeting with clients/executives	.64
Managing public relations programs	.58
Implementing new programs	.53
Conducting or analyzing research	.53
Meeting peers	.51
Handling correspondence/telephone calls	.35
Implementing event planning/logistics	.32
Disseminating messages	.15
Implementing the decisions of others	.15
Making media contacts	.14
Writing, editing, producing messages	.08

1995

Planning public relations programs	.78
Managing public relations programs	.74
Making communication policy decisions	.60
Counseling management	.53
Implementing new programs	.53
Planning and managing budgets	.48
Implementing event planning/logistics	.47
Evaluating program results	.39
Supervising the work of others	.38
Meeting with clients/executives	.35
Making media contacts	.33
Conducting or analyzing research	.27
Disseminating messages	.21
Handling correspondence/telephone calls	.22
Writing, editing, producing messages	.16
Meeting with peers	.15
Implementing the decisions of others	.06

Factor 2: Technical activities for men[b]

1990

Writing, editing, producing messages	.82
Disseminating messages	.82
Implementing decisions made by others	.76
Making media contacts	.75
Handling correspondence/telephone calls	.64

(*continued on next page*)

TABLE 9.2. (*continued*)

Implementing event planning/logistics	.63
Implementing new programs	.60
Managing public relations programs	.56
Meeting with peers	.48
Planning public relations programs	.44
Meeting with clients/executives	.38
Planning and managing budgets	.29
Evaluating program results	.24
Making communication policy decisions	.22
Supervising the work of others	.10
Counseling management	.09
Conducting or analyzing research	.06

1995

Disseminating messages	.84
Writing, editing, producing messages	.82
Making media contacts	.53
Handling correspondence/telephone calls	.50
Implementing event planning/logistics	.43
Implementing the decisions made by others	.41
Implementing new programs	.36
Managing public relations programs	.34
Planning and managing budgets	.32
Planning public relations programs	.24
Meeting with peers	.20
Making communication policy decisions	.19
Evaluating program results	.14
Meeting with clients/executives	.11
Conducting or analyzing research	.11
Supervising the work of others	.02
Counseling management	−.11

[a] Eigenvalues for the men's managerial profile in 1990 and 1995 were 7.98 and 7.10, respectively.
[b] Eigenvalues for the men's technical profile in 1990 and 1995 were 1.94 and 1.67, respectively.

changed to those involving others (meeting with peers and implementing the decisions of others). Instead, female managers seemed to be doing more writing, editing, and producing of messages.

The men's managerial profile shifted toward their doing more editorial work, but still with fewer such activities than reported by female managers. In 1990, four activities had such low factor loadings as to be insignificant: disseminating messages; implementing the decisions of others; making media contacts; and writing, editing, and producing messages. In 1995, there were three. Writing, editing, and producing messages and implementing the decisions of others continued to have low factor loadings. Disseminating messages and making media contacts became more a part of the managerial profile. Meeting with peers dropped out.

In short, the men and women we sampled seemed to have lost ground in terms of the level of functions for which they were responsible. To take just two indicators, notice how the scores for counseling management and making policy decisions dropped for women and men alike.

Several of the men reacting to these statistics in a 1995 focus group attributed the gender differences to biology. More specifically, they believed at least some women turned down management opportunities to have families. One man said: "I've had babies, babies, babies all over the place and the work is being shifted around. People are taking second thoughts about applying for positions that open because [they] might have more responsibility." Some in the group agreed that professional women react to motherhood in highly individualistic ways. One man put it this way: "I've seen some women who will not want to go to the next level because they want to have a baby next year. I also know of women who rush back from maternity leave to get back to work, to get on with their life. And that's totally . . . who they are." However, the majority opinion was expressed this way:

> "In my office right now two individuals are going through having babies in the last couple of years and I find them, the females in our office, being more reluctant to take on those managerial roles knowing that they're not going to be in the office, that they're going to have more responsibilities at home."

Later in the discussion, that same man pointed out an inconsistency in his thinking. We belabor this because we believe his ambivalence or confusion may be shared by other men doing public relations. He had agreed that leadership was an individual, rather than a gender-based, characteristic. However, he heard himself saying that even women who seemed driven to lead, to accept the managerial role in public relations, failed to do so because of what he called "social issues" related to home and family and organizational issues that include "a little bias."

Even acknowledging the societal and organizational pressures that may work to keep qualified women out of management, this same man expressed unhappiness over what he considered the result of working with young mothers:

> "I certainly have frustration with this. I don't express it to them, but internally I'm going, 'God, you know, I'm picking up the slack.' Six

months off of work, 5 months off of work, and I'm deluged. I can barely get done what I'm trained to do. . . . I'm glad there are more women in the profession, but for me, it's like, 'Can you bring some other people in?' "

Men in his group agreed that although several are angry inside, they (1) do not express that resentment and (2) admit that family responsibilities affect women's progress.

How did women analyze these same statistics? To many, having a family often was incompatible with corporate life at the managerial level. Many with children left for a career in freelancing, which they said "men perceive to be a step backward." By contrast, they saw freelance consulting as an opportunity—one that makes public relations attractive to them as a flexible field. Women who create their own companies enjoy what one woman called "a sense of freedom."

Women also talked about how the situation had changed over time. Several years ago, they agreed, women downplayed the fact that they had children. They explained absences from work because of their child's sickness in some other way. Today, more women feel confident about explaining why they're headed for home. The reason, according to one woman, is that more women are in senior-level positions and they, too, have children so they understand. The result is a sense of empowerment and control over their careers and their lives "when you're not sneaking around, trying to be a mother, trying to be a wife, and trying to live up to this expectation of being this loyal corporate employee or agency employee."

Still, at least some women even in the mid-1990s found themselves dissembling about why they miss work. As one woman explained:

> "You cannot say, 'The school just called, my child's got a sore throat, I've got to leave.' You've got to lie. You've got to say, 'I forgot to pick up something from the printer.' Or just [get] the secretary to cover for you."

From these free-flowing discussions, we could not determine causation but we speculated about what led to what. Overall, women obviously were growing in confidence. Did that confidence lead to what one woman called "a stronger voice as consumers . . . in corporations . . . [and] in public relations"? Or, does the new confidence result from the burgeoning role for women in the marketplace, in organizations, and in communication management? Our sense is that each factor feeds on the other; as women gain in confidence, they work toward the managerial role. Junior women gain confidence as senior women become highly visible as managers of public relations. Regardless of causation, what we heard in the focus groups of women clearly reflects the situation in the new millennium: "The playing field is leveled a little bit . . . women . . . [are] getting a bigger piece of the pie."

Qualities of Managers

Two of our three survey questions related to managerial qualities and gender exposed significant differences between men and women. In hindsight, perhaps one of these queries was double-barrelled and thus inappropriate for statistical testing. We asked respondents to react to this statement: "Men are more apt than women to back down or seek compromises in public relations–office conflict situations." The structure of the sentence suggests that to "back down" is the same as to "seek compromises." However, we do not consider compromising backing down. Thus, although we report the responses in Table 9.3, we find these data difficult to interpret.

The strongest disagreement from women and men alike came from the statement, "Men are better suited for public relations management positions than women." However, women were even more vehement in their opposition. Opinions became somewhat less extreme by 1995.

Men and women did not differ significantly on the question of whether men are more assertive than women in defending proposals and winning consent for decisions, either in their organizations or in the field; and this did not change over the 5 years of the study.

Participants in the focus group research were divided on whether they would prefer to work for a male or for a female manager. Their comments related to individual experience, to the point where we found it difficult to tease out meaningful patterns. To some women, men were easier to work for because they are more direct. Female managers, by contrast, strike some other women as indirect because they worry about hurting their employees' feelings. Women also could be "very brutal" in trying to avoid the female stereotype of being more emotional and softer. One female participant had worked for such a woman and learned a great deal from her: "I learned how *not* to manage." She believed that this particular woman was threatened by her competence and, because the manager was controlling, she wanted to "hold me back in my position."

To other women, female bosses can be just as direct and a whole lot more helpful than men. This remark from one women's focus group is characteristic: "The woman I worked for was very direct, very adroit, very

TABLE 9.3. Mean Scores of Managerial Qualities Broken down by Gender

Qualities	All	Men	Women

1. Men are more apt than women to back down or seek compromises in public relations office conflict situations.

In Your Organization

	All	Men	Women
1990 $t = -.87, p = .382$	3.30 ($n = 812$)	5.26 ($n = 344$)	3.34 ($n = 460$)
1995 $t = 4.66, p < .001$	3.15 ($n = 661$)	5.22 ($n = 240$)	5.72 ($n = 418$)

Throughout Public Relations

	All	Men	Women
1990 $t = .70, p = .485$	3.38 ($n = 812$)	3.42 ($n = 344$)	3.36 ($n = 460$)
1995 $t = 4.01, p < .001$	3.30 ($n = 661$)	5.18 ($n = 240$)	5.60 ($n = 418$)

2. Men are more assertive than women in defending proposals and winning consent for organizations.

In Your Organization

	All	Men	Women
1990 $t = .53, p = .596$	3.34 ($n = 812$)	3.36 ($n = 344$)	3.32 ($n = 460$)

Throughout Public Relations

	All	Men	Women
1990 $t = -.59, p = .558$	3.67 ($n = 812$)	3.64 ($n = 344$)	3.69 ($n = 460$)

3. Men are better suited for public relations management positions than women.

In Your Organization

	All	Men	Women
1990 $t = 8.06, p < .001$	2.17 ($n = 812$)	2.60 ($n = 344$)	1.84 ($n = 460$)

Throughout Public Relations

	All	Men	Women
1990 $t = 8.36, p < .001$	2.35 ($n = 812$)	2.82 ($n = 344$)	1.99 ($n = 460$)

Note. Responses are coded 7 = agree very strongly, 6 = strongly agree, 5 = agree, 4 = uncertain/not sure/don't know, 3 = disagree, 2 = strongly disagree, 1 = disagree very strongly.

hands-on, very involved. The man I worked for was totally passive–aggressive, barely said two words to me, let me work totally on my own, didn't give me feedback." Other male managers were considered overly authoritarian and less likely than women to be team players. We also heard that women are more relationship-oriented, find it easier to communicate (especially in offering compliments), are less likely to take credit for what others do, and give needed support to their direct reports.

If one word could best describe how women and men characterized female bosses, it would be "nurturing." However, even this seemingly positive characteristic could work against women, both superiors and their subordinates. When employees are "needy," and the manager is a nurturer, others in the office may perceive the needy ones as favorites.

Few participants in the focus group discussions were comfortable with what they considered generalizations about the way women and men managed their public relations programs. They typically concluded that management style was less "a gender thing" and more a personality trait. As one woman put it: "Both men and women have masculine and feminine traits. You have assertive women; you have sensitive men." In light of previous chapters of this book, we have to agree that sex role rather than biological gender may explain the most about the ways in which we manage. We also heard about the unfairness of stereotyping managers according to gender-linked traits such as women being insecure or men being political. However, one woman who claimed "all I want to do is work" was frustrated that she could not smoke cigars, play golf, or even talk about sports the way the male managers do.

Another woman described herself as manager in a way that suggests an optimal approach to the kind of two-way, symmetrical public relations we described earlier in this book as the most effective and ethical way to practice:

> "I am the type of person who wants to listen . . . instead of going in with my set agenda and knowing what I'm going to stand on. . . . I also listen to my clients' side of it and I sympathize with what they say and I find myself in a situation where basically I'm taking in both sides and then going back and analyzing again."

She said her male colleagues, by contrast, "go in there and basically what they say is, 'That's the way it goes.'"

Other women seemed to understand what it took to be an effective manager yet were unable to play that role. For example, one participant in a focus group explained her inability to delegate by the fact that if she didn't do the work, it would not be done the way she wanted it. As a result, she said: "I kill myself . . . all the time. I feel badly and I'm constantly apologizing to the person that works with me: 'I'm sorry, I'm sorry. I'm not managing you.'" Another woman in her group acknowledged what she considered a different managerial shortcoming: being overly concerned about whether the women reporting to her and to whom she reported liked her. She said she didn't care whether she "hit it off with a man," but her personal relationships with women at work were critically important.

Outwardly masculine characteristics may lead to the perception that men are "naturally" the managers. We heard of the man in his mid-40s who was at the same level as one female participant in our focus group. She said, "It's really funny because . . . a lot of the people if they've never met anybody in the department assume he's the director and he kinda likes it." Indeed!

One unexpected turn in a couple of the focus group discussions was to the issue of sexism and secretaries. In one of the few areas of agreement between the genders and among participants in the groups, female secretaries were portrayed as considerably more helpful to male than to female bosses. Discussants also tended to agree that female managers were more amenable than their male counterparts to do the work normally considered part of the secretary's job. They attributed this to two main factors: women's acceptance of their dual role as manager and tactician and women's willingness to help out wherever needed. At least one woman questioned whether this latter proclivity helps or hurts women (and even the profession of public relations):

> "Are we undermining ourselves when they come to me and say, 'How come you haven't had time to do these strategic-level things?' and it's because I've been taking care of the technical things that need to be done. I think we are doers. We'll do whatever needs to be done without regard for whether this is beneath me or not. But in the grand scheme of things, does that work against us in the perception of others . . . when they see us typing labels?"

Finally, as part of the discussion of managerial qualities, we learned that female managers mourned the loss of perks they associated with male managers—even though they had not enjoyed those tokens of success themselves. In talking about the need for leadership training geared especially to women, they were disappointed to find that such professional development opportunities were largely a perk of the past. So, too, was the company car. As one woman put it, "As soon as we got there, they said, 'Eh.'" Others in her session agreed that "all of that stuff was taken away" and "those things have just gone by the wayside." They believed that public relations was inordinately denied such opportunities, whereas other organizational functions such as finance and information systems continued to enjoy their perks.

The Technical Profile

Similar to the findings over time for the managerial profiles, the technical profiles of men and women in 1995 illustrated a loss of activity. In the 1990 study, as Table 9.1 shows, women seemed to do all but the four very senior types of public relations work: making communication policy decisions, planning and managing budgets, supervising the work of others, and counseling management. By 1995, women had gained in making communication policy decisions but lost as technicians conducting or analyzing results and meeting with clients or executives. Still, female technicians were more likely than male technicians to be engaged strictly in technical tasks. Men in that role tended to take on some additional managerial work.

For the men in the technical profile, the change over time was dramatic. In 1990, men evidenced a technical role that included all but three of the most senior types of public relations activities: supervising the work of others, counseling management, and conducting and analyzing research. However, by 1995, men reported little work in these three areas and also in three more activities: making communication policy decisions, evaluating program results, and meeting with clients or executives. This shrinking of types of technical activities for the men makes their factor look more like the women's. The bottom line here is that male technicians are doing less management than they were in 1990.

A Combination of Roles

In addition to confirming the two-factor construct depicting roles of public relations practitioners, the 1990 sample reflected a number of activities that loaded relatively highly on both manager and technician dimensions. For example, in 1990 the factor loadings for implementing new programs were over .50 for both men and women on the management dimension and .60 and .63, respectively, for men and women on the technical dimension. There was crossover as well on such activities as meeting with peers, planning public relations programs, and managing public relations programs. These findings support Broom and Dozier's (1986) qualification that public relations practitioners do combine a number of roles in practicing public relations (Toth & L. Grunig, 1993).

These results provide evidence that despite the two broad profiles of manager and technician, many public relations people do both types of activities to some degree. Many do so extraordinarily well. As one participant in a men's focus group said, fewer hands to work with means working smarter. Perhaps another man explained it best: "As organizations downsize their public relations functions, you see people having to take on more roles." As middle management is decimated, technicians take on greater responsibility; to maintain their positions, top managers are pressured to provide evidence of results.

However, this kind of role multiplicity affects women and men differently. This is how one man explained what he has experienced. Technical work such as answering phones, running the copy machine, and stacking envelopes is included as part of female management's "daily repertoire." However, he said, "The male managers that I know seem to delegate that."

Women, on the other hand, typically define themselves by how well they do their work and by *how much of it they do*. They believe that others in the organization judge them primarily on the latter basis. As one woman put it, "You can spend as much time as you want on strategy; but if you don't get placement, if you don't get whatever your task is, . . . then you're in trouble."

Women also agreed that men tend to delegate more than they do. Here is the take on the question of how much or how little men actually do from one woman: "I find that senior men in PR have defined for themselves the role that is one part counselor, crisis communications king, hand-holder. They don't do much of anything." A second participant in the same group considered men "diddlers." A third added, "They look like they're so busy and then you're like, 'What did you do all day?'" To her, this explained the CEO's (unfortunate) perception of what public relations is: "Saving us from some hideous disaster in the press which you know rarely happens." As a result, women may envy men the 2- to 3-hour lunch but find it impossible to spend that long away from their desk.

The Third Factor

What was unexpected in the second audit was a third factor profile to emerge. Especially for the men's profile, items loaded high enough on this factor for us to report it here in Table 9.4. We call this third dimension the "agency" profile because it suggests the work of a practitioner in the public relations agency or firm (including the entrepreneurial counselor). Its activ-

TABLE 9.4. Agency Profile (Factor 3) for Women and Men, 1995

Women

Meeting with peers	.57
Meeting with clients/executives	.55
Handling correspondence and making telephone calls	.40
Counseling management	.28
Evaluating program results	.26
Implementing decisions made by others	.22
Making media contacts	.21
Making communication policy decisions	.20

Men

Meeting with peers	.72
Meeting with clients/executives	.69
Evaluating program results	.63
Conducting or analyzing research	.57
Counseling management	.47
Handling correspondence and making telephone calls	.38
Making communication policy decisions	.37
Supervising the work of others	.37
Implementing new programs	.35
Planning and managing budgets	.32
Planning public relations programs	.28
Making media contacts	.23

Note. Eigenvalues for the women's agency profile and for the men's agency profile were .54 and .71 respectively.

ities reflect the expert prescriber role introduced by Broom and Smith in 1979; but it also includes the skills of handling correspondence, making telephone calls, and making media contacts. As such, we also can link it to the role of communication liaison. In this factor—more collaborative and research-based than the two major roles—we see such additional activities as meeting with clients, executives, and peers; counseling management; and doing research.

The men's profile shows 12 of the 17 activities surveyed as loading above .20. The activities with the highest factor loading on the agency profile are meeting with peers and meeting with clients or executives. Evaluating program results loaded above .60 as well. Men in this role do more work associated with the managerial role than do women. The women's agency profile is not so deep, with only 8 of the 17 activities loading above our cutoff point of .20. None of these activities is above .60, although meeting with peers and meeting with clients or executives loaded close to that critical point.

Conclusions

The most striking change in this trend study of roles is the reduction of se-nior-level activities reported by both women and men in our sample of PRSA members. The men's and women's managerial profiles are less robust and more concentrated on middle-management types of activities. One focus-group participant described the situation as an "increase in low-level positions and a decrease across the board."

We (Toth et al., 1998a) concluded that this change could result from the economic downswing of the early 1990s, when there were many reports of senior public relations managers losing their jobs. Those who remained, both men and women, were doing less strategic problem-solving and in-stead became more responsible for carrying out the day-to-day operations. This conclusion seems supported by the stagnant salaries of men over the same 5 years and the shift to work in the "other" category.

We might conclude also that top-level male communicators left their organizations and women were hired in their place. Women's salaries went up, but not so high as to match the salaries of the men who left. Finally, the change might be attributed to a loss of status or prestige for the public rela-tions function, as explored at some length in Chapter 7. That chapter also establishes the connection between devaluation of public relations and the problem of encroachment or sublimation of the function.

Whereas the senior-level activities declined in importance on the man-agerial factor, they appeared instead on the third, or agency, factor. This factor looks like the "expert prescriber" role conceptualized by Broom and Smith (1979). This third factor is considerably more robust for men than for women in the 1995 audit. The agency profile might have emerged as organizations lost internal public relations people and these practitioners established their own consulting firms. The consultants were more influen-tial in this period because out-sourcing the counseling was more efficient than retaining highly paid counselors on staff.

Dozier (1992) argued that agency consultants should be excluded from research on public relations roles because "external consultants play differ-ent roles than do practitioners inside organizations" (p. 333). To depict public relations roles, Dozier studied only internal practitioners for a sec-ond reason. He considered their roles more stable, more enduring: "Exter-nal consultants likely shift roles for different clients" (p. 333). However, our findings of change in both the managerial profile and the emerging agency profile also could be a function of the sample itself. It may be that in 5 years, PRSA became more an organization of interest to middle manag-ers, female and male alike, who would not be responsible for the more strategic activities of public relations. PRSA also may have become a society of public relations consultants because of the economic downturn and other factors we discussed in Chapter 4 on entrepreneurship.

The managerial role for women includes a broader range of activities than reported by men in that role. However, women seem almost isolated on the job; they are less likely than their male counterparts to meet with peers or clients. Women lost ground in the range of activities performed that could have helped their professional advancement. In other words, the picture that emerges between 1990 and 1995 suggests that *women are farther from, rather than closer to, breaking through the glass ceiling in public relations.*

At that same time, men's and women's technical role activities seemed to converge. The men's technical profile lost three activities, encompassing 11 instead of 14 main activities. The profile for female technicians shows a loss of a single activity from the cutoff of .20 over that same span of 5 years. However, there was greater change within this factor for women. Two activities dropped below the .20 floor (conducting or analyzing research and meeting with clients or executives). One, making communication policy decisions, rose from below that floor to above our cutoff point. Thus factor analysis shows that in 1995 women continued to engage in only one more activity (12 vs. 11) than did men within this technician's role.

If these results were influenced by an economic downturn, the possibilities for advancement for both men and women would have been affected. Although the agency profile seems to indicate a change in role for the entire profession, men were more likely to gravitate to counseling than were women. Still, male and female practitioners should consider how they may need to retool and reinvent themselves to work in different organizational settings. The question of whether they will be able to advance in tenuous economic times remains problematic.

One theoretical aspect of significance in this study is the need to look beyond number of years of professional experience as the major factor influencing career advancement. We should consider alternative explanations for promotion, such as how women and men are assigned (or choose for themselves) specific activities on their jobs. They could be performing diverse activities that prepare them to advance, as was illustrated in 1990 with the men's technical profile. However, 5 years later, women and men in public relations performed different activities—perhaps driven or constrained by the U.S. economy. At that time, there may have been little advancement potential into senior roles for anyone. Instead, the public relations practice illustrated in this survey seems limited to middle management.

Sublimation and encroachment, as described in Chapter 7, also are limiting factors. One woman clearly was sublimated beneath the marketing umbrella. Although she had the responsibilities of a public relations manager, she reported to the manager of corporate communications, which primarily entailed marketing communications. The boss explained to her that she could not have the title of "manager" because a manager could not report to a manager. Ultimately, the woman left the organization. A woman in another focus group was similarly disadvantaged because of the encroachment of human resources (HR) on the communication function in her company. As a result of the close association of those two functions, she said, public relations was stigmatized. She also was frustrated because the HR perspective did not recognize the importance of public relations in helping build the integrity and credibility of the organization.

One final explanation for the shifting role statistics came from participants in the second wave of focus groups. Several men made the argument that although women had gained ground as managers, their doing so has had the unfortunate result of pulling back both men and women in this field. Typical of the men who held this view is the following comment (from a man who acknowledged that he was not being politically correct):

> "Look at the traditional structure of the family. The man . . . was the breadwinner . . . so that the women did not need to work and [could] stay home and raise children. So, what's happening here is that in order to accommodate a greater influx in the profession (by and large it's women), everything has dropped so that the position that the man once had, where he was making a lot of money in PR, is not as valuable."

A second man in the same focus group agreed: "We're getting the six-figure income from two people at jobs that don't pay as much whereas it was once just a one-person job with a high salary." A third man in that discussion mentioned the negative impact of new technology on managerial role-enactment.

Few of our focus group participants considered gender the determining factor in the "ideal" manager. Instead, they agreed on key abilities such as delegation, facilitating the development of staff, communicating effectively with employees, listening, leading, and working well with different types of publics. They considered this an appropriate *blending* of managerial traits and activities stereotypically associated with women and men. However, men's conversations focused more on the strategic aspect of management, whereas women talked more about "people" concerns (Serini et al.,

1998b). Women said they felt pressured to *do* more, rather than to *strategize* more.

We conclude our discussion of findings related to roles by answering the two main research questions. First, we questioned how the roles of men and women in public relations changed between 1990 and 1995. By the second phase of our glass ceiling research, both men and women were engaging in significantly fewer tasks associated with the managerial role. At the same time, women in that role were taking on more responsibilities associated with the communication technician—primarily message production and dissemination. This addition of technical tasks was characteristic of male managers in our sample as well, but to a lesser extent.

The change over time for men in the technician's role was more obvious. Factor loadings showed a loss of some activities associated more with the communication manager than with the technician—making policy decisions, conducting evaluation research, and meeting with clients or executives. These results suggest a pessimistic outlook for all practitioners in our field, women and men alike, because taken together they portray a field that may be losing any hard-won gains at the management table.

Finally, the 5-year span of our longitudinal study showed a shift in the "purity" of the initial two-role construct. By 1995, a third factor had emerged as significant. More respondents in the second stage of the research than in the first may be responsible for activities associated with expert prescription, liaison work with others, or freelance work in public relations.

Our second research question asked whether women and men receive professional experience on the job that prepares them for more advanced managerial assignments. Unfortunately, the changes we observed in the technician's role factor do not bode well. Women in the managerial role tend to take on both technicians' and managers' tasks. Increasingly, however, the same cannot be said for men or women in the technician's role. Whereas in 1990 many technicians had the opportunity to engage in at least some managerial-level work—such as meeting with executives or environmental scanning—by 1995 those activities had dropped beyond the point of discussion.

We heard repeatedly from our focus group discussants that the ideal manager would blend traditional roles for women and for men. If they fail at the managerial role, they may have been pushed into that position before they had adequate experience or, more importantly, leadership training. If so frustrated and demoralized, such women may opt out into freelance consulting. This option struck several woman we talked with as an attractive alternative to corporate life, but men typically perceived it as a step down or backward.

On the whole, however, woman were beginning to succeed in breaking the glass ceiling at least to achieve midlevel management roles. With their success came a burgeoning confidence and sense of empowerment, which could be "contagious." Junior women, seeing women in senior roles in their organization, were encouraged.

Taken together, these roles data provided some of our most significant findings. Over time, both men's and women's managerial profiles became less robust; the activities of the typical public relations practitioner today are more concentrated on midlevel management than in the recent past. Further, women continue to "do it all," playing both the managerial and the technical role almost to the point of exhaustion. The emergent agency profile may be a fall-back position for women, but men seem to be taking greater advantage of the opportunity to go into business for themselves. As a result, one could conclude that women actually have made little gain in breaking through that glass ceiling. Of course, all practitioners are constrained by lack of understanding from members of their dominant coalition. However, with the added burden of juggling home and work, women find it particularly difficult to ascend to the level of highest responsibility.

We do well to consider the environmental impact of the economy on how public relations is structured. Women gained something in the exchange but may not have found the role activities of public relations that we believe lead to excellence in public relations. Organizations will structure and restructure according to what their leaders believe will keep them profitable or successful (or both). Public relations people may feel they can counter the economy by becoming consultants or expert prescribers. However, our theory suggests that this role does not have the same leverage as the role of the problem-solving facilitator who collaborates with top management through a strategic management process.

Chapter Ten

The Glass Ceiling

W omen have entered public relations in impressive numbers, yet their role in management has not kept pace.
Like women in the U.S. work force generally, they encounter a glass ceiling
to overcome when seeking leadership positions in their organizations. To
wit, in 1996 women accounted for only 37% of *managers* in marketing,
advertising, and public relations although they comprised 62% of all public
relations specialists in this country (U.S. Bureau of the Census, 1997).

This chapter presents the bulk of the research on the glass ceiling in
public relations, a longitudinal study conducted for the PRSA (Wright, L.
Grunig, Springston, & Toth, 1991; Serini, Toth, Wright, & Emig, 1997;
Serini, Toth, Wright, & Emig, 1998a; Toth, Serini, Wright, & Emig 1998a;
Toth, Serini, Wright, & Emig, 1998b). In addition to studying the roles and
salaries discussed in previous chapters, this two-part project audited PRSA
members' level of job satisfaction and their perceptions of relevant work-
place issues. More specifically, we explored hiring and promotion, mentoring, sexual harassment, and flexibility at work. We consider these the additional factors that create and maintain or serve to mitigate the glass ceiling
in the field.

WHAT IS THE GLASS CEILING?

The glass ceiling, as we explained earlier in this book, refers to a real yet invisible barrier that blocks women from obtaining top jobs. More than 10
years ago, an article in *The Wall Street Journal* (Hymowitz & Schellhardt,
1986) reported on the argument that "brains and competence" work only
to a certain point as a means of achieving promotion. Then, CEOs promote

those with whom they feel comfortable: people who have passed such imperceptible tests as getting along in the business world, having an "appropriate" temperament, demonstrating adequate commitment, and having an acceptable management style. The result of these indiscernible tests is the creation of an invisible glass ceiling over upper-management jobs and ultimately "a caste system in Corporate America of men at the top and women lower down" (Hymowitz & Schellhardt, 1986, p. D1). Hymowitz and Schellhardt speculated that the glass ceiling would crumble in some fields, such as ours, more quickly than in others: "It could happen relatively soon in banking and communications, where sizable numbers of women hold top posts in middle-management" (p. D1).

An article in *Business Week* made a similar argument; but it speculated that communication at least was a safe place, a "velvet ghetto," where female managers could be counted as such but would not threaten men for top managerial jobs. *Business Week* reported on this tactic more than 20 years ago:

> When is affirmative action not so affirmative? When companies load their public relations departments with women to compensate for their scarcity in other professional or managerial capacities that usually lead more directly to top management . . .
>
> Certainly, the women themselves are keenly aware that they threaten no one. "PR is a very safe, ladylike position because you are not in competition for upper-management jobs," says Elly M. Pick, former manager of public relations for Tiger Leasing Group of Chicago, a division of Tiger International. "There's no route up inside the company," says Cheryl Wells, former director of public relations for Mogen David Wine Corp. in Chicago. "Unless you want to go into agency work or open your own agency, PR is a fast track for a short career." ("PR: 'The Velvet Ghetto' of Affirmative Action," 1978, p. 122)

In 1992, Catalyst added to our understanding of this phenomenon by introducing the "glass wall" concept, meant to describe how organizations keep women in staff positions, "such as public relations and human resources, steering women away from jobs in core areas such as marketing, production, and sales" (as cited in Lopez, 1992, p. B1). Women get stuck in dead ends, deprived of the lateral movement through an organization's operating functions that they need to climb the corporate ladder. However, Myra H. Strober, a labor economist at Stanford University, discounted this analogy: "The glass wall is just a new name for an old phenomenon called occupational segregation. . . . Jobs get segregated when women begin to move through them. . . . That's just a way of maintaining old types of discrimination" (as quoted in Lopez, 1992, p. B1). Throughout this chapter, we'll use the term "glass ceiling" to depict the barriers to advancement experienced by women who aspire to manage an organization's public relations function.

Job Satisfaction

The first and second phases of the glass ceiling audit sought to determine how satisfied men and women are with their work. We knew that learning about the relative degree of career satisfaction between men and women could provide further information about the vitality of public relations as a career for all.

Pincus and Rayfield (1989) defined job satisfaction as "an organizational member's perceptual response to the aspects of his or her job and organization environment considered most important to meeting his or her needs/expectations" (p. 189). Price and Mueller (1986) offered a compatible definition: "the degree to which employees have a positive affective orientation toward employment by the organization" (p. 215). Job satisfaction may be broken into two domains: individual satisfaction and satisfaction with the organization. Dozier, L. Grunig, and J. Grunig (1995) defined individual job satisfaction as "the inherent satisfaction employees derive from the work content itself" (p. 140). They defined organizational job satisfaction as "the external rewards or recognition that organizations give employees" (p. 140).

The social science literature has provided mixed results in comparing men's and women's job satisfaction, whether individual or organizational. Mottaz's (1986) meta-analysis established that whereas some studies find women to be more satisfied than men, other research discovers just the opposite. However, Mottaz concluded that the bulk of research in this area establishes no significant difference between men's and women's overall satisfaction with their work.

The literature of public relations, too, suggests little difference between men and women in their satisfaction on the job. Broom and Dozier (1986), exploring the relationship between role and satisfaction, found that public relations managers were more satisfied than technicians in 1979 but this difference seemed to disappear when they replicated their study in 1985. Why? "Managers had decreased in their satisfaction and technicians had increased, closing the gap" (p. 351).

Dozier (1992) attributed the technician's satisfaction to his or her affinity for the creative aspects of public relations. This conclusion was echoed in the findings of Phelan (1994), who identified the paradox of the contented female worker. Women can be paid less and have less authority than men, but they could be equally satisfied: "The paradox results from the fact that although organizational satisfaction is related to subjective factors such as intrinsic and important rewards, it is not related to salary grade for either women or men" (p. 103).

Selnow and Wilson (1985) found that male public relations practitioners value security more than do female practitioners, who value social relationships more than do men. They also found women to be significantly more likely to report the creative challenge and pay as being less satisfying than they are for men. Finally, Selnow and Wilson established that satisfaction with opportunities for promotion is lower for women than for men.

Additional factors related to job satisfaction in public relations include perceived status, importance or value (or both) of the work, personal gratification, enjoyment, and feelings of accomplishment (Broom & Dozier, 1986; Dozier, 1992). Job satisfaction in our field also has been linked to excellence in public relations (Dozier et al., 1995); pay and job security (Selnow & Wilson, 1985); creative artistic beliefs and the challenges thereof (Dozier, 1992); the structure of the organization and a symmetrical communication system (J. Grunig, 1992a); the ability to influence superiors in the organization (L. Grunig, 1992a); autonomy (J. Grunig, 1992a); and the organization as a whole (J. Grunig, 1992a).

In the glass ceiling research, we assessed our participants' level of satisfaction by asking for responses to a 14-item index that encompasses many of these factors. We used a Likert-type scale ranging from 1 (extremely dissatisfied) to 5 (extremely satisfied), with the midpoint of 3 (uncertain/not sure/don't know). Items include satisfaction with present job, public relations as an occupation, income, prestige of working in public relations, perceived value of the job to society, job security, the way participants' family and friends feel about their working in public relations, advancement opportunities, future prospects, autonomy, recognition, and knowledge of communication skills and public relations.

Again, the preponderance of literature suggests little, rather than major, difference in terms of job satisfaction between men and women. Still, we could not ignore the work of Phelan (1994) and Selnow and Wilson (1985), who teased out distinctions we considered important enough to explore further. Thus the research questions related to job satisfaction for the glass ceiling study were:

1. Is there a difference in overall satisfaction between men and women over time?
2. What variables, if any, changed significantly between 1990 and 1995 for the men and women of the sample?

Differences in Job Satisfaction over Time

Based on average scores for men and for women in the list of job-satisfaction indicators, we found that in 1990 women were significantly less satisfied than men with their work in public relations. At that time, women also tended to be less optimistic than men about the future with their current employers. Five years later, women and men expressed equal levels of job satisfaction (see Table 10.1). Men had a 3.8 mean score in 1990 and a 3.7 mean in 1995. In 1990 the mean for women was 3.4 and in 1995 3.7. Thus we see that in general, job satisfaction for male respondents declined somewhat and for female respondents it grew.

The good news is that almost all respondents (92% of the women and 89% of the men) like the work they do. Their level of satisfaction decreased to the moderate level, though, with many aspects of their job and profes-

TABLE 10.1. Comparison of Mean Scores on Job Satisfaction by Gender, 1990, 1995

	Men		Women	
	1990	1995	1990	1995
How satisfied are you with:				
Present public relations job	4.0	3.8	3.7	3.8
Public relations as an occupation	4.1	4.0	4.1	4.0
Income as a public relations person	3.5	3.3	3.1	3.3
Prestige of working in public relations	3.4	3.3	3.4	3.3
Knowledge of public relations/ communication skills	4.1	4.2	3.9	3.9
Overall knowledge of public relations	4.1	4.1	3.9	3.9
Future prospects with present employer	3.7	3.4	3.3	3.5
Value of your job to society	3.7	3.6	3.5	3.4
Autonomy and freedom in present job	4.2	4.1	4.0	4.1
Prospects for your future in public relations	3.9	3.8	3.8	3.8
Advancement opportunities with present employer	3.3	3.0	3.0	3.2
Job security in present position	3.9	3.7	3.8	3.7
Recognition received from superiors	3.6	3.5	3.4	3.5
How you think your family and/or friends feel about your working in public relations	3.8	3.9	4.0	4.0
Job Satisfaction Score	3.8	3.7	3.4	3.7

Note. Responses are coded as follows: 1 = extremely dissatisfied, 2 = dissatisfied, 3 = uncertain/not sure/don't know, 4 = satisfied, 5 = extremely satisfied

TABLE 10.2. Mean Scores for Men on Job Satisfaction, 1990, 1995

	1990	1995
1. How satisfied with present public relations job?	4.00	3.81
$t = 2.32, p < .05$	(n = 342)	(n = 237)
2. How satisfied with prospects with present employer?	3.70	3.42
$t = 2.65, p < .01$	(n = 339)	(n = 230)
3. How satisfied with opportunities for advancement with present employer?	3.26	3.03
$t = 2.22, p < .05$	(n = 329)	(n = 227)
4. How satisfied with job security?	3.89	3.70
$t = 2.00, p < .05$	(n = 339)	(n = 236)

Note. Responses are coded as follows: 1 = extremely dissatisfied, 2 = dissatisfied, 3 = uncertain/not sure/don't know, 4 = satisfied, 5 = extremely satisfied.

sional status. They were most dissatisfied with the prestige and recognition accorded public relations, their advancement potential with the current employer, and their pay.

More specifically, Table 10.2 shows that between 1990 and 1995, men reported significant differences in four variables related to job satisfaction. Satisfaction with all of these aspects declined: their present job; prospects with their current employer; opportunities for advancement with that employer; and job security. None of the measures of satisfaction showed a significant increase for men over the 5-year span.

Table 10.3 shows that in that same period, women also reported significant differences in four variables. On two dimensions, prospects with their present employer and opportunities for advancement with that employer, satisfaction increased. On the other two, income and job security, it went down. In 1995, respondents reported less satisfaction than had respondents 5 years earlier on prospects with their current employer, opportunities for advancement, and job security. However, we found a gender-based difference in terms of satisfaction with income and with one's job in public relations. Men remained satisfied with their income but not with their jobs. Women remained satisfied with their jobs, but not with their income.

Members of the second glass ceiling research team designed a set of focus groups to gain a greater understanding of these results. Participants in the group discussions were invited to comment on relevant findings from the first phase of the study. More specifically, they were asked:

TABLE 10.3. Mean Scores for Women on Job Satisfaction, 1990, 1995

	1990	1995
1. How satisfied with present public relations job?	3.04	3.27
$t = 3.06, p < .01$	($n = 458$)	($n = 416$)
2. How satisfied with prospects with present employer?	3.28	3.51
$t = 2.77, p < .01$	($n = 452$)	($n = 405$)
3. How satisfied with opportunities for advancement with present employer?	3.02	3.23
$t = 2.32, p < .05$	($n = 452$)	($n = 400$)
4. How satisfied with job security?	3.89	3.70
$t = 2.00, p < .05$	($n = 339$)	($n = 236$)

Note. Responses are coded as follows: 1 = extremely dissatisfied, 2 = dissatisfied, 3 = uncertain/not sure/don't know, 4 = satisfied, 5 = extremely satisfied.

- How do you account for the change in both women's and men's satisfaction during the past five years?
- Does this reflect your experience and the experience of public relations practitioners you know?
- Are there any other comments you would like to make about job satisfaction? (Serini et al., 1997, p. 106)

Focus group results showed some similarities and some differences between men's and women's talk about job satisfaction. Men tended to discuss (1) the entry of women into the field, skewing opportunities for men; (2) the lack of prestige accorded them from peers outside the field; (3) the effects of cutbacks that left those with more to do with less pay and fewer perks; (4) the justice of being paid what you are worth; (5) cynicism, rejection, and disillusionment toward the field; (6) defining themselves by their jobs; and (7) their belief that public relations was a good profession for women, because of its relatively low educational requirements and accommodation of women who want to have a family.

Men believed they were more dispirited than women about downsizing in particular because of two main reasons: having to get used to doing more with less and men's close identification with their job. As one man put it, "One of the first things to get hit is public relations, so the profession can't have a lot of prestige if you have no bottom-line impact and, you know, what is it you do all day?" Several men agreed that because women were relatively new to the profession, they had not experienced the benefits of corporate life before downsizing.

By contrast, women's talk focused on (1) the entry of women into the field as beginning to clear the way for the new generations of women to follow; (2) concern for respect from their bosses, their organizations, and the public; (3) cutbacks as a mixed bag, in some cases making fewer upper-level positions available and in others providing opportunities to obtain these positions; (4) the significance of pay as more important than compensation alone; (5) feelings of recognition for their contributions to the organization; (6) a need for personal satisfaction and deeper meaning in their work; (7) the importance of challenging work; (8) the necessity of autonomy; (9) the malecentric nature of the work place; and (10) explaining men's nervousness because of the entry of women into public relations.

Shirley Serini and her colleagues (1997), who were primarily responsible for this second series of focus groups, found that the two elements of greatest common concern were the effects of the recession of the early 1990s and of the entry of women into the field. Both women and men believed these factors not only shape the job market but their individual jobs. The research team also discovered that men tend to be more competitive than women about their work, whereas women bring a wider range of needs to the discussion. Serini and her team concluded that women also seem to be "more positive" about the field (p. 116). They speculated:

> What does seem to be emerging about the midcareer cohort defined for this study is a greater understanding of and sensitivity toward the demons and successes of the other gender. Both groups appear to be willing to respect the other, and, perhaps more importantly, to engage in dialogue on the issues in ways that will result in collaboration and benefits of both. (p. 116)

Departing now from these gender-related nuances, what did we hear about satisfaction that was common to women and men? Not surprisingly, some participants in the men's focus groups questioned the survey results establishing any gap between male and female respondents related to satisfaction. As an outspoken member of one discussion said: "Show me somebody that's satisfied with their income and I'll show you somebody who probably needs to look for another job. Does anybody here think they make enough money?"

One of his colleagues agreed that satisfaction for everyone, male and female alike, should decline over time because of the ubiquitous devaluation of the function. He complained, "We're so often times looked upon as publicists, spin doctors, and not really strategic partners in business." Early in one's career, a wide-eyed enthusiasm may carry the day but as one gains experience, in his view, the public relations practitioner becomes discour-

aged because "you look at the other people who've got the respect and recognition and you don't."

A second cause of what members of one men's group considered an inevitable decrease in job satisfaction over the years is also directly attributable to this field, rather than to gender. These men experienced growing
frustration with the society they interact with day in and day out. The media segment of that society was singled out as a cause of dejection because
seasoned professionals have had to deal with rejection from the press as
much as 99% of the time over the years.

Women in one focus group agreed with the participant who had
become unhappy at work because of the balancing act necessary to handle
both managerial and technical tasks. Like the men's responses, women
tended to believe the problem stems more from organizational factors such
as downsizing than from discrimination. Women who reported experiencing more—not less—satisfaction with their work in public relations attributed this largely to the same cause: the added responsibility of fulfilling the
managerial role. In the case of one woman, this happened not because of
downsizing but because of "helping the CEO to understand the value of
public relations in the [banking] business." She works closely with that
chief executive. Other women enacting the manager's role came from the
Northwest's high tech industry. Otherwise, regional differences among focus groups were virtually nonexistent on this and other questions.

We heard an interesting comment from one woman, describing the importance of doing managerial-level work. In explaining her frustration, she
said "I still don't fully understand what putting a brochure together does in
the bigger scheme of things." We are baffled as well. Failing to tie the work of
technicians in with greater organizational objectives not only frustrates the
practitioner, it diminishes the overall effectiveness of the organization—and
ultimately can lead to devaluation of the profession (Dozier, L. Grunig, & J.
Grunig, 1995). Similarly, women who work under senior executives whose
notion of public relations differs markedly from theirs experience tremendous frustration and, undoubtedly, ineffectiveness. One woman said:

> "I know, speaking from experience, where our top management has a
> certain vision, and maybe you are or aren't privy to it, but you have
> to sort of go along with what they want even though you know that's
> not the way to do it; but if you want your job, you don't have a
> choice."

On the other hand, practitioners whose contributions are recognized
experience more fulfillment than those whose organizations fail to appreci-

ate what they do. One woman told her focus group that her husband, also in public relations, became so discouraged he left the field. Another woman, unhappy over her sense that public relations is one of the first functions axed during tough economic times, considered bailing out herself:

> "I can't help but think if I'm in a profession that's not valued such that as soon as they look for a way to cut . . . among the first five places they cut is public relations . . . maybe that's not where I belong, because I'm going to give my all to my job."

Women trying to explain the reasons behind the shifting levels of satisfaction for men and women over time agreed that women's satisfaction increased primarily because they have made great strides in the field and that men's decreased because they are nervous over both the growing number of women and women's achievements in the field. "Nervous" may be too mild a term. What at least one woman considered a redefinition of roles for men, resulting from women's moving up in public relations, "would make anyone . . . lose control." On the other hand, some women said they never had the sense men were threatened by the feminization of "their" field.

Conclusions

So, did we indeed find a difference in overall satisfaction between men and women and if so, did that change over time? Women we surveyed in the second stage of the glass ceiling research indicated a higher level of satisfaction than had their counterparts in round one. Men's scores on job satisfaction went in the other direction. Perhaps this major change means that women's growing fulfillment on the job comes at the expense of their male colleagues' contentment. Certainly, the growing female majority in the field is a major factor affecting both genders' level of satisfaction with their careers. By 1995, levels of job satisfaction for women and men had become identical.

We also asked whether specific variables changed significantly between 1990 and 1995 for the men and women of the sample. We found that men had become significantly less satisfied with their current job, their overall prospects with their organization, and their job security. Over time women became significantly more satisfied with their advancement opportunities with their current employer, but their satisfaction both with pay and job security declined.

Perceptions of the Glass Ceiling in Public Relations

By 1992, several studies had documented the increasing number of women entering the U.S. labor force (e.g., U.S. Department of Labor, Bureau of Labor Statistics, 1992; "Dreams and Realities," 1990; Marsh, 1991; Miller, 1991). However, studies of women entering public relations and the impact of gender on the field generally had been limited to secondary research, some qualitative work, and salary data (Cline et al., 1986; Toth & Cline, 1989a; Toth, 1994).

Among the earliest and most representative surveys of the growing legions of women coming to public relations was research by Toth and Cline (1991) that depicted the attitudes of 443 randomly selected public relations practitioners from two professional organizations, IABC and PRSA. Their study found a salary disparity based on perceptions of gender. That is, women faced special problems when attempting to advance into managerial positions and to combat sexual bias. Respondents also perceived differences in women's managerial motivation, their willingness to sacrifice when work and family demands conflict, and their ability to command top dollar.

Two influential research reports that had brought attention even earlier to Broom and Dozier's (1986) conclusion that gender related to roles were *The Velvet Ghetto* (Cline et al., 1986) and *Beyond the Velvet Ghetto* (Toth & Cline, 1989a). Both studies were commissioned by the Foundation of the IABC. They explored a breadth of gender issues, including perceptions of issues related to the feminization of public relations, gender bias in employment, and the salary disparity between men and women. Since role advancement had been linked to salary, the authors of *The Velvet Ghetto* also asked questions about women's opportunities for promotion. They concluded that women chose the technician's role over the managerial role because of the societal expectation that women be "less managerial"—less serious-minded, less aggressive, and less likely to be part of the "good old boys" (Cline et al., 1986).

The authors of *The Velvet Ghetto* based their conclusions primarily on focus group discussions conducted in Atlanta; Dallas; Halifax, Nova Scotia; Indianapolis; New Haven; and San Francisco. The groups, composed of men and women, acknowledged that women were underrepresented in the upper levels of public relations. Why?

> Some saw women as following "normal" career tracks, while the men were able to "fast track." Some said that women have the "titles," but not the same level of authority as men, and some also reported that women were not taken seriously. (Cline et al., 1986, p. VIII-27)

These themes reemerged in the focus group research conducted for *Beyond the Velvet Ghetto*, in which many of the same participants from the same cities gathered again. Authors of *Beyond the Velvet Ghetto* concluded that perceptions of barriers to women seeking advancement had not changed over the years. They proposed solutions for women who wanted to move from the technical role to the managerial role. Ambitious women were encouraged to accept the velvet ghetto as real, learn to play the game, and develop a career plan (Cline, 1989).

In 1990 and again in 1995, we glass ceiling researchers returned to perceptions of public relations professionals regarding several work-place issues: hiring, promotion, networking or mentoring, sexual harassment, and work-place flexibility. Our primary research question in this area explored any differences between men and women on their perceptions of work-place issues, in their organizations and throughout public relations. We also were interested in any trends that might have emerged over time.

Results of two focus groups were included in the 1991 *Under the Glass Ceiling* report. Volunteer participants came from that year's PRSA convention. One focus group encompassed all male participants with a male moderator; the other was all women. From these first two focus groups, we concluded:

1. Men do not perceive as much inequality in their organizations (with regard to women being in a one-down position) as do women.
2. Men and women feel that there is more sex discrimination in the field generally than in their own organizations.
3. Women perceive a much greater degree of discrimination than do men (Wright et al., 1991, p. 14).
4. Women consider flexibility in the work schedule, such as flexible locations, child care, leave policy, and so on, as being considerably more important than do men (Wright et al, 1991, p. 16).
5. Scores on the gender perception scale items suggest female perceptions differ significantly from male perceptions. Higher scores on these scales reflect the perception that women are professionally oppressed and are entrenched in a secondary status when compared to men (Wright at al., 1991, pp. 16–17).

Thus we learned that perceptions are of critical importance, and that they vary significantly by gender. For example, women see themselves in a one-down position relative to men in terms of pay, promotion, and exploitation by management. In particular, women consider gender a significant determinant of whether practitioners function as technicians or managers. What frustrates men is their perception that women frequently are hired as a result of affirmative action policies. Some of the men we talked with seemed to think they are better suited than women for management-level positions in public relations.

In 1995, we (Toth, Serini, Wright, & Emig, 1998b) repeated our set of questions on perceptions of the work place. With only a few added questions about sexual harassment, the scale items were presented in the same way as 5 years earlier. We found many more similarities than differences between the 1990 and 1995 perceptions of men and women on work-place issues. That is, neither group changed its positions in any significant way. What follows is a description of how men and women compare on several important perceptions related to the glass ceiling: hiring, promotion, mentoring and networking, notions of success, sexual harassment, work-place accommodations, and the qualities of a manager.

Hiring

In both 1990 and 1995 we established several significant differences in perceptions of men and women on issues pertaining to hiring. Table 10.4 shows that in 1995, few women relative to men believed women were more likely than men to be hired for public relations management positions. On the other hand, women more than men perceived that women were more likely to be hired for public relations positions involving mainly communication skills in their organizations. This perception held for women's views of the entire field of public relations.

Men continued to believe that if an equally capable woman and man applied for the same public relations job, the woman would be hired. As one male participant in a 1995 focus group put it, "I still hear the phrase, 'We need a woman in a visible position.'" Another said that "being a white male is a liability when looking for a job." A third agreed: "We're [white males] the worst minority group." Still another man denigrated the question by equating it with the tooth fairy: "I've never been beset with a problem of having an equally capable woman or man, or two men. Never. Somebody has the edge."

At both points in time, women disagreed that they are advantaged. Men were more uncertain than women that women often were hired as a result of affirmative action policies in their organizations. The men in 1995 were even more uncertain that throughout public relations women were often hired as a result of affirmative action. At least one man in a focus group discussion held in 1995 brought up the question of whether women were

TABLE 10.4. Mean Scores on Perceptions of Hiring Broken Down by Gender, 1990, 1995

Perceptions	All	Men	Women

1. Women are more likely than men to be hired for public relations management positions involving problem solving and decision making.

In your organization

	All	Men	Women
1990	3.39	3.23	3.50
$t = -2.62, p < .001$	($N = 812$)	($n = 344$)	($n = 460$)
1995	3.60	3.44	3.69
$t = -2.27, p < .05$	($N = 661$)	($n = 240$)	($n = 418$)

Throughout public relations

	All	Men	Women
1990	3.32	3.34	3.30
$t = .50, p = .620$	($N = 812$)	($n = 344$)	($n = 460$)
1995	3.60	3.70	3.54
$t = 1.67, p = .095$	($N = 661$)	($n = 240$)	($n = 418$)

2. Women are more likely than men to be hired for public relations positions involving mainly communication skills.

In your organization

	All	Men	Women
1990	4.13	3.58	4.53
$t = -7.99, p < .001$	($N = 812$)	($n = 344$)	($n = 460$)
1995	4.19	3.85	4.38
$t = -3.82, p < .001$	($N = 661$)	($n = 240$)	($n = 418$)

Throughout public relations

	All	Men	Women
1990	4.80	4.44	5.07
$t = -6.72, p < .001$	($N = 812$)	($n = 344$)	($n = 460$)
1995	4.78	4.58	4.90
$t = -3.09, p < .05$	($N = 661$)	($n = 240$)	($n = 418$)

3. If an equally capable woman and man applied for the same public relations job, the woman would be hired.

In your organization

	All	Men	Women
1990	3.59	3.65	3.54
$t = 1.11, p = .269$	($N = 812$)	($n = 344$)	($n = 460$)
1995	3.68	3.90	3.55
$t = 2.92, p < .001$	($N = 661$)	($n = 240$)	($n = 418$)

Throughout public relations

	All	Men	Women
1990	3.53	3.80	3.31
$t = 5.79, p < .001$	($N = 812$)	($n = 344$)	($n = 460$)
1995	3.74	4.21	3.47
$t = 8.19, p < .001$	($N = 661$)	($n = 240$)	($n = 418$)

(continued on next page)

TABLE 10.4. (*continued*)

4. Women often are hired as a result of affirmative action policies.

In your organization

1990	3.31	3.33	3.27
$t = .54$, $p = .590$	($N = 812$)	($n = 344$)	($n = 460$)
1995	3.26	3.48	3.13
$t = 2.67$, $p < .05$	($N = 661$)	($n = 240$)	($n = 418$)

Throughout public relations

1990	3.92	4.01	3.84
$t = 1.83$, $p = .067$	($N = 812$)	($n = 344$)	($n = 460$)
1995	3.84	4.21	3.63
$t = 5.68$, $p < .001$	($N = 661$)	($n = 240$)	($n = 418$)

Note. Responses are coded as follows: 7 = agree very strongly, 6 = strongly agree, 5 = agree, 4 = uncertain/not sure/don't know, 3 = disagree, 2 = strongly disagree, 1 = disagree very strongly.

discriminated against in hiring because "it is assumed that they will take off every time there's a sick kid."

What do we make of these distinctions in perceptions related to hiring? Some aspects of the gap have begun to close.

Men and women still disagree on whether women are more likely than men to be hired for management positions—those involving problem solving and decision making—but that disagreement has moved toward uncertainty. (Focus groups established that men disagree with each other about who has the advantage.) A second gap that is narrowing relates to the question of whether women are more likely than men to be hired for jobs involving mainly communication skills. Initially, men disagreed and women agreed. By 1995, women had come to agree less than they did before; men agreed more than they did in 1990.

Of course, we explored this question in our focus groups as well as in the survey. We learned that participants saw tremendous complexity here. For example, the mix of existing staff and individual personalities would be key factors in hiring decisions. One man admitted having violated the law to hire a man. He said: "I, as illegal as it was, deliberately set out to try to find a male because there are so many women." He explained that he was searching for balance. Also important, though, is the notion of visibility. Participants in his group agreed that they knew from personal experience that senior management had specified that women be hired for top communication jobs.

We also found that men believed women have the edge in hiring in our field because they work for less. As one man said: "The company would see that they have two equally qualified candidates and they could get one for lower pay. That's the one they hire." Women are willing to take less money because of "maybe something that's ingrained in women" as a result of women's long struggle to be hired in professional jobs in the first place. This line of reasoning should remind readers of the human capital model we discussed at some length in Chapter 2 of this book.

Men were quick to reject the explanation of women having the advantage in hiring to make up for past inequities. One group agreed that, as one man put it, if organizations "were truly concerned with affirmative action ... we'd see a lot more ethnic minorities in the profession which ... we know is not the case." He considered this a "huge problem" for PRSA to look into. Others in his group added women and people with handicaps to the equation.

To another person, questions about hiring were particularly knotty because of his own experience. He had found it tough to earn as much as a new woman brought into the organization without having to risk exposure and mistakes he made working his way up there. As a result, he sees inequity. He did acknowledge, however, that women in other organizations are still playing catch up from the postwar era when men dominated most fields.

Women who think *others* think they were hired under affirmative action suffer what approaches a crisis of confidence. The perception is more often subtle than overtly expressed, but here is how one woman described her experience:

> "Sometimes I'm asked, 'Were you hired under affirmative action, because you certainly can't be qualified.' Not directly, but just asking, if you're sitting down at a cocktail dinner or some reception or even in a staff meeting ... and people are constantly asking you questions about your background. You're trying to really figure out why I have this job and then you want to understand the relationship I have with the CEO."

One men's group talked about life in the public relations firm and how that could be detrimental to ambitious women. One man even acknowledged that he had been hired not for his expertise but for the industrial clients, "who happened to be very sexist in their ways and the last thing they wanted to see was a young woman sitting across the table from them." His colleagues speculated that the experience must have left him feeling "used and cheapened." They also agreed that men might continue to enjoy breaks in hiring, though, because so many women are drawn to public relations today.

Some of the most poignant testimony in this research came from women in response to questions about hiring equity. One woman said her company typically would hire a woman for an entry-level job in public relations because:

> "We knew she could work her butt off and we wouldn't have to worry about feeling guilty that here we were [hurting] some poor man whose future income could be tied to whether he was rising in the organization. We didn't talk about it in this way, but I know that we always felt that a woman's going to work harder and we could ask her to work harder.
>
> "Once we got to more midlevel communications and public relations managers, the men—because there were fewer of them—stood out, although I didn't think their skills were as good mostly. I thought that there were probably three really qualified women to every male candidate, but because they were different and because there were inevitably men on the hiring committee . . . once you get to midlevel, the man probably has more of an advantage. . . . They'd take any man that comes along. Got to have one, you know."

As part of this discussion of hiring, we first heard participants' explanation of why both men and women perceive problems to be worse in the field than in their own organizations. Their answer lies with selectivity, or the fact that they are not representative of public relations as a whole. Rather than being chosen randomly to take part in the focus groups, they were—as one man called it—"warm bodies" willing to sacrifice a significant amount of time to talk. Survey respondents, too, fail to mirror the field because as members of PRSA they can be considered more professional than their counterparts who do not embrace the professional norms associated with such membership.

To understand the worst, rather than the best, of this business one man suggested including in the focus groups a Hollywood press agent, a sweatshop PR person, or a tobacco company staffer. Otherwise, he said, what we heard came from "a very cutting-edge society." That society also has geographical dimensions. Others in the group alluded to Seattle, for example, as being distinctly more positive for women than, say, Philadelphia, New York, or Dallas (denigrated for its "good old boy network"). Our findings, in these participants' view, are skewed by this enlightenment bias. Finally, men in one group expressed skepticism about how honest any of

the written answers had been—in large part because of the legalities involved with questions of hiring and promotion.

Promotion

Two issues related to promotion continue to indicate that men and women
perceive the situation differently. Table 10.5 exposes the sharp contrast between female and male respondents on the questions of who gets promoted
more quickly and who has a harder time reaching the top in public relations.

In 1990, and again in 1995, women agreed more strongly than men in
our sample that men are promoted more quickly in most public relations
employment situations in their organizations. Women also believed this to
be the case throughout public relations, although they were divided in their
responses and tended to see the situation more positively for the field than
in their own organization. Men disagreed that they are promoted more
quickly than are female public relations practitioners in their organizations,
but they were uncertain about the field itself.

In both 1990 and 1995, women considered it more difficult for them
than for men to reach the top in public relations in their organizations and
throughout our industry. Men disagreed about their own organization but
expressed uncertainty about who has a tougher time getting to the top
throughout the industry. Between the two points in time, men tended to
disagree more strongly and women tended to agree more strongly about
their employers.

We also asked for reactions to this statement: "If there is an opportunity for advancement in my organization, I feel I'll have a fair chance at it."
In 1990, men agreed to a significantly greater extent than did women that
they had a fair shot at promotion in their organization. Any other distinctions between women's and men's mean responses to this item and between
1990 and 1995 are statistically insignificant. The bottom line here? Men
and women fall somewhere between uncertainty and at least a modest belief that they have a fair chance to advance within their organization (mean
score on the 7-point Likert-type scale was 4.39 in 1995).

These differences were apparent in the focus group studies as well.
Several of the men expressed the belief that women and racioethnic minorities are getting ahead in the field because they establish their own
agencies—taking advantage of outsourcing and consulting opportunities.
Some men also believed that public relations has become an equal-
opportunity profession in large part to make up for past inequities. As a result, men considered their own chances for promotion diminished. This sit-

TABLE 10.5. Mean Scores of Promotion Issues Broken Down by Gender, 1990, 1995

Issues	All	Men	Women
1. Men are promoted more quickly than women in most public relations employment situations.			
In your organization			
1990	3.66	3.16	4.04
$t = -7.84$, $p < .001$	$(N = 812)$	$(n = 344)$	$(n = 460)$
1995	3.62	3.11	3.91
$t = -6.49$, $p < .001$	$(N = 661)$	$(n = 240)$	$(n = 418)$
Throughout public relations			
1990	4.65	4.06	5.10
$t = -11.70$, $p < .001$	$(N = 812)$	$(n = 344)$	$(n = 460)$
1995	4.42	3.73	4.82
$t = -11.28$, $p < .001$	$(N = 661)$	$(n = 240)$	$(n = 418)$
2. It is more difficult for women than it is for men to reach the top in public relations.			
In your organization			
1990	4.17	3.54	4.64
$t = -9.06$, $p < .001$	$(N = 812)$	$(n = 344)$	$(n = 460)$
1995	3.99	3.36	4.35
$t = -6.85$, $p < .001$	$(N = 661)$	$(n = 240)$	$(n = 418)$
Throughout public relations			
1990	4.94	4.19	5.32
$t = -10.64$, $p < .001$	$(N = 812)$	$(n = 344)$	$(n = 460)$
1995	4.69	3.97	5.10
$t = -9.69$, $p < .001$	$(N = 661)$	$(n = 240)$	$(n = 418)$
3. If there is an opportunity for advancement in my organization, I feel I'll have a fair chance at it.			
In your organization			
1990	4.80	4.94	4.72
$t = 1.96$, $p < .05$	$(N = 812)$	$(n = 344)$	$(n = 460)$
1995	4.86	4.74	4.92
$t = -1.38$, $p = .169$	$(N = 661)$	$(n = 240)$	$(n = 418)$
Throughout public relations			
1990	4.34	4.40	4.30
$t = 1.41$, $p = .159$	$(N = 812)$	$(n = 344)$	$(n = 460)$
1995	4.39	4.41	4.37
$t = .54$, $p = .591$	$(N = 661)$	$(n = 240)$	$(n = 418)$

Note. Responses are coded as follows: 7 = agree very strongly, 6 = strongly agree, 5 = agree, 4 = uncertain/not sure/don't know, 3 = disagree, 2 = strongly disagree, 1 = disagree very strongly.

uation can provoke what a man in one group called "violent tension," perhaps healthy for public relations because it forces everyone to become a better practitioner but threatening to men who for the first time encounter what he called "a real competitive battle" with women vying for top spots.

In an interesting contradiction, most men also said they believe promotion in public relations hinges more on ability than on gender. At the same time, they believed that promotion for women into the highest ranks is inevitable as more and more top management positions are filled by women who would—in turn—advance other women. They attributed the difference of opinion between male and female survey respondents to women's *perception* that it is more difficult for them to reach the top because their bosses are men. (However, as one man pointed out, "It's easy for men to, if you don't see a problem, it doesn't exist . . . we're not in their shoes.") On the whole, though, men attributed women's survey responses in this area to the fact that they are surrounded by men who continue to occupy the top spots in their organizations. As one man put it, "I don't see a whole lot of women cracking the code, so to speak."

When women they know actually have been barred from promotion, men tend to blame the woman's industry as male-dominated. One man described a client who is the marketing director for a coffee company. He said, "They call her 'girl,' " and he predicted that because of the masculine bias of the company "she's not going to go anywhere."

Individual bosses, individual companies, individual industries—all of these were blamed for any roadblocks to women's career advancement in public relations. We heard surprisingly little about patterns of bias or societal, political, or structural impediments. Instead, industries considered traditional or "masculine" such as banking, engineering, accounting, and manufacturing often took the heat. One man called these "unenlightened companies." (Banking, however, has a significant proportion of women in positions of communication management [Hymowitz & Schellhardt, 1986], which underscores the importance of perceptions.) By contrast, men perceived nonprofits, high tech, and what one called "upstart industries" as more willing to promote women.

In addition to arguing that certain industries are male- or female-friendly, several participants in the focus group research blamed history as a barrier to women's ascension in the typical organization. As one man said, "Men have been at this [public relations] a lot longer." Others in his group agreed that women have been present in the field in significant numbers only since the 1950s—which one man characterized as "a relatively short amount of time." He added, "You know, as far as the industrial history of the world and country, men have just always dominated the work force." Two decades ago in Chicago, one man said, women in public relations were limited to what he called "the home furnishings, food, and fashion ghetto." Women's progress, men in all three 1995 groups were convinced, would be "evolutionary."

Men also agreed that for the most part, though, women would have to make their own opportunities in "emergent" fields. At the same time, men said with considerable emphasis that everyone in public relations has "fair opportunity." This quote from one focus group is illustrative: "[You] gotta, gotta earn your opportunities." Many of the male participants also emphasized the importance of men and women relying on evaluative research to show the results of their work.

Because public relations as an organizational function is often devalued, some men chose to frame their discussion of promotion in terms of getting the *department* promoted—despite their earlier comments about the increasing need for communication management. Rather than focusing on women's or men's chances for advancement, these men talked about the need to educate CEOs who have come up through finance and have little working knowledge of either marketing or public relations.

We detected a final contradiction in men's conversation about promotion. On the one hand, they said there is more opportunity for women to reach the top in public relations today because, as the field increasingly is credited with bottom-line contributions, the number of senior-level positions grows. On the other hand, they said there are fewer chances for women—and men—to reach those director slots because downsizing has reduced their number.

A minority viewpoint espoused in the men's focused discussions was that men continue to enjoy an advantage in promotion. Here is how one man expressed this notion:

> "The public relations function is being called to the round table. And that voice is being listened to by management. I would say that it's probably more likely that a man gets called to the round table . . . gets called up to the next level . . . men are dominating upper management right now."

A second man in the same group talked about the fact that even women in his organization may be reluctant to promote other women, not because of history, management style, capability, or the industry, but because of family responsibilities:

> "In the last 3 years, we've had to keep on bringing in new people who come in, they work for a year, they have children, and then they quit.

And I think that our vice president of public affairs, who's female, is getting to the point where she's gone, 'You know what? I'm going to hire a male next time, because this is just becoming too much of an issue, too much time, money.' "

On the other side of the family coin, we heard the scenario of a woman on maternity leave who was promoted. Why? Her boss, a focus group participant explained, "We had the sense that if we didn't promote her now, there would be the perception that she was penalized because she was still out due to taking full advantage of the maternity leave that the agency offers." Another participant in this same group mentioned that women promoted into the managerial rank may undergo closer scrutiny than men. The assumption, he explained, is akin to that of the boss's son—advanced for reasons other than competence or experience.

We compared these conversations with what women in the three 1995 focus groups were saying. Those who feared they would not have an equal shot at promotion despaired, to the point of considering leaving their companies. As one woman put it:

"I think our company is . . . very male-dominated. Out of probably 20 . . . people at the director level, only two are women and that says a lot right there because . . . for me to look at the way the company operates and consider my future prospects, I'm probably going to have to leave the company in order to advance."

Women, like men, were looking for opportunities to make a real difference in their organizations. Working in a small organization or in a larger one whose public relations function was downsized limits what they perceive as a good chance for promotion. One woman explained, "If I want to move up, I move out because there is nowhere for me to move up." Another woman elaborated: "If there's only one or two people in PR and you're either No. 1 or No. 2, there's no where to go. You've got to move to an organization that's bigger, has more offices." She considered the situation "a hazard of being a PR professional." Others agreed, and many women considered the problem endemic across types of organizations: associations, corporations, and even public relations firms.

On the other hand, at least one woman had experienced what she initially thought was the "waiting for someone to die" syndrome but discovered was sexism in her organization. When she was hired, her boss said that he was almost 60 and planned to retire at that age. She worked very hard for the next 5 years. His 60th birthday came but he failed to retire. Why? She concluded that "people were very uncomfortable with a woman in the upper level." She stayed as long as she did because of what we determined was the typical socialization of mainstream American women: "After a while you start to think, 'Well, I'm lucky to have a job,' and so you . . . say, 'Do I want to make a big fuss about this situation?'" We have to point out, of course, that not all women feel fortunate just to be employed. At least one woman stated quite the opposite: "I don't feel that, gosh, I'm so lucky to be where I am and shut up and appreciate it. If I don't find what I'm doing to be satisfying, I feel now I can look around and, you know, control my own career."

Even people who had enjoyed working in a particular company alluded to leaving as a requisite move for promotion. A woman described the exploitation possible in this scenario:

> "The women will come in, and they'll work like hell thinking they're going to get promoted, and when they don't they'll be mad and they'll leave and they'll [the organization] take the next one, work her for 5 years. . . . It's very, very clear to me."

Job title without responsibility and little possibility for increasing responsibility were all too characteristic of the situation for both women and men we talked with. One midlevel manager explained the essence of her job as "coordinating publicists," and she doubted that in that role she would reach true managerial status. Another woman in her group suggested she wait for a crisis, when management may call for advice and thus see her as more central to the organization's success.

As was the case in our discussions about job satisfaction, women looked at who was above them, beyond their glass ceiling, when assessing their own chances for moving up in the organization. One woman tried to balance optimism with the reality of her workplace: "Women can [do well] here . . . but if you look at the top echelon of management, it's all men."

What would it take for women to break the glass ceiling and be promoted to those visible spots at the top? According to women in one group, doing twice as much as men. They considered the inequity "incredible." Reacting to the excuse that young women, the majority in public relations practice, are too "green" to be promoted, one woman said: "I am 30 years old. Like I had to run around and tell people 'I'm old enough; you can promote me.'"

These women had numerous suggestions for helping women get ahead, primarily through self-promotion: blowing their horn as "loudly as men do," making sure the "right people" know what is going on, networking (with which few were comfortable), and finding champions in the organization. Few women are socialized to do these things. As one woman said:

> "I have to be told by women vice presidents to go tell the president what I've done. It just never occurs to me that I have to go down there and say, 'I just wanted to let you know what happened,' 'cause that's what I was hired to do and I do it and I guess I feel like through osmosis he's going to find out."

Fundamentally, though, the problem of promotion for women in public relations boils down to the field itself. Women believed that because public relations is "at the bottom," few in the typical organization think about promoting anyone in that department. Public relations firms, of course, are different. People do get promoted, but women we talked with believed that men had a slight edge over women in terms of agency promotions. They believed this advantage stems in large part from how account executives begin. For women, one common career path is to be hired as a secretary or an intern. Men, in their opinion, rarely begin in this support role or adopt these strategies for getting their foot in the door.

For too many typical staffers outside of firms, the field represents a revolving door. Here is how one woman characterized her experience: "People leave their positions and new people come in but there was nothing set up to promote people."

Mentoring, Networking, and Success

We questioned whether having a mentor and networking with professionals outside the organization contributed to our respondents' success. Women and men agreed that these connections help somewhat. However, there was a significant difference in their perceptions. Table 10.6 shows that women credited both mentors and networks significantly more than did men for their professional achievement.

Focus group discussions exposed a difference of opinion on whether networking comes to men or women more naturally. It may be more natural for women, but that doesn't necessarily make it attractive. One woman who was acknowledged as effective at networking was compared with lower life forms: slug, bloodsucker, shark, and barracuda. A woman in this focus group conceded that the networker also was considered a hard worker, very busy, high powered, and high energy. Nevertheless, she resented her efforts (and perhaps her effectiveness!) at monopolizing the time and attention of the dominant coalition in their organization.

TABLE 10.6. Mean Scores of Networking Issues Broken Down by Gender, 1990, 1995

Issues	All	Men	Women
1. Having a mentor has contributed to my professional success.			
1990	3.60	3.37	3.79
$t = -4.88, p < .001$	(N = 812)	(n = 344)	(n = 460)
1995	3.52	3.27	3.66
$t = -3.90, p < .001$	(N = 661)	(n = 240)	(n = 418)
2. Networking with other practitioners outside my organization has made an important contribution to my success in public relations.			
1990	3.68	3.51	3.81
$t = -3.77, p < .001$	(N = 812)	(n = 344)	(n = 460)
1995	3.76	3.60	3.85
$t = -2.77, p < .05$	(N = 661)	(n = 240)	(n = 418)

Note. Responses are coded as follows: 5 = strongly agree, 4 = agree, 3 = uncertain/not sure/don't know, 2 = disagree, 1 = strongly disagree.

Women agreed on the importance of this "face time," yet few were so aggressive at hobnobbing with their power elite. They also worried over the balance they considered inherent in a "perfect management style": an appropriate amount of networking without "clinging to every single executive that walks in the door." "Pushing it," in their opinion, may lead to the perception that the networking woman has slept with the boss. At the very least, it leads to "questions."

To some participants, networking was principally a male domain. Women said they believed men who network at least a bit are respected because it is expected of men. When women join networking organizations, in at least one man's opinion, "They're copying what men have done." One man said he believed women's groups within PRSA, at least, do the profession a disservice because "we need to be united." He did have a suggestion for PRSA's management, however: "Next time you're asked about whether or not women's issues are important, say 'Yes.' At least learn the lip service part of it, Ray [Gaulke, PRSA's COO]."

In contrast, the experience of a man in another focus group led him to believe that seeking help and asking for advice come more readily to women. He said, "I've had a lot of experience with people calling me for informational interviews, and most of them are women." Others in his group agreed. A second man there elaborated on what he considered a gendered difference: "It's real interesting what women ask versus men. Men just ask . . . if there's a job open today. Women are more long term and showing me their resume, saying, 'What do you think?' Seeking out information and help." A third man in the same group said: "You see more women at PRSA meetings; I think you see more female participation on PRSA committees. That's all networking."

Most men agreed that women are "naturally" better at talking with others. Women, they believed, do so more effectively and more frequently—whether consciously or not, although at least one man thought women probably network "with a little more forethought than men." Men, in his opinion, may be almost inhibited from doing so. Another man explained why he thought women were more likely than men to seek professional mentors:

> "Men . . . tend to find their mentors in their fathers, or in their fraternity brothers, or in older men that they may have worked for; but I don't necessarily feel that women have that same infrastructure of mentoring available to them at this point."

He also blamed men for not making themselves available to mentor younger women in their offices. His agency had made a deliberate effort to hire a woman who could serve as a role model for other women. Sure enough: "She's got a steady stream of customers who are coming to her for professional advice." It turned out that these mentees were men as well as women, so apparently the "infrastructure" of family and college buddies he referred to earlier does not apply to all men.

Surprisingly few women spoke of the benefits of being mentored. Several of the women we spoke with alluded to the growing number of women in senior positions who would be available to mentor them. One of the few who expressed her enthusiasm for the role was very specific. She had found the mentoring of two men about how to negotiate invaluable. She said: "They just find it amazing that I don't know how to negotiate, that I just don't go in and ask for what I feel I deserve, but I had a mother that never did that either. So I learned a pattern: that you don't rock the boat." Once again, then, socialization helps explain a large part of the situation for women who work outside their homes for pay.

Despite its potential value, the mentoring relationship between a senior man and a junior woman may be problematic, we heard, because of perceptions of intimacy. Several men in one group attributed men's reluctance to enter into such a professional relationship to today's concerns about sexual harassment. This caution saddened them, because they believed they had acquired skills in their 2 or 3 decades of experience that would be useful to neophytes. As one man explained what he called "this garbage":

"Intimacy sometimes can be misunderstood, misinterpreted, not only by the two people who are in the middle of it but by the people who are watching it going on. So I think you have to be awfully careful."

Yet another man mourned the loss of personal and professional relationships with female coworkers. During the 1960s and 1970s in New York, he and his eight female professional staffers enjoyed a special camaraderie: "We drank together, worked together. We cursed together. I loved them, and they loved me . . . in a non-Biblical sense." Could that happen now? "Let's just say it's a heck of a lot more difficult today."

Questions about what public relations professionals consider "success" were posed exclusively in our focused discussions. There we learned that men and women have different perceptions—and that those perceptions change with age and experience. Men cited as indicators of success money, advancement, challenge, happiness on the job, greater and greater responsibility, and being in control of their time. One man who emphasized that salary was not his priority attributed this to "the more feminine side of myself." At least one man considered success a means to an end: "What I've chosen to do for a living is a way of funding the rest of my life." Another simply answered, "I'd be in Hawaii."

As people work longer, their notions of success take on broader dimensions. One man seemed to capture the sentiment of his group when he explained:

"Initially you want to climb the corporate ladder, get to the top. It becomes more you're looking for personal achievement, a sense of accomplishment, you've made a contribution. You've helped society. It isn't all just money. Some of it is . . . professional recognition."

Men in another group echoed this notion, talking at length about what they considered the societal trend of people trying to achieve balance in their lives. They spoke of money as a wedge that may come between one's professional and ultimate goals. Those goals, in their view, included giving back to the profession and to society. Interestingly, most of the men believed that their idea of success is universal. As one man put it, "I always want to work less, make more. . . . Everybody does."

Women had surprisingly little to say about what success means to them. They spoke only in vague terms, alluding to concepts such as "appreciation," "being valued," and "playing the game."

Sexual Harassment

Serini and her colleagues (1998a) explored in depth the perceptions of public relations practitioners toward sexual harassment. They concluded that our field is characterized by a great deal of uncertainty about the problem. Also, women and men disagreed on all five dimensions of the phenomenon we studied (see Table 10.7).

Not surprisingly, women were more likely than men to recognize sexual harassment issues in public relations. Both genders agreed that harassment exists in the field, if not in their own organizations. These perceptions changed little over time.

In 1995, the glass ceiling research team added four questions related to sexual harassment. We found that men tended to believe its incidence is on the decline, but women were not so sure. Women more than men agreed that sexual harassment limits women's opportunities for advancement in their organizations and throughout public relations. Women agreed more than men that people who report sexual harassment lose career opportunities. Men considered sexual harassment a minor issue relative to other problems in the work place today; women disagreed.

Focus group discussions about the matter were intriguing. Men acknowledged that attitudes have changed little over time. They believed that there is more reporting of harassment today, rather than more actual instances. They alluded to greater awareness brought about by public service announcements on television and radio—"All the time," according to one male participant. However, they also believed men pay greater lip service to sexual harassment than in the past. In some cases, as one participant put it, "people are walking on eggshells." Why? A second participant in his group explained, "They just know they're going to get caught more likely than they were 5 years ago." They characterized the problem as one of male ego and power—not an inherently important concern but a major issue in the contemporary work place. Men in another focus group questioned the veracity of survey respondents who acknowledged that harassment is a problem—but not in their own organizations. One man characterized the response as "not in my backyard, someone else's problem."

Women are more likely to perceive the problem, men said, because women expect to encounter it. Men, on the other hand, consider the problem relatively minor because it so rarely happens to them. At the same time, some questioned whether men also are victims of harassment, given the growing number of women in the field. They wondered whether men are as likely to report such victimization and whether it bothers male victims in

TABLE 10.7. Mean Scores of Sexual Harassment Issues Broken Down by Gender, 1990, 1995

Issues	All	Men	Women
1. Sexual harassment exists in public relations.			
In Your Organization			
1990	3.33	3.09	3.49
$t = -3.42, p < .001$	$(N = 812)$	$(n = 344)$	$(n = 460)$
1995	3.22	3.01	3.33
$t = -2.33, p < .05$	$(N = 661)$	$(n = 240)$	$(n = 418)$
Throughout PR			
1990	4.39	4.18	4.54
$t = -4.41, p < .001$	$(N = 812)$	$(n = 344)$	$(n = 460)$
1995	4.38	4.21	4.48
$t = -10.38, p < .001$	$(N = 661)$	$(n = 240)$	$(n = 418)$
2. There is less sexual harassment in public relations work environments today than there was five years ago.			
In Your Organization			
1995	4.37	4.53	4.28
$t = 2.31, p < .05$	$(N = 661)$	$(n = 240)$	$(n = 418)$
Throughout PR			
1995	4.33	4.50	4.24
$t = 3.22, p < .001$	$(N = 661)$	$(n = 240)$	$(n = 418)$
3. Sexual harassment limits women's opportunities for advancement in public relations.			
In Your Organization			
1995	3.33	2.91	3.56
$t = -4.89, p < .001$	$(N = 661)$	$(n = 240)$	$(n = 418)$
Throughout PR			
1995	3.78	3.42	3.99
$t = -4.79, p < .001$	$(N = 661)$	$(n = 240)$	$(n = 418)$
4. People who report sexual harassment lose career opportunities.			
In Your Organization			
1995	3.87	3.48	4.08
$t = -5.01, p < .001$	$(N = 661)$	$(n = 240)$	$(n = 418)$
Throughout PR			
1995	4.46	4.02	4.70
$t = -7.26, p < .001$	$(N = 661)$	$(n = 240)$	$(n = 418)$

(*continued on next page*)

TABLE 10.7. (*continued*)

5. Sexual harassment is a minor issue when compared with other problems in the
   workplace today.

In Your Organization

1995	4.08	4.38	3.90
$t = 3.49, p < .001$	$(N = 661)$	$(n = 240)$	$(n = 418)$

Throughout PR

1995	3.82	4.09	3.65
$t = 3.62, p < .001$	$(N = 661)$	$(n = 240)$	$(n = 418)$

Note. Responses are coded as follows 7 = agree very strongly, 6 = strongly agree, 5 = agree, 4 = uncertain/not sure/don't know, 3 = disagree, 2 = strongly disagree, 1 = disagree very strongly.

the same way that it bothers women. Men acknowledged that the very discussion embarrassed them. However, they agreed—as one participant put it—that the "Demi Moore, Michael Douglass movie is the exception rather than the rule."

Several male participants in one focus group acknowledged that the trauma associated with an actual incidence would be severe enough to make the issue a big one—especially for public relations. As one man put it, "You're dealing with the profession that is supposed to be highly sensitive to these issues."

One man who said he had never seen a "real" sexual-harassment issue on the job did refer to a growing awareness about how individuals interact. He complained that employees are not given training about what constitutes sexual harassment—training he would find increasingly helpful as his staff becomes feminized:

> "Starting a new job with half the staff being women, I was very careful at the beginning of the year about how I was socially with many of the women. You know, simple things like the tone, like their dresses, or, 'Gee, you look nice today,' or whatever. That became a real issue."

His colleagues in the group agreed that the line between flirtation and harassment differs between the sexes.

Men in this same group, too, seemed to agonize over exactly what constitutes harassment. They considered it a knotty problem, as one put it, because of perceptions:

> "One man putting his arm around the woman's shoulder while having a conversation is perfectly okay and acceptable, and another man

does the same thing and it's an untoward advance—because it's how it's perceived."

One man offered this instance of sexual harassment—interesting, because it illustrates the insidiousness of the problem. Two women reported that a man was harassing them at work. The participant in our focus group, who was a shop steward, went to the man to "make sure and put things in the women's file . . . about that they filed these charges against him . . . saying that these women will report sexual harassment all the time . . . as a behavioral pattern." He did this, he told the group, because he thought the charges against his male colleague were unfair.

Somewhat predictably, some men questioned whether women brought on harassment themselves. One participant mentioned receiving three resumes that included photographs of "incredibly attractive women" in the previous 9 months. No men had included pictures with their vitae, leading him to assume that women who "can't sell your skills" may promote their sexuality instead—as he put it, "anything to get that upper edge."

Woman as perpetrator rather than as victim of harassment is a disturbing proposition. Perhaps socialization leads some women to blame themselves even when others consider them blameless for the harassment they face. One man described a female colleague who had been invited by two different male coworkers to spend the night when they were traveling on business. She asked her colleague what she was doing wrong. He told the group: "I almost wanted to slap her over the phone. 'You're not doing anything wrong. I mean, it's them, not you.' "

Virtually every woman in the focus groups told a story of sexual harassment, either her own or that of an acquaintance. Because they had experienced some form of harassment, and few if any men they knew had, they were not surprised at the men's responses. They anticipated backlash as the problem gained in visibility.

Women also expected increasing attention to the problem of sexual harassment as more and more female managers emerge in public relations. Here is one example: "I was probably the only female at a lot of the top management meetings and someone would turn and say, 'Please take notes,' and I'd say, 'No.'" Even incidents women considered fairly innocuous, such as a man complimenting a woman on her appearance, could be traumatic. Over time, women experiencing such treatment come to feel they are seen primarily as women, not as professionals. One woman explained it best:

"Men think they're giving women compliments. And sometimes [they are]. . . . I don't mean to be sensitive about every single thing, but when it's repeated and that's their way of acknowledging you when you walk in a room . . . that really angered me after a while, because that wasn't what I was there for."

Finally, women seemed to blame sexual harassment not so much on lust as on the insecurities some men feel about women. As a result, one woman told us, "They have to kind of bring [women] down a little bit." Women who are "brought down in this way" may be reluctant to report the incidents when they distrust their upper management. Just as women assess their chances at promotion in an organization by seeing how many women the company has promoted before, they look at how the organization has handled previous complaints of harassment. They consider whether they might lose career opportunities as a result of exposing the harasser, although the survey data on this point were inconclusive.

Several women in the focus groups emphasized that they would have to walk, rather than file suit or take a settlement, in too many organizations they had worked for. In fact, fear of losing their job or of being stuck in a dead-end position prompts some women to put up with harassment and hope for the best. We heard from women who had endured the unwanted attention of "slimy, gross" guys who were both coworkers and clients, in the case of public relations firms. Even then, the organization may "kind of push you out," as one woman put it, when superiors are aware of the problem. It becomes an embarrassment and a source of guilt. One woman imagined her boss thinking: "Maybe I should have done something to stop it but I didn't stop it and every time I see you, I'm reminded of that."

Flexibility

We included four questions about accommodation in the work place on our survey instrument. They tapped into perceptions of parental leave policies, flexible hours and locations, and employer-provided child care. In other words, we were asking about issues related to the family.

Child care provided by the organization was least important to our sample. Table 10.8 shows that most respondents agreed that flexibility is critical in their own organizations and in all of public relations. Flexible hours were considerably more important than changeable locations to both women and men—and the perceived importance of such flexibility grew over time. However, every one of the four issues was more important to women than to men—and that significant difference persisted over time. By 1995, the gendered gap had narrowed somewhat.

Participants in our focus groups had much to say about the question of

TABLE 10.8. Mean Scores of Flexibility Issues Broken Down by Gender, 1990, 1995

Issues	All	Men	Women
1. It is important that public relations people be permitted to work flexible hours.			
In your organization			
1990	5.17	4.90	5.36
$t = -4.41, p < .001$	$(N = 812)$	$(n = 344)$	$(n = 460)$
1995	5.54	5.22	5.72
$t = -4.66, p < .001$	$(N = 661)$	$(n = 240)$	$(n = 418)$
Throughout public relations			
1990	5.19	4.88	5.41
$t = -5.45, p < .001$	$(N = 812)$	$(n = 344)$	$(n = 460)$
1995	5.44	5.18	5.60
$t = -4.01, p < .001$	$(N = 661)$	$(n = 240)$	$(n = 418)$
2. It is important that public relations people be permitted to work in flexible locations.			
In your organization			
1990	4.40	4.12	4.60
$t = -4.43, p < .001$	$(N = 812)$	$(n = 344)$	$(n = 460)$
1995	4.94	4.58	5.14
$t = -4.33, p < .001$	$(N = 661)$	$(n = 240)$	$(n = 418)$
Throughout public relations			
1990	4.55	4.24	4.78
$t = -5.72, p < .05$	$(N = 812)$	$(n = 344)$	$(n = 460)$
1995	4.99	4.66	5.18
$t = -4.62, p < .001$	$(N = 661)$	$(n = 240)$	$(n = 418)$
3. It is important that public relations employees have child care provided by their employer.			
In your organization			
1990	3.80	3.53	4.02
$t = -4.27, p < .001$	$(N = 812)$	$(n = 344)$	$(n = 460)$
1995	3.74	3.36	3.96
$t = -4.77, p < .001$	$(N = 661)$	$(n = 240)$	$(n = 418)$
Throughout public relations			
1990	4.00	3.71	4.22
$t = -4.71, p < .001$	$(N = 812)$	$(n = 344)$	$(n = 460)$
1995	3.92	3.55	4.13
$t = -4.88, p < .001$	$(N = 661)$	$(n = 240)$	$(n = 418)$

(*continued on next page*)

TABLE 10.8. (*continued*)

4. It is important that organizations employing public relations practitioners have parental leave policies.

In your organization

1990	4.51	4.15	4.79
$t = -5.70, p < .001$	(N = 812)	(n = 344)	(n = 460)
1995	4.92	4.58	5.11
$t = -4.39, p < .001$	(N = 661)	(n = 240)	(n = 418)

Throughout public relations

1990	4.58	4.19	4.88
$t = -6.59, p < .001$	(N = 812)	(n = 344)	(n = 460)
1995	4.88	4.56	5.06
$t = -4.38, p < .001$	(N = 661)	(n = 240)	(n = 418)

Note. Responses are coded as follows: 7 = agree very strongly, 6 = strongly agree, 5 = agree, 4 = uncertain/not sure/don't know, 3 = disagree, 2 = strongly disagree, 1 = disagree very strongly.

flexibility at work. Men acknowledged the issue as more important to women because, as one man said, "Men are afraid to state their preference for it because it's viewed as, 'Oh, you're not interested in a career; you're not serious.' " Others in his group concurred that making a case for flexibility is considered a negative for men—especially expressing interest in parental leave policies. One participant in a men's group offered this anecdote: "I know a man who took 6 months off to be a house husband . . . and it was a career breaker for him." A man in another group summed up the sense of most of his colleagues: "I would hazard a guess that most men would be perfectly fine working the 9 to 5 or 7 to 7 schedule downtown in the office . . . and that women are probably more interested in the flexible work-place type arrangements."

Of course, we found no universal agreement among men on this point. Another man complained about the distance he travels to work. As a result, he said, "I'm very interested in transporting those tasks out of the office." A bachelor, too, voiced a somewhat different perspective. He expressed resentment that flexibility to accommodate home or family concerns disadvantaged him:

"As a single guy, I hate being dumped on. What happens is I got bosses who've been women who have kids, who get sick. Who does all their work? I do, but I don't have any kids to worry about. There's no equal benefit that I get from the company. . . . When people leave the office early for family it's to go home; when a single person leaves it's to go out. There's a different perception about that—you're not working really hard."

The seemingly obvious solution came from another man in the same group: create a "level playing field," where family responsibility does not fall solely on women. One way to do that is the day-care center touted by a male participant in one of our focus groups. His organization converted a spare office for children. The result?

> "It's been great. We've been able to keep female workers that are very valuable, sometimes management-level people, with the company as opposed to them leaving because they couldn't spend time with their child."

At least one other single man appreciated work-place flexibility, although he did not have the responsibility of child or elder care. He chose to work four 10-hour days, which he acknowledged as more important for people with families, but he liked the arrangement very much. Also, we heard about men who shared the responsibility for their families. For them, work-place accommodation was critical. One manager explaining today's realities said:

> "I have as many men in my employ as women who bring up family issues, who want to be home with their children, who we make accommodations for simply because we want them to have the fullest of their life. That's what they demand of us, what an employee demands in every organization."

Technology may help. As one participant speculated, when "people can work from home, it's not going to matter." Online computer services, e-mail, fax, voice mail, and beepers all were mentioned as helping free employees from the tyranny of the 9-to-5 office. Still, although men alluded to women they knew who worked from home, they agreed that most homes offer too many distractions to be productive. One man went so far as to say, "If I stayed at home, I'd never work." Some worried about feeling isolated away from the office. Also, they argued that the agency business in particular depends on face-to-face interactions and immediate response— thus eliminating the possibility of account people who stay home. (Another man countered, "That's why you gotta wear a beeper!") The fact remains that new technology creates the capability for nontraditional working arrangements. What matters is finding a way to accommodate workers who need flexibility on the job, especially with elder care looming.

Even now, lack of flexibility or unreasonable inflexibility is a problem for women who are mothers. Women we talked with described real suffering, as in the cases of the two who knocked themselves out to do "everything right" when they were on maternity leave and then came back with the assistance of nannies. The result? When they came back, they "were told that unless they were in their desks, in their office at 7 o'clock at night whether they were done with their work, whether they had anything to do or not, it didn't look good for them."

Thus women typically considered parental leave a double-edged sword. As one woman explained, "We really want it and we need it but it's not going to help us in terms of our career advancement." Women who take advantage of flexible hours in general believe they are held back as a result. Even female bosses may disadvantage them, saying (as another woman put it), "You're not getting ahead because you didn't give up as much as I did."

Significant Changes Between 1990 and 1995

Remarkably few changes characterize the perceptions of men and women on these issues presented to them in 1990 and again in 1995. Both groups were more likely to believe women received lower salaries than men throughout public relations than in their own organizations. However, women and men tended to disagree on the relative strengths each brought to the bargaining table during times of salary negotiation. Socialization may be working to disadvantage women, although our analysis of the data suggests a female work force growing in the self-confidence necessary to demand more and not settle for less. Some women consider this newfound assertiveness unsettling for men, which might account in part for men's diminishing satisfaction with their work in pubic relations.

We also concluded that having a mentor and learning to network are not a panacea for getting ahead in public relations. Both are fraught with the potential for misunderstanding. Likewise, affirmative action was rejected as a significant factor in women's being hired or promoted in the field; focus group participants alluded to how such equity policies had not resulted in more racioethnic minorities and people with disabilities gaining ground in the field. The major factor inhibiting the advancement of public relations professionals seems to be the devaluation of the entire field, rather than its practitioners themselves. Still, women continued to believe that men have an easier and quicker time getting to the top in their field.

Women (and men) who felt at a disadvantage in terms of their likelihood of being promoted typically left their employers, reinforcing again the understanding that (1) public relations stands to lose major talent when these professionals go into other fields and (2) organizations risk the loss of ambitious staffers who go into business for themselves. Women typically gauged their chances for success by checking for senior-level women in the company.

In much the same way, women often decided whether to report an incidence of sexual harassment by reviewing how their employer had handled similar problems in the past. The specter of harassment loomed significantly larger in the work life of female than male practitioners in our research. Astute participants in our focus groups understood the significance of the issue of sexual harassment, even if they disagreed along gender lines about its pervasiveness and its causes. They recognized that of all organizational functions, public relations can least afford to be painted with the brush of harassment.

The clearest change in perceptions over the 5-year period of our longitudinal study came in the area of work-place flexibility. With the passage of time, both men and women perceived it was more important that public relations be permitted to be carried out in flexible locations and to have the option of parental leave. We heard much enlightened discussion on this topic, and the champions for accommodation included men as well as women who were concerned about their employees' quality of life at the office and at home.

Given the pervasiveness of these issues related to the glass ceiling, and how little perceptions had changed over time, we echo the question of one woman: "Where are all the women that are really pushing for women's issues?" In the concluding section of this chapter, we enlarge the challenge to encompass men as well as women, and our professional associations as well as their individual members.

CONCLUDING THOUGHTS

The results of this audit of men and women in public relations suggest several conclusions. First, there has been an impact on the field of public relations beyond what the practitioners themselves controlled. The economic downturn of the early 1990s led to or exacerbated a restructuring of the internal public relations function from senior management to middle management. Many professionals left staff jobs and started their own consulting businesses. Those who left seemed to be more often men than women as evidenced by the third, or agency, factor to emerge in the roles analysis. That it was the men who left is further evidenced by the decreasing number of men in PRSA's membership who took part in the survey. The men who participated in the focus groups spoke somewhat longingly about the good old days and the perks and authority that were no longer a part of their jobs. As a result, in part, their level of satisfaction at work declined, whereas for women it increased. The emergence of women in significant numbers in this field was a second significant factor affecting men's satisfaction negatively.

The change in organizational use of public relations provided opportunities for women to advance, although what they found was more midlevel management positions and pay. Their satisfaction was evident in the focus group findings. Women perceived fewer barriers to advancement in public relations than they had 5 years earlier. Like men, they remain most dissatisfied with the prestige and value attributed to their chosen field, public relations.

Even after 5 years, many of the results suggested that men and women perceive work-place issues along the same lines of the specific instances in which they have personal experience. Some men believed women were given favored treatment because of affirmative action requirements. At the same time, others in the focus groups expressed surprise at the large disparity between men's and women's average salaries. Women more than men perceived the existence and damage of sexual harassment.

If there was a breakthrough, it was in the area of flexibility. Both men and women saw the need for a flexible work place that provided time and location choices rather than the traditional organizational requirement that people be on the job between 9 and 5 (or later). Women and men alike acknowledged the need for parental leave policies.

Educating top management was a thread woven throughout our focus group discussions. Participants across the country, male and female, urged PRSA to work toward CEOs' appreciation for the potential of the public relations function. They considered this outreach, in the words of one man, "almost an insurmountable task." However, few of their personal or professional goals could be realized if public relations remains isolated from the top tier of organizational decision making. One focus group participant suggested a second role for PRSA: serving as the public conscience for the profession. His fellow participant in a group called for the industry's launching of a "management sensitivity program" to overcome the negative perceptions (and in some cases, reality) of public relations. Participants in our research seemed to agree that the long-term credibility of the field is at stake. Finally, they hoped PRSA programs would showcase more women. As we learned in one women's group, "I'm tired of hearing from the 50- or 60-year-old male executive." She acknowledged that she could learn many things from these people, who typically form the panels at professional development sessions, but "I cannot relate to them on another level." She wanted to see more female panelists. Others in her group agreed, and added they hoped PRSA would continue to conduct its all-important salary surveys.

These results could provide for a dialogue between the men and women of public relations who will have to collaborate if public relations is to maintain and even gain in status. The practitioners we surveyed saw things differently because of their own experiences. Many of them expressed this understanding in the focus groups. As a result, we think they are open enough to understand the experiences of the other sex and to benefit the entire practice of public relations.

Chapter Eleven

Explaining Gender Inequality in the Work Place

I n this chapter, we turn to explanations for discrimination against women in public relations. Results from our survey, interviews, and focus groups combine to provide a revealing portrayal of the barriers female practitioners face. The portrait painted in this chapter draws most heavily on long talks with female practitioners and focus groups conducted with women selected from among those interviewees in Maryland and Florida, rather than reiterating much of the survey and focus group data we describe in detail in the Appendix.

Most research has shown that women earn less than men because they are willing to accept less, because society values male employees more highly, because women have greater caretaking demands, and because women work in lower paying organizations such as nonprofits (Toth, 1989b). Research specifically in public relations has shown gender-based differences among practitioners in their perceptions of a double standard for work, opportunities for advancement, making personal sacrifices, encounters with sex discrimination, expression of emotions, networking with the "good old boys," and ability to command top salary (Toth & Cline, 1991; see also Hon, L. Grunig, and Dozier, 1992). Broom and Dozier (1986) documented that the number of women in technician roles within public relations provides a partial explanation for salary discrimination. However, they consistently have found that female managers are paid less than male managers, indicating that pure gender discrimination also is involved.

Our findings parallel these explanations but present a fuller picture. Importantly, none of our research participants believed that *overt* discrimination against women in public relations was the major problem. Rather, they thought women face a complex system of *indirect* barriers to advancement. This argument is consistent with evidence from a 6-year international study of public relations that found little explicit gender bias (J. Grunig, 1992). The authors of IABC's velvet ghetto study also maintained that discrimination in public relations is linked to subtle biases rather than to obvious anachronisms such as sexist language and male-only perks (Cline et al., 1986).

Most of the obstacles our respondents cited are not unique to public relations, but instead they can be found throughout the public sphere. We have discussed these issues in earlier chapters. Now, we turn to a discussion of these problems as they relate specifically to women in public relations.

THE MALE-DOMINATED WORK PLACE

Masculine Value Systems

Many of our female research participants considered the work place still a man's world. They made the point that at work "maleness" is valued, whereas women's concerns rarely are taken seriously. Feminist scholars (e.g., Acker, 1990; "Feminists to Bring Broader Perspective," 1988), too, have argued that masculinity and organizational values are one and the same. For them, masculine institutions form the system of oppression feminists call "patriarchy."

Organizational theorists also have documented that organizations are masculine entities (Conrad, 1990; Morgan, 1986). That is, organizational value systems typically reflect attributes that are associated with masculinity, such as rationality, competition, and independence. Addressing this issue, the communication manager for a state solar energy center mentioned how she wanted to establish a communication program geared toward children but her idea was squashed. What was important to her as a woman was dismissed by organizational leaders who want her to direct her communication efforts only to those with money and power. Another interviewee commented on this reality when she pointed out that "the values that are important [in organizations]—conflict, confrontation, power, dominance, macho strength—have been socialized into men." At the same time, women's traditional concerns—such as educating children—are devalued.

Some of our research participants also believed that women's contributions are often not even noticed. Several women mentioned how their male bosses have taken credit for their work. Others talked about how they often feel ignored during meetings.

Many of the women we interviewed agreed that all organizations tend to be male-dominated, but several believed that these problems are more pronounced in some types of organizations than in others. The director of corporate communication for a professional and technical services firm considered her industry particularly male-dominated. So did a manager of public relations for a firm that manufactures shuttle booster rockets. She said her company is led by a "good old boy network" of mostly retired military personnel who are very close-knit and are "recycled again and again."

A senior counselor at a national agency argued that the glass ceiling is felt more in traditional, for-profit institutions, whereas an agency such as hers is more progressive. The advantages of women working in agencies also were reported in one survey of public relations professionals ("Survey Reveals Insights," 1991). These practitioners believed that women have a far better chance of advancement in the typical firm than in a corporate department. For a second example, a director of news information at a private, technical university said that she has not experienced problems related to gender discrimination. She commented that universities seem to be made up of people who are more open-minded and "freethinking" than those in many corporate environments. The retired vice president of a national firm noted regional differences in "tolerance for women," stating that certain parts of the country (e.g., the Rust Belt) are less accepting than others. She may be right, given that regional discrepancies in salaries for male and female practitioners were documented in our survey. The largest gaps were in New Jersey and the six New England states. Differences also were significantly greater than the norm in the central and upper midwestern states.

Some of the women noted that organizational size also makes a difference. One said that her male clients in smaller companies have no problem accepting a woman into their fold whereas larger companies may be more conservative. As another noted, the more red tape in an organization, the less risk men can take. Or, as still another believed, most small companies are new and therefore do not have an "entrenched [male] culture."

Women's Exclusion from Men's Networks

Almost all of our interviewees and focus group participants talked about women's isolation from the inner circle where important business gets done. Most referred to this clique as the "good old boy" network and said that it shuts them out at the management table as well as on the basketball court or on the golf course. A director of external affairs for a telephone company was particularly vocal about discussing women's exclusion because so much of her job entails building relationships in the community. Because she is a woman, she does not get invited to do a lot of informal things with men. She has to find other ways to gain access and visibility. So she joins groups that place her within the "leadership pool" of the community and performs extra volunteer and community work. But she must do all of these in a way that is "not threatening" to the men's wives.

An associate director of research at a national firm explained that she misses input into the "off the cuff" discussions or "buddying up" among men. She believed that these friendships put other men "top of mind" when it comes to recommending people for jobs and promotions. How the "golf syndrome" helps men also was a topic raised. Most of the focus group participants believed that women must earn credibility solely through their work, whereas men sometimes recommend one another simply because they are friends. One focus group also addressed the benefits men enjoy by having nonworking access to other men. One participant noted that women trying to break into this network are "damned if you do, damned if you don't." That is, women trying to be "one of the guys doesn't play well."

Most of our research participants implied that women's exclusion is not a male conspiracy. Rather, men are just more comfortable dealing with other men. As one woman in a PRSA focus group said, there are "more men in the inner circle," and men "wouldn't feel comfortable seeing women and men with the same experience in that management role." Many of our female respondents acknowledged that, similarly, women tend to be more comfortable working with women.

The director of promotions for a professional sports team argued that women sometimes purposely reject the networking strategies of men: "The golf scene is the level men have worked at. Women are more professional, more direct. . . . They choose not to participate at that level." Not all of our female participants felt excluded from men's networks. As the college publications director said, even though she works in a male-dominated environment, she feels that she is part of the team. The men there involve her in decision making and other managerial functions. She believed that this inclusion is especially notable because she only works part time.

All of these comments about gender and networking are important because of the "similarity preference," or people's tendency to hire, groom, and promote people like themselves (Conrad, 1990). Given this tendency, male managers are more likely to groom other men, not women. A participant in one men's PRSA focus group noted this dilemma. He said:

"[Women] don't automatically have credibility—[it's] a delicate personal relationship. People tend to trust people like themselves."

The owner of a publications design business argued that men generally consider male students better prepared than female students for management slots. However, she did recognize some men's efforts toward fostering women's careers but said these actions were hardly "revolutionary change." This practitioner's assertion seems to be supported by our survey data. Male respondents appeared to think they are better suited than women for management-level positions in public relations. However, one woman argued that the subjective nature of public relations can lead to ambiguous evaluations of practitioners' competence. Some of the other participants in her group thought that this ambiguity factor causes lackluster men to be promoted while outstanding women are passed by.

A related issue also was raised by some women: Men may avoid championing women out of fear that others will think their interests are romantic. As one interviewee explained, "They [senior men] can be more personal with men; they pull back from women. . . . It comes into play with my interactions with men. . . . It means you don't have the personal interaction."

Networking among women was another topic discussed by many of our female research participants. Some worried that opportunities are so limited that some women are forced to promote themselves at the expense of other women. This situation causes "catfighting" among women or the elevation of only the "meanest" women. The convergence of these two problems was referred to several times as the "queen bee syndrome."

Many of the women believed, though, that successful women are neither harsh nor do they undermine other women. For example, one participant said that women always have been open to sharing and have done a lot for each other. Or, as other women argued, individual personality—not gender—determines people's relationships with others.

One agency owner cited Kanter's (1977) argument that women's so-called catty behavior is linked to the roles women typically play in organizations—and not to their gender. Blum and Smith (1988) explained that "traits that are often cited as *causes* of women's subordinate status are better understood as *results* of subordinate positions in organizations" (p. 533). For example, Kanter (1977) found in her study of clerical workers in one firm that female secretaries' low aspirations and low level of commitment to the company and their careers were not aspects of their feminine self-image. Rather, these characteristics were a *response* to their minimal opportunity for advancement and the low level of power inherent in their positions (see also Doyal, 1990).

Women's Lack of Self-Esteem and Undervaluing Their Worth

Many of our research participants believed that women lack self-esteem and undervalue their worth. As one business owner noted, many women seem to have an unjustified lack of confidence. She believed that when women enter the professional work force, many question their place there, believing they are not ready for success or family pressures will not allow them to succeed. Women's perceptions of their competence in this new arena of public relations suffered as a result.

Some researchers (e.g., L. Grunig, 1989b) attribute women's lack of confidence to the "impostor syndrome." This occurs when women feel like "fakes," realizing they are working in a man's world, according to men's rules. The psychological result can be self-doubt (Bell & Young, 1986). One interviewee said that women's questioning themselves is tied to the "societal mind-set" that women "constantly have to improve" themselves. She also believed that women's sagging self-esteem stems in part from college professors whom she described as "discouraging." As she stated, "You get indoctrinated in school that you are going to be perceived that way [not worthy]."

Some women argued that women's devaluation begins much earlier than college. One cited research that shows that girls and boys start elementary school with high self-esteem. By the time these students have graduated from high school, the girls' confidence has slipped dramatically. This practitioner said that women carry this feeling of inadequacy with them into the work place and then "disappear in the boardroom."

Powers (1991) made the same argument, citing a 1989 report issued by the Mid-Atlantic Equity Center and the New England Center for Equity Assistance. This report concluded that women's doubts linger as women enter their careers and contribute "to the economic penalties they encounter in the workplace" (as quoted on p. 7). One participant in a focus group mentioned that women she knows are capable of rising to higher posts, but these women's uncertainty about themselves keeps them from applying for top jobs. This occurs even when these women already have been performing the job duties of the higher position.

Women's Timidity About Salary Negotiation

Women's low self-esteem was linked by many of our female respondents to women's timidity about salary negotiation. This finding is consistent with research by Mathews (1988), who found that some female practitioners were embarrassed to admit they were inexperienced with the basic techniques of salary negotiation. Several interviewees said that women are much more likely than men to take a smaller salary than they deserve. As the editor for an association's member magazine put it, "Women are too grateful."

Related to this are the differences in men's and women's expectations about salary in public relations. DeRosa and Wilcox (1989) found that male students of public relations expect to earn from $5,000 to $10,000 more than women in their entry-level jobs. The director of community relations for a county school system acknowledged that, in her first job, she settled for too little money. She admitted that she should have looked for more, but she suffered from a "crisis of self-confidence" that left her unsure of herself.

Another example is the associate director of research for a national agency, who revealed that she sometimes lacks self-confidence and "tolerates a little more responsibility" than she is being paid for. She said:

"Women have this bad habit of letting people pile work on them without saying, 'What are you going to do for me?' or 'How is it going to be paid for?' Women will just do things without asking for more pay or promotion. Men don't do that."

Several women in her focus group agreed. As one said: "Women don't know how to ask for raises. We don't know how to ask for what we want." Another explained that this timidity is part of female socialization. That is, women learn that "it's not nice to talk about money; it's embarrassing."

Several women brought up another, related point: The salary problem for women is exacerbated by the "dual-career issue" or "second-income syndrome." Some women accept less pay because they see their income as complementary to or secondary to their spouse's salary. Or, employers offer women less because they assume women can rely on their spouses' check.

Stewart (1988) criticized female practitioners who make their careers secondary to their partner's career. She said that when women do so, organizations are justified in not considering women for top posts. However, this argument ignores the reality that generally men make more money than women and do not participate equally in domestic chores, even when their wives work full time outside the home (Hochschild, 1989). Thus, the logic of finances or the burden of home responsibilities (or both) causes some women to make their jobs secondary to their spouses'.

Not all of our female respondents undervalue themselves, nor are they all uncomfortable with salary issues. For example, the vice president of a national firm said that she never has felt timid about her abilities and has been outspoken when it comes to salaries and raises. But, she said she does this "without being a bitch." Her approach involves "strategic thinking, convincing people, mothering, nurturing." One agency owner has learned to play the money game, too, by becoming much more "deliberate" and "brazen" about her business after realizing that she had been undervaluing her services. She said that "women need to learn what is a lot of money to [men]."

A related issue—women's fear of risk taking—also was mentioned by research participants. For example, the women in one PRSA focus group discussed their beliefs that men were more conditioned to take risks than women. Some research has shown that, as children, girls are less inclined toward risks than boys; as adults, women are given fewer opportunities to take risks (Bell & Young, 1986; Slovik, 1966). Several of the women we talked with believed women's trepidation can result in their staying in jobs they dislike. Some mentioned their own fear of risks, acknowledging that they have gotten comfortable in positions and stayed too long.

A Dearth of Female Role Models and Mentors

Men's stranglehold on power in the work place also translates into too few female role models and mentors who might guide other women. Almost all of our female research participants said that women need to have mentoring to "move up." Several women pointed out that the shortage of female role models contributes to women's not getting groomed in business skills. The women in one focus group discussed how the presence of high-ranking women can make a real difference for other women. One recalled attending a meeting of a board of directors that included women. She said that simply having other women to join in the bathroom was affirming: "You suddenly realized what the men knew all along."

In earlier work we (L. Grunig, 1989b) explained gender discrimination in public relations by highlighting the importance of role models and mentoring for women. This research is consistent with the velvet ghetto study, which concluded that linking junior women with top-level female practitioners should be a major initiative for professional associations in public relations.

A related issue was raised by several research participants who have been role models: They are tired of having to be the "representative" for women and fighting for women. This problem usually is referred to as "tokenism," whereby women who have "made it" are coerced into representing womankind; these women must excel for all women (L. Grunig, 1989c). However, successful women often lack female peers with whom they can share their feelings of isolation, of not being heard, or of having their ideas ignored (Lyles, 1985).

The owner of a publications design business admitted her frustration at being the lone voice for women at meetings. She wondered why she should still be grappling with women's issues after all this time. Another woman expressed the same sentiment, confessing that after 15 years of fighting, she is tired. Still another said that constantly having to speak up for women gets tedious and has made her jaded. "You get so tired," she said. "You think, 'I shouldn't have to do this.' You either say, 'Just screw it,' or keep fighting back."

Related to the dearth of women at high levels may be some women's lack of professionalism—a problem cited by several of the interviewees and female focus-group participants. These women believed that too often "women can be their own worst enemy" by undermining themselves by "sneaky" behavior or sabotaging themselves by the inadvertent sexual or "little girl" messages they send.

In one focus group a female participant called some women "crybabies." She said such women blame gender for their problems rather than acknowledging their poor performance. She also said that because of these women's unprofessional behavior, other women suffer through "guilt by association." Another woman in the same group said that women's worst enemy is other women, the "blonde bimbos" who do not act professionally. Still another woman said that the field might end up with "a cadre of old broads who have worked hard to establish credibility" while a set of young "powderpuffs" undoes the older group's efforts. Participants agreed that public relations attracts women like this.

Stewart (1988) also questioned some female practitioners' professionalism. She recounted how a woman complained to her about not being taken seriously:

> "I stood there and looked at her multicolored dress, lace hose, cute little earrings shaped like cats and green eye shadow and wondered how on earth she even got employed by the conservative corporation she is with. . . . If she does not have enough sense and seasoning to project a serious image, why should top management have confidence in her?" (p. 23)

On this point, we consider it important to note that men define what is appropriate behavior (and, by extension, what is means to be "professional") in organizations. So, as long as standards continue to be defined by men, women may come up short no matter how they act or dress. At the very least, women are forced to spend an inordinate amount of time at work trying to fit in (Morgan, 1986). Further, some women's lack of professionalism probably does not stem from unique female sensibilities. Rather, this behavior no doubt is linked to the social norm that women's glamour and sexuality are more valued than women's professionalism. As Wolf (as cited in Kleiman, 1991a) pointed out, the only occupations where women are paid more than men are modeling and prostitution.

Socialization and Women's Ambivalence Toward Careers

Several research participants asserted that the choice some women have about whether or not to have a career contributes to the glass ceiling. As an independent consultant said, as long as society grants women that choice and not men, "potential employers will wonder about women." One agency owner added that, because of women's motherhood role, women are not socialized toward a long-term career and often choose staff jobs. She conceded, however, that this tendency is changing.

Cline and her colleagues (1986) also argued that socialization helps explain why female practitioners tend to stay technicians. Socialization may be the reason why some management scholars claim that "women don't crave power enough" (Gallese, 1991, p. 19). Studying 24 corporate women in a variety of fields, Gallese theorized that women's advancement is stymied in part because of the way women and their male peers perceive women's capability for attaining and using power. As one of Gallese's interviewees explained: "There are glass ceilings for women because women won't fight in the same way that a man will fight. Women won't demand the same things. Even more importantly, the male hierarchy doesn't expect women to demand the same things" (p. 19).

Related to socialization is some women's ambivalence toward their careers (Cline et al., 1986; R. Simpson & I. Simpson, 1969). The velvet ghetto study (Cline et al., 1986) found that some women express less involvement in their jobs than men do. For these women, work is a less central part of their lives. R. Simpson and I. Simpson (1969) suggested that some women see their job as just a temporary haven before marriage.

Some women's lesser commitment to their careers may lead to women's not being "career pathed" to the same degree their male counterparts are. Several interviewees said that women are more likely to be hired merely to do a "job" than begin or enter a career path. A female participant in one focus group agreed, saying women are not aggressive enough about "strategic pathing" in their careers. She believed that men expect and plan for quick movement whereas women get stuck or do not demand movement. Mathews (1988) also argued that some female practitioners have "a steady, if somewhat timid, approach to career pathing" (p. 25). Instead of believing a career path is a vertical climb, women may see their path as "a winding road that travels up a small slope and then levels off with positions as manager or senior manager" (p. 26).

However, several students in an undergraduate class in public relations at the University of Maryland who read Mathews' article questioned her arguments. One student (as quoted in L. Grunig, 1990c) challenged Mathews' point that "women in public relations 'lack focus' about their personal and professional lives" (p. 30). This student said that any lack of focus among women is because women are "victims of their traditional roles in society." She also said that men need to "play a role in helping women lessen the price women must pay to attain their professional goals" (pp. 31–32).

Rush, Kaufman, and Allen (1995) made the same point even more forcefully:

> Now is the time for men to begin their hard labor by correcting the structural inequities and societal symbols they have erected. . . . Men now need to pour *their time, their energy, their money, their knowledge* of the construction and maintenance of structural inequities into disassembling and restructuring those same systems. (p. 6; emphasis in original)

The women in an early PRSA focus group discussed a related issue: whether women in public relations "choose" the technician role. "[They] can't see themselves in management," one said. Another said that practitioners must be able technicians as well as managers, but the two roles are very different: "Few technicians can be managers—but managers must be able to do [the] technical." Still another added:

> "It's the same in other fields and it's similar personality characteristics that get you beyond the technical. . . . if you want to be a manager, you have to train to be a good manager; [you] have to be respected as a senior manager—managing people, budgets, not as a PR person."

Ryan (as quoted in Lukovitz, 1989) disputed the assertion that female practitioners' choosing or getting stuck in lower or midlevel posts is of their own doing: "All of the women I know perceive themselves as far transcending the roles they are obliged to occupy" (p. 20). For her, a discriminatory environment—not women's lack of aspirations—explains women's lower status. Bolstering this point is research by Goldin, Blau, and O'Neill (as cited in Nasar, 1992a) that showed young women's expectations about work have shifted profoundly since the first wave of baby boomers entered the work force. These scholars found that since the mid-1980s, women expect a lifelong career and are preparing themselves with the necessary credentials.

Some of our female respondents agreed with this characterization. For example, one practitioner, who previously taught public relations at a state university, said that her female public relations students were as serious if not more serious about their careers than the male students. She added that these women are no longer strictly "maternally motivated"; they are "career primary."

Powell (1988) cited research that shows socialization differences between women and men favor women as managers and are contrary to gender stereotypes. Chusmir (1985) found that female managers have a higher need for achievement than male managers. Similarly, Donnell and Hall (1980) reported that compared to men, women are more concerned with opportunities for growth, autonomy, and challenge and less concerned with work environment. Powell (1988) believed that findings such as these indicate that, because women have had to overcome stereotypical attitudes about their unsuitability for management, those who secure management positions are actually more motivated toward achievement and self-actualization than men are.

Women's Discomfort with or Lack of Knowledge About Organizational Advancement

Male dominance of the work place means that men have defined the rules for advancement. Many of our female interviewees pointed out that women are either uncomfortable with "playing the game" by men's rules or have not been schooled in the political strategizing men learn from one another (or both). An example is the coordinator of community relations for a county school system, who acknowledged her discomfort with the "stressful politics" in the male-dominated sphere of educational administration. She said that men aspire to these positions for money and power. Thus, advancing involves competition and confrontation. She contended that women are there for "more accurate reasons": They want to help children. Given this, men's games for succeeding are at odds with her female values. A former communication liaison, who works in the same school system, described the frustration she experiences over the male-centered politicking that thwarts her efforts to work for the children of her school district. That is, her priorities are constantly clashing with "the good old boys" who value enhancing their own stature above all else.

The associate director of research at a national agency summed up women's trepidation well: "I'm not sure women are always comfortable [with the rules of the game] because they weren't socialized that way. . . . Some women learn to play by the rules, but it bothers them; they react more."

The director of external affairs for a telephone company thought that, for women, "business is a different animal." Thus, "women don't know how to get what they want." She said that women are too direct; they do not realize that things are accomplished by coalition building—not by going and asking for something point blank. She explained that "coalition building is not our [women's] natural talent." Similarly, several other women argued that women are not socialized to develop the contacts they will need for advancement.

Several women mentioned another disadvantage when it comes to political strategizing: Women are not team players. Several women said that men can wound one another and walk off the field arm-in-arm. However, women in the same situation would personalize the exchange and feel hurt. The manager of public relations for a shuttle booster rocket manufacturer cited herself as an example. She said: "When you are playing with the boys, you had better be tough. You have to . . . keep the competition on the playing field and not take it personally." She admitted, though, that playing the game sometimes leaves her feeling "devastated."

Turk (1986c) also drew a link between advancement in public relations and team-playing skills. For her, female practitioners are disadvantaged because they do not bring the experience of team sports to their work. Yet the director of communication for a state solar energy center disagreed with the assertion that men have special talents for team interaction. She said men may have played team sports, but the experience did not do them much good. That is, except for collegiality, men have no edge in team-building skills. Several research participants said that if women are disadvantaged when it comes to playing organizational politics, it is only because they lack experience. Once women learn the rules, they can be as politically astute as men.

Negative Attitudes Among Senior Men

Another obstacle for women is the outmoded and unchanging attitudes of the senior set of men at the top of organizations. Several women contended that the managerial generation, or men 45 and up, are "anti-women" who see women as a threat. The director of public relations for an accounting firm said her organization wants to be progressive about dealing with women. But, she explained, the "older men are standing in the way."

Moore (1986a) argued that older men for the most part do not intentionally discriminate against women; they are just following their customary way of choosing people to advance. After all, the "successful PR executive" has been defined—on paper—as a corporate or agency decision maker who earns more than $175,000 a year, is more than 45 years old, has more than 20 years of experience, works a 50-hour week, and is male ("Survey Reveals Insights," 1991).

The anachronistic attitudes of senior men were discussed in our focus groups. One participant thought that older men do not promote women because these men still have the perception that women are going to have a baby and leave. Another noted that women do leave rather than stay in a low-paying, unchallenging job. The women in this group thought that the only solution was these men's eventual death. As one participant recalled, a sympathetic senior man once told her, "Sometimes you just have to wait until all those people who hold those attitudes die off."

The director of promotion for a professional sports team pointed out an exception. She explained that, although her boss harbors traditional attitudes about women, he wants to learn and change. She recalled how, in an effort to become more enlightened, he asked her with sincerity, "Now, you're not a secretary, are you?" His ignorance provided her an opportunity to explain how her job differs. She said that he and she have exchanges like this every day.

Most of the women believed that younger men are more egalitarian than the senior set. For example, an agency owner said that men 35 and younger have grown up with women in the work force and do not consider women's presence there an issue. Arguing that young men are different, one woman cited an example of a male intern who did hold not stereotypes about women. Another participant in the same group was not so sure. She believed that "the sons of the old boys have learned some of the same attitudes." As she said, "Look at MTV [Music Television]; I don't see a lot of enlightened attitudes."

Miller and Kruger (1990) also questioned the popular belief that young men are free of chauvinistic attitudes and behaviors toward working women. As Cram (as quoted in Miller & Kruger, 1990) pointed out: "These men may have 'intellectually' changed their views about what is appropriate in the workplace. But, their emotions and behavior have not quite caught up with what they want to believe" (p. 96). Dubbing these men the "new old boys," Miller and Kruger believed that the prejudices of these men are even more insidious than those of traditional chauvinists. This is because younger men really believe they are enlightened. At the same time, though, these men find subtle ways of perpetuating discrimination against women. Their techniques include male bonding (e.g., talking about sports) and "innocent" jokes about women's appearance (p. 96).

One participant commented on this trend, arguing that the 1970s saw progress for women. It was socially unacceptable to be sexist then. The 1980s, however, brought a resurgence of "Neanderthal" attitudes toward women, which indicates that the "pendulum is swinging back." Thus, she worried that chauvinists are still "alive and breeding." Another participant in that group raised a related issue. She wondered if because the 1970s did effect progress for women, men are no longer making a conscious effort to deal with discrimination. That is, too many men might assume erroneously that they no longer have to.

However, Nasar (1992a) cited a fresh body of research that dispels the argument that the 1980s brought a backlash against feminism and that women's progress was stalled. Conducted for the most part by female economists, this research showed that women made impressive economic strides in the 1980s. Further, the results suggested that women's gains would continue in the 1990s regardless of which party ruled the White House. These economists attributed women's progress to their higher expectations and better education as well as fewer women dropping out of the work force and for less time.

Conflicting Messages for Women

A final barrier related to a male-dominated work place is conflicting messages for women. Many of our female respondents pointed out that masculine attributes for managers are esteemed; but when women display these traits, they are evaluated negatively. For example, several women commented on the "whiner assumption." That is, assertiveness is prized in organizations; but when women assert themselves, too often they are dubbed "whiners."

Some women said that people perceive women's strength as "bitchiness." As the director of development for a state university explained, when a man is aggressive, others believe he is acting appropriately. But when a woman displays aggressiveness, others believe something is wrong; she must be suffering from "PMS," for example. One woman said that her assertiveness has not been well received by top management. She noted that several of her female staff members also have been tagged "aggressive" and "probably won't get ahead." She expressed frustration about not knowing when "crossing over" and displaying masculine attributes is appropriate and when this should be avoided.

In the same group, another participant revealed that she finds herself "monitoring" her behavior to avoid being perceived as too female. She recalled how, after reprimanding male subordinates for what she thought was obnoxious behavior, these men later "coddled" her as if her reaction were inappropriate. That is, the men seemed to think she was having some "female problem" that made her overly sensitive.

Morrison, White, and Van Velsor (1987) pointed out that the range of "appropriate" behavior for women at work is narrow. If women display too many masculine traits—assertiveness, ambition, risk taking—they are perceived negatively since these qualities are not consistent with female roles. However, if women display too many feminine traits—passivity, dependence, emotionality—they are perceived as lacking in the characteristics needed for leadership positions in organizations (Conrad, 1990). Morrison et al. (1987) concluded that these inconsistencies leave many professional women walking an uncomfortable tightrope.

WOMEN'S BALANCING ACT

Many of our research participants believed that women's advancement in organizations is impeded because of women's traditional role as the caregivers in society. Some women noted that the "balancing act" is made more difficult by the societal myth that the "fast track" is right for everyone. The vice president of public relations for a health care organization made the point that women feel guilty about neglecting the parenting role. As the communication manager for a scientific instruments manufacturer pointed out, if she had kids she would want to be with them. She would "feel the pressure and tug."

One participant in a focus group said that women with children at home do not have it so easy as men in a similar situation. But, as she commented, "You make those choices." Seconding this point, a senior counselor at a national agency asserted that the "idea of the superwoman is a myth." She said that women have to make choices; they cannot do it all. Toth (1988) pointed out the catch-22 inherent in this dilemma: Women often are forced to make choices between their professional and personal lives that men might not face in equal numbers. Women's making these choices, of course, may inhibit their careers. As one agency head explained, "the system" is not set up for managing a career and a family. She conceded, however, that women are finding creative ways such as job sharing to strike a balance.

The participants in the first women's PRSA focus group discussed the trade-offs career success implies. One woman said:

> "Organizations won't accommodate individual needs. We make trade-offs. Many who are making it don't have great home lives. Those with great home lives have spouses not working—and I don't know women with spouses not working."

Another woman in that group described her organization changing to provide flex-time to accommodate families. But, a third participant responded: "The trade-offs are real—the biggest gifts are being conscious of what the trade-offs are."

The director of community relations for a family entertainment park spoke at length about the balancing act. As a single mother, she has "babysitters on hold everywhere." She often works late at night. Given this, she went on to argue that the "personal aspect" of women's lives is an important factor in determining whether or not women can be successful in a career. Another interviewee agreed, maintaining that women's aspirations are as high as men's; but children are a "stumbling block" that management notices. She pointed out that this may mean women "strive harder."

The director of community relations for a county school system revealed that trying to manage children and work has stopped her from considering other, more demanding positions. It also means that she does not "do evening functions." She commented that a supportive boss and husband help. Still, as she said, "some days are better than others." A college publications director, too, acknowledged her devotion to family (she has three young children) is a factor in her career plans. She said she "would go for the directorship [of public relations]" if there were no personal barriers.

One participant in a focus group said that, for older women, these issues are "moot." Now that she is beyond childbearing, her career "continues to gain momentum." She conceded, though, that even though her children are grown and she is divorced, she is still the caretaker; she still feels responsible. There are still so many "have to dos." An independent consultant also said that having children is a "bump"—not a "stop"—in women's careers. But, she acknowledged that female socialization makes women consider their children their first responsibility.

One participant was uncomfortable with making broad generalizations about women, career, and family. She pointed out that, like herself, many women are choosing not to have children. Another woman countered that, even though all women may not have divided loyalties, others perceive that they do and evaluate them accordingly. One of the youngest participants in the initial women's PRSA focus group said that, although she now puts her career first, she would like to think that someday she could have a balance. She mentioned the example of her female counterparts saying, "Let her stay late; she's not married."

The director of public relations for a children's hospital, a woman who was recently married, was beginning to think about the balancing act. She said that the hospital has on-site day care. She also has thought about giving up her formal position and doing fundraising for the hospital on a contract basis. Whatever she chooses, this practitioner is encouraged because she believes public relations allows for options such as freelancing and re-entry into the field.

Female respondents to our survey considered flexibility in the work schedule—such as flexible hours and locations, child care, and parental leave policy—considerably more important than men did. Both the women's and men's initial PRSA focus groups addressed the survey's finding that women were attracted to public relations because of the flexible work schedule. One man said: "Look at the average female—[she] would favor a flexible situation. Females are primary caretakers of young children. Males [are] more oriented toward a career path, a long day." However, another man said, "I don't think of this as a flexible field." When he was questioned about the field if he had child-care responsibilities, he responded, "I wouldn't be in public relations," citing travel and weekend demands. "If you have that responsibility, I don't know how you'd function!" Likewise, all of the women in the first PRSA focus group questioned the notion of "flexibility." One woman said that "[this notion] must be the technicians [talking], not the managers. [I] can't imagine that's a managerial response."

The stress of the career–family balancing act is worsened when there is little support at home. Several of our interviewees revealed that the chauvinistic attitudes of their spouses were constraining and, in some cases, a major factor in their divorces. Three of the four participants in the first women's PRSA focus group had been divorced over their careers.

When the men in the PRSA focus group were questioned about having a wife who wants a career, the reply was "conflict." One man said that he wouldn't marry "someone like that." Another said, "We got a divorce . . . because she wanted to change roles." These men generally agreed that it was hard on their self-confidence to make less money than their wife. One man said, "I can't imagine anything worse to self-esteem than to have the wife come home with the paycheck." One man gave the example of his wife, who had a bigger budget and staff than he did. She advised him to hire a middle-aged woman married to a blue-collar man, "an example of a professional woman going through the same stereotypes." Following this, one man said: "As roles change, women move up. They'll have similar needs as men have had."

Women's home life also may make them geographical "captives" because women traditionally have been more committed to the career of their husband than vice versa (Landau & Amoss, 1986). Even though men's reluctance to accommodate their wife's career may be diminishing (Kleiman, 1991b), women still are perceived as less mobile than men. As a result, some women may be at a disadvantage when negotiating promotions. Several female respondents said that they have turned down some career opportunities because their partner was unwilling to accommodate their plans. The director of development for a state university complained that she is always the one who has to compromise her career for personal reasons. Unlike her husband, she is the one expected to make sacrifices. She acknowledged, however, that the "inbred" female in her pushes her to do so.

Some interviewees thought that the trend toward men's greater participation in domestic duties would ease the tension of the balancing act for women. Several women said that their male colleagues increasingly seem concerned with family. These women see men leaving the office earlier than they used to, transporting children to and from day care, and staying at home when children are sick. A group manager for a national agency also said that gender roles are becoming more balanced. She believed that men are participating in the domestic scene more, and women no longer have to "compromise" their careers more than men. She pointed out that she is the major breadwinner in her family. The director of community relations for a family entertainment park also believed the rules are being rewritten. She said that the new generation of workers will expect more androgyny in the work place and at home.

Others took exception to this viewpoint. The director of external affairs for a telephone company said that "men definitely have an advantage in the working world" because women do more than their share of domestic duties. She said, "I don't see a lot of change." The associate director of research for a public relations firm also said that "a lot more stress gets put on women because they are doing the domestic work; their sole purpose in life is not to go to work like men."

Research on division of household duties seems to confirm this picture. Hochschild (1989) noted that many women work a full day at the office and then come home to their "second shift." Similarly, others also have pointed out that women are disadvantaged in the office because they continue to do more than their share of work around the home (Heins, Hendricks, & Martindale, 1982).

GENDER STEREOTYPES

Still another major impediment for women mentioned by our respondents was pervasive gender stereotypes. This finding is consistent with our (Wright, Lewton, Springston, & L. Grunig, 1991) earlier discussion of the effects stereotyping has on female practitioners' careers. We argued that widely held beliefs about what is appropriate behavior for men and women pigeonhole people and contribute to much of the gender discrimination in public relations. Schwartz (1989) also found that stereotyping is a major problem for women. As she said, preconceptions, stereotypes, and other expectations men have concerning women as managers contribute to the resistance in promotion women face.

The most ominous of these stereotypes for our female respondents was others' misconceptions about women's abilities at work. As many of these women stated, women have to "prove" themselves because others are too quick to assume women's inferiority. Some women expressed this dilemma in terms of women's having to try harder. This finding parallels other research. A study by Clutterbuck and Devine (1987) showed that, among 128 female corporate directors, 91% said they had to work harder to get ahead because of their sex. One participant in a focus group provided an example of this dilemma. She said that, when dealing with a new man at the office, she repeatedly has to demonstrate that she is "just as bright" as any man.

Other women maintained that women still are not being taken so seriously as men by male managers. A senior counselor at a national agency argued that men continue to be uncertain about women's skills. She said, "Men's psyche has been traumatically challenged," and it "takes a long time for stereotypes to change; prejudice still exists."

The director of news information for a private university pointed out that "people are more apt to think that you lack intelligence if you are a woman." She observed that terminology exists for stupid women, such as "airhead," but not for men. Given this, she is more of a "perfectionist" to avoid being seen as "ditzy" or "flaky." Although she conceded that this caution is a good thing, she said that it makes her work harder and she feels more pressured. The director of community relations for an airport, too, made the point that women have to work harder. As a high-ranking woman, she bemoaned the psychological and personal price of being on call 24 hours a day.

Most of our female respondents believed that, for women to succeed, women must counter gender stereotypes about women's inadequacies by being "superwomen." The owner of a design business said that some of the men she sees in vice presidential slots are "questionable," but the women in these positions "have earned it." As she joked, she will know equity has been achieved "when an incompetent women can get as far as an incompetent man."

An independent consultant, however, denied ever feeling like she had to prove herself (although she acknowledged that women have to work harder). She remembered working on a major account with a predominately male team and maintained that these men never treated her like a "woman." In one focus group, a participant called this experience "privatization." That is, successful women are "privatized," or considered separate from women in general.

Several of our female respondents mentioned another problem related to gender stereotypes: Some men are not comfortable working for women. Some women commented that their male staff members have not liked taking orders from a woman. For instance, the director of public relations for a children's hospital mentioned that her male subordinate always bypasses her in the chain of command.

Another gender stereotype was brought to light in our focus groups. One participant told how her husband sent her flowers at the office to congratulate her on a new job offer. However, all of her colleagues—women and men—assumed she was pregnant. This practitioner lamented that not one of her coworkers ever considered that a woman would receive flowers for something related to her career.

Still another gender stereotype was mentioned by the director of development at a state university: others assuming that women's success was bought with sexual favors. This practitioner finds herself frequently having to prove her integrity. As she said, "I've heard people say I'm sleeping with someone to get money or a job." When this happens, "I lose total control on impact; I'm appalled."

This same woman raised a related concern: Is the problem of gender stereotyping compounded by women's being set up to fail? She wondered if perceptions about women's incompetence may stem from the performance of poorly prepared women who have been "pushed forward" through affirmative action. Other women in her group disagreed. One said she cannot recall any instance that fits this scenario. Another participant maintained that the opposite usually happens: The women who are allowed to advance are typically superior to men in those positions. Some other research substantiates this argument. Leonard (as cited in Carr-Ruffino, Baack, Flipper, Hunter-Sloan, & Olivio, 1992) examined government data from 1966 and

1977 and found that employee equity initiatives increased organizational productivity. This is because women who were hired as a result of affirmative action were more productive than their male counterparts.

Not all of our female respondents, though, believed that gender stereotypes are an issue for women. Several women argued that individual credibility—not gender—is the key to success. That is, advancement is linked to individuals' ability to present themselves in an acceptable way, irrespective of gender. Several of the women, too, explained how their masculine attributes have helped them overcome gender stereotypes. These women described themselves as a "manly woman," and "not a real woman's woman." Another commented that she has "masculine vibes going out."

SEXUAL HARASSMENT AND "LOOKISM"

Blatant sexual harassment was cited as a problem by several of our interviewees. A development director provided the most pronounced example of overt harassment. In her position as fundraiser, she had encountered uncomfortable situations so often she described her work environment as a "den of wolves." She explained how some men—particularly older ones—still believe that, if a woman is traveling alone or out after dark by herself, she is available. One agency head also described being sexually harassed. For her, this abuse was "the straw that broke the camel's back" in her previous job, prompting her to open her own firm. The editor of an association magazine also mentioned receiving unwanted sexual advances from men. For her, out-of-town conferences have been particularly perilous.

This practitioner also mentioned "lookism," a form of covert sexual harassment. This problem refers to others' tendency to focus more—either positively or negatively—on women's appearance than on their job performance. Some in her organization harass her in this way by referring to her as a "bimbo" and the "sex kitten." She attributed some of this to professional jealousies; the tension became so bad that she subsequently was forced out.

Other female respondents also have felt the brunt of lookism. The director of external affairs for a telephone company said that being attractive has been a hindrance for her because other people think she will not work so hard as a plain woman would. She added that men are sometimes so uncomfortable around an attractive woman that they do not hear what she is saying.

An independent consultant, too, has noticed that her looks affect others' perceptions of her. She said she has had to overcome the "blond" and "southern" stereotypes. Although she did not believe lookism had been a problem for her, a college publications director said that this tendency does exist to some degree, especially in initial encounters. She decided, "It's best [for women] to be moderately not ugly."

Several women believed that lookism is more a problem for attractive women than for good-looking men. One participant in a focus group contended that when a woman walks in a room, men see "body parts first." The same is not true for women regarding men, though.

A participant in another group thought that men's focusing on women's physical attributes was the "ultimate power play" by men to demean women's professionalism. Another participant recalled how men frequently comment on her clothing although it never occurs to her to mention theirs. Humor is her strategy for defusing these uncomfortable situations. Still another participant, however, said that she retorts when men say things such as, "Gee, you're wearing one of those short skirts today." In the same group, one woman complained about women's having to take energy away from their work to manage "crap" such as lookism. She said that many women already outperform their male peers. Thus, if women could recover this lost energy, their performance would shoot through the roof.

Other female respondents pointed out that women are guilty of lookism, too. As one woman acknowledged, she "might expect a really pretty woman to prove herself." Another said that she might not take a very beautiful woman so seriously as an average-looking woman—especially if the beautiful woman is "too feminine." She said, "Big hair and a sweet voice turn me off."

Some women argued that lookism can be used to women's advantage. One participant said that women's looks "can captivate them [men] long enough to see we [women] have brains." Another said that lookism can be helpful if women's appearance gets men's attention. "Use all your resources," was one participant's advice.

MARKETPLACE FACTORS

Still another explanation for the glass ceiling in public relations was marketplace factors. As one business owner pointed out, organizational downsizing has occurred at the same time the baby boomers are primed to fill management posts. Further, the downsizing has hit the ranks (middle and upper-middle posts) where public relations typically is located. The result is stiffer competition for fewer jobs and, possibly, lower salaries for both women and men.

The men in the first PRSA focus group also discussed corporate downsizing and suggested that corporate public relations is being devalued because of mergers and buyouts. One participant alluded to resultant encroachment when he said, "They cut public relations and put other people in." Another suggested that younger women don't get the pay, just the responsibility after "the old guy retires."

One agency head argued that the economy makes the marketplace "more cutthroat." On this point, the college publications director recalled that more than 100 people applied for one public relations position in her department.

The director of communication for a state solar energy center linked the glass ceiling problem in part to a labor pool in public relations that is abundant, young, and female. One participant in a men's PRSA focus group said: "More women tend to drive down salaries; employees are seen as commodities. When there are a lot, they cost less." Another man in the same group also pointed to "the sheer numbers of women entering the field and what this influx was doing to the actual structures and status of the job."

A related concern is that because men have become a rarity in public relations, men increasingly are prized at the expense of qualified women. As a senior counselor at a national agency argued, women's devaluation might be explained in part by supply and demand—that is, "men are more valuable because they are scarce." Several female respondents explained how they have been pressured to hire a man. One participant in a focus group stated that others have asked her, "Can't you get a man in this [corporate communications] department?" However, she and several other women mentioned that they have had difficulty finding qualified men to hire.

Taking the opposite position, several women in another focus group argued that marketplace factors will help advance equity for women. One pointed out that white men soon will be a minority in the U.S. work force, implying that hiring and promoting women increasingly is a necessity. Another thought that more women will be needed to fill positions, and as women gain experience gender gaps will erode.

The women in a third focus group did not agree on how marketplace factors affect women's status in public relations. One thought that changing demographics suggest fewer people in the work force, so female practitioners will enjoy a seller's market. Several others, however, were skeptical. One said that there are already too many people for the number of jobs.

One interviewee raised a related issue: Since there are so many women in public relations, affirmative action "falls out." That is, other fields are being forced to seek and promote women. But, within public relations, there is little pressure to adhere to equal opportunity rules. The men in the initial PRSA focus group, however, believed female practitioners are being used to achieve affirmative action goals. For example, one said that, in his organization, "the vice president of public relations was known to be a 'female job.'" Another said: "That's why I'm in the agency business. What's my future here? The job you want has been taken for affirmative action." Several other men, though, gave counterexamples of companies where jobs were given on the basis of merit, not gender.

AGEISM

A final work-place barrier mentioned by some research participants was ageism. This problem usually refers to discrimination against seniors, but several female respondents felt that, because of their youth, they have been or are shut out of positions they are qualified for. Some of these women recalled how glad they were to turn 30. As one interviewee said, when she was in her 20s and in a maternity dress, people did not take her seriously. She pointed out, however, that some people still refuse to do business with her. "Being young, female, and pretty are three liabilities," she said.

One participant in a focus group said that she often has heard the excuse "You're too young." Another said that her youth might be part of the reason why the management team where she works has not accepted her. She added that if she waits around until she is considered "old enough," ageism then might resurface and she will be considered too old. As she joked, there may be just a "3-year slot" during which women are considered the appropriate age.

This catch-22 also was addressed by another focus group. One participant said that a double standard exists when it comes to gender and age. As she noted, television journalism is dominated by older men, but they [media decision-makers] "wouldn't allow old women on TV."

MARGINALIZATION OF THE PUBLIC RELATIONS FUNCTION

Our research participants mentioned several problems specific to public relations, all of which are related to the marginalization of the function. Because their colleagues often do not understand the importance and purpose of public relations, practitioners are assumed to be organizational lightweights—the "party planners." As a vice president for public relations at a health organization pointed out, the glass ceiling in public relations may be related to misconceptions about the field. Her solution was to "become savvy in marketing." She said that since "public relations does not have irrefutable evidence" of its effects on the bottom line, her link to marketing—a function that can show direct effects—elevates her credibility.

An independent consultant echoed this argument, pointing out that "until we clearly define public relations better, it always will be a stepchild to the business-centered organization." She, too, wants to move from public relations to marketing because marketing has more credibility. She said, "Public relations isn't quantitative enough."

A director of news information said that it is sometimes harder for her to overcome the perception of being a public relations person than being a woman. She added that public relations people—women and men—are "perceived as stupid." The manager of public relations for a rocket manufacturer said that she constantly fights "attitudes against public relations." As she explained, the "very white, Anglo-Saxon, military, southern, chauvinist" managers of her organization "don't even know they are not operating in the real world." She still hears things such as, "Give it to the PR girl."

This practitioner also said that, in her organization, the director of human resources is part of the inner management circle because others believe human resources has something valuable to bring to the management table. The efforts of the public relations department, however, are not recognized in the same way. "How do you do that [demonstrate your worth] in a business that is so hard to measure?," she wondered.

This practitioner did point out, though, that her new boss is "more enlightened" and sees the department as "more than public relations. . . . She sees it as the epitome of formal communications." So the public relations department is trying to "work strategically" with the "archaic dinosaurs" who do not understand its importance.

Perhaps no research participant expressed frustration over the marginalization of public relations so deeply as the manager of corporate communication for a national real estate company. She spoke at length about feeling like an outsider, or "on an island" by herself, because she is not part of top management. She voiced her impatience about management's failing to recognize the validity of public relations and to give her the resources she needs.

This practitioner went on to say that, despite her formal education in public relations and proven track record, the management group in her organization continues to "pigeonhole" her as the "newsletter editor," the position for which she originally was hired. She believed this problem stems in part from the ineffectiveness of professional organizations in public relations. She contended PRSA is unknown among CEOs. Although IABC has "some credibility," its potential for advocacy hardly rivals that of other professional associations such as the American Medical Association. She also thought that neither PRSA nor IABC has an overall vision for improving public relations's stature and their professional designations (APR and ABC, for "Accredited Public Relations" and "Accredited Business Communicator," respectively) carry little weight with people outside (and some people inside) the field.

An editor at a trade association said that she is relegated to outsider status at her organization. She said that she feels like a "lone ranger" because her job "isn't taken seriously." Even though she is the managing editor of the member magazine, she often finds herself excluded from management's discussions about the magazine. The physical isolation of her office reinforces the separation.

The coordinator of communication for a county school system provides still another example of others' delusions about public relations. The school board members for whom she works still think community relations can and should be done by a secretary. So she considered her status as an administrator tenuous ever since her position was created.

Marginalization of public relations also was addressed in the first men's PRSA focus group. One man was concerned about the irrelevance of public relations in the corporate equation: "We come in all too often, soft and fuzzy stuff. Holy shoot, if all [of that is] true, and [there is] an implied lack of credibility of women to men, then how on earth do we strengthen public relations? That's what's worrisome."

A related problem is that public relations's job responsibilities do not provide the operational (or even management) experience needed for top posts. Several research participants believed that the glass ceiling was a result of the "staff" (as opposed to "line") status of public relations. Also making this point, Blumenthal (as cited in Toth, 1989a) explained that women in public relations may encounter an especially impregnable ceiling: Public relations is perceived as a nonoperational area that seldom leads to top management.

The director of community relations for a school system described her situation in this way. As a member of the superintendent's staff, she is a "director," whereas all of the male staff members (she is the only female staff member) are "assistant superintendents." Although she does report directly to the superintendent, she said that her inferior status relative to the men is linked to her job.

Other women said that public relations rarely feeds to the head of organizations; and the function often is placed under others, such as development. They also wondered if feminization would compound this problem of sublimation. As one said, discriminatory attitudes toward women as senior managers might keep public relations in the middle of organizational hierarchies. Another explained how her organization was restructured "to make public relations less than senior management." Her department now reports to human resources, which in turn reports to the chief financial officer. When she asked the CFO why, he said, "There are no women directors and we're not sure whether upper management will accept you."

A participant in the first women's PRSA focus group also noted that "human resources has taken in public relations." She argued that the power in organizations goes into the "market, profit-making positions—finance, areas understood on a historical basis. Staff positions are lower." For her, "the value of the activity, far more than the individuals in it" is how others evaluate any organizational function. Two other women in the group countered, though. One said: "There's a trade-off. If you want to be separate, it means less power and influence." Another proposed that getting into the "mainstream" is getting into the profit section. She said: "Support the bottom-line effort—not just women—but the profession as a whole. There is a fear that as public relations becomes more feminized, this means that public relations will be less mainstream."

Some members of another focus group drew an explicit link between the marginalization of public relations and feminization. One said that feminization and the devaluation of public relations go hand in hand: "Women's work and their products are not valued as much." Another agreed, arguing that the influx of women has brought a lower value to public relations—but for a different reason. She said that because public relations is so easy for women (because women are so well suited to the function), others do not perceive that female practitioners work very hard. The result is that the value of the work is diminished.

Several other female respondents said that the marginal status of public relations explains why so many women are in the field. Women are attracted to public relations because it is an "acceptable" role for them in the corporate stream; the function is not seen as a "strong" position. A vice president of a public relations firm made the same point, saying that women are entering the field because they want to be in business; and low on the organizational hierarchy is where women "fit." Whereas women used to go into the secretarial pool, the logical move now is public relations.

In another focus group one participant said that, because of gender stereotypes, men have an easier time accepting women's proficiency at communication than they do with other, operational functions. For this reason, she thought that public relations may be women's smoothest entree into organizations.

The men in the initial PRSA focus group also discussed whether women are attracted to public relations because the profession is more open to women than other careers. One said that the field is attracting women because women are hiring other women. Another suggested that "women see more women in it and are attracted to that." Still another said, "It's not just PR—women go where they think they'll have a shot at careers." However, one man questioned the assumed droves of women entering the field. "I find tremendous numbers of young men looking for jobs," he said.

Raising another issue, several research participants worried that feminization might hinder the development of public relations as a management function because of encroachment. This trend, as we explained in Chapter 7, refers to people (typically men) from outside the public relations ranks (e.g., MBAs and lawyers) being recruited to manage public relations rather than promoting qualified practitioners ("PR People Deplore Encroachment by Marketers and 'Feminization,'" 1984; Broom & Dozier, 1985; Lauzen, 1990a, 1990b). A vice president at a national agency noted that encroachment by lawyers is already a problem in public affairs and issues management. One participant in the men's PRSA focus group said that encroachment by lawyers and CFOs is happening "because public relations people lacked a bottom-line background."

However, not all of the women and men we talked with considered the marginalization of public relations and its link to feminization problems for the field. One woman in a focus group said that quality—irrespective of gender—is appreciated. She said that the more women "surprise people and convince them [of women's competence]," the more progress women make. She also pointed out that "many higher level managers choose a woman when they want the job done." A participant in another focus group said that, at the same time public relations is finally being accepted as a management function, women are making progress in the field. She forecasted that women "will position the industry as an excellent opportunity for women to go on the executive track, and they [women] will come to the field for that."

Several of our research participants said that public relations's credibility is improving as the measurement of results becomes more precise. One female participant made this point, countering the argument that because of feminization public relations increasingly is seen as the "fluff" department. One male participant in the PRSA focus-group study also made this point when he said that research would improve the status of the profession by bringing "hard" data to decision making.

Women were optimistic about the future of the field. They said that, far from being marginalized, public relations is outstripping traditional advertising and marketing because the same results can be achieved through public relations at a lower cost. They believed that agency mergers between advertising and public relations as well as in-house integration are evidence of this reality.

Chapter Twelve

Liberal Feminist Strategies for Women's Advancement

This chapter addresses liberal feminist strategies for overcoming discrimination against women in public relations. However, the chapter should not be read in isolation. The radical feminist strategies proposed in Chapter 13 should be considered along with the suggestions here since both liberal and radical feminist tactics are needed to produce equity for female practitioners.

Liberal feminist approaches typically focus on characteristics of women themselves such as their personality traits (Hennig & Jardim, 1977), communication behavior (Fitzpatrick, 1983), and management style (Ezell, Odewahn, & Sherman, 1982). These strategies suggest that women abandon the attitudes and behaviors associated with stereotypical feminine socialization so they may blend more effectively into the (male) work-place. Restructuring of the "system" itself is not emphasized. The strength of liberal feminist strategies lies in the empowering effect these tactics can have since liberalism assumes women as individuals can and do overcome discrimination. Further, they offer women immediate strategies for securing advancement while working toward the institutional transformations that radical feminism prescribes.

BUYING INTO AND WORKING THE SYSTEM

Many of our female respondents said that women should learn to work "the system" to their advantage rather than fighting it. One believed that this plan involves making a choice: "Buy into the system and work twice as

321

hard as your male colleagues or refuse to and give up the rewards." This interviewee said that most of the women she knows are buying in even though doing so often leaves them "exhausted." She admitted that this strategy is no panacea for women, but she argued that it improves women's chances for breaking through the glass ceiling. Another respondent made the point that women need power before they can make changes in the work place. Therefore, women must assimilate into the power structure even if doing so demands personal compromise.

Impression Management

Most suggestions for working the system involve women monitoring their behavior and appearance. Or, as one interviewee said, women need to take on the attributes of maleness they are perceived to be lacking. An agency owner spoke at length about what these characteristics are. She suggested women think before speaking up, align themselves with politically strategic people, take business politics seriously, and dress appropriately. Women should not apologize for family concerns, nor should they play the victim.

No doubt, these and other impression management techniques (Conrad, 1990; Leong, Snodgrass, & Gardner, 1992) have helped many women. However, these strategies may be limited if the psychological cost to women involves feeling like impostors (Bell & Young, 1986). That is, techniques of impression management reinforce women's outsider status by highlighting their difficulty in demonstrating their "appropriateness" for organizational advancement. The stress caused by having to act out male-defined standards may be debilitating for women in the long run.

Another point is that suppressing women's "natural" communication and management styles may not be in the best interests of organizations. A lot of research has shown that women and men approach their work and relationships at work differently (see, e.g., Konner, 1990; Levine, 1990; Mann, 1986). Moreover, women's tendency toward an empowering style of communicating and managing is more responsive to organizational environments of the 1990s and beyond (Doyle, 1990; Teegardin, 1991; Varadan, 1991; "Women Managers 'Superior,' " 1988).

Many interviewees and several focus group participants believed that women tend to have progressive communication and management methods. They argued that women are uniquely qualified for public relations because women generally are more detail-oriented and are more verbal, less egocentric, and more intuitive than men. These arguments imply that organizations might prosper by taking advantage of women's unique talents rather than by requiring women to conform to male molds.

Finding the Right Place

Another aspect of working the system that several female participants mentioned is selecting the right institution to work for. A group manager for a national agency considered some places better for women than others but cautioned against women's "jumping around" too much. She argued that women should "stick out" a less-than-perfect situation, at least temporarily. While they are doing so, women should use their "instincts to get involved in other projects, walk around and talk to people, look for people who are in areas they want to work in, and begin to develop relationships."

Several interviewees who had young children believed that a flexible work environment is key. These women noted how their bosses (all men) give them the necessary support and flexibility to perform the balancing act successfully. One woman recalled how several times when she was working late, her boss encouraged her to go home. Another mentioned that her boss understood her need to limit work-related evening functions.

Results from our quantitative survey showed that flexibility in the work environment was more important for women than for men. However, participants in both early PRSA focus groups challenged the idea that a public relations career and flexibility are compatible. One agency owner made the point that female professors should help women find the right place by providing a realistic picture of opportunities for women. Professors also should encourage women to go into areas such as health care where they have a better chance for advancement.

Ford's (1986) discussion of discrimination and structural features of organizations is relevant to many of the points our female respondents made about finding the right place. The structural factors she examined include type of business (defense, space, and industrial manufacturing are identified as oppressive), the size and age of the organization (large and old organizations are less promising for women), a large number of men lacking a high degree of education, female managers in low visibility positions and generally supervising other women, a strong "old boy network," and depressed salaries for women.

Unfortunately, Ford merely listed these oppressive attributes to suggest that women try to avoid organizations bearing these traits. She might have pointed out that the latter three characteristics describe almost *all* organizations in the public sphere. Further, many women do not have the option of steering clear of organizations where women have had and continue to have difficulties advancing.

An alternative approach involves reforming organizational characteristics that are defeating for women. Although the age of an organization and its type of business are fixed, most organizational features are amenable to change. In support of this metamorphosis, organizational psychologists have argued that organizations benefit when they abandon procedures that discriminate against women and establish policies aimed at eliminating gender inequities. For example, Canter (1982) documented that affirmative action policies promote motivated and well-qualified women, which, in turn, raises women's aspirations and encourages them to be more productive. Similarly, Gutek (1982) found that strict guidelines and procedures that prohibit sexual harassment eliminate costly "role spillover" (treating valuable women employees as dates or wives wastes time they otherwise spend on their jobs). Organizational efficiency also is enhanced by worksite child care, flextime, job sharing, generous maternity benefits, and dependent illness leave, as well as a tolerance for the needs of dual-career couples (Bailyn, 1982). Finally, Koprowski (1983) found that when members of an organization believe that they are being treated fairly, creative productivity is optimized.

Denying the Existence of Discrimination

Several female participants raised still another issue related to working the system: Women's success would be inhibited if they worry too much about discrimination. That is, women's concerns may become a self-fulfilling prophecy. Therefore, women should not assume they are being discriminated against. One interviewee said women should aim as high as they want and refuse to acknowledge discrimination. "What has always worked for me is to go and do it and prove myself," she explained.

However, Mathews (1988) decried female practitioners' "flat, almost frightening denial that a problem exists" (p. 1). She worried that denial among those most disadvantaged by discrimination—women themselves— would only make inequities worse. Similarly, Jones (1991) found that, among her focus group participants, female undergraduates were either unaware of gender discrimination or unconcerned about it. She concluded that these women were unprepared for the challenges they would face in public relations.

Denying gender-related problems is evident throughout public relations (Zoch & Russell, 1991). Men in the first PRSA focus group spent a large part of their session expressing doubts about the accuracy of the gender disparities reported in our quantitative survey. The questioning continued despite assurances by one group member and the moderator that our survey results parallel many other studies.

The male focus group participants also seemed unconvinced that the sample could be generalized to the entire field. They compared PRSA and IABC memberships, insisting that women who were not PRSA members but known to the men would have changed the results if they had been included in the survey. One said that "the data hasn't caught up with the situation." He knew of women heading agencies: "[We're] missing those people from the survey—also [they're] not PRSA members." Denying the existence of discrimination, however, may be a faulty approach for both women and men. The weight of the evidence suggests that sexism in public relations does exist. By acknowledging this, women could empower themselves to look for discriminatory practices and devise strategies for eliminating these biases (or, at the very least, maneuvering around them). Men accepting this reality could make them more active in breaking down barriers for women.

One problem, though, may be that many people believe it is sexist to suggest that feminization will affect public relations (either negatively or positively). This sentiment is grounded, no doubt, in the false assumption that men and women are equal (or can or should be). People want to believe that the nature of public relations and its stature will not change simply because the sex of the majority of practitioners has changed (for examples of this sentiment, see Toth & Cline, 1991).

Again, though, evidence suggests that this belief is risky. Researchers have documented that when women become the majority of an occupation, or a division of an organization is more than half women, salaries plummet (Cline et al., 1986; Conrad, 1990; Pfeffer & Davis-Blake, 1987). Touhey (1974) found that the status of an occupation declines when people even *think* more women than men would enter the field. Further, as women gain numbers within an occupation, a "splintering" occurs: Women are restricted to or choose the lower paying, less desirable positions within the profession (for a discussion of this dynamic, see Raymond, 1989 [real estate and commercial banking]; Adler, 1991 [psychology]; and Herman, 1991 [psychiatry]). Given these trends, we believe that practitioners' false hopes should be set aside. By doing so, more energy can be directed toward enhancing public relations' effectiveness.

Recruiting Male Practitioners

Another strategy for working the system that several research participants proposed was attracting men back into public relations. All of the women in the initial PRSA focus group were concerned about maintaining gender balance. "If the profession is feminized, we're going to pay the price—the women at the managerial ranks will get lower salaries," one said. Another admitted to hiring a male over a more qualified female so that the owners would not view the area as a "fluff" department. Yet another woman said, "I've had a hard time finding qualified men and have hired less-qualified men."

Some scholars have suggested tactics for making public relations more appealing to male college students. As Hunt and Thompson (1987, 1989; Hunt, 1989) explained, feminization of the field means many men will not consider it appealing. This is because, among other things, men have no desire to work for women, the salaries offered are too low, and affirmative action programs favor women applying for entry-level positions (Hunt, 1989).

Hunt (1989) argued that this male flight could lead to a drop in salaries and prestige for practitioners and should be countered by a "concerted effort to make the profession appeal to males" (p. 212). His efforts to do so at Rutgers University involved establishing quota systems to ensure that males appear in each class and the same proportion of males could be found in each section, developing internships and a "mentor" program designed to match male students with role models in the field, and selecting clients that interest males for class projects.

However, the weakness of Hunt and Thompson's (1997) approach lies in not acknowledging that if the status of public relations is deflating, the real problem lies in societal devaluation of women—*not in women themselves or the feminine*. Thus their suggestions for making public relations "more macho" in the long run may worsen the underlying problem: institutional policies and norms that privilege men and penalize women. So, although we herald diversity among practitioners, we believe that strategies for courting male students may be shortsighted. A more fruitful approach involves exploiting the positive effects on the field, organizations, and society that public relations's swing to the feminine could bring. These effects, however, will be realized only to the extent that discrimination against women and public relations because of its association with women stops.

Making Choices

Some research participants mentioned another aspect of buying into and working the system: making choices. A senior counselor said that women cannot be traditional mothers and corporate executives at the same time. Similarly, the communication manager for a hospice organization argued that women must make sacrifices to advance in their careers, and that women generally are less willing than men to do so.

Making choices also emerged as an issue in the women's PRSA focus groups as participants discussed our survey results that showed a significant gap in pay after the fourth year of employment. These women agreed that the period between the fifth and tenth year of employment is especially difficult because women have to make decisions about allocating time to career and family. One woman said, "That's the reality of the world—young women are foolish not to recognize that." Another said: "Many women don't want to pay the price you pay for getting ahead. You have to make up your mind that you'll pay the price, do what you have to do—moving, not staying home with your babies."

Turk (as quoted in Lukovitz, 1989) explained this reality further:

> Any woman in any business who sets her sights on top management must be willing to give up some things—spend less time with family, or cut back on social or additional professional activities—or decide not to have children. (p. 22)

Mathews (1988) also suggested that women must choose between having a good career in public relations and having a good family life. However, after reading Mathews's piece, students in a public relations course at the University of Maryland challenged this trade-off. "We always read that women must choose between career and children," one student said. "Do men ever have to make these decisions?" (as quoted in L. Grunig, 1990c, p. 30).

Schwartz (1989) explained this choice when she referred to "career-primary" women versus "career-and-family" women (p. 68). However, Schwartz was criticized for suggesting that organizations develop a separate "mommy track" for women who must balance work and family.

Inclusion in Management Decision Making

Still another tactic for women to work the system is insisting on inclusion in management decision making. One participant in a focus group argued that getting into the managerial role ultimately is up to women. A participant in the first women's PRSA focus group agreed that women's advancement "takes some person to take it to task, to force it—[the] push thing—men are pushed into it, women aren't pushed; men can't stay at technical levels." The women in that focus group discussed specific strategies for moving women into management. One participant said: "If you want to move ahead, you have to have courage, to constantly push. One clear step is to go to the immediate supervisor and then list ways you can help the organization."

Networking with Men

A final strategy involves women's creating opportunities to network with men. Several female participants denounced any sort of women's separatist movement by pointing out that nurturing alliances with men is crucial. One participant in a focus group said that, although women should not give up their female friends, they need to bring men into their circles, associate with men, and be seen with men. This tactic should extend to informal scenes as well. The communication manager for a scientific instruments manufacturer argued that women may not be able to (or want to) do sports with men. But women should be "brazen enough" to find something they *can* do with male colleagues (such as driving to company functions together) and then "fill in the gaps."

DEVELOPING COMPETENCE IN PUBLIC RELATIONS

Many of the women in our study said that equity for female practitioners will happen only if women develop the skills and knowledge needed to advance in public relations. They believed that being highly skilled helps keep doors open to women. Since information is power, women must constantly strive to learn more and refuse to be intimidated.

Several research participants believed that learning how to conduct research is key. That is, female practitioners need to evaluate the results of communication programs and then educate management about public relations's contributions. One agency owner said that the "true test" of women's success in public relations will be in the results women can show. Part of this is letting others know about good work. One participant in a focus group said that public relations is being tested. If female practitioners can show results, women will be accepted by management—gender notwithstanding.

Echoing this theme, Dozier (1988) argued that female practitioners could gain the power they need to break through the glass ceiling by conducting scanning research—social scientific methods practitioners use "to find out 'what's going on' among internal and external publics" (p. 6). He explained that environmental scanning is important for all practitioners because it gives them control over a scarce resource (information) that is useful to the dominant coalition of an organization. Armed with this information, practitioners are more likely to be included in management decision making.

A critical point that Dozier (1988) made, though, is that scientific scanning is more important for women than for men. Since the stereotypi-cal manager possesses stereotypical masculine characteristics, male practi-tioners are more readily accepted by the predominately male top brass. In addition, male practitioners are "groomed for the manager role through mentoring" and by male managers' taking them under their wing as "infor-mal assistants" (p. 12). Because of these advantages, male practitioners do not need the power that comes from controlling scarce resources (i.e., in-formation) so much as female practitioners do. Dozier's recommendation for women, then, is to do more scanning research.

Dozier's suggestion seems viable on the surface, but Toth (1988) cited several studies that cast doubt. In the first of these, Ghiloni (1987), who coined the phrase "velvet ghetto," studied women in the public affairs de-partment of a corporation. She found that although women were playing an increasingly important role in maintaining corporate power, they were not likely to gain power as a result. She explained that this was because the women were stereotyped in a way that kept them as second-class citizens despite their contributions to power holders. Ghiloni's description of how corporate women were granted many privileges but were still dominated was paralleled in the work of Messner (1987), who found that organiza-tional communication practices dominate and demean women.

A crucial issue here may be the difference between the masculine no-tion of *power* and its feminine alternative, *empowerment*. Knappenberger (as quoted in Swoboda, 1990b) explained the distinction:

> There is a big difference between the kind of involvement that draws employ-ees into the debate but does not involve them in the actual decision making and empowerment, which gives them *both* the *tools* and the *right* to make the decision. (p. H3; emphasis added)

Knappenberger pointed out, however, that the empowerment of employees usually is not done with the blessing of management. He explained that when managers are used to "barking out the orders," empowering others is difficult to impossible (p. H3).

Given this resistance, extra research efforts by women may be of little value. The alternative is an organizational value system that assumes em-powerment is the essence of effective management. Unlike power, which usually operates as a zero-sum game (the more power one has, the less oth-ers have), empowerment involves building up one's own strength by build-ing up the strength of others (Helgesen, 1990).

Related to doing research is the suggestion that women get an ad-vanced degree. The communication manager for a state solar energy center went so far as to say that an advanced degree acts as a "surrogate penis." Or, as one independent consultant advised women, "If you want an advanced salary, get an advanced degree." However, this recommendation was not echoed by participants in the quantitative survey. Neither women nor men thought that a graduate degree would hasten entry into management.

A senior vice president at a health care corporation suggested that women who want to advance in public relations get operational experience. Part of doing so, she said, involves women overcoming their predisposition for verbal rather than quantitative tasks. Similarly, one agency head also thought that aspiring women need to get into a line position. She recommended that women major in public relations, enter organizations via communication, and then jump off to a line slot. However, the weakness of this approach is that the public relations department is robbed. A more appealing option may be for practitioners to develop a variety of business skills that lead to advancement for them as well as increased stature for public relations.

DEMONSTRATING PROFESSIONALISM

Several research participants cited a commitment to professionalism as another strategy for female practitioners' advancement. Membership in professional associations was cited as one way for women to demonstrate professionalism. Several women commented that participating in these groups has given them networking opportunities, professional development, and more self-confidence. All of these benefits carry over into their work.

Taking advantage of occasions for professional development within associations might be especially important for women. Activities such as chairing committees, organizing events, and making presentations provide women the requisite management skills and experience that they may not have a chance to develop at work. Successfully accomplishing these endeavors helps build women's self-confidence. Networking with peers also might provide women a better perspective for salary negotiations since getting to know peers and staying in touch with them can be effective tactics for gaining a sense of what the market will bear.

Some female respondents also mentioned professional accreditation, saying that the process was helpful to them as individuals and that accreditation might help bolster the stature of public relations in general. Our quantitative survey found that accreditation is the third (after age and gender) strongest predictor of practitioners' salaries. Among women and men, those professionals who are APR earned on average almost $20,000 more than those who are not ($65,147 vs. $46,750). Among women only, those with PRSA accreditation had average salaries of $53,000, while non-APR women earned an average of $38,000. Further, individuals who are not PRSA-accredited were more likely to be technicians than those who are accredited. However, PRSA accreditation did not appear to affect whether or not individuals function as public relations managers.

WOMEN EMPOWERING THEMSELVES

Many of our research participants believed that female practitioners could empower themselves by connecting with other women. As Novek (1991) noted, feminism "has long emphasized the special enabling qualities of connectedness for women" (p. 2). She found that when women rally together, they can produce social change. In doing so, "women forge new social bonds, develop new abilities, learn to respect skills they already possess, and test their capacities for leadership and confrontation" (p. 10).

One aspect of this empowerment that many female interviewees mentioned was mentoring and role modeling other women. Several women suggested inviting women who have "gone through the hard knocks" to be guest speakers in college classrooms. The owner of a publications business said that women in high positions in particular "have to be constantly reminded to pull the next [woman] along." As she insisted, women helping one another has "got to have a positive effect." On this point, an independent communication consultant believed that women's networks are growing. To help foster contacts, she makes a point of taking someone different to lunch every day.

The advantages of having mentors and role models have been documented by research that shows people with sponsors earn more at a younger age, are more satisfied with their job, and have more job mobility and visibility (Wright, L. Grunig, Springston, & Toth, 1991). These relationships are especially important for women, since research also indicates they need such ties to offset the lack of stability and power their positions typically offer (Keele, 1986).

The mentor–protege relationship, however, can be problematic if others believe the protege is too dependent on the mentor (Conrad, 1990; Edson, 1980). For this reason, building a coalition of supporters can be helpful to women (Kanter, 1977). Through this network women have access to the same information men traditionally have gained via the "good old boy" clique (p. 340; see also Barbieri, 1991b). This pipeline helps women decide whether "the risks they take are reasonable, learn when to pull out of an unsuccessful project before it becomes a public failure, and develop strategies for making their success known and accepted" (Conrad, 1990, p. 340).

Another strategy many women have at their disposal is starting their own public relations business. A communication manager for a scientific instrument manufacturer said that such "boldness" can be strengthening for a woman. An agency co-owner agreed, explaining that she has empowered herself by becoming an external consultant. She said, "I can manage my way more than I could as an insider."

Moore, Buttner, and Rosen (1992) explained that women have selected "the entrepreneurial alternative" for several reasons (p. 85). They include frustration over the glass ceiling, disenchantment with corporate politics, and a desire for autonomy. As Bryant (1984) reported, ambitious, self-confident women with business acumen get tired of waiting for the top positions they deserve. So they bail out of corporate life and open their own businesses.

Being the boss also gives some women more control over managing work and family simultaneously (Barbieri, 1991a). As Vernon (as quoted in Barbieri, 1991a) explained: "A lot of women who are forming organizations are doing it so they can have more flexible time. That doesn't mean they're working less; that means they're working more effectively" (p. E5).

The entrepreneurial alternative is not for everyone, though. As Grogan (as quoted in Barbieri, 1991a) pointed out, "Running a business requires an ability to solve problems, a willingness to take risks, . . . [and] a burning desire to be one's own boss" (p. E5). Further, this venture can be lonely, the days can be long, and sometimes the cash flow is inconsistent (Barbieri, 1991a).

Still more problems for female business owners have to do with the disparate treatment they receive from government and banks, as we explained in Chapter 4. Moore et al. (1992), too, pointed out that female entrepreneurs still experience discrimination in Social Security benefits disbursement and taxation of annuities and business income. Women also face sexism in banks' processing of credit applications. They concluded, "Equality of entrepreneurial opportunity based on sex remains a distant goal" (p. 104; see also Loscocco & Robinson, 1991).

Despite these handicaps, women's opting for the entrepreneurial track no doubt will continue. As Matthews (1991) documented, women in the work force are starting companies at three times the rate of men. This trend may continue to provide opportunities for many women in public relations. However, the downside is that in-house public relations is stripped of precious talent when ambitious women flee. Further, the most able women are the most likely to strike out on their own. As Humphrey (1990) found, the most competent, admired, and professional women in public relations are the ones who tend to become entrepreneurs.

Huberlie (1997) added another concern related to female practitioners striking out on their own if the status of public relations becomes more threatened. She said: "Female practitioners who choose the entrepreneurial route should recognize that the initial benefits of operating outside the organizational structure may start to diminish as public relations potentially becomes a more external and dispensable function in many organizations" (p. 28). Because of these problems inherent in entrepreneurship, along with most of the liberal feminist strategies explored in this chapter, we turn next to the alternative, radical approach.

Chapter Thirteen

Feminist Strategies with Radical Intent

T his chapter continues the discussion of solutions for advancing equity for women in public relations. Here we focus on radical feminist strategies, those geared toward the institutional
transformations that must take place before discrimination against female
practitioners stops. However, most of our research participants did not
mention as many radical approaches for battling discrimination as they did
liberal feminist ideas. This may stem from the pervasiveness of society's devaluation of women. Without realizing it, many women (and men) assume
that sex-based discrimination stems from women's deficiencies alone.
Male-centered institutions that devalue women are often overlooked as
sources of gender bias.

Here we examine the institutional bases of discrimination at three levels: societal, organizational, and public relations. Whereas liberal feminist
prescriptions suggest how women need to change themselves to assimilate
into the (male) status quo, radical feminism calls for changes in the "system" itself. The ultimate goal is a new form of organizations where women
are valued in their own right. Explaining this radical approach, a participant in one focus group said that some of the obstacles women face are systemic: "To expect a woman no matter how good she is to hurdle all these
barriers is unrealistic." Thus, she called for refusing to "let institutions off
the hook" for discrimination. She worried that although liberal feminism
may bring success for some women, the numbers may not be significant
and the costs for these women may be too high.

We believe the most inclusive plan for advancing equity for women in
public relations combines liberal and radical strategies. As feminist scholar

334

Condit (1988) pointed out, the extent of problems that women face and the "power and wiliness of the forces arrayed against" feminist interests lead to a combined liberal/radical solution rather than a fixation with one or the other (p. 7). The most effective approach for battling discrimination is probably incremental—one compatible with liberal feminism but with the radical intent of changing society so that the masculine ethos no longer pervades the organizations in which public relations practitioners operate. For this reason, we present the radical solutions in this chapter as the *complement* to the liberal tactics discussed earlier.

SOCIETAL REFORMS

Levels of Awareness

A fundamental barrier to women's progress is denial that gender discrimination exists. Yet Bureau of Labor Statistics indicate that the median weekly earnings of full-time working women are just under 75% of the men's median, which is a 2-point downturn since 1993 (Lewin, 1997a). A National Academy of Sciences report documented that only 40% of any closure in the gender gap comes from women's improved earning power. The other 60% comes from men's lost earning power (Mann, 1997; Kuhn, 1992). Moreover, only two of the CEOs of Fortune 500 companies are women, and women make up only 10% of corporate officers (Bellafante, 1998). All these figures suggest that renewed energy directed to raising awareness levels about sexism is not misguided.

Related to levels of awareness about sexism is educating others about the feminist movement. The stereotypical image of feminists as strident and anti-men continues to be a problem for feminism because many women (especially young women) are reluctant to call themselves feminists. They fear being stigmatized or they do not consider feminism relevant to their lives (Olen, 1991). Ironically, only one of our female respondents in a PRSA focus group identified herself as a feminist.

A 1998 *Time*/CNN poll (Bellafante, 1998) found that more women said they were not a feminist than said they were (about 65% and 25%, respectively). The percentage who denied being a feminist has grown in the last decade (up from about 55%). In the same poll, more women said they had an unfavorable image of feminists than a favorable one (43% vs. 32%); and the percentage of unfavorable impressions has increased since 1989 (up from 29%).

Faludi (1991) addressed feminism's taint in *Backlash: The Undeclared War Against American Women*. She documented how the media, popular culture, and advertising have undermined the feminist movement by falsely portraying feminist goals as damaging to women and proposing a return to home and hearth as women's true road to happiness. In 1992, commenting on the much hyped "Year of the Woman," Faludi grimly pointed out the persistent lack of progress toward feminist goals:

> Women did not break through the glass ceiling. (More than 95 percent of executive suites are still inhabited by men.) Women did not break down the doors of political power. ("Tripling" our representation in the U.S. Senate is no triumph when the female faces go from two to six.) Women did not make a dent in Hollywood's rotten portrayal of women. Women did not win even the most basement level basics—modest, very modest, federal bills for (unpaid) family leave, (minimal) child-care assistance and freedom of choice went by the boards. (p. 31)

Some feminists themselves have questioned the efficacy of the movement. For example, Ebeling (1990) discussed "the failure of feminism," suggesting it has produced little more than "frenzied and overworked women often abandoned by men" (p. 9). She concluded that women would be a lot better off if they had stayed out of the executive office and home with their children.

Goodman (1992), however, took issue with such claims. She argued that feminism has not failed; instead, society has failed to give women the support they need to succeed. In our opinion, tensions related to feminist goals may stem in part from many people's exclusive focus on liberal strategies rather than a combined liberal/radical approach. For example, in public relations, women's ascension to managerial ranks is a hollow triumph if women in these positions are successful only to the extent that they support the status quo.

We believe this scenario is happening too often in public relations. Women who rise to top posts do so for the most part by "buying in" (as many women in our study say they have done). Efforts at fundamental organizational transformation are lagging. Some women may even begin to benefit from the status quo and thus defend it, which is counterproductive for women in the long run.

In a study of female lawyers, Rosenberg, Perlstadt, and Phillips (1993) identified women in their sample as either *feminists* or *careerists*. The feminists are those who believe in collective action to alter the distribution of power in the field, are members of women's organizations, and support only candidates for bar and bench offices who espouse feminist objectives. The careerists were women who believe in equal economic rights with men but reject the notion that gender affects their experiences at work. Rosenberg et al. found that contrary to their expectations, the careerists were more likely to face work-place harassment. They concluded:

> For years, women . . . have been advised to be patient, to play down women's issues, and to take on the values of the men who have preceded them (Rhode, 1988). But those women who play the careerist game may unintentionally reinforce those aspects of organizational and professional culture that encourage men to believe they can control women or drive them out through discrimination and sexual manipulation. (p. 431)

Federal Initiatives

Another societal mandate is federal laws that support working. The most obvious step is comprehensive family leave legislation that allows employees to take time off to care for children, an ailing partner, or elderly parents. The United States lags far behind other industrialized countries in offering family leave benefits as a fundamental right (Thompson, Thomas, & Maier, 1992). For example, nations of the European Community guarantee women at least 14 weeks (many European countries allow more) of pregnancy leave at wages higher than sick pay and some at full pay ("Paid Maternity Leave in Europe," 1991). Safe working conditions for pregnant women are required, and organizations are forbidden from firing women because of pregnancy.

In the United States, unpaid family leave is now federally mandated. However, unpaid leave helps only those with enough money to take time off without pay. Since most workers cannot afford this option, a more progressive policy as well as federal initiatives for assistance with dependent care are needed. Surprisingly, only one woman in our study pointed out that such policies would be helpful for women. This may be because many of our participants can afford quality child and elder care. Then, too, several of the women had no dependent-care responsibilities.

Federal legislation also is needed to ban sexual harassment. Other countries are taking the lead in instituting strict legislation for dealing with sexual harassers. For example, within the European Community, Spain and France have made sexual harassment at work a criminal offense; offenders can be jailed and fined (Gordon, 1991). The U.S. Supreme Court has expanded potential liability for harassment by ruling that employers can be held liable if a supervisor threatens to retaliate against a subordinate who spurns his or her sexual advances, even if the retaliatory action was not carried out. The ruling has prompted major companies, such as Nabisco and Lockheed-Martin, to reevaluate their sexual harassment policies (Greenhouse, 1998).

Many of our female respondents felt strongly that sexual harassment is a problem in public relations. Earlier in this book, we reported that nearly one-fourth of the female and male practitioners we surveyed believed the same, although these practitioners were unsure about the magnitude of the problem. We underscored the important point that to the extent women are degraded by sexual harassment, the public relations function also is devalued:

> As long as sexual harassment is implicitly or explicitly tolerated in an organization, women will be marginalized in every strata. Not only does this lead to ineffectiveness and upset in organizational functioning, it indirectly impacts the public relations position and role in an organization. . . . If it [sexual harassment] is used to continue to control women in the organization, then women who do rise to managerial positions, who do sit with the dominant coalition, will be powerless. (Serini, Toth, Wright, & Emig, 1997, pp. 9–10)

Another federal directive is stopping the erosion of affirmative action. In 1991, the U.S. Department of Labor's Office of Federal Contract Compliance Programs, which is responsible for ensuring that organizations holding government contracts do not discriminate in employment decisions, found that a number of companies "were not living up to the good faith efforts to meet affirmative action requirements" (p. 4). The Equal Employment Opportunity Commission, which investigates work-place discrimination, has a 100,000-case backlog (Fletcher, 1997). The federal government has problems of its own. At the end of fiscal 1995, there were 30,682 discrimination complaints pending from federal workers (more than a 20% increase over the previous year) and 12 class-action employee lawsuits on file or about to be filed.

Despite these figures, several of our male participants believed their careers had been stymied because women are advantaged by affirmative action. In 1997 only 3% of the cases filed with the EEOC were for reverse discrimination (Clinton, 1997). So, even if some men have felt slighted, the argument that women in general are advantaged in the work force is fallacious. The salary and role advantages that most men in public relations typically enjoy underscore this point.

Gender Stereotypes

Still another societal strategy has to do with breaking down gender stereotypes. Several of the women in one focus group considered traditional gender socialization a fundamental roadblock for women. They argued that too many parents continue to raise daughters to be passive about salary issues and narrow in their career ambitions. One pointed out that some young women remain ignorant about opportunities for women; these women believe that getting married and having children are their only options.

Bureau of the Census figures suggest, though, that women are making progress along these lines, even outdistancing men. Its report "Educational Attainment in the United States, March 1997" documented that 29.3% women aged 25 to 29 had completed 4 years or more of college as of 1997, compared to 26.3% of men. Census population expert Jennifer Day explained that these statistics indicate more women than ever before want careers and recognize the economic value of education. "I think, historically, men were the breadwinners, and now it's two-earner couples," she said (as quoted in "Women, Blacks Soar in Schools," 1998, p. 2A). Or, as Lawlor (1997) reported, women are the primary breadwinners in one out of four marriages.

The participants in the first women's PRSA focus group also discussed gender socialization. One woman said, "We have to raise women's expectations." Another agreed: "As long as women are willing to take the technical roles, salaries are going to stay lower. Women have to be willing to rise. Otherwise, the management aspect is going to suffer."

One participant in another focus group stressed the importance of raising enlightened sons. She believed boys' attitudes must change too. However, some of the women in a different focus group wondered just how malleable children really are. Two noted that their children—even at a very young age—showed gendered behavior. Thus, they wondered if genetic predispositions might be an immutable factor in children's later choices. Some researchers have suggested that parents' ability to mold children's attitudes and behaviors may be limited by biology (for a discussion of the nature vs. nurture debate, see Cherry, 1992, and Shapiro, 1990). Boys may be genetically programmed to like playing with guns, for example; girls may be predisposed toward dolls. And, as Cherry (1992) pointed out, gender stereotypes serve an important function for children. Gender typecasting helps children make sense of the world and figure out their own identity. Cherry went on to note, though, that by adolescence children's adherence to stereotypes becomes less rigid. Thus, this may be the critical period for inspiring girls to reject limited notions about appropriate roles for women in the work place.

Related to breaking down gender stereotypes is another societal change advocated by several of our research participants: renegotiating gender roles at home. As the coordinator of community relations for a county school system pointed out, women's entrance into the work place means that both men and women have to negotiate new positions in the domestic sphere. The county director of external affairs for a telephone company believed that, for the most part, women have wanted to keep the peace at home by continuing their traditional roles. Women typically have accommodated their spouses by taking on more than a fair share of housework or by making their careers subordinate. For her, women need to realize it is okay to let their spouses do some adjusting.

Some societal trends indicate that this adjustment is happening in many families. As James A. Levine, director of the Fatherhood Project at the Families and Work Institute, said: "The way men define success has shifted in the last generation—it's not just being a provider, it means being involved with your kids" (as quoted in Spencer, 1997, p. 78). A 1994 Roper poll for the Family Research Council found that the time fathers spend one-on-one with their kids had increased to 38 hours a week, up from 5 hours in 1989. And a University of North Texas survey documented that the amount of time men spend on child care and domestic chores, although still less than what women spend, has been increasing over the last 30 years. During this same period, the amount of time women spend has been dropping proportionately.

Despite these trends, some of the younger women in our study seemed to hold onto traditional gender ideologies about the division of labor at home. They expressed interest in public relations as a career because they believed it would enable them to engage in paid work while still being the primary manager of the domestic sphere.

Wharton (1994) studied this dynamic among female real estate agents, since many women are attracted to careers in real estate because of the flexible work hours. Wharton found, though, that the women were overburdened, given the sheer number of hours they had to dedicate to their jobs to be successful. This dilemma was compounded by the women's (and their husband's) belief that despite who does what at home, women still are responsible for managing what needs to be done and when. Wharton concluded that flexible work schedules were inadequate for helping women balance paid and domestic work, arguing for more radical changes in work and family patterns to achieve gender equality. These might include expanded households with extranuclear and intergenerational social networks; simplification of lifestyles; and the development of noncontinuous, part-time, or shared work roles—or all three (from Hunt and Thompson, 1987).

ORGANIZATIONAL REFORMS

Work-Life Policies

A major step for organizations is establishing innovative work-life policies. We use the term *work life* to emphasize the whole range of initiatives that organizations might undertake—from family-friendly benefits to support for employees' returning to school (see Harris, as cited in "Backlash to Work-Family Benefits," 1997). Beck (1991) emphasized that organizations that are supportive of employees' total lives enjoy competitive advantages because these organizations are better able to attract and retain the best employees.

Carpenter (as quoted in Barbieri, 1992) discussed the organization–family connection, arguing that family-friendly benefits do not amount to a "do good" scheme; they bring a direct financial boost to employers because employees with child- or elder-care issues are more likely to be absent, to experience more stress, and to have more health problems than those without such responsibilities.

Several of our participants agreed. As one interviewee argued, organizations' lack of support for families may jeopardize employees' emotional health. Another interviewee concurred, predicting that more time for family would result in more content employees. Workers also would feel more kinship with and loyalty to their organizations. Still another made the same point in a different way. She questioned whether women's gaining equal representation in a work-obsessed environment is really a victory for anyone. That is, a large paycheck may not make up for the loss of a meaningful existence beyond work.

Suggestions for work-life initiatives usually include child-care and elder-care assistance and policies for making the work place more flexible. Recommendations for child-care assistance take the form of financial aid, resource-referral services, and employer-sponsored day-care centers. Elder-care service entails financial aid, counseling services, long-term-care insurance, and employee-sponsored adult day-care (Hewitt Associates, as cited in Barbieri, 1992). Suggestions for making the work place less rigid include flextime, extended leaves, job sharing, telecommuting, quality part-time work, phase-back-in programs for employees (Beck, 1991), and spousal relocation and job-locator programs (Lelen, 1997; Thompson et al., 1992).

Some of our research participants considered such policies necessary. However, one woman said that these initiatives will occur only on the heels of "a lot of writing and talking about" the need for modifications. She argued that fields in which there are a lot of women, such as public relations, can make a difference. That is, when women dominate a function, organizational policy-makers more readily can see that they must accommodate women or face the possibility of losing their work force.

A related suggestion has to do with organizations devising alternative career paths. The need for more options is supported by evidence showing that 70% of women with schoolage children and 50% of women with children under 1 year are working. These figures mean that the average working mother's office and home duties total 84 hours a week (Rodgers & Rodgers, as cited in "New Career Paths for Women," 1990).

Several of our participants noted that inflexible career paths stem in large part from the dated assumption that all employees have a "wife" at home who is managing the domestic sphere. Although at one point this presumption may have been accurate, it has become unrealistic. One example of the gap between organizational assumptions and work-force reality is the structure of advancement within universities, or what Sekaran and Kassner (1992) called the "old male tenure model" (p. 175). Following this scheme, faculty members typically are granted a 6-year period during which they are expected to have a minimum number of publications in refereed journals in addition to acceptable performance in teaching and an adequate service record. As Sekaran and Kassner pointed out, these expectations "might have been realistic when the faculty were all men, with wives at home to keep house on a full-time basis" (p. 175). Now, however, such expectations have constrained both men and women.

Most often, advancement within other organizations follows (at least implicitly) a plan similar to the university model. The first few years of an employee's career are the period of "paying dues." During this time, employees are expected to perform at top speed and demonstrate loyalty and commitment by putting work above all else (Conrad, 1990). The underlying problem with this scheme is that the start-up period typically occurs around the time when workers are starting a family or caring for small children (and sometimes aging parents). For women, this mismatch is particularly vexing because often they are dealing with the physical and mental trauma of pregnancy, childbirth, and perhaps breastfeeding. As Cobb (as quoted in Sekaran and Kassner, 1992) stated, women's resumes "do not list the marriage, the miscarriage, the first baby and the second baby, [and] the exhausting and fruitless search for perfect day care" (p. 162).

Organizations providing alternatives to rigid career paths would help workers balance these demands. An example mentioned by several of our female respondents is the nonpartner track that has developed within law firms. Employees on this track work a strict 40-hour week; neither the firm nor they expect performance that would qualify them to be partners. At a later date, however, employees can change directions and enter a more demanding line. Presumably the firm benefits, too, from arrangements such as this by retaining quality employees who otherwise might have been forced to leave, given their outside demands.

The scenario we are proposing, however, does not translate into a "mommy track." As Thompson et al. (1992) argued, differential consideration for those with family responsibilities, in the absence of realigning society's priorities, does little to resolve discrimination against women: "As long as such responsibilities are socially devalued and seen as the sole domain of women, women will remain second-class citizens in the workplace" (p. 72). Vanderfolk (as quoted in Barbieri, 1992) agreed, contending that a mommy track is merely an excuse for treating women disparately. One of our interviewees pointed out that her agency "gives lip service to job sharing, but there is this unspoken feeling that everyone else gives 120 percent, why can't you [the job sharer]?" Further, the Economic Policy Institute (as cited in "Part-time Employees Receive Low Priority," 1991) found that employees who work part time fare poorly in terms of employee rights and benefits. As DuRivage (as quoted in "Part-time Employees Receive Low Priority," 1991) explained, "Flexible forms of employment relieve employers of obligations under federal safety, pension, unemployment, and affirmative action laws" (p. C1).

Discussing a related issue, several of the women in one focus group called for reevaluating the organizational assumption that everyone can and should aspire to top levels. As one participant argued, "being the very best at the middle level" should be legitimate. Another participant, too, believed that people need to look beyond salaries and status; people should ask themselves whether they are happy.

However, one participant in a discussion brought out the importance of some women continuing to aspire to and achieve top billing: Women who do so demonstrate to others that women can and do succeed at high posts. Several women made the same point in another focus group. As one stated, others seeing women's successes will help the "cause of women." Or, as another contended, other women "gain by association."

Valuing the Feminine

Another organizational reform is transforming organizational cultures so that feminine values are esteemed. Organizations then need to communicate these values in several ways: through the socialization process, symbolic communication, linking values to specific behaviors, and using financial resources (Clampitt, 1991). The socialization period, or the phase when new members are becoming acclimated to an organization, is one opportunity for organizations to establish that they are supportive of women. For example, during the "interviewing" phase, organizations should not employ the thinly veiled strategy of inviting token women to apply for positions for which a man is already slated. Nor should organizations have prospective employees interview only with men; female managers should be included. Symbolic communication also can get a pro-women message across. For example, women should not be excluded from executive clubs (Gallagher, 1992) or be assigned the dingiest offices. Linking values to specific behaviors is also important. An example here might be organizations instituting training seminars in gender sensitivity and then requiring employees to attend. Finally, new values can be communicated using financial resources such as ensuring women's salaries and opportunities for raises are equal to men's.

Several of our research participants also had ideas for how organizations could move toward valuing the feminine. The easiest route, according to one communication manager, is to have more women in charge. She asserted that organizational culture is an "outgrowth of the personality of the people in top level." Thus, as long as men dominate those levels, masculine values will be the norm. A step toward changing this situation, according to one interviewee, is women refusing to accept the status quo. She explained that if women see a situation where all the participants are white men, women need to be aware and "call people" on it. This woman also pointed out that organizations need to stress gender-neutral language. She said this makes a difference in how people conceptualize gender and work.

REFORMS IN PUBLIC RELATIONS

Combating Marginalization

According to many of our research participants, the most fundamental problem within public relations is overcoming others' misconceptions about the field. An obvious recommendation here is educating others—particularly top management—about the importance of public relations. As the marketing communication director for a private university said, this is the first step toward rectifying public relations's marginalization. The communication manager of a hospice organization called this "PR for PR." One agency owner agreed, stating that "public relations needs to sell itself to upper-level management." She went on to explain how she does this as a consultant by "co-opting" the internal public relations staff. The result, she said, is the elevation of the public relations function in the eyes of management.

This practitioner thought that another step should be instituting media relations courses in business schools. She believed this would help expose future managers to public relations and bolster the credibility of communication. Similarly, in another focus group, one woman stressed the importance of practitioners educating the business community about public relations. She believed that in general, public relations has not done enough "cross-industry fertilization." She said practitioners should take their skills and "give them to the rest of the world."

A corresponding suggestion put forth by several research participants was that professional associations in public relations play a role in educating management about public relations. As the vice president of a local agency pointed out, professional associations need to start communicating with CEOs and enlighten them about the importance of public relations.

Some female respondents also argued that professional associations can and should specifically address the problem of the glass ceiling. As a senior counselor at a national agency contended, professional organizations have an obligation to keep gender issues "on the table." She said these groups need to empower women by helping them develop salary negotiating skills. Another interviewee deemed professional associations uniquely suited for advancing equity for female practitioners because, unlike most organizations, many associations are headed by women. Similarly, a public relations educator (as quoted in L. Grunig, 1989a) explained that, although opportunities for women may be limited elsewhere, "opportunities within the professional organizations are unlimited" (p. 229). One participant in a focus group said initiatives taken by professional associations would filter down to universities.

The director of public relations for a national accounting firm concurred, but provided one caveat. She thought that organizing within professional associations would be beneficial as long as these attempts did not turn into "gripe" sessions. As another female respondent said, professional associations should not become too "obsessed" with women's issues. She called for dealing with prejudice but also seeing past it by sticking to "business at hand." She believed this is a more effective strategy than any broad-scale movement.

At least one interviewee was a little skeptical about the role professional associations could play. She argued that these groups have many other fires to fight. Also, there are more pressing issues such as addressing the credibility of the field irrespective of feminization. However, we believe public relations's stature cannot be examined in a gender void. That is, the credibility of public relations has become a gender issue.

Reassessing Undergraduate Education

Another initiative within public relations should be reassessing undergraduate education. One suggestion is more required coursework in business, a recommendation made by many research participants and one that surfaced in several focus groups. In general, participants believed that the stakes for entering public relations should be raised by requiring practitioners to be communicators *and* managers.

Several female respondents went even further by wondering if public relations should assimilate into business schools. As one participant stated in a focus group, if public relations is really part of management, then perhaps public relations should be taught in management schools. She wondered whether universities even should have undergraduate programs in public relations, given what she considered the weaknesses of the typical curriculum. For her, majoring in business and then getting a master's degree in communication might be a better approach.

A vice president of a national agency wondered if the disintegration of public relations per se might help. Pondering the future of the field, she thought, "Maybe public relations won't be public relations anymore." She speculated that "public relations" might (and possibly should) give way to a more generalized "communications" approach. On this point, she believed a student's majoring in business and minoring in communication would provide opportunities that a public relations major would not. The vice president of marketing and public relations for a nonprofit health care organization made a similar point in a focus group. Stating she never liked the term "public relations," she argued for redefining the field as "communications." However, we believe that changing public relations's name is merely a cosmetic solution. A more effective strategy is bolstering students' and practitioners' management skills. By doing so, public relations could be practiced to its fullest potential and would be most likely to make a valued contribution to organizations.

A related suggestion involves incorporating women's perspectives into the curriculum (Jones, 1991). As one female respondent lamented, "Men have written the textbooks; they have defined the field." Research supports this practitioner's claim. Creedon (1989a) found that textbooks have either omitted altogether or distorted the story of women's contribution to public relations's history. Similarly, Kern-Foxworth (1989c) discovered in her content analysis of textbooks that the number of references to women was limited (38 mentions in 3,447 pages). Further, she found that most texts focused only on the increased number of women in the profession and the gender–salary connection. She concluded that public relations textbooks are failing to prepare students for the reality that "society is not monolithic but a pluralistic dynamic in which women are central components" (p. 35).

For Kern-Foxworth, biases toward women in textbooks could be erased in part if schools hired more female faculty to teach public relations. These women might then write and edit public relations textbooks that accurately reflect women's status in public relations. Further, these female professors could provide the positive role models for women that current public relations materials do not.

Few transformations in public relations curricula and textbooks will occur, however, unless women in public relations are encouraged to pursue academics. A move toward ensuring this would be to warm the "chilly" climate for women on college campuses. One aspect of this warming should be supporting women who do feminist or gender-related research. Part of the "ice" some women in academe may feel no doubt stems from the constant reminder that women's experiences and interests carry little worth within university structures. Female graduate students who pursue feminist or gender-related research often have a hard time finding interested and supportive faculty (Sekaran & Kassner, 1992). This situation stems in part from the pervasive attitude within academe that feminist scholarship is not legitimate research. Thus, some women may perceive a gap between women's interests and the priorities of universities. This disjuncture does little to encourage women to pursue the academic route.

We (L. Grunig, 1989a) have listed several strategies for moving beyond this disjuncture. A positive message for women would be sent by universities enhancing research support funds and opportunities specifically for women and junior faculty. Another step would be developing courses especially for women who want to study women and communication. A related suggestion raised by some of our research participants was addressing the gender imbalance in university faculty. As one interviewee contended, the power structure within most communication faculties continues to be male. She went on to point out, however, that new scholars are infusing communication and public relations departments with fresh perspectives. She believed that positive changes for women will be effected as "more people with a vision of a different future articulate that vision every chance they get." Further, even if female faculty have to "buy in" to be promoted and tenured, their individual successes filter to the larger community of women.

MEN AND WOMEN WORKING TOGETHER

We conclude this list of strategies by proposing that all of these solutions must come from men as well as women. Why? Although the minority in terms of numbers, men dominate the field of public relations in positions of power and responsibility. Women may draw strength from themselves and from each other to challenge such powerful institutions as departments of corporate communication and public relations firms nationwide, but any transformation of employment practices will require the involvement and the commitment of women and men alike.

That dedication to equality may emanate from an emerging sensitivity to the ways in which previously unexamined attitudes or stereotypes about women and public relations have led to the unintentional bias in decision making that has characterized the field. It should lead to a politics of affiliation. This argument for partnership is consistent with Harraway's (1991) notion that those who are or who look like they belong to a constructed category, such as "woman," and those who are sympathetic to and want to empower the lives of those people should join together to effect change.

Chapter Fourteen

Final Thoughts

Times certainly have changed since the classified ads were placed in columns headed by "Help Wanted: Men" and "Help Wanted: Women." Since its inception, PRSA's membership in some senses has mirrored the changing times for women and work in this country. By 1997, the typical member ("Special Report," 1997) was female (60%) and of the baby-boomer generation (63%). However, many of these young women are still segregated—only more subtly than in the days when job categories were advertised as gender-specific—into lower paying, less-prestigious subspecialties of the field. Almost all of PRSA's members are still white (93%).

How can this be? If you have read to this point, you are well acquainted with factors such as stereotyping, socialization, tokenism, isolation, and the triple shift at home and in the office that disadvantage even the most super of superwomen. Add to these influences working at the *individual* level the *organizational* forces that include the sublimation of public relations to related areas such as marketing or human relations and the encroachment on the function by lawyers, personnel experts, or MBAs. Top off this confluence of elements with societal or organizational cultures that advantage masculine values and devalue women, regardless of their chosen field. We must conclude, then, that despite the educational and professional opportunities that have opened to women in this country, the glass ceiling continues to oppress us.

OPPRESSION AS A SOCIAL CONSTRUCT

The root of the word *oppress* is *press*. When we thought about this, we first envisioned women of older generations working at home, in the private sphere, nurturing their families by cooking, cleaning, and—yes—washing and *pressing* their clothes. We thought next about the women who still do it all—working outside the home while continuing to take on more than their share of household responsibilities. Women stand beside their male colleagues in the office on weekdays and at their ironing boards at night and on weekends at home. Thus we found ourselves questioning whether women have gained or lost. Have women in public relations, in particular, been oppressed or liberated by the potential for a management role in this exciting career field?

To begin to answer this question, we return to the origin of *oppression*. Frye (1992) explained that the *press*—root of the term—is used to mold, flatten, or reduce things in bulk: "Something pressed is something caught between or among forces and barriers which are so related to each other that jointly they restrain, restrict or prevent the thing's motion or mobility" (p. 38).

In a sense, then, yes—women in public relations are caught between pressures imposed both from within themselves and from the outside. They aspire to "be all that they can be," given their brains, advanced education, and motivation. Society, too, expects women to contribute to the family income. Most families at this turn of the century need two paychecks even to survive. Of course, families also rely inordinately on female members to take care of children and elderly relatives. In this book, we hope we have underscored the dignity of motherhood, daughterhood, and intimate partnerships right along with management or any other way in which women choose to enter and survive in the marketplace.

In fact, many of the anonymous women we studied were *central* to the lives of their families. At the same time, they were *marginalized* in the organizations that employed them. Operating on the periphery of the company, rather than at its core, may result from the devaluation of the entire staff function of public relations. However, we also know that marginalization is particularly likely when the staffers are women.

Women face barriers subtle and not so subtle that may constrain them to the technician's role. They encounter stereotyping about what women want or are capable of handling. Our own research and that of other scholars has established that female public relations practitioners typically are relegated to a ghetto within the larger ghetto of this organizational function. O'Neil (1999) reviewed 20 years of our trade press to reveal the social and cultural patterns disadvantaging women. Her content analysis established the masculine values of individualism, competition, and objectivity as privileged. Women may be perceived as "too soft" for top-level management or just soft enough to be attractive to the sexual harassers still found in the U.S. work force. Socialization may have kept white women, in particular, out of the managerial pipeline until too recently for their salaries to catch up to their ambitions or abilities.

An androgynous managerial style—one that combines the strengths of what our culture considers masculine and feminine—has empowered African American women in public relations. Perhaps, then, this approach would foster the careers of white women as well. After all, we know that many female practitioners enact the dual role of technician and manager (and for considerably less pay than their male colleagues typically earn).

With this understanding of oppression, then, we can replace any notion of women as victimized by individual supervisors, employers, or spouses with the reality that oppression is structured into the fabric of our social institutions: political, educational, and organizational. Throughout this book, in fact, we have tried for the so-called big picture rather than emphasizing personal solutions for or individual gains of women in public relations. Just as women are not responsible for their oppression, they alone should not be expected to remedy this pressing situation.

We cannot underscore enough the importance of social constructs. We explained early on how gender is socially constructed. We need to emphasize as well how sexism and racism go beyond individual malfeasance to what amounts to an institutionalization of sexism and racism in this country. Thus we need more than individual solutions for the perpetrators and for the victims of those biases. Education, moral training, attitude readjustment, trying harder—are all inadequate to the task of overcoming the themes, the social constructs and patterns, that our research has traced.

Inequality is structural, built into our institutions and corporations. It is constructed through the intersection of gender, racioethnic, and age relations. The result is that groups with power and privilege, such as the dominant coalition of any organization, can control those who enjoy less power and influence, such as female public relations practitioners. Is that relationship of domination innate? Not at all. Because it is socially constructed, it can be reconstituted.

If such a restructuring of society fails to occur, we fear that as in most professional occupations, female public relations practitioners will "choose" roles, specializations, and types of organizations that pay less but allow greater flexibility for family responsibilities than the higher paying jobs. Or, to the detriment of the organizations that formerly employed them, women may opt for entrepreneurship.

Rather than apologizing for our subjectivity as female scholars studying sexism and choosing words like "fear," we hope that our narrative is credible because it is born of authenticity. In one sense, we are telling others' stories: those of the men and women who took part in our two-stage investigation, as well as those about whom we read in others' research. In another and more critical sense, though, we are telling our own story as women who teach and do public relations. That story is exceedingly complex. It called for an equally complex methodological approach, relying on a plethora of primary and secondary sources.

As a result, our research has been able to expose a number of seemingly contradictory notions. For one important example, the glass ceiling studies highlight how the material conditions of women's lives—especially our gender but also the very fact that we work in public relations—constrain our choices. At the same time, we heard much about the *agency* of women encountering and overcoming substantial personal and professional limitations on their choices. Thus we come to understand that how people see themselves—as agent of their own fate or as object of oppression—has a great deal to do with their satisfaction at work (if not their salary or level of job responsibility).

WOMEN'S AGENCY

Is this situation, then, a real "either/or" between actual conditions and self-perception or stereotyping? Our answer, after analyzing the data we collected with our colleagues over a period of several years, is that both factors are operating at once on female public relations practitioners. We learned that many professionals in this field, especially women, face incredible constraints that do limit their career options. What continues to intrigue us the most is what women, in particular, do in those cases.

Of course, we do not deny that structural systems of oppression exist; we do not let our "good politics" disavow that reality. We choose instead to celebrate the strides women have made in the work place since public relations entered the U.S. scene at the turn of the 20th century. Among them have been pioneers, such as Doris Fleischman Bernays, who from the field's contemporary inception have been effective and influential. We have profiled as well a larger group of women, those who accepted what they could achieve at the moment and looked forward with optimism to a better day ... a time when their salaries would equal men's, when they would have a chance to be hired and promoted on the basis of their expertise rather than their gender or racioethnic background, and when they would be empowered to speak for the publics for whom they felt responsible. We cannot name all these competent, courageous women because, for the most part, they do their work quietly. Their victories are more long term than highly visible at any moment. Still, their successes steadily have created opportunities for the ambitious women who will follow. Their stories say that anything is possible.

Some of these women, disadvantaged by social and political structures but advantaged by their own education, experience, endurance, and ambition, were championed by male partners, coworkers, and bosses. So we must question whether women through their own agency alone find rewarding work in public relations—managing, along the way, to overcome the blatant sexism we remember from earlier decades. Undoubtedly not. Instead, we believe that women have collaborated with like-minded people of both sexes—working with men like so many of those male PRSA members who spoke candidly in our focus groups around the country.

We also know that, queen bee syndrome not withstanding, women have worked together. Through informal networking and more structured, association-based women's groups, they have engaged in a kind of "strategic essentialism." That is, they may—consciously or subconsciously—deny the complexity of their individual situations for professional gain. We have tried throughout this book to expose all the differences among women, rather than to suggest any essential nature of women or essential differences between women and men. However, there are times, both historically and in professional life, when the unique aspects of each woman may need to be downplayed to achieve some goal only attainable through *collective* action. Thus we are convinced by the participants in our research, both women and men, who encouraged societies such as PRSA to continue to support women's opportunities in public relations.

We are convinced as well of the need to decenter the experiences of men and of whites in public relations. Too much of our literature to date has assumed, typically implicitly, that men's career plans and opportunities are universal. The statistically significant differences reported by our survey respondents suggest otherwise. Even a cursory demographic analysis also establishes the ubiquity of whiteness in public relations. The problem, in both the case of race and of gender, is one of power: dominance of the group considered the "norm" over that which is considered "different." Our intent is not to discourage young women preparing for a career in this field, nor any of our African American, Asian American, or Hispanic American students. Rather, we hope to raise awareness of the constraints imposed by that power dynamic at the same time we introduce students to people of color and women whose own agency has led them to success as entrepreneurs or managers of the staff function.

Nor should women in communication management feel alone in being squeezed from inside and outside. We have demonstrated that many groups

354 WOMEN IN PUBLIC RELATIONS

of women—from the highest echelons of professional practice in law, education, government service, journalism, corporate management, and medicine to the bottom of the socioeconomic ladder where blue- and pink-collar workers toil—have been excluded from top-level pay and promotions.

Despite the fact that most U.S. women work outside the home, our society—including its political institutions and leading organizations—has made few relevant concessions to ease the double or triple burden these women endure. Further, despite women's increasing numbers and influence on the way work is done, women and men alike have suffered from what may be an inevitable backlash. In *The Decline of Males*, anthropologist Lionel Tiger (1999) attributed an erosion in the confidence and power of men to women's rising confidence and power. Consider also sexual harassment litigation. Fear of class-action suits in the work place may lead to more guarded interactions between women and men than ever before. As a result, some employers are buying liability coverage to protect themselves against claims of harassment that have soared as high as $10 million ("Odd Jobs," 1998a). At the very least, a burgeoning nontraditional work force has left bosses and workers alike confused and often resentful.

SO WHERE DO WE STAND?

All the news is not negative, of course. Changing social attitudes, free-market forces, political victories, and educational opportunities all have served to help shrink the pay gap and crack the glass ceiling for women in public relations. Management training programs, including those designed to manage multicultural diversity, should keep the sponge ceiling from drying out. Growing diversity in the work force and in consumer markets has released some practitioners from their acrylic vaults.

At the same time, the U.S. Congress in place as this manuscript was being finalized voted against issues that directly affect women's progress in education and at work. We worry because the 105th Congress passed a bill to eliminate funding for specific vocational education programs designed to help girls and women. More relevant to the concerns of public relations professionals, congressional leaders have targeted affirmative action for elimination. They also have proposed legislation that would end equal opportunity in education, employment, and contracting.

Such cuts undoubtedly would disadvantage women and people of color who need equal opportunity to compete for jobs and the education in public relations that is now so readily available. Thus we worry about regression, not progress, for women working outside their homes. We cannot assume that "things" inevitably get better the longer women work in non-traditional fields such as public relations. At the same time we take pride in contributing to the record of women's accomplishments as communication managers and technicians, we caution against complacency.

So back and forth we go, between the good news and the bad, the gains and the reversals. How to sort it all out?

We have presented survey data that should allow you, the readers, to assess the situation as it exists for women in public relations. We also have included the testimony of a range of women who talked of their feelings in these pages. We hope that their words, in turn, inspire our readers to explore their own feelings.

Along the way, we have answered the research questions posed in the introductory chapter of the book. In so doing, we hope to have corrected distortions and filled gaps in information available about the experience of women in contemporary public relations. By including the admittedly narrow picture available for different minority groups, we hope to have helped transform the understanding of everyone—men and women and people of diverse racioethnic backgrounds—in communication management.

FUTURE DIRECTIONS FOR RESEARCH

Still, the job of exploring, describing, and understanding the work life of women in public relations remains incomplete. We trust PRSA's Foundation will continue to support this longitudinal research. The work force in public relations is more like a passing parade than a standing army, and so a periodic, systematic surveying of its membership seems critical. We hope, too, that the next phase of the glass ceiling research will probe more deeply into issues of cultural inclusivity. Given the pivotal importance of relationship building in this field, the concept of requisite variety looms large. This is not to say that only people of like racioethnic backgrounds can communicate with each other. That would mean pigeonholing, which can limit the careers and impinge on the self-esteem of minority practitioners. (It also lets white practitioners off the hook, implying that they need not become culturally sensitive.) It is to suggest, rather, that realizing the potential of public relations as a two-way, symmetrical process of establishing, maintaining, and enhancing relationships will require "multicultural communicators" of all races and genders. Women, perhaps because they have been socialized differently from men, seem especially well suited to nurture such collaborative relationships.

Future editions of a book like this undoubtedly will feature discussions we barely have hinted at. In particular, we envision a growing need for future study of three distinct areas: harassment, globalization, and new communication technologies.

Sexual Harassment

Two-thirds of the 17,000 respondents to a survey of the country's largest corporations cited evidence of sexual harassment more than a decade ago (Houghton, 1988). Our female survey respondents strongly believe that sexual harassment exists in public relations. Women Executives in Public Relations (WEPR Memo, 1991) found that 95% of those who responded to its questionnaire indicated that, at some point in their careers, they had been sexually harassed at the office or by clients. Only 13% reported the problem to management (although one woman brought suit through the Equal Employment Opportunity Commission).

We consider sexual harassment more an issue of *power* than of sex or gender. Perhaps because women as a group enjoy less power at work than do men, they typically are the harassed rather than the harassers. Only recently have our society and our legal institutions addressed the power imbalance at work or in school and what that means for women subjugated by men.

We hope scholarship in the future explores another important dimension of harassment, however. *Backlash* harassment occurs as a reaction against women entering nontraditional fields in increasing numbers. Men may react with suspicion, derision, or even violence if they perceive these women enjoying attention or special favors. We saw the ugly effects of backlash in Montreal in 1990, when 14 female students were shot to death by a disgruntled white male student. Apparently he resented their admission into an engineering program. Two years later, female professors of engineering at a Minnesota university received death threats simply for disrupting the status quo there. A professor of communication on another Minnesota campus received a hostile communication warning her against her outspoken feminist standpoint—and the fact that she had begun to teach in a technical area. These three incidents, varying in severity, all speak to the abuse and violence women may encounter as they enter men's turf. If women ascend to the managerial ranks of public relations, once considered "only-man's-land," we worry about the backlash harassment they may experience. The resentment against them may be particularly pronounced if they work in types of organizations, such as corporations, where female managers have been the exception longer than in the nonprofit sector.

Only recently have we begun to understand the different forms sexual harassment may take. Here we are guided by the insightful work of Benokraitis (1997), who developed a preliminary taxonomy of types of harassment. We know sexual harassment may be *subtle*, less obvious than the more blatant types of sex discrimination discussed throughout this text yet still harmful to women because it entails unequal treatment—intentional or not. It also may be *covert*, hidden yet purposeful and often maliciously motivated. Covert harassment typically involves manipulation or sabotage. Sexual harassment even may be thought of as *"friendly,"* seemingly harmless or even playful, yet it too is a form of discrimination because it creates embarrassment, discomfort, or humiliation.

Whatever its manifestation, we need to explore the ways in which sexual harassment affects women in public relations. We can't be sure whether this type of sex discrimination actually has increased, or whether women are more likely to report the problem today than in the past. We know only that it has become increasingly visible throughout the time we have spent preparing this manuscript.

Globalization

Sexual harassment and globalization may be linked as issues of concern. As domestic organizations increasingly "go global," sexual harassment may present an even greater problem for women who work in the international context. In some countries, such as Zimbabwe, where U.S. women undoubtedly will find themselves doing public relations, sexual harassment is considerably more widespread than in the United States. This "crime of enormous proportion" has major consequences for professional women (Khan, 1997).

Less fierce but also of concern are cultural inclusivity and sensitivity throughout public relations. The ramifications are both external and internal. Customers, suppliers, and competitors of the typical United States-based organization are more heterogeneous than ever before. So, too, are employees. Thus what some consider women's "natural" talents as communicators, integrators of information, negotiators, educators, and even healers should be increasingly valued. Fisher (1999) went so far as to suggest that women, if not held back by societal or organizational constraints, will reshape many professions and corporations worldwide.

Diversity on an international scale becomes a greater challenge for communication managers all the time. As the work forces of other countries become as heterogeneous as that in the United States has been for some time, we—with our responsibility for internal relations—need to help ensure fair hiring and promotion opportunities for all employees in countries outside the United States where our organizations may do business. Increasing diversity of religion, racioethnicity, and gender in cultures previously marked by more sameness than difference brings with it the potential for a changing work environment at the least and legal actions at most. We know the challenge this represents, especially in countries historically more masculine than feminine in their cultural values. Thus we see a real need to study the interactive effects between feminization and globalization.

New Technology

The implications of new technology for public relations practice are legion. So, too, are the concerns for women in communication management. Future scholars undoubtedly will explore questions such as whether the computer further relegates women to the technician's role, how sexual harassment inhibits women on the Internet, and whether the information superhighway is bound to remain a road primarily traversed by men.

Warnick (1999), for one, believed that some online chat groups and gateway websites have marginalized women and even excluded them, as latecomers in what she considered a more established and hostile male environment. She recommended noncommercial, alternative websites more supportive of women and girls because they provide humor and an avenue for self-expression. At the same time, we are aware that already the Internet offers one critical resource for women who feel isolated, so much in the minority that they are tokens at work. That resource is camaraderie.

Relationships can be built in cyberspace, as communication scholars around the country are beginning to discover. Walther and Parks (1998), for example, used the Internet to publish their research on how e-mail, newsgroups, and online chat rooms are conducive to creating good friendships. They theorized that cyberspace offers a way to connect like-minded people, people who are not distracted by physical first impressions but who share a common interest. Although e-mail does allow for potential misrepresentation, users can feel safe in withdrawing from the conversation if they sense a threat. Conversing online also is characterized by more and earlier self-disclosure—characteristics Walther and Parks considered vital to developing good quality relationships.

This program of research certainly resonated with the three of us. Our personal relationship as well as our professional one has grown throughout our book project. Because we live and work thousands of miles apart and because we have numerous and often conflicting role responsibilities, we question whether we could have conceived, written, and edited our manuscript offline. The documented isolation of at least one of us (L. Grunig, 1989b) as a woman on a faculty dominated by men led her to value the larger "invisible college" of colleagues in public relations research across the country—a group linked daily by electronic communication. This virtual college extends her working relationships and friendships with other women beyond the border of her campus or any one project, such as writing a book.

Chatting online offers a professional as well as personal benefit, especially for increasing numbers of home-based workers in public relations. It allows for the important networking we have alluded to throughout this book. Using e-mail to communicate regularly with others who have virtual firms helps create what Joshua M. Peck, director of public relations for a Washington, DC, company called the "virtual water cooler" (as quoted in Ginsberg, 1998, p. 9). It overcomes the lack of face time that challenges all telecommuters—people who are, after all, social creatures needing personal contact as well as a professional group of supporters.

A third major advantage the new media offer public relations practitioners may be the most important of all for women in this field. Kornegay and L. Grunig (1998) proposed that *cyberbridging* may help boundary spanners go beyond their tactical, craft-based function to contribute to the dominant coalition. The cyberbridge, in their view, is an Internet or electronic means for public relations practitioners to collect information valuable to top-level decision makers in their organizations. By using online databases to monitor issues or conducting e-mail surveys of members of strategic publics, communication managers have the potential to connect with and influence the power elite. This cyberscanning, of course, furthers one's own power base—critically important to women who have been relegated inordinately to the technician's role. Environmental scanning via online databases (Choo, 1994) and other electronic means also helps make organizations women work for more effective, because excellent organizations empower public relations professionals to contribute to strategic management at the highest levels (Dozier, L. Grunig, & J. Grunig, 1995). Finally, research activities that support strategic planning provide a way for members of the dominant coalition to become attuned to their publics— thus giving voice to constituencies that otherwise may have been unheard in the decision-making process.

In effect, then, the World Wide Web provides not so much a sales or marketing tool as a two-way medium through which the organization both seeks information from and provides information to its publics. Pavlik and Dozier (1996) found that innovative firms already use the Web for all of these purposes.

For these reasons, we believe that the Web has immediate and positive value for most women. We suggest you bookmark these established resources:

- Advancing Women—http://www.advancingwomen.com
- The Electra Pages: Directory of Women's Organizations—http://www.electrapages.com
- Feminist.com—http://www.feminist.com
- UM Women's Studies Page—http://www.inform.umd.edu/EdRes/Topic/WomensStudies
- The Women's Bureau Fair Pay Clearinghouse—http://www.dol.gov/dol/wb
- Working Woman's Web site—http://www.womenconnect.com

THE LAST WORD

Most feminist treatises end with the notion that the solution to sex discrimination hinges on political, institutional, and organizational policies. Women alone, even women aligning themselves with like-minded men, cannot overcome either the blatant or the subtle sexism we have described here. We agree. We also acknowledge, as have most writers before us, that societal transformation is not so easy as it might seem on paper. Change takes longer than anyone expects. Without moving toward equity for women in public relations, however, the field risks losing the talents of well more than half of what we have established as its most effective practitioners.

Appendix

Research Design

This appendix outlines the four components of the design for the research we and our colleagues conducted on the glass ceiling phenomenon. We explored the situation for women in public relations using survey research, focus groups made up of PRSA members (including both female and male participants), lengthy interviews with female practitioners, and additional focus groups conducted with women chosen from our group of interviewees. The interviews and three focus groups with female practitioners were part of Linda Hon's (1992) doctoral dissertation. The survey and focus group research with PRSA members was conducted for the society's research foundation. Research team members for the initial stage of the PRSA study were Donald K. Wright, Elizabeth L. Toth, Larissa A. Grunig, and Jeffrey K. Springston. Team members for the second stage were Wright, Toth, Shirley A. Serini, and Arthur G. Emig.

A combined methodology such as this is one of the hallmarks of feminist scholarship (see Fine, 1988; Brannen, 1992). By relying on a variety of methods, feminists try to produce "new and better (more comprehensive) research" (L. Grunig, 1988, p. 49).

More specifically, feminism's recognition of connectivity in research suggests several important implications for this book. First, its mandate for responsibility toward research participants required that we constantly consider the effects our research might have on women in public relations. As a result, we have tried deliberately to validate women's experiences and contributions and to avoid disparaging or trivializing their beliefs. Finally, we strived for a methodology that would provide an open and egalitarian relationship between researchers and participants through which knowledge could be cocreated.

This combined methodology is outlined next. We describe the first phase of the PRSA research in greater detail than the second, because of the close similarity between the two stages of our survey and focus group analyses.

THE SURVEYS

The survey instruments were six-page mail questionnaires, nearly identical, sent to a large random sample of PRSA members. The instruments' questions tapped into roles, job satisfaction, and respondents' perceptions of the field of public relations. This two-stage research was conducted in 1990 and again in 1995.

The 1990 study represented 20% of the association's membership, or 2,785 members. One thousand twenty-seven (N = 1,027) usable responses were received, yielding a return rate of 37%. The 1995 study reached a smaller random sample of PRSA members. However, the completion rate of 45%, or 678 members, still matched the expected return for a lengthy survey of this kind.

Most of the questions addressed gender-related professional issues such as participants' perceptions of the impact of gender-related professional issues within their organization and these same issues throughout the overall field of public relations. The questionnaire included a job satisfaction index, as well as questions about demographic and organizational characteristics.

Several statistical procedures were used to determine scale reliability and whether or not there were differences between women and men in response to survey questions. Items concerning gender-related professional issues were assessed in relation to how those issues were perceived in organizations respondents worked in, as well as how individuals perceived the issues in the overall field of public relations. Those scoring high on the gender scales viewed women in a one-down position relative to men. These internal and external perceptions also were measured relative to the issue of flexible work environments.[1]

Practitioner roles were established by examining the percentage of time respondents spent performing 17 particular functions.[2] Respondents were grouped in categories according to whether they had high, medium, or low involvement in manager and technician activities.

---

[1]In 1990, the gender perception scale (inside the organization) obtained an alpha of .73, whereas the gender perception scale (throughout the field) only reached .56 alpha. Flextime scales (inside the organization and throughout the field) reached .72 and .75 alphas, respectively. Reliability of the job satisfaction scale was .85.

[2]Reliability coefficients (Cronbach's alpha) were used for all indices. When alpha scores made it clear that roles reflected either a manager or a technician dimension, we decided to take advantage of the number of cases in the study's database and take measurement beyond dominant role categories. Three levels of dimensional involvement—"high," "medium," and "low"—were established for both public relations manager and public relations technician roles. This yielded a more comprehensive role matrix, with sufficient cell sizes to conduct more detailed statistical analysis, than appears to have been possible in previous public relations role research.

PRSA FOCUS GROUPS

The survey research supplied only as much insight as participants would share via pen and paper. Also, additional research needed to be done to identify the critical variables that help *explain* gender inequities. So, focus group interviews were conducted to gather more and different kinds of information.

Some focus group research findings already had been reported on the perceptions of public relations practitioners toward gender issues in *The Velvet Ghetto* (Cline et al., 1986) and in *Beyond the Velvet Ghetto* (Toth & Cline, 1989a). In both of these studies, though, male and female focus groups members were combined. At the time of the research, it had been a conscious choice on the part of the scholars to represent the membership of IABC. However, Toth (1989b) concluded that her results were influenced by having both males and females in the same group. The men tended to dominate the discussion and did not perceive gender and public relations to be so important an issue as did the women. Thus, our focus group research separated male and female participants in part to determine whether putting both sexes together had muted or changed the focus on the issues that surfaced.

The previous focus group research on perceptions of gender issues and public relations (Cline et al., 1986; Toth & Cline, 1989a) also had been carried out by volunteer moderators without the researchers present. It was audiotaped for later transcription. Clearly, it is important to use experienced moderators who go through briefings before the focus group sessions and to videotape the sessions. The 1990 PRSA focus groups had the advantage of doing both: using trained moderators and videotaped documentation. There was a male moderator for the men's focus group and a female moderator for the women's focus group. We believe that the focus group data reported here are less susceptible than previous research to gender or moderator influences (or both) and that data analysis was improved because of the videotape.

Focus group research has several disadvantages that should be kept in mind when considering the results reported here. Again, experts such as Broom and Dozier (1990) and Pavlik (1987) point to the inability to generalize from focus group findings to the larger population of the study; the potential domination of a participant that could reduce the emergence of issues; the actual group dynamics that should permit deeply held ideas to emerge but may work instead to reflect group rather than individually held feelings and beliefs; and the subjectivity of the researcher that might surface during data analysis. The researcher must maintain an open mind in the face of so much material and not choose to interpret what is there according to personal biases. To avoid this problem, many of the results reported here were confirmed by two independent coders.

Research Questions

Six general research questions, based on the survey, were used in the PRSA focus groups. These questions dealt with roles, salaries, attraction to public relations work, and perceptions of working conditions and career opportunities of the survey respondents. Focus group participants also answered the question: "What do you consider the impact of female practitioners' lower salaries on public relations?" Finally, the participants responded to the question: "How do you define success?"

Procedures

All survey participants from the 1990 study were invited to take part in focus groups held during the November 1990 PRSA national conference. More than 100 practitioners expressed an interest in participating. These respondents received follow-up letters inviting them to attend the focus group sessions. Although several women responded by phone that they would volunteer, eventually they did not attend the scheduled focus groups. Male volunteers came from an announcement at the PRSA Assembly meeting and from actual conference contacts. The final focus group of men consisted of 11 PRSA members. The final focus group of women consisted of four PRSA members.

After the 1995 mail survey in the second phase of our research, two focus groups (one of women and one of men) were conducted in each of three cities: Chicago, Seattle, and Washington, DC. These sites were chosen because they represent major public relations markets and are geographically diverse. The six focus groups were held from October through December of 1995; they were preceded by a pretest conducted in September of that year. They were videotaped and those tapes later were transcribed. Size of the focus groups conducted in the second stage ranged from 5 to 10 participants.

Procedures were similar in the two series of focus groups. Shortly before the sessions began, each focus group member received a set of questions focused on responses to the survey and a "waiting room" questionnaire to complete before the sessions started. A research team member facilitated the session by introducing the purpose of the sessions and the moderators. The moderators for each of the focus groups had previous focus group experience. They had received the questions to review beforehand and were given an advance briefing. The moderators went over ground rules for the session, explained how the session would be conducted, and started by having the group members introduce themselves.

Participants

All participants in the two initial focus groups worked as managers or consultants and had considerable experience in public relations. Most were 40 years of age or older and earned more than $50,000 annually.

In the men's focus group, the average number of years working in public relations was 18, with a range of 6 to 31 years. Six of the participants majored in journalism as undergraduates. One majored in public relations. The other four had liberal arts degrees. All of the participants had either BA or BS degrees. There were two with master's degrees, one with a PhD, and one with a law degree. The participants' average age was 47 years, with a range of 31 to 58 years. Eight of the participants earned annual salaries of more than $50,000. All 11 participants were managers or worked as consultants in public relations. None of the job titles or descriptions given at the beginning of the focus group sessions suggested that these participants were employed as technicians.

In the women's focus group, the average number of years in public relations was 15, with a range of 7 to 24 years. Two of the participants majored in liberal arts as undergraduates, one majored in journalism, and one had no response. There were two participants with BA/BS degrees, one participant with a master's degree, and one participant with an MBA. The participants' average age was 39 years, with a range of 29 to 47 years. Three of the four participants earned salaries of more than $50,000. Three were managers or consultants in public relations. One taught and did public relations consulting. As in the men's group, none of the job titles or descriptions given at the beginning of the focus group session suggested that these participants were employed as technicians.

In the second series of six focus groups, participants ranged in age from 25 to 45 years and in experience from 5 to 15 years. They were mostly white and came from a variety of kinds of organizations.

Although such focus group research is not generalizable to any larger population, the results of this total of eight group discussions provided important insights into the quantitative data. So, too, did our long interviews with selected professionals.

LONG INTERVIEWS WITH FEMALE PRACTITIONERS

McCracken's (1988) methods for conducting "long" interviews provided the basis for the next phase of our research design. Long interviews are similar to in-depth interviews except that long interviews go beyond studying individual feelings; identifying shared beliefs among a group of people is the primary goal. This goal meshed well with our interest in exploring women's (both individually and as a group) experiences as communicators and their perceptions about discrimination in public relations.

The long interview's emphasis on providing an opportunity for interviewees to speak for themselves attracted us to this research technique (see also Cotterill, 1992). As McCracken (1988) pointed out, the most important principle to keep in mind when conducting open-ended interviews is "the recognition that the first objective . . . is to allow respondents to tell their story in their own terms" (p. 34). We believe this approach empowered our female research participants by showcasing their perceptions and experiences as they want them told. The flexibility provided by long interviewing also was an advantage because interviewees were able spontaneously to discuss experiences and issues that did not surface in the survey or even in the focus groups. This unanticipated information enriched our data immeasurably.

We should point out, however, that interviewing as a research method has several disadvantages (Marshall & Rossman, 1989). One is misinterpretation between the interviewer and the interviewee. We attempted to avoid distortions by collaborating with selected participants while writing up the findings. This exchange helped ensure that if inaccurate interpretations were being made, they were brought to light and corrected before conclusions were reached.

Marshall and Rossman (1989) listed researchers' dependence on the cooperation and honesty of a typically small group of interviewees as another limitation of interviewing. Securing cooperation, however, was not a problem. Every single woman who was contacted agreed to be interviewed. As for honesty, we have already discussed feminism's rejection of the search for objective "truths." We believe that these women's views of their world, however subjective, are valid. So the integrity of our findings lies in the extent to which we have presented their experiences accurately.

Selection of Interviewees

McCracken's (1988) plan suggests that when choosing respondents "less is more" (p. 17). As he pointed out, working longer and more carefully with a smaller number of people usually yields richer data than working superficially with many people.

Interviewing a small number of women in depth may seem counterintuitive for understanding a lot about women in public relations in general. Yet deep probing allows researchers to uncover the categories and assumptions according to which respondents make sense of their world. This depth is especially important for studying women in public relations. Plenty of studies already have examined impressive numbers of practitioners (e.g., *pr reporter*'s and the former *Public Relations Journal*'s annual surveys). Despite their breadth, these studies have revealed little useful knowledge for effectively confronting the issues surrounding discrimination against women in public relations.

Keeping this in mind, our selection of 34 female interviewees obviously was not meant to be a "sample" as that word is commonly used in research. Any female practitioner with enough experience (which we thought should be about 5 years) to shed light on the research questions was considered a credible choice. Most of the interviewees were located through contacts. Others were suggested by several of the interviewees.

One principle, however, was kept in mind: diversity. Although this group is not statistically representative of any larger population of women in public relations, as diverse of a group as possible (with regard to age, type of organization, organizational level, and so on) was assembled. But, even so, this group is narrow. Like ourselves, these women were middle class and mostly Caucasian and American. However, included were one American Asian (she prefers this order), one African American, and one Briton. So although we believe these women's experiences speak powerfully about gender discrimination in public relations, their stories are just part of a larger picture.

Interviewees ranged in age from mid-20s to over 60. Their positions spanned from the midlevel to the top; most were high ranking (directors and above). The kinds of organizations for which these women worked varied: corporations, government, public relations agencies, associations, and nonprofits. All of the women had at least a bachelor's degree, and 12 had a master's degree. Most studied public relations or an allied field, such as English.

Procedures

Thirty-seven interviews ultimately were conducted. Several of the first women to be interviewed were interviewed more than once, which helped to identify the major topics and issues women wanted to talk about most. All of the interviews were audiotaped so respondents' exact words could be retrieved, and all but seven were conducted face to face. At the request of one interviewee, we spoke over the phone. Six telephone interviews were completed with women who were located too far away to be interviewed in person. The interviews took place at different times (during work, lunch, after hours, and the weekend) and at different places (their offices, restaurants or cafes, and a library). Interviews lasted from 1 to 3 hours. The average was about 90 minutes.

Data Analysis

There is no clear-cut formula for analyzing the results of long interviews. However, feminists' concern with showcasing women's stories presupposes that participants speak for themselves. Thus, these women's "voices" in paraphrases and direct quotations provide the data for this phase of our research design.

With this is mind, notes and tapes from the interviews were reviewed. Responses were transcribed either verbatim (when the response demanded direct quotation) or in summary form. Next, themes were identified, comments were arranged under these categories, and differing opinions were documented (see Lindlof, 1995).

ADDITIONAL FOCUS GROUPS

At this point, three additional focus groups were conducted with a total of 13 women (those who could be clustered geographically) chosen from the group of interviewees. These focus groups were held in College Park, MD (with four women), Gainesville, FL (with four women), and Melbourne, FL (with five women). A member of the research team moderated the sessions after studying the videotapes of the initial PRSA focus groups. However, these three midpoint focus groups did not follow the same list of questions that the PRSA focus groups used (although there was some overlap). Instead, a set of general questions areas derived from the interviews was used.

Research Questions

The overriding question for these focus groups was, "What are the factors that explain gender discrimination in public relations?" Participants also were asked to discuss strategies that they thought would be effective for women as individuals to use in overcoming discrimination. These women then were asked about institutional strategies, or what society in general, organizations, and the public relations industry could do to advance gender equity.

Procedures

Participants spoke for about 90 minutes at each session. All of the groups were videotaped. A member of the research team analyzed the data using the same procedures as those used for the PRSA focus groups.

Participants

All of these focus group participants belonged to at least one professional association in public relations; several had held positions as high as president. These women's tenure in public relations ranged from 6 to more than 20 years. As undergraduates, four of the women majored in journalism, six majored in public relations, one majored in technical communications, one majored in English, and one majored in sociology. The participants' ages ranged from mid-20s to over 50. Eight of the participants were managers whose positions varied from midlevel to high ranking. Three women owned their own business, and one woman worked for one of the business owners. One woman was a reentry doctoral student who previously had held a managerial post in a national association. None of these women's job titles or descriptions of their jobs during their interview or interviews suggested that participants were employed as technicians.

References

Abel, E. (1981). Collective protest and meritocracy: Faculty women and sex discrimination lawsuits. *Feminist Studies, 7*(3), 505–538.

Abrahams, E. (1998, April 5). One woman against the tide. *Washington Post Education Review*, pp. 22–23, 25.

Aburdene, P. (1990, November). Speech to the Public Relations Society of America, New York.

Aburdene, P., & Naisbitt, J. (1992). *Megatrends for women*. New York: Villard Books.

Acker, J. (1990). Hierarchies, jobs, bodies: A theory of gendered organizations. *Gender and Society, 4*(2), 139–158.

Acker, J., Barry, K., & Esseveld, J. (1983). Objectivity and truth: Problems in doing feminist research. *Women's Studies International Forum, 6*, 423–435.

Adams, H. F. (1983). Work in the interstices: Woman in academe. *Women's Studies International Forum, 6*(2), 135–141.

Adelman, C. (1991). *Women at thirtysomething: Paradoxes of attainment*. Washington, DC: Office of Educational Research and Improvement, U.S. Department of Education.

Adler, N. J. (1997). *International dimensions of organizational behavior* (3rd ed.). Cincinnati, OH: South-Western College Publishing.

Adler, T. (1991). Will feminization spell decline for field? *APA Monitor*, page unknown.

Advice for soon-to-be working mothers. (1998, May). *Tactics*, p. 30.

Alba, R. D., & Chamblin, M. (1983). A preliminary examination of ethnic identification among whites. *American Sociological Review, 48*, 240–247.

Aldoory, L. (1998). The language of leadership for female public relations professionals. *Journal of Public Relations Research, 10*(2), 73–101.

Aldrich, H. E., & Herker, D. (1977). Boundary spanning roles and organization structure. *Academy of Management Review, 2*, 217–230.

Andersen, M. L., & Collins, P. H. (1992). *Race, class, and gender: An anthology* (2nd ed.). Belmont, CA: Wadsworth.

Anderson, J. A. (1993, April). Thinking about diversity. *Training and Development*, pp. 59–60.

Ang, I., & Hermes, H. (1991). Gender and/in media consumption. In J. Curran & M. Gurevitch (Eds.), *Mass media and society* (pp. 307–328). London: Edward Arnold.

Angrist, S. A. (1969). The study of sex-roles. *Journal of Social Issues, 15*, 215–232.

Anshen, M. (Ed.). (1974). *Managing the socially responsible corporation*. New York: Macmillan.

Associated Press. (1992, June 3). World's women work more, get little pay, much stress. *Washington Post*, p. A24.

Awanohara, S. (1990, November). Spicier melting pot. *Far Eastern Economic Review*, pp. 30–33.

Babington, C. (1993, August 15). In bid for Md. governor, Boergers sets no limits: Senator aims to crack "glass ceiling" for women. *Washington Post*, pp. B1, B4.

Backlash to work-family benefits. (1997, October 20). *purview* (Supplement to *pr reporter*), p. 1.

Bailyn, L. (1982). The apprenticeship model of organizational career: A response to changes in the relation between work and family. In P. Wallace (Ed.), *Women in the workplace* (pp. 45–58). Boston: Auburn House.

Bakan, D. (1966). *The duality of human existence: Isolation and communion in Western man*. Boston: Beacon.

Baker, L. C. (1996). Differences in earning between male and female physicians. *New England Journal of Medicine, 334*, 960–964.

Baker, M. A. (1991). Gender and verbal communication in professional settings: A review of research. *Management Communication Quarterly, 5*, 36–63.

Balchen, A. S. (1987). *Consumer market development*. New York: Fairchild.

Bales, R. W. (1984, May). *Organizational interface: An open systems, contingency approach to boundary-spanning activities*. Paper presented at the meeting of the International Communication Association, San Francisco.

Barbieri, S. M. (1991a, February 5). Women advance as entrepreneurs. *Orlando Sentinel*, pp. E1, E5.

Barbieri, S. M. (1991b, February 5). Women increasingly band together to create their own "old boy network." *Orlando Sentinel*, p. E5.

Barbieri, S. M. (1992, February 13). 4C promoting child care. *Orlando Sentinel*, p. E5.

Baron, A. S. (1977). Selection, development, and socialization of women into management. *Business Quarterly, 42*, 61–67.

Bartol, K. (1973). *Male and female leaders in small work groups*. East Lansing: Michigan State University Press.

Bates, D. (1983, July). A concern: Will women inherit the profession? *Public Relations Journal*, pp. 6–7.

Baxter, B. L. (1986). Public relations professionals offer course recommendations. *Journalism Educator, 40*(4), 9–10.

Baxter, W. (1980). *Our progress and our potential* (Working paper). Norman: School of Journalism, University of Oklahoma.

Baytos, L. (1992). Launching successful diversity initiatives. *HRMagazine, 37*(3), 91–97.

Beck, J. (1991, April 9). Make room for mommy: More U.S. firms must do it. *Orlando Sentinel*, p. A7.

Becker, L. B. (1989). Enrollment growth exceeds national university averages. *Journalism Educator, 44*(3), 3–15.

Becker, L. B. (1990). Enrollments increase in 1989, but graduation rates drop. *Journalism Educator, 45*(3), 4–15.

Bell, L., & Young, V. (1986). Impostors, fakes, and frauds. In L. L. Moore (Ed.), *Not as far as you think* (pp. 25–52). Lexington, MA: Lexington Books.

Bellafante, G. (1998, June 29). Feminism. It's all about me. *Time*, pp. 54, 56–62.

Bem, S. L. (1974). The measurement of psychological androgyny. *Journal of Consulting and Clinical Psychology, 42*(2), 155–162.

Bem, S. L. (1976). Probing the promise of androgyny. In A. J. Kaplan & J. P. Beans (Eds.), *Beyond sex-role stereotypes: Readings toward a psychology of androgyny* (pp. 48–62). Boston: Little, Brown.

Bem, S. L. (1977). On the utility of alternative procedures for assessing psychological androgyny. *Journal of Consulting and Clinical Psychology, 45*(2), 196–205.

Benderly, B. L. (1987). *The myth of two minds: What gender means and doesn't mean*. New York: Doubleday.

Benokraitis, N. V. (1997). *Subtle sexism: Current practice and prospects for change*. Thousand Oaks, CA: Sage.

Bernard, J. (1964). *Academic women*. University Park: Pennsylvania State University Press.

Bernard, J. (1976). Sex differences: An overview. In A. G. Kaplan & J. P. Bean (Eds.), *Beyond sex-role stereotypes: Readings toward a psychology of androgyny* (pp. 10–26). Boston: Little, Brown.

Berryman-Fink, C. (1985). Male and female managers' views of the communication skills and training needs of women in management. *Public Personnel Management, 14*(3), 307–313.

Beyer, C. (1986, June). Salary survey. *Public Relations Journal*, pp. 26–29.

Bianchi, S. (1990). America's children: Mixed prospects. *Population Bulletin, 45*, 3–41.

Bird, R. E. (1987, June 28). Unequal partners: We still haven't decided whether all women are created equal, too. *Washington Post Magazine*, pp. 44–48.

Blau, F. D., & Ferber, M. A. (1987). Occupations and earnings of women workers. In K. S. Koziara, M. H. Moskow, & L. D. Tanner (Eds.), *Working women: Past, present, future* (pp. 37–68). Washington, DC: Bureau of National Affairs.

Blau, P. M. (1964). *Exchange and power in social life*. New York: Wiley.

Blee, K. M. (1991). Women in the 1920s' Ku Klux Klan movement. *Feminist Studies, 17*(1), 57–77.

Block, J. H. (1973). Conceptions of sex role: Some cross-cultural and longitudinal perspectives. *American Psychologist, 28*(6), 512–526.

Blum, L. M. (1987). Possibilities and limits of the comparable worth movement. *Gender & Society, 1*(4), 380–399.

Blum, L., & Smith, V. (1988). Women's mobility in the corporation: A critique of the politics of optimism. *Signs: Journal of Women in Culture and Society, 13*(3), 528–546.

Bonacich, E. (1972). A theory of ethnic antagonism: The split labor market. *American Sociological Review, 37,* 547–559.

Boowie, N. E. (1988). *Equal opportunity.* Boulder, CO: Westview Press.

Bovet, S. F. (1993, March). Midsize firms take new shapes to suit service, profit goals. *Public Relations Journal,* pp. 14, 16–18, 36.

Bovet, S. F. (1994, September). Minority-owned firms seek mainstream acceptance. *Public Relations Journal,* p. 12.

Braddy, P. K. (1989). Evaluation of child care alternatives as an employee benefit. *Health Care Supervisor, 7*(2), 33–41.

Brannon, J. (1992). *Mixing methods: Qualitative and quantitative research.* Aldershot, UK: Ashgate.

Braus, P. (1993). What does "Hispanic" mean? *American Demographics, 15*(6), 46–49.

Brody, E. M., Litvin, S. J., Albert, S. M., & Hoffman, C. J. (1994). Marital status of daughters and patterns of parent care. *Journal of Gerontology: Social Sciences, 49*(2), 95–103.

Broom, G. M. (1982). A comparison of sex roles in public relations. *Public Relations Review, 8*(3), 17–22.

Broom, G. M., & Dozier, D. M. (1985, August). *Determinants and consequences of public relations roles.* Paper presented at the meeting of the Public Relations Division, Association for Education in Journalism and Mass Communication, Memphis, TN.

Broom, G. M., & Dozier, D. M. (1986). Advancement for public relations role models. *Public Relations Review, 12*(1), 37–56.

Broom, G. M., & Dozier, D. M. (1990). *Using research in public relations: Applications to program management.* Englewood Cliffs, NJ: Prentice-Hall.

Broom, G. M., & Smith, G. D. (1979). Testing the practitioner's impact on clients. *Public Relations Review, 5*(4), 47–59.

Brosco Christian, M. (1996). *The use of management from below by female public relations practitioners at Maryland community colleges.* Unpublished master's thesis, University of Maryland, College Park.

Broverman, I. K., Vogel, S. R., Broverman, D. M., Clarkson, F. E., & Rosenkrantz, P. S. (1972). Sex-role stereotypes: A current appraisal. *Journal of Social Issues, 28*(2), 59–78.

Brown, D. A. (1980). Public affairs/public relations. *Public Relations Journal, 36,* 11–14.

Brown, L. K. (1979). Women and business management. *Signs: Journal of Women in Culture and Society, 5,* 266–288.

Bryant, G. (Ed.). (1984). *The working woman report: Succeeding in business in the 80s.* New York: Simon & Schuster.

Buchholz, R. A. (1989). *Business environment and public policy* (3rd ed.). Englewood Cliffs, NJ: Prentice-Hall.

Buchwald, A. (1992, March 21). Women are best bearers of bad business news. *Atlanta Journal and Constitution*, p. A10.

Buffington, P. W. (1986, August). The powers that be. *SKY*, pp. 97–100.

Burch, D. (1998, Spring). The "f" word: Evolution of a revolution. *College Park* (The University of Maryland Magazine), pp. 26–31.

Burger, C. (1983). How management views public relations. *Public Relations Quarterly, 27*(4), 27–30.

Burgess, N. J. (1994). Gender roles revisited: The development of the "women's place" among African American women in the United States. *Journal of Black Studies, 24*(4), 391–401.

Burlew, A. K. (1982). The experiences of black females in traditional and nontraditional professions. *Psychology of Women Quarterly, 6*(3), 312–325.

Burlew, A. K. (1992). Career and educational choices among black females. *Journal of Black Psychology, 3*(2), 88–106.

Burton, J. (1993, January 21). Targeting Asians: Agencies in US tailor messages to new immigrants. *Far Eastern Economic Review*, pp. 40–41.

Camden, C., & Witt, J. (1983, May–June). Manager communicative style and productivity: A study of female and male managers. *International Journal of Women's Studies, 6*(3), 258–269.

Canning, K. (1991). An interdisciplinary approach to analyzing the managerial gender gap. *Human Relations, 44*(7), 679–695.

Canter, R. (1982). Achievement in women: Implications for equal employment opportunity policy. In B. Gutek (Ed.), *Sex role stereotyping and affirmative action policy* (pp. 9–64). Los Angeles: Institute of Industrial Relations, University of California.

Cantor, B. (1989, July–August). Minority hiring shows problems in corporate America. *IABC Communication World*, pp. 22–25.

Caplan, P. J. (1985). Introduction to special issue on sex roles and sex differences and androgyny. *International Journal of Women's Studies, 8*(5), 437–440.

Carlson, R. (1985, June). Masculine/feminine: A personological perspective. *Journal of Personality, 53*(2), 384–399.

Carr-Ruffino, N., Baack, J. E., Flipper, C., Hunter-Sloan, K., & Olivio, C. (1992). Legal aspects of women's advancement: Affirmative action, family leave, and dependent care law. In U. Sekaran & F. T. L. Leong (Eds.), *Womanpower: Managing in times of demographic turbulence* (pp. 113–158). Newbury Park, CA: Sage.

Chadwell, T. (1993, June 4). Marketing/PR freelancers enjoying new freedom. *Business Journal*, p. 5.

Chang, C. S., & Chang N. J. (1994). *The Korean management system: Cultural, political, economic foundations.* Westport, CT: Quorum Books.

Changing American workforce: Impact on women and PR. (1993, May–June). *WEPR network*, pp. 1–2.

Chapman, S. (1990, December 27). The gender gap on payday—There's less than meets the eye. *Orlando Sentinel*, p. A13.

Check out your gender dynamics. (1992, Winter). *WEPR network*, p. 1.

Cheney, K. (1998, April). 10 hottest careers for working moms. *Working Mother*, pp. 24–28.

Cheng, B. D. (1988). *A profile of selected women leaders: Toward a new model of leadership*. Burlington, VT: Trinity College.

Cherry, S. S. (1992, March 20). Kids are sexist—Is it biology or training? *Orlando Sentinel*, pp. E1, E4.

Chesanow, N. (1985). *The world-class executive*. New York: Rawson Associates.

Chesler, P. (1998). *Letters to a young feminist*. New York: Four Walls Eight Windows Press.

Childers, L. L. (also see L. C. Hon). (1986). *Gender and salary: A panel study of public relations practitioners*. Unpublished master's thesis, University of Florida, Gainesville.

Choo, C. W. (1994). Perception and use of information sources by chief executives in environmental scanning. *Library and Information Science Research, 16*(1), 23–29.

Christensen, J. B. (1993). *The effect of gender on preference for public relations models*. Unpublished master's thesis, San Jose (California) State University.

Christensen, K. (1988). *Women and home-based work*. New York: Holt.

Chusmir, L. H. (1985). Motivation of managers: Is gender a factor? *Psychology of Women Quarterly, 9*, 153–159.

Cindoglu, D., & Onkal, D. (1993, November). *Women academicians in medical education: The Turkish case*. Paper presented to the meeting of the Association for the Advancement of Policy, Research and Development in the Third World, Cairo.

Clampitt, P. G. (1991). *Communicating for managerial effectiveness*. Newbury Park, CA: Sage.

Clanton, G. (1990). *Minority public relations practitioners: Their experiences and perceptions*. Unpublished master's thesis, University of Maryland, College Park.

Clark, M. J., & Centra, J. A. (1985). Influences on the career accomplishments of Ph.D.'s. *Research in Higher Education, 23*, 256–269.

Clark, S. M., & Corcoran, M. (1986). Perspectives on the professional socialization of women faculty: A case of accumulative disadvantage? *Journal of Higher Education, 57*, 20–43.

Cline, C. G. (1989). What now? Conclusions and suggestions. In E. L. Toth & C. G. Cline (Eds.), *Beyond the velvet ghetto* (pp. 299–308). San Francisco: IABC Research Foundation.

Cline, C. G., Masel-Walters, L., Toth, E. L., Turk, J. V., Smith, H. T., & Johnson, N. (1986). *The velvet ghetto: The impact of the increasing percentage of women in public relations and business communication*. San Francisco: IABC Foundation.

Clinton, W. J. (1995, July 20). *Give all Americans a chance* (Speech). Reprinted in *Washington Post*, p. A12.

Close, H. W. (1980, April). Public relations as a management function. *Public Relations Journal*, pp. 15–17.

Clutterbuck, D., & Devine, M. (1987). *Businesswomen: Present and future*. London: Macmillan.

Cohn, D., & Vobejda, B. (1992, December 21). For women, uneven strides in workplace: Census data reflect decade of white-collar progress, blue-collar resistance. *Washington Post*, pp. A1, A12.

Cole, D. (1989, June). The entrepreneurial self. *Psychology Today*, pp. 60–67.

Cole, J. B. (1992). Commonalities and differences. In M. L. Andersen & P. H. Collins (Eds.), *Race, class, and gender: An anthology* (pp. 128–134). Belmont, CA: Wadsworth.

Condit, C. M. (1988). What makes our scholarship feminist? A radical/liberal view. *Women's Studies in Communication, 11*, 6–8.

Conley, F. K. (1998). *Walking out on the boys*. Gordonsville, VA: Farrar, Straus & Giroux.

Conrad, C. (1990). *Strategic organizational communication: An integrated perspective*. New York: Holt, Rinehart & Winston.

Constantinople, A. (1973). Masculinity–femininity: An exception to a famous dictum? In A. G. Kaplan & J. P. Beans (Eds.), *Beyond sex-role stereotypes: Readings toward a psychology of androgyny* (pp. 28–46). Boston: Little, Brown.

Cook, K. S. (1977). Exchange and power in networks of interorganizational relations. *Sociological Quarterly, 18*, 62–82.

Cose, E. (1993). *The rage of a privileged class*. New York: HarperCollins.

Cotterill, P. (1992). Interviewing women: Issues of friendship, vulnerability, and power. *Women's Studies International Forum, 15*(5–6), 593–606.

Cottone, L. P. (1992). Women's issues . . . They keep knocking. *PRIDE (Public Relations Innovation, Development and Education Newsletter), 5*(2), 2.

Cover. (1993, July). *Public Relations Journal*.

Cox, S. (1976). *Female psychology: The emerging self*. Chicago: Science Research Associates.

Cox, T. (1990). Problems with research by organizational scholars on issues of race and ethnicity. *Journal of Applied Behavioral Science, 26*(1), 5–23.

Creedon, P. J. (1989a). Public relations history misses "her story." *Journalism Educator, 44*(3), 26–30.

Creedon, P. J. (Ed.). (1989b). *Women in mass communication: Challenging gender values*. Newbury Park, CA: Sage.

Creedon, P. J. (1991). Public relations and "women's work": Toward a feminist analysis of public relations roles. *Public Relations Research Annual, 3*, 7–84.

Cuban American National Council. (1989). *The elusive decade of Hispanics*. New York: Ford Foundation.

Culbertson, H. M. (1991). Role taking and sensitivity: Keys to playing and making public relations roles. *Public Relations Research Annual, 3*, 37–63.

Davis, A. Y. (1981). *Women, race and class*. New York: Vintage Books.

Deaux, K. (1976). *The behavior of men and women*. Monterey, CA: Brooks/Cole.

DeRosa, D., & Wilcox, D. L. (1989). Gaps are narrowing between female and male students. *Public Relations Review, 15*(1), 80–90.

DeStefano, L., & Colasanto, D. (1990, February). Unlike 1975, today most Americans think men have it better. *Gallup Poll Monthly*, pp. 25–36.

Dewar, H. (1993, August 4). 5 female senators engineer rejection of abortion ban. *Washington Post*, p. A4.

Dexter, C. R. (1985). Women and the exercise of power in organizations: From ascribed to achieved status. In L. Larwood, A. H. Stromberg, & B. A. Gutek (Eds.),

Women and work: Vol. 1. An annual review (pp. 239–258). Beverly Hills, CA: Sage.

Digest: Women in Europe and North America. (1994, September 20). *Washington Post*, p. C2.

Diggs-Brown, B., & Zaharna, R. (1995). Ethnic diversity in the public relations industry. *Howard Journal of Communication, 6*(1–2), 114–123.

Dipboye, R. L. (1987). Problems and progress of women in management. In K. S. Koziara, M. H. Moskow, & L. D. Tanner (Eds.), *Working women: Past, present, future* (pp. 118–153). Washington, DC: Bureau of National Affairs.

Direction of trade statistics yearbook. (1990). Washington, DC: International Monetary Fund.

Diversity in action v. diversity inaction: Is the "second sex" finally being heard? (1991, November 25). *pr reporter*, p. 3.

Dobbins, G. H., & Platz, S. J. (1986). Sex differences in leadership: How real are they? *Academy of Management Review, 11*(1), 118–127.

Doctoral recipients: U.S. citizens by ethnic group. (1990). *NWSAction, 3*(1–2), 5.

Doig, S. K. (1992, August 16). Women, blacks dominate work force. *Syracuse Herald American*, pp. D5, D10.

Donato, K. M. (1990). Keepers of the corporate image: Women in public relations. In B. F. Reskin & P. A. Roos (Eds.), *Job queues, gender queues: Explaining women's inroads into males' occupations* (pp. 129–144). Philadelphia: Temple University Press.

Donnell, S. M., & Hall, J. (1980). Men and women as managers: A significant case of no significant difference. *Organizational Dynamics, 8*, 60–77.

Doonan, A. L. (1993). *The role and status of women in higher education fund raising.* Unpublished master's thesis, University of Maryland, College Park.

Doyal, L. (1990). Waged work and women's well being. *Women's Studies International Forum, 13*(6), 587–604.

Doyle, J. M. (1990, October 14). Men rule—but how much longer? *Orlando Sentinel*, p. E15.

Dozier, D. M. (1981, August). *The diffusion of evaluation methods among public relations practitioners.* Paper presented at the meeting of the Association for Education in Journalism and Mass Communication, East Lansing, MI.

Dozier, D. M. (1988). Breaking public relations' glass ceiling. *Public Relations Review, 14*(3), 6–14.

Dozier, D. M. (1990). The innovation of research in public relations practice: Review of a program of studies. *Public Relations Research Annual, 2*, 3–28.

Dozier, D. M. (1992). The organizational roles of communications and public relations practitioners. In J. E. Grunig (Ed.), *Excellence in public relations and communication management* (pp. 327–356). Hillsdale, NJ: Erlbaum.

Dozier, D. M., & Broom, G. M. (1995). Evolution of the manager role in public relations practice. *Journal of Public Relations Research, 7*(1), 3–26.

Dozier, D. M., Chapo, S., & Sullivan, B. (1983, August). *Sex and the bottom line: Income differences among women and men in public relations.* Paper presented at the meeting of the Public Relations Division, Association for Education in Journalism and Mass Communication, Corvallis, OR.

Dozier, D. M., Grunig, L. A., & Grunig, J. E. (1995). *Manager's guide to excellence in public relations and communication management.* Mahwah, NJ: Lawrence Erlbaum Associates.

Dozier, D. M., & Lauzen, M. M. (1990, July). *Antecedents and consequences of marketing imperialism on the public relations function.* Paper presented at the meeting of the Public Relations Division, Association for Education in Journalism and Mass Communication, Minneapolis, MN.

Dreams and realities: The state of women, 1990. (1990, December 2). *Syracuse Herald American*, p. A4.

DuBois, E. C., Kelly, G. P., Kennedy, E. L., Korsmeyer, C. W., & Robinson, L. S. (Eds.). (1985). *Feminist scholarship: Kindling in the groves of academe.* Urbana: University of Illinois Press.

DuBois, W. E. B. (1903). *The souls of Black folk: Essays and sketches* (2nd ed.). Chicago: McClurg.

Dunham, R. S. (1993, August 2). A different kind of launch for McDonnell: A new program is catapulting women into the political arena. *Business Week*, pp. 66, 70.

Eadie, W. (1997, April 9). *Organizational culture.* Unpublished lecture, University of Maryland, College Park.

Ebeling, K. (1990, November). The failure of feminism. *Newsweek*, p. 9.

Edson, A. S. (1980, July). Mentors: Do they work in PR? *Public Relations Journal*, pp. 18–19.

Edwards, P., & Edwards, S. (1985). *Working from home.* Los Angeles: Tarcher.

Ehling, W. P. (1992). Estimating the value of public relations and communication to an organization. In J. E. Grunig (Ed.), *Excellence in public relations and communication management* (pp. 617–638). Hillsdale, NJ: Erlbaum.

Eilperin, J. (1998, April 29). More women finding a place in the House. *Washington Post*, p. A19.

Eisler, R. (1987). *The chalice and the blade: Our history, our future.* San Francisco: Harper & Row.

Emerson, R. M. (1962). Power–dependence relations. *American Sociological Review, 27*, 31–43.

Emerson, R. M. (1972). Exchange theory, part 2: Exchange relations, exchange networks, and groups as exchange systems. In J. Berger, M. Selditch, & B. Anderson (Eds.), *Sociological theories in progress* (Vol. 2, pp. 58–87). Boston: Houghton Mifflin.

Epstein, C. (1970). *Woman's place: Options and limits in professional careers.* Berkeley and Los Angeles: University of California Press.

Epstein, C. (1973). Positive effects of the multiple negative: Explaining the success of black professional women. *American Journal of Sociology, 78*, 912–935.

Ervin, D., Thomas, B. J., & Zey-Ferrell, M. (1984). Sex discrimination and rewards in a public comprehensive university. *Human Relations, 37*(12), 1005–1028.

Etaugh, C. (1984). Women faculty and administrators in higher education: Changes in their status since 1972. *Journal of the National Association for Women Deans, Administrators, and Counselors, 48*, 21–25.

Evangelauf, J. (1984, January 18). Women's average pay trails men's by 19 percent in three top professor ranks. *Chronicle of Higher Education*, p. 20.

Exter, T. (1993). The largest minority. *American Demographics, 15*(2), 59.

Ezell, H. F., Odewahn, C. A., & Sherman, J. D. (1982). Women entering management: Differences in perceptions of factors influencing integration. *Group and Organization Studies, 7*, 243–253

Faludi, S. (1991). *Backlash: The undeclared war against American women.* New York: Crown.

Faludi, S. (1992, December 28). Looking beyond the slogans. *Newsweek*, p. 31.

Feild, H. S., & Caldwell, B. E. (1979). Sex of supervisor, sex of subordinate, and subordinate job satisfaction. *Psychology of Women Quarterly, 3*, 391–399.

Feminists to bring broader perspective to disciplines. (1988, September). *Outlook*, p. 2.

Feminization of the new profession may not occur after all. (1987, May 18). *pr reporter*, p. 4.

Fenyvesi, C. (Ed.). (1992, May 25). Washington whispers: No hablo? *U.S. News & World Report*, p. 30.

Ferber, M. A., Loeb, J. W., & Lowry, H. (1978). The economic status of women faculty: A reappraisal. *Journal of Human Resources, 13*, 385–401.

Ferguson, M. (1990). Images of power and the feminist fallacy. *Critical Studies in Mass Communication, 7*(3), 215–230.

Ferguson, M. A. (1987, May). *Utility of roles research to corporate communications: Power, leadership, and decision-making.* Paper presented at the meeting of the International Communication Association, Montreal.

Fernandez, J. (1988, July–August). New life for old stereotypes. *Across the Board*, pp. 24–25.

Ferreira, J. (1993). *Hispanic public relations practitioners and the glass ceiling effect.* Unpublished master's thesis, University of Maryland, College Park.

Field, J., & Wolff, E. N. (1990). The decline of sex segregation and the wage gap, 1970–80. *Journal of Human Resources, 26*(4), 608–622.

Fierman, J. (1988, November 21). Child care: What works and what doesn't. *Fortune*, pp. 165–176.

Fine, M. G. (1988). What makes it feminist? *Women's Studies in Communication, 11*, 18–19.

Fish, S. (1992, February 2). Girls get a 2nd-class education, study says. *Orlando Sentinel*, pp. A1, A7.

Fisher, H. E. (1999). *The first sex: The natural talents of women and how they are changing the world.* New York: Random House.

Fishman, J. (1988, April). Starting your own business. *Capital PR News*, pp. 1, 3.

Fitzpatrick, M. A. (1983). Effective interpersonal communication for women of the corporation: Think like a man, talk like a lad. In J. J. Pilotta (Ed.), *Women in organizations.* Prospect Heights, IL: Waveland Press.

Fletcher, M. A. (1997, July 8). Lawmakers urge Clinton to address discrimination in federal workplace. *Washington Post*, p. A4.

Footnotes. (1997, November 28). *Chronicle of Higher Education*, p. A12.

Ford, K. B. (1986). *Women in public relations: Barriers and bridges*. Unpublished manuscript, University of Maryland, College Park.

Forsythe, N. (1998, April 15). *Where and when is "women"?: Knowledge/power and "women's" movements*. Talk presented at the Program in Social Theory Colloquium, University of Maryland, College Park.

Fox, M. F. (1985). Publication performance and reward in science and scholarship. In J. Smart (Ed.), *Higher education: Handbook of theory and research* (pp. 255–282). New York: Agathon.

French, M. A. (1992, August 22). Distorted reflections: Mainstream media still short on minorities. *Washington Post*, pp. D1, D7.

Friedl, E. (1975). *Women and men: An anthropologist's view*. New York: Holt, Rinehart & Winston.

Frieze, I. H., Parsons, J., Johnson, P. B., Ruble, D. N., & Zellman, G. L. (1978). *Women and sex roles*. New York: Norton.

Fry, S. (1991, February). Reaching Hispanic publics with special events. *Public Relations Journal*, pp. 12–13, 30.

Frye, M. (1992). Oppression. In M. L. Andersen & P. H. Collins (Eds.), *Race, class, and gender: An anthology* (pp. 37–42). Belmont, CA: Wadsworth.

Fullerton, H. N. (1987, September). Labor force projections: 1986 to 2000. *Monthly Labor Review, 110*, 19–29.

Galbraith, J. K. (1967). *The new industrial state*. Boston: Houghton Mifflin.

Gallagher, K. (1992, March 20). Club doors may open for women. *Orlando Sentinel*, pp. A1, A12.

Gallese, L. R. (1991, April). Why women aren't making it to the top. *Across the Board*, pp. 18–22.

Garen, M. E. (1982). A management model for the '80s. *Training and Development Journal, 36*(3), 41–49.

Gaski, J. F. (1984). The theory of power and conflicts in channels of distribution. *Journal of Marketing, 48*, 9–29.

Gender differences in communication originate at the physical level, says gender expert. (1990, September 24). *pr reporter*, p. 4.

Gerhart, B. (1990). Gender differences in current and starting salaries: The role of performance, college major, and job title. *Industrial and Labor Relations Review, 43*(4), 418–433.

Gerhart, B., & El Cheikh, N. (1991). Earnings and percentage female: A longitudinal study. *Industrial Relations, 30*(1), 62–78.

Ghiloni, B. W. (1987). Women, power, and the corporation: Evidence from the velvet ghetto. In G. W. Domhoff & T. Dye (Eds.), *Power elites and organizations* (pp. 38–45). Newbury Park, CA: Sage.

Giddings, P. (1984). *When and where I enter: The impact of black women on race and sex in America*. New York: Bantam Books.

Gilligan, C. (1982). *In a different voice*. Cambridge, MA: Harvard University Press.

Ginsberg, S. (1998, April 13). Making networking work for you: A guide to rubbing shoulders with the right people. *Washington Post Washington Business*, p. 9.

Glass ceiling update: All sticks, no carrots. (1992). *Ragan Report, 23*(1), 1.

Gomez, M. (1992, October). A place at the table. *Hispanic*, pp. 16–20.

Gonzalez, C. (1998, November 10). Ranks of women executives grow. (Portland) *Oregonian*, pp. E1-E9.

Goodman, E. (1992, February 27). The women's movement (cont'd): New set of raised expectations. *Orlando Sentinel*, p. A15.

Gordon, G. (1991, December). A worldwide look at sexual harassment. *IABC Communication World*, pp. 15–19.

Gorney, C. M. (1992, November). *The changes in China for working women*. Paper presented at the Association for the Advancement of Policy, Research and Development in the Third World, Orlando, FL.

Gorney, S. K. (1975, May). Status of women in public relations. *Public Relations Journal*, pp. 10–13.

Gose, B. (1998, April 24). The feminization of veterinary medicine. *Chronicle of Higher Education*, pp. A55-A56.

Goss, K. A. (1989, March 21). Influx of women into fund raising poses paradox: They're effective, but pay and prestige could suffer. *Chronicle of Philanthropy*, pp. 2, 10.

Gould, S. J. (1981). *The mismeasure of man*. New York: Norton.

Greenhalgh, L., & Gilkey, R. W. (1986). Our game, your rules: Developing effective negotiating approaches. In L. L. Moore (Ed.), *Not as far as you think* (pp. 135–148). Lexington, MA: Lexington Books.

Greenhouse, S. (1998, June 28). Companies set to get tougher on harassment. *New York Times*, p. 1.

Greyser, S. A. (1981, March). Changing roles for public relations. *Public Relations Journal*, pp. 18–25.

Grimsley, K. D. (1997, May 12). Strategies, struggles, successes: Difficult choices, different paths that have changed the picture of working Washington. *Washington Post*, pp. K11, K15.

Grimsley, K. D. (1998, March 24). MBA no ticket to top for women. *Washington Post*, pp. A1, A8.

Gross, S. (1985). Public relations and the minority thrust. *Public Relations Quarterly, 30*(2), 28–30.

Grove, L. (1993, March 19). The limited life of a political wife: For the spouse, avoiding conflict may be the top job. *Washington Post*, pp. C1, C9.

Grunig, J. E. (1984). Organizations, environments, and models of public relations. *Public Relations Research and Education, 1*, 6–29.

Grunig, J. E. (1987, May). *Symmetrical presuppositions as a framework for public relations theory*. Paper presented at the Conference on Communication Theory and Public Relations, Illinois State University, Normal.

Grunig, J. E. (1992a). Symmetrical systems of internal communication. In J. E. Grunig

(Ed.), *Excellence in public relations and communication management* (pp. 531–576). Hillsdale, NJ: Erlbaum.

Grunig, J. E. (Ed.). (1992b. *Excellence in public relations and communication management*. Hillsdale, NJ: Erlbaum.

Grunig, J. E., & Grunig, L. A. (1989). Toward a theory of the public relations behavior of organizations: Review of a program of research. *Public Relations Research Annual, 1,* 27–63.

Grunig, J. E., & Grunig, L. A. (1992). Models of public relations and communications. In J. E. Grunig (Ed.), *Excellence in public relations and communication management* (pp. 285–325). Hillsdale, NJ: Erlbaum.

Grunig, J. E., & Hunt, T. (1984). *Managing public relations.* New York: Holt, Rinehart & Winston.

Grunig, J. E., & White, J. (1992). The effect of worldviews on public relations. In J. E. Grunig (Ed.), *Excellence in public relations and communication management* (pp. 31–64). Hillsdale, NJ: Erlbaum.

Grunig, J. E., Grunig, L. A., Dozier, D. M., Ehling, W. P., Repper, F. C., & White, J. (1991, September). *Initial results of survey confirm value of communication and the components of excellent public relations.* Report to the IABC Research Foundation, San Francisco.

Grunig, L. A. (1988). A research agenda for women in public relations. *Public Relations Review, 14*(3), 48–57.

Grunig, L. A. (1989a). The glass ceiling effect on mass communication students. In P. Creedon (Ed.), *Women in mass communication: Challenging gender values* (pp. 125–147). Newbury Park, CA: Sage.

Grunig, L. A. (1989b). Sex discrimination in promotion and tenure in journalism education. *Journalism Quarterly, 66*(1), 93–100, 229.

Grunig, L. A. (1989c, August). *Toward a feminist transformation of public relations education and practice.* Paper presented at the Seminar on Gender Issues and Public Relations, Association for Education in Journalism and Mass Communication, Washington, DC.

Grunig, L. A. (1990a). Power in the public relations department. *Public Relations Research Annual, 2,* 115–155.

Grunig, L. A. (1990b). Using focus group research in public relations. *Public Relations Review, 16*(2), 36–49.

Grunig, L. A. (1990c, January). Inquiring (student) minds want to know. *IABC Communication World,* pp. 27–31.

Grunig, L. A. (1991). Court-ordered relief from sex discrimination in the Foreign Service: Implications for women working in development communication. *Public Relations Research Annual, 3,* 85–113.

Grunig, L. A. (1992). Power in the public relations department. In J. E. Grunig (Ed.), *Excellence in public relations and communication management* (pp. 483–502). Hillsdale, NJ: Erlbaum.

Grunig, L. A., Toth, E. L., & Hon, L. C. (1999, June). *Feminist values in public relations.* Paper presented at the meeting of the Public Relations Division, International Communication Association, San Francisco.

Gutek, B. (1982). A psychological examination of sexual harassment. In B. Gutek (Ed.), *Sex role stereotyping and affirmative action policy* (pp. 131–163). Los Angeles: Institute of Industrial Relations, University of California.

Haberfeld, Y. (1992). Employment discrimination: An organizational model. *Academy of Management Journal, 35*(1), 161–180.

Hacker, H. M. (1951). Women as a minority group. *Social Forces, 30,* 60–69.

Hage, J. (1980). *Theories of organizations: Form, process, and transformation.* New York: Wiley.

Halberg, L. J. (1987). *A comparison of sex-role stereotypes, achievement, motivation and decision-making styles of college and university women chief student affairs officers and women middle managers.* Unpublished doctoral dissertation, University of Iowa, Iowa City.

Hall, M. (1986). The lesbian corporate experience. *Journal of Homosexuality, 12*(3–4), 59–75.

Hall, M. (1989). Private experiences in the public domain: Lesbians in organizations. In J. Hearn, D. L. Sheppard, P. Tancred-Sheriff, & G. Burrell (Eds.), *The sexuality of organizations* (pp. 125–138). London: Sage.

Hamilton, M., & Burgess, J. (1992, July 11). Local firms look to help employees in child and elderly care. *Washington Post,* p. F1.

Hannon, S. W. (1998, February). A comparative analysis of ethnic inclusion in public relations textbooks and reference books. *Teaching Public Relations, 45,* 1–4.

Hare-Mustin, R. T., & Maracek, J. (1988). The meaning of difference: Gender theory, postmodernism, and psychology. *American Psychologist, 43*(6), 455–466.

Harragan, B. L. (1977). *Games mother never taught you.* New York: Warner Books.

Harraway, D. J. (1991). *Simians, cyborgs, and women: The reinvention of nature.* New York: Routledge.

Harrington, W. (1993, January 24). The secret of her success. *Washington Post Magazine,* pp. 9–11, 18–22.

Harris, P., & Moran, R. (1987). *Managing cultural differences* (2nd ed.). Houston, TX: Gulf.

Harwood, J., & Seib, G. F. (1997, December 9). Female Democrats lack issues that led to '92 success. *Wall Street Journal,* p. A24.

Haseley, K. A. (1993, April). Raising awareness precedes changing attitudes. *Public Relations Journal,* pp. 36–37.

Hawes, J. (1998, April 7). Standing on the shoulders of sky pushers: Barbara Finkelstein named outstanding woman of the year. *Outlook* (University of Maryland faculty and staff weekly newspaper), pp. 1, 3.

Haworth, D. A., & Savage, G. T. (1989). A channel-ratio model of intercultural communication. *Journal of Business Communication, 26*(3), 231–254.

Heath, T. (1994, September 9). Sexism still on ticket, female candidates say: More women are running, but they're still stumbling over stereotypes. *Washington Post,* pp. B1, B4.

Hefner, C. (1993, Fall). Expanding influence through strategic alliances. *Brandeis Review,* pp. 49–51.

Heins, M., Hendricks, J., & Martindale, J. (1982). The importance of extra-family support on career choices of women. *Personnel and Guidance Journal, 60*, 455–459.

Helgesen, S. (1990). *The female advantage: Women's ways of leadership*. New York: Doubleday.

Helping women rise through the ranks. (1998, May). *Tactics*, pp. 30–31.

Hennig, M. (1971, March). What happens on the way up. *MBA—Master of Business Administration*, pp. 8–10.

Hennig, M., & Jardim, A. (1977). *The managerial woman*. New York: Anchor Press.

Henry, S. (1988, July). *In her own name? Public relations pioneer Doris Fleischman Bernays*. Paper presented at the meeting of the Association for Education in Journalism and Mass Communication, Portland, OR.

Henzl, S., & Turner, L. (1987). Rationalizing conflict choices: Do men and women speak the same language? In L. B. Nadler, M. K. Nadler, & W. R. Todd-Mancillas (Eds.), *Advances in gender and communication research* (pp. 175–187). New York: University Press of America.

Herbert, S. J. (1990, August–September). Black public relations movers and shakers in the entertainment industry. *Crisis*, pp. 16–18, 38.

Herman, R. (1991, October 23). Changing the face of psychiatry. *Orlando Sentinel*, pp. E1, E2.

Herman, R. (1993, February 16). Sex stereotypes in medicine. *Washington Post*, Health section, p. 7.

Hersch, J. (1991). Male–female differences in hourly wages: The role of human capital, working conditions, and housework. *Industrial and Labor Relations Review, 44*(4), 746–759.

Higginbotham, E. (1992). We were never on a pedestal: Women of color continue to struggle with poverty, racism, and sexism. In M. L. Andersen & P. H. Collins (Eds.), *Race, class, and gender: An anthology* (pp. 183–190). Belmont, CA: Wadsworth.

Hine, D. C., & Thompson, K. (1998). *A shining thread of hope: The history of black women in America*. New York: Broadway.

Hines, B. (Ed.). (1994). *Directory of multicultural professionals and firms*. New York: Public Relations Society of America.

Hirschman, C., & Wong, M. G. (1981). Trends in socio-economic achievement among immigrant and native-born Asian-Americans. *Sociological Quarterly, 22*(4), 495–513.

Hochschild, A. (1989, September–October). Second shift. *New Age Journal*, pp. 60–64.

Hofstede, G. (1980). *Culture's consequences: International differences in work-related values*. Newbury Park, CA: Sage.

Hon, L. C. (1992). *Toward a feminist theory of public relations*. Unpublished doctoral dissertation, University of Maryland, College Park.

Hon, L. C. (1993, August). *Toward a feminist theory of public relations*. Paper presented at the meeting of the Association for Education in Journalism and Mass Communication, Kansas City, MO.

Hon, L. C., Grunig, L. A., & Dozier, D. M. (1992). Women in public relations: Problems and opportunities. In J. E. Grunig (Ed.), *Excellence in public relations and communication management* (pp. 419–438). Hillsdale, NJ: Erlbaum.

Houghton, J. R. (1988, July). To add corporate value, break the glass ceiling. *Financier*, pp. 32–36.

Howe, F. (1984). *Myths of coeducation: Selected essays, 1964–1983*. Bloomington: Indiana University Press.

Hoxie, R. C. (1992). *Cost–benefit effects and the role of excellent public relations for electric utilities faced with environmental or consumer activist situations*. Unpublished master's thesis, University of Maryland, College Park.

Huberlie, M. H. (1997, July). *Women in public relations: How their career path decisions are shaping the future of the profession*. Paper presented at the meeting of the Public Relations Division, Association for Education in Journalism and Mass Communication, Chicago.

Humphrey, K. S. (1990). *Entrepreneurial women in public relations: Why open collars?* Unpublished master's thesis, University of Maryland, College Park.

Hung, C. J. (1998, Spring). *Professional code of ethics for United Pacific International, Inc. in Taiwan*. Unpublished paper, University of Maryland, College Park.

Hunt, T. (1989). Making PR-communication management macho. In E. L. Toth & C. G. Cline (Eds.), *Beyond the velvet ghetto* (pp. 203–217). San Francisco: IABC Research Foundation.

Hunt, T., & Thompson, D. W. (1987, August). *Making PR macho: Reversing the sex gap in undergraduate public relations programs*. Paper presented at the meeting of the Public Relations Division, Association for Education in Journalism and Mass Communication, San Antonio, TX.

Hunt, T., & Thompson, D. W. (1988). Bridging the gender gap in PR courses. *Journalism Educator, 43*(1), 49–51.

Hymowitz, C. (1997, November 11). Colleagues often have the wrong ideas about why women quit. *Wall Street Journal*, p. B1.

Hymowitz, C., & Schellhardt, T. D. (1996, March 24). The glass ceiling: Why women can't seem to break the invisible barrier that blocks them from the top jobs. *Wall Street Journal*, pp. D1, D4.

IABC's Profile '97: The most comprehensive survey of communicators and their work. (1997). San Francisco: International Association of Business Communicators.

Ibarra, H. (1992). Homophily and differential returns: Sex differences in network structure and access in an advertising firm. *Administrative Science Quarterly, 37*, 422–447.

Ibarra, H. (1993). Personal networks of women and minorities in management: A conceptual framework. *Academy of Management Review, 18*(1), 56–87.

Ilgen, D. R., & Youtz, M. A. (1986). Factors affecting the evaluation and development of minorities in organizations. In K. Rowland & G. Ferris (Eds.), *Research in personnel and human resources management* (Vol. 4, pp. 307–337). Greenwich, CT: JAI Press.

Ingley, K. (1993, January 31). Feminism turns 30: Women realize dreams—and drawbacks—since *Mystique*. *Arizona Republic*, pp. A1, A18-A19.

Ingraham, L. A. (1995, April 19). Enter, women: What glass ceiling? *New York Times*, p. A3.

Isaac, S. (1990, December 29). Seminole's top school jobs elude women. *Orlando Sentinel*, pp. B1, B5.

Jaatinen, M. (1998, Spring). *Public relations and lobbying: Division of labor in different organizations and environments.* Unpublished paper, University of Maryland, College Park.

Jablin, F. M. (1980). Superior's upward influence, satisfaction, and openness in superior–subordinate communication: A reexamination of the "Pelz" effect. *Human Communication Research, 6*(1), 210–220.

Jacklin, C. N., & Maccoby, E. E. (1975). Sex differences and their implications for management. In F. E. Gordon & M. H. Strober (Eds.), *Bringing women into management* (pp. 23–38). New York: McGraw-Hill.

Jacobson, D. Y., & Tortorello, N. J. (1990, June). PRJ's fifth annual salary survey. *Public Relations Journal*, pp. 18–25.

Jacobson, D. Y., & Tortorello, N. J. (1991, June). PRJ's sixth annual salary survey. *Public Relations Journal*, pp. 14–21.

Jacobson, D. Y., & Tortorello, N. J. (1992, August). *PRJ's seventh annual salary survey. Public Relations Journal*, pp. 9–21, 26–30.

Jacobson, M. B., & Effertz, J. (1974). Sex roles and leadership: Perceptions of the leaders and the led. *Organizational Behavior and Human Performance, 12*, 383–396.

Jelinek, M., & Adler, N. J. (1988). Women: World-class managers for global competition. *Academy of Management Executives, 2*(1), 11–19 (Abstract No. 11783).

Johnson, D. J., & Acharya, L. (1982, July). *Organizational decision-making and public relations roles.* Paper presented at the meeting of the Association for Education in Journalism and Mass Communication, Athens, OH.

Johnson, P. (1976). Women and power: Toward a theory of effectiveness. *Journal of Social Issues, 32*(3), 99–110.

Johnson, P. (1978). Women and interpersonal power. In I. H. Frieze, J. E. Parsons, P. B. Johnson, D. N. Ruble, & G. L. Zellman (Eds.), *Women and sex roles: A social psychological perspective* (pp. 301–320). New York: Norton.

Johnston, W. B., & Packer, A. H. (1987). *Workforce 2000: Work and workers for the 21st century.* Indianapolis: Hudson Institute.

Jolly, D. L., & Grimm, J. W. (1990). Patterns of sex desegregation in managerial and professional specialty fields, 1950–1980. *Work and Occupations, 17*(1), 30–54.

Jones, C. A. (1991). *Obstacles to integrating scholarship on women into public relations education: Strategies for curriculum transformation.* Unpublished master's thesis, University of Maryland, College Park.

Jordan, E. C. (1998, March 26). Black women, into the light of history. *Washington Post*, p. B9.

Jordan, M. (1992, February 12). Wide gender gap found in schools: Girls said to face bias in tests, textbooks, and teaching methods. *Washington Post*, pp. A1, A8.

Joseph, D. (1992, July 14). Pay for hospital fund raisers grew by 8.2%. *Chronicle of Philanthropy*, p. 37.

Joseph, T. (1985, Winter). The women are coming, the women are coming: Results of a survey. *Public Relations Quarterly*, pp. 21–22.

Kahn, N. (1997, November). *Sexual harassment of women at the workplace: Legal and ethical considerations*. Presentation to the International Public Relations Association Professional Development Seminar, Harare, Zimbabwe.

Kanter, R. M. (1977). *Men and women of the corporation*. New York: Basic Books.

Kanter, R. M. (1979, July–August). Power failure in management circuits. *Harvard Business Review*, pp. 18–21.

Kaplowitz, S. A. (1978). Towards a systematic theory of power attribution. *Social Psychology, 41*, 131–148.

Katz, D., & Kahn, R. L. (1966). *The social psychology of organizations*. New York: Wiley.

Katz, D., & Kahn, R. L. (1978). *The social psychology of organizations* (2nd ed.). New York: Wiley.

Kaufman, D. R., & Richardson, B. L. (1982). *Achievement and women: Challenging the assumptions*. New York: Free Press.

Keele, R. (1986). Mentoring or networking? Strong and weak ties in career development. In L. L. Moore (Ed.), *Not as far as you think* (pp. 53–68). Lexington, MA: Lexington Books.

Keller, E. F. (1985). *Reflections on gender and science*. New Haven, CT: Yale University Press.

Keller, R. T., Szilagyi, A. D. Jr., & Holland, W. E. (1976). Boundary-spanning activity and employee reactions. *Human Relations, 29*(7), 699–710.

Kelly, R. M. (1991). *The gendered economy*. Newbury Park, CA: Sage.

Kennedy, G. (1985). *Doing business abroad*. New York: Simon & Schuster.

Kern-Foxworth, M. (1989a, August). Minorities 2000—The shape of things to come. *Public Relations Journal*, pp. 14–18, 21–22.

Kern-Foxworth, M. (1989b). Status and roles of minority PR practitioners. *Public Relations Review, 15*(3), 39–47.

Kern-Foxworth, M. (1989c). Public relations books fail to show women in context. *Journalism Educator, 44*(3), 31–36.

Kern-Foxworth, M. (1990). Ethnic inclusiveness in public relations textbooks and reference books. *Howard Journal of Communication, 2*(2), 226–237.

Kern-Foxworth, M. (1991). Black, brown, red, and yellow markets equal green power. *Public Relations Quarterly, 36*(1), 27–30.

Kern-Foxworth, M. (1993). Minority practitioners' perceptions of racial bias in public relations and implications for the year 2000. In *Diversity in public relations education: Issues, implications and opportunities: A collection of essays* (pp. 35–51). Florida International University, North Miami, and University of South Carolina, Columbia: Diversity Committee, Educators Section, Public Relations Society of America.

Kern-Foxworth, M., & Miller, D. A. (1992, May). *Embracing multicultural diversity: A preliminary examination of public relations education*. Paper presented at the meeting of the Public Relations Interest Group, International Communication Association, Miami, FL.

Kern-Foxworth, M., Gandy, O., Hines, B., & Miller, D. A. (1994). Assessing the managerial role of black female public relations practitioners using individual and organizational discriminants. *Journal of Black Studies, 24*(4), 402–434.

Kilpatrick, R. (1984). International business communication practices. *Journal of Business Communication, 21*(4), 33–43.

Kim, J. (1991, October 17). Mom-preneurs tend to kids, corporate accounts at home. *USA Today*, p. 4B.

King, B., & Scrimger, J. (1993). Public relations, fund raising, and marketing in Canadian hospitals: The potential for encroachment. *Public Relations Quarterly, 38*(2), 40–45.

King, L. R. (1973). *The politics of higher education: The Washington lobbyists*. Unpublished doctoral dissertation, University of Connecticut, New Haven.

Kipnis, D., & Schmidt, S. M. (1988). Upward-influence styles: Relationship with performance evaluations, salary, and stress. *Administrative Science Quarterly, 33*, 528–542.

Kitano, H.H.L., & Daniels, R. (1988). *Asian Americans: Emerging minorities*. Englewood Cliffs, NJ: Prentice-Hall.

Kleiman, C. (1991a, July 28). Too pretty, too heavy—Women battle workplace discrimination. *Orlando Sentinel*, pp. D1–D2.

Kleiman, C. (1991b, November 26). Whose paycheck is bigger doesn't always dictate where couples live. *Orlando Sentinel*, p. C1.

Kleiman, C. (1991c, August 28). Eek and yuck can't explain gender gap. (Portland) *Oregonian*, p. B1.

Kleiman, C. (1991d, September 22). Changing workplaces adapt to women. *San Jose Mercury News*, p. 2PC.

Kleiman, C. (1992, April 22). There's a way to rise above boss from hell. (Portland) *Oregonian*, p. B1.

Knowles, O. S., & Moore, B. A. (1970, Fall). Today's woman executive. *Business and Public Policy Administration Student Review*, p. 72.

Kohlberg, L. (1966). A cognitive developmental analysis of children's sex-role concepts and attitudes. In E. E. Maccoby (Ed.), *The development of sex differences* (pp. 82–173). Stanford, CA: Stanford University Press.

Kolodny, A. (1998). *Failing the future: A dean looks at higher education in the twenty-first century*. Durham, NC: Duke University Press.

Konner, J. (1990, May 5). *Women in the marketplace: The values of collaboration, comments, and cure*. Speech given to the New Jersey Press Women's Association, Paterson, NJ.

Koprowski, E. (1983). Cultural myths: Clues to effective management. *Organizational Dynamics, 12*, 39–51.

Kornegay, J., & Grunig, L. A. (1998). Cyberbridging: How the communication manager role can link with the dominant coalition. *Journal of Communication Management, 3*(2), 140–156.

Kosicki, G. M., & Becker, L. B. (1998). Annual survey of enrollment and degrees awarded. *Journalism and Mass Communication Educator, 53*(3), 65–82.

Kovacs, R. (1992, May). *The organizational woman as communicator in reality and in films: A literature and video review.* Unpublished paper, Towson State University, Towson, MD.

Kramarae, C., Schultz, M., & O'Barr, W. M. (1984). *Language and power.* Newbury Park, CA: Sage.

Kremgold-Barnett, A. (1986). *Women mentoring women in an academic nursing faculty.* Unpublished doctoral dissertation, Boston University, Boston.

Kucera, M. (1994). *Doing it all: Why women public relations managers tend to fulfill both the managerial and technical roles.* Unpublished master's thesis, University of Maryland, College Park.

Kuhn, B. (1992, April 16). Wage gap persists, survey finds. *Orlando Sentinel,* pp. C1, C6.

Lamphere, L. (1977). Review essay: Anthropology. *Signs: Journal of Women in Culture and Society, 2,* 612–627.

Landau, J., & Amoss, L. (1986). Myths, dreams, and disappointments: Preparing women for the future. In L. L. Moore (Ed.), *Not as far as you think* (pp. 13–24). Lexington, MA: Lexington Books.

Lannon, J. M. (1977). Male vs. female values in management. *Management International Review, 17,* 9–12.

Latinos on the rise. (1993). *Futurist, 27*(1), 48–49.

Lauzen, M. M. (1990a, June). *The effects of gender on professional encroachment.* Paper presented at the meeting of the Public Relations Special Interest Group, International Communication Association, Dublin, Ireland.

Lauzen, M. M. (1990b, August). *Losing control: An examination of the management function in public relations.* Paper presented at the meeting of the Association for Education in Journalism and Mass Communication, Minneapolis, MN.

Lauzen, M. M. (1992). Public relations roles, interorganizational power, and encroachment. *Journal of Public Relations Research, 4*(2), 61–80.

Lauzen, M. M., & Dozier, D. M. (1992). The missing link: The public relations manager role as mediator of organizational environments and power consequences for the function. *Journal of Public Relations Research, 4*(4), 205–220.

Law school diversity is rising, study finds. (1999, March 12). *Chronicle of Higher Education,* p. A8.

Lawlor, J. (1997, June). The new breadwinner. *Working Mother,* pp. 12–14, 16–17.

Layton, M. (1980, April). Blacks in public relations: A growing presence. *Public Relations Journal,* pp. 64–67.

Lee, G. (1993a, February 1). Breaking the color barrier in PR: Minority firms mobilize to expand their role in D. C. *Washington Post,* Washington Business section, pp. 1, 20–21.

Lee, G. (1993b, February 15). Black PR firms charge business bias. *Washington Post,* Washington Business section, p. 7.

Lee, S. M. (1989). Asian immigration and American race relations: From exclusion to acceptance? *Ethnic and Racial Studies, 12*(3), 368–390.

Lelen, K. (1997, July 12). For women on the move, help to cross the miles. *Washington Post,* pp. E1, E15.

Len-Rios, M. E. (1998). Minority public relations practitioner perceptions. *Public Relations Review, 24*(4), 535–555.

Leong, F.T.L., Snodgrass, C. R., & Gardner, W. L. (1992). Management education: Creating a gender-positive environment. In U. Sekaran & F.T.L. Leong (Eds.), *Womanpower: Managing in times of demographic turbulence* (pp. 163–191). Newbury Park, CA: Sage.

Lesly, P. (1981, May). The stature and role of public relations. *Public Relations Journal*, pp. 14–17.

Lesly, P. (1988). Public relations numbers are up but stature down. *Public Relations Review, 14*(4), 3–7.

Levine, B. (1990, October 28). Female bosses' non-traditional approach may set leadership style of future. *Baltimore Sun*, p. 10C.

Lewin, T. (1997a, September 15). Wage difference between women and men widens. *New York Times*, pp. A1, A8.

Lewin, T. (1997b, September 15). Women losing ground to men in widening income difference. *New York Times*, pp. A1, A12.

Lewton, K. L. (1989, December 13). Unpublished *memo to members of the PRSA Ad Hoc Task Force on the Status of Women in Public Relations*.

Leyland, A. (2000, March 27). Competition drives PR salaries up 8% in '99. *PR Week*, p. 1.

Lilienthal, S. (1999, February 22). Black future. *PR Week*, pp. 18–19.

Limaye, M. R., & Victor, D. A. (1991). Cross-cultural business communication research: State of the art and hypotheses for the 1990s. *Journal of Business Communication, 28*(3), 277–299.

Lindenmann, W., & Lapetina, A. (1981). Management's view of the future of public relations. *Public Relations Review, 7*(3), 3–13.

Lindlof, T. R. (1995). *Qualitative communication research methods*. Thousand Oaks, CA: Sage.

Lippman, T. W. (1997, March 25). State Dept. seeks gains for women: Albright is stressing rights concerns in foreign policy agenda. *Washington Post*, pp. A1, A9.

Lively, K. (1994, January 5). Shaking up business education for women. *Chronicle of Higher Education*, p. A5.

Locke, E. A. (1992, January). Survey finds junior female faculty suffer research anxiety. *Faculty Voice*, p. 6.

Locksley, A., & Colten, M. E. (1979). Psychological androgyny: A case of mistaken identity? *Journal of Personality and Social Psychology, 37*(6), 1017–1031.

Lodahl, T., & Kejner, M. (1965). The definition and measurement of job involvement. *Journal of Applied Psychology, 49*, 361–368.

Loden, M. (1985). *Feminine leadership*. New York: New York Times Press.

Loden, M. (1986). Feminine leadership: It can make your business more profitable. *Vital Speeches of the Day, 2*(15), 472–475.

Lomenzo, A. J. (1993, December). Diversity drive discomfort. *American Journalism Review*, p. 5.

Lopez, J. A. (1992, March 3). Study says women face glass walls as well as ceilings. *Wall Street Journal*, pp. B1-B2.

Loscocco, K. A., & Robinson, J. (1991). Barriers to women's small-business success in the United States. *Gender and Society, 5*(4), 511–532.

Lott, B. C. (1981). *Becoming a woman*. Chicago: Thomas.

Lublin, J. (1997, November 28). How one woman manages in world of male directors. *Wall Street Journal*, pp. B1, B7.

Lueck, T. L., Endres, K., & Caplan, R. E. (1993, August). *Mass communication course evaluations: An exploratory study on the effect of gender*. Paper presented at the meeting of the Committee on the Status of Women, Association for Education in Journalism and Mass Communication, Kansas City.

Lukovitz, K. (1989, May). Women practitioners: How far, how fast? *Public Relations Journal*, pp. 14–22, 34.

Lusterman, S. (1987). *The organization and staffing of corporate public affairs: A research report*. New York: Conference Board.

Lyles, M. A. (1985). Strategies for helping women managers—or anyone. In B. A. Stead (Ed.), *Women in management* (2nd ed., pp. 16–27). Englewood Cliffs, NJ: Prentice-Hall.

Lyra, A. (1991). *Public relations in Greece: Models, roles, and gender*. Unpublished master's thesis, University of Maryland, College Park.

Mainiero, L. A. (1986). Coping with powerlessness: The relationship of gender and job dependency to empowerment-strategy usage. *Administrative Science Quarterly, 31*, 633–653.

Mallette, W. A. (1995). *African Americans in public relations: Pigeonholed practitioners or cultural interpreters?* Unpublished master's thesis, University of Maryland, College Park.

Mann, J. (1986, April 4). Hand that rocks the cradle. *Washington Post*, p. B3.

Mann, J. (1997, July 2). Taking another crack at the wage gap. *Washington Post*, p. D10.

Marin, G., & VanOss Marin, B. (1991). *Research with Hispanic populations*. Newbury Park, CA: Sage.

Marsh, B. (1991, October 18). Women in the workforce. *Wall Street Journal*, p. B3.

Marshall, C., & Rossman, G. B. (1989). *Designing qualitative research*. Newbury Park, CA: Sage.

Mason, M. A. (1988). *The equality trap: Why working women shouldn't be treated like men*. New York: Touchstone.

Mathews, J. (1993, August 15). The street with a glass ceiling: Brokerages see gains. A fired Goldman Sachs executive and other women see otherwise. *Washington Post*, pp. H1, H5.

Mathews, W. (1988). Women in public relations: Progression or retrogression? *Public Relations Review, 14*(3), 24–28.

Mathews, W. (1989). Killing the messenger. In E. L. Toth & C. G. Cline (Eds.), *Beyond the velvet ghetto* (pp. 1–6). San Francisco: IABC Research Foundation.

Mathias, B. (1993, January 15). Focus: The derring-doers: Chronicling the deeds of our foremothers. *Washington Post*, p. B5.

Matteson, M. T., McMahan, J. F., & McMahan, M. (1974). Sex differences and job attitudes: Some unexpected findings. *Psychological Reports, 35*, 1333–1334.

Matthews, A. (1991, April 17). Alma maters court their daughters. *The New York Times Sunday Magazine*, pp. 40, 73, 77.

McAdams, K. C. (1981). *Some effects of sex role socialization on women entering journalism careers.* Unpublished master's thesis, University of North Carolina, Chapel Hill.

McAllister, B. (1992, October 29). Government women, too, seen facing glass ceiling: Relatively few get access to top federal jobs. *Washington Post,* pp. A1, A4.

McCarthy, C. (1991, September 28). Academia's stoop laborers. *Washington Post,* p. A27.

McCracken, G. (1988). *The long interview.* Newbury Park, CA: Sage.

McDermott, J. (1993, August 11). Publisher takes the "next step." (Portland) *Oregonian,* pp. E1, E3.

McElrath, K. (1992). Gender, career disruption, and academic rewards. *Journal of Higher Education, 63*(3), 269–281.

McGoon, C. (1993, January–February). Life's a beach, for communicators. *IABC Communication World,* pp. 12–15.

McIntyre, D. J. (1991, June). When your national language is just another language. *IABC Communication World,* pp. 18–21.

McKay, E. G. (1982). *Hispanic statistics summary: A compendium of data on Hispanic Americans.* Washington, DC: National Council of La Raza.

Melton, R. H., & Grimsley, K. D. (1998, March 23). Work climate warmer for women. *Washington Post,* pp. A1, A8-A9.

Merida, K. (1993, August 2). Sisterhood of the Hill "shaking up the place": Black female lawmakers have early impact. *Washington Post,* pp. A1, A10.

Messner, M. (1987). The reproduction of women's domination in organization communication. In L. Thayer (Ed.), *Organization—Communication* (pp. 51–70). Norwood, NJ: Ablex.

Micheli, R. (1988, July). Home is where the office is. *Money,* pp. 69–79.

Milbrath, L. W. (1963). *The Washington lobbyists.* Chicago: Rand-McNally.

Miles, R. H. (1977, August). *Boundary relevance.* Paper presented at the meeting of the Academy of Management, Kissimmee, FL.

Miller, A., & Kruger, P. (1990, April). The new old boy. *Working Woman,* pp. 94–96.

Miller, A., Springen, K., & Tsiantar, D. (1992, August 24). Now: The brick wall. *Newsweek,* pp. 54–56.

Miller, B. W., & Schroeder, C. K. (1983). Women administrators in higher education: Cooperation or conflict? In B. W. Miller, R. W. Hotes, & J. D. Terry Jr. (Eds.), *Leadership in higher education: A handbook for practicing administrators* (pp. 227–234). Westport, CT: Greenwood Press.

Miller, D. A. (1991, August). *Multicultural communications: Sensitizing public relations students to multicultural society.* Paper presented at the meeting of the Public Relations Division, Association for Education in Journalism and Mass Communication, Montreal.

Miller, D. A. (1993). *Multicultural communications: A bibliography.* New York: PRSA Foundation.

Miller, J. B. (1976). *Toward a new psychology of women.* Boston: Beacon Press.

Miller, M. E. (1992). *Politicians and their spouses' careers.* Washington, DC: Congressional Management Foundation.

Miller, W. H. (1991, May 6). A new perspective for tomorrow's workforce. *Industry Week*, pp. 7–9.

Minority entrepreneurs challenge the barriers. (1989, August). *Public Relations Journal*, pp. 19–20.

Moore, D. P., Buttner, E. H., & Rosen, B. (1992). Stepping off the corporate track: The entrepreneurial alternative. In U. Sekaran & F.T.L. Leong (Eds.), *Womanpower: Managing in times of demographic turbulence* (pp. 85–110). Newbury Park, CA: Sage.

Moore, L. L. (1986a). Introduction. In L. L. Moore (Ed.), *Not as far as you think* (pp. 1–12). Lexington, MA: Lexington Books.

Moore, L. L. (1986b). *Not as far as you think: The realities of working women.* Lexington, MA: Lexington Books.

Morgan, G. (1986). *Images of organizations.* Newbury Park, CA: Sage.

Morgenthau, H. (1960). *Politics among nations.* New York: Knopf.

Morin, R. (1993, February 21). Female aides on the Hill: Still outsiders in man's world. *Washington Post*, pp. A1, A18-A19.

Morley, M. (1998). *How to manage your global reputation: A guide to the dynamics of international public relations.* London: Macmillan.

Morris, M., & Siegel, A. (1992, January). The thirteenth annual working woman salary survey 1992. *Working Woman*, pp. 49–53.

Morrison, A. M., White, R. P., & Van Velsor, E. V. (1987, August). Executive women: Substance plus style. *Psychology Today*, pp. 18–27.

Mottaz, C. (1986). Gender differences in work satisfaction, work-related rewards and values, and the determinants of work satisfaction. *Human Relations, 39,* 359–378.

Multi-Connections (PRSA's Professional Interest Section Newsletter). (1997, Fall). New York: Public Relations Society of America.

Multiculturalism is debated at PRSA meeting; Sides far apart. (1994, January). *O'Dwyer's PR Services Report*, pp. 1, 8.

Must busy professionals be concerned about education in the field while battling issues like achieving top management decision making? (1984, November 28). *pr reporter*, p. 1.

Myrdal, G. (1944). *An American dilemma: The Negro problem in modern democracy.* New York: Harper & Row.

Name withheld. (1992, June 8). Glass ceiling update: All sticks, no carrots (Letters). *Ragan Report*, p. 1.

Nasar, S. (1992a, October 18). Women's progress stalled? Just not so. *New York Times*, section 3, pp. 1, 10.

Nasar, S. (1992b, October 22). Women move closer to pay equality with men: Research shows major gains in '80s. *Atlanta Journal and Constitution*, pp. G1, G3.

National Council of La Raza (NCLR). (1991). *The Hispanic population: 1990. A chartbook "snapshot."* Washington, DC: Author.

Nelton, S. (1992, May). Showing their staying power. *Nation's Business, 80,* pp. 65–70.

New career paths for women. (1990, March 12). *pr reporter*, p. 1.

The new face of America: How immigrants are shaping the world's first multicultural society. (1993). Special issue, *Time, 142*(21).

New job burnout research identifies 2 specific assignments for pr. (1992, June 1). *pr reporter*, pp. 3–4.

Newman, L. (1980, April). Public relations phase II: Adviser becomes decision maker. *Public Relations Journal*, pp. 11–13.

Newsom, D. A., & Carrell, B. J. (Eds.). (1995). *Silent voices*. Lanham, MD: University Press of America.

Nieva, V. F., & Gutek, B. A. (1981). *Women and work: A psychological perspective*. New York: Praeger.

Nilson, L. B. (1976). The occupational and sex-related components of social standing. *Sociology and Social Research, 60*, 328–336.

Nollen, S. P. (1989). The work–family dilemma: How human resource managers can help. *Personnel, 66*(5), 25–30.

Novarra, V. (1980). *Women's work, men's work: The ambivalence of equality*. London: Marion Boyars.

Novek, E. (1991, May). *Getting together: How does empowerment happen?* Paper presented at the meeting of the International Communication Association, Chicago.

Oakley, A. (1974). *Women's work: The housewife past and present*. New York: Rentheon Books/Random House.

O'Briant, D. (1992, July 23). Columnist sees women gaining power. (Portland) *Oregonian*, p. F1.

Odd jobs: Harassment insurance. (1998a, April 5). *Washington Post*, p. H4.

Odd jobs: How work-life programs help. (1998b, April 12). *Washington Post*, p. H4.

Olasky, M. N. (1987). *Corporate public relations: A new historical perspective*. Hillsdale, NJ: Erlbaum.

O'Leary, V. E., & Hansen, R. D. (1982). Trying hurts women, helps men: The meaning of effort. In H. J. Bernardin (Ed.), *Women in the workforce* (pp. 100–123). New York: Praeger.

Olen, H. (1991, July 11). Mellower than mom: Daughters of women's lib. *Orlando Sentinel*, pp. E1, E5.

Olerup, A., Schneider, L., & Monod, E. (1985). *Women, work, and computerization: Opportunities and disadvantages*. New York: Elsevier Science.

O'Neil, J. W. (1999, August). The Strategist: *Positioning women as "outsiders within" the public relations profession*. Paper presented at the meeting of the Public Relations Division, Association for Education in Journalism and Mass Communication, New Orleans.

Orazem, P. F., Mattila, J. P., & Yu, R. C. (1990). Communications: An index number approach to the measurement of wage differentials by sex. *Journal of Human Resources, 26*(1), 125–136.

Organizations want diversity: A culture change job for pr. (1994, January 24). *pr reporter*, pp. 1–2.

Overall salaries remain flat, gender discrepancies continue. (1992, December 7). *pr reporter*, p. 2.

Paglin, M., & Rufolo, A. M. (1990). Heterogeneous human capital, occupational choice, and male–female earnings differences. *Journal of Labor Economics,* 8(1), 123–144.

Paid maternity leave in Europe: 14 weeks. (1991, November 7). *Orlando Sentinel,* p. A19.

Parsons, P. R. (1989). Values of communication students and professional self-selection. *Journalism Quarterly,* 66(1), 161–168.

Part-time employees receive low priority. (1991, December 21). *Orlando Sentinel,* pp. C1, C6.

Patterson, M., & Engleberg, L. (1978). Women in male-dominated professions. In A. H. Stromberg & S. Harkess (Eds.), *Women working: Theories and facts in perspective* (pp. 266–293). Palo Alto, CA: Mayfield.

Pavlik, J. V. (1987). *Public relations: What research tells us.* Newbury Park, CA: Sage.

Pavlik, J. V., & Dozier, D. M. (1996). *The new technology.* Gainesville, FL: Institute for Public Relations Research and Education.

Peacock, J. L. (1986). *The anthropological lens.* Cambridge, NY: Cambridge University Press.

Pedhazur, E. J., & Tetenbaum, T. J. (1979). Bem sex role inventory: A theoretical and methodological critique. *Journal of Personality and Social Psychology,* 37(6), 996–1016.

Pendelton, M. (1996, December). *Racial and ethnic diversity in public relations: A literature review.* Unpublished paper, University of Maryland, College Park.

Pfeffer, J. (1981). *Power in organizations.* Boston: Pitman.

Pfeffer, J., & Davis-Blake, A. (1987). The effect of the proportion of women on salaries: The case of college administrators. *Administrative Science Quarterly,* 32(1), 1–24.

Phelan, J. (1994). The paradox of the contented female worker: An assessment of alternative explanations. *Social Psychology Quarterly, 57,* 95–100.

Pincus, J. D., & Rayfield, R. E. (1989). Organizational communication and job satisfaction: A metaresearch perspective. In B. Dervin & M. J. Voigt (Eds.), *Progress in communication sciences* (pp. 183–208). Norwood, NJ: Ablex.

Pincus, W. (1994, September 9). CIA and the "glass ceiling" secret: Female, black operatives report harassment; Reprisals "seem to go unchecked." *Washington Post,* p. A25.

Pollack, J. C., & Winkleman, M. (1987, June). Salary survey. *Public Relations Journal,* pp. 15–17.

Popovich, J. C. (1992). *From participation to empowerment: Employee perceptions of participatory decision making and employee effectiveness.* Unpublished master's thesis, Cornell University, Ithica, NY.

Powell, G. N. (1988). *Women and men in management.* Newbury Park, CA: Sage.

Powers, D. C. (1991, June 13). Changing school gender roles. *Prince George's Sentinel,* pp. 1, 7.

Powers, M., & Oliver, M. (1992). Courting the Hispanic dollar. *Human Ecology Forum, 20,* 25–27.

PR/Ketchum Public Relations Survey on Diversity in Public Relations. (1994, November). New York: Author.

PR people deplore encroachment by marketers and "feminization" of the field. (1984, December). *Marketing News,* p. 12.

PR: "The velvet ghetto" of affirmative action. (1978, May 8). *Business Week,* p. 122.

Pratt, A. (1990). Academic discrimination: The Supreme Court rules in favor of opening tenure files. *NWSAction,* 3(2), 1, 6.

Presentation by multicultural panel member A. Bruce Crawley, president, Crawley Haskins & Rogers PR, Philadelphia. (1994, January). *O'Dwyer's PR Services Report,* pp. 10–11, 13.

Presentation by multicultural panel member Jack O'Dwyer, publisher and editor of this magazine. (1994, January). *O'Dwyer's PR Services Report,* pp. 12–13.

Presentation by multicultural panel member Lynne Choy Uyeda, principal, Lynne Choy Uyeda and Assocs., Los Angeles. (1994, January). *O'Dwyer's PR Services Report,* p. 14.

Preston, A. E. (1990). Women in the white-collar nonprofit section: The best option or the only option? *Review of Economics and Statistics, 72,* 560–568.

Price, J. L., & Mueller, C. W. (1986). *Handbook of organizational management.* White Plains, NY: Longman.

Provan, K. G. (1980). Recognizing, measuring, and interpreting the potential/enacted power distinction in organizational research. *Academy of Management Review, 5, 549–559.*

Public participation: Antithesis of political correctness? (1994, January 3). *pr reporter,* pp. 1–6.

Public relations must pave the way for developing diversified work force. (1992, January). *Public Relations Journal,* pp. 12–13.

Public Relations Society of America. (N.d.). *Summary of 1990 gender survey.* New York: Author.

Q & A: On the future of PRSA with Ray Gaulke, newly-appointed COO of the association. (1993, July 19). *Ragan Report,* 24(7), 3.

Rabin, P. (1990). Does your salary measure up? *Currents, 1*(1), 14–15.

Rabin, P., & Myles, P. (1991, November 27). PR society polls membership on gender-pay issue. *Washington Times,* p. B1.

Ragins, B. R., & Sundstrom, E. (1989). Gender and power in organizations: A longitudinal perspective. *Psychological Bulletin, 105*(1), 51–88.

Rakow, L. (1989). From the feminization of public relations to the promise of feminism. In E. L. Toth & C. G. Cline (Eds.), *Beyond the velvet ghetto.* (pp. 287–298). San Francisco: IABC Research Foundation.

Rakow, L. (1991). Gender and race in the classroom: Teaching way out of line. *Feminist Teacher, 6,* 10–13.

Raspberry, W. (1989, June 14). Ruling in favor of white males. *Washington Post,* p. A23.

Rationale for black PR groups given by Goss of PRSA/LA. (1994, January). *O'Dwyer's PR Services Report,* p. 14.

Raymond, C. (1989, October 11). Shift of many traditionally male jobs to women. *Chronicle of Higher Education*, pp. A4, A6.

Raynolds, E. H. (1987). Management women in the corporate workplace: Possibilities for the year 2000. *Human Resources Management, 26*, 265–276.

Rebello, K. (1990, July 13). Women execs crash into "glass ceiling." *USA Today*, pp. 1B-2B, 7B-8B.

Reif, W. E., Newstrom, J. W., & Monczka, R. M. (1978). Exploding some myths about women managers. In B. A. Snead (Ed.), *Women in management* (pp. 11–23). Englewood Cliffs, NJ: Prentice-Hall.

Reitz, H. T., & Jewell, L. N. (1979). Sex, focus of control, and job involvement: A six country investigation. *Academy of Management Journal, 8*, 330–312.

Rensberger, B. (1992, August 26). Women's place: On the podium. *Washington Post*, p. A21.

Reskin, B. F., & Roos, P. A. (Eds.). (1990). *Job queues, gender queues: Explaining women's inroads into males' occupations*. Philadelphia: Temple University Press.

Reuters. (1993, August 9). 2 women on court will make a difference, Ginsburg says. *Washington Post*, p. A7.

Riffe, D., Salomone, K., & Stempel, G. H. III. (1998). Characteristics, responsibilities, and concerns of teaching faculty: A survey of AEJMC members. *Journalism and Mass Communication Educator, 52*(4), 102–120.

Rigdon, J. E. (1993, June 9). Three decades after the Equal Pay Act, women's wages remain far from parity. *Wall Street Journal*, pp. B1, B6.

Riger, S., & Galligan, P. (1980). Women in management: An exploration of competing paradigms. *American Psychologist, 35*(10), 902–910.

Robbins, S. P. (1987). *Organization theory: Structure, design and process* (2nd ed.). Englewood Cliffs, NJ: Prentice-Hall.

Rocha, V. A., & Frase-Blunt, M. (1992, May). Coming to America. *Hispanic*, pp. 15–20.

Rosaldo, M. Z. (1980). The use and abuse of anthropology: Reflections on feminism and cross-cultural understanding. *Signs: Journal of Women in Culture and Society, 5*, 121–133.

Rosaldo, M. Z., & Lamphere, L. (Eds.). (1974). *Woman, culture, and society*. Stanford, CA: Stanford University Press.

Rosen, B. (1982). Career progress of women: Getting in and staying in. In H. J. Bernardin (Ed.), *Women in the workforce* (pp. 70–99). New York: Praeger.

Rosenberg, J., Perlstadt, H., & Phillips, W.R.F. (1993). Now that we are here: Discrimination, disparagement, and harassment at work and the experience of female lawyers. *Gender and Society, 7*(3), 415–433.

Rosener, J. B. (1994). Ways women lead. In N. A. Nichols (Ed.), *Reach for the top* (pp. 13–23). Boston: Harvard Business Review.

Rothschild, C. S. (1978). Women and work: Policy implications and prospects. In S. Harkess & A. Stromberg (Eds.), *Working women* (p. 429). Palo Alto, CA: Mayfield.

Rudavsky, S. (1992, August 12). A status report on the glass ceiling: Invisible barrier to top-level promotions is still there, Martin says. *Washington Post*, p. A19.

Rush, R. R. (1993). A systemic commitment to women in the academy: Barriers, harassment prevent "being all that we can be." *Journalism Educator, 48*(1), 71–79.

Rush, R., Kaufman, S. J., & Allen, D. (1995). Toward a humanly decent theory of communications for the 21ˢᵗ century. In D. A. Newsom & B. J. Carrell (Eds.), *Silent voices* (pp. 1–16). Lanham, MD: University Press of America.

Russell, V. (1988, June). Salary survey. *Public Relations Journal*, pp. 26–30.

Ryscavage, P., & Henle, P. (1990, December). Earnings inequality accelerates in the 1980s. *Monthly Labor Review*, pp. 3–16.

Salary Survey of Public Relations Professionals. (1995). New York: Simmons Market Research Bureau for the Public Relations Society of America.

Sanders, G., & Schmidt, T. (1980). Behavioral discrimination against women. *Personality and Social Psychology Bulletin, 6*, 484–488.

Sanders-Thompson, V. L. (1994). Socialization to race and its relationship to racial identification among African Americans. *Journal of Black Psychology, 20*(2), 175–188.

Sargent, A. G. (1981). *The androgenous manager.* New York: Amacom.

Savenye, W. C. (1990). Role models and student attitudes toward non-traditional careers. *Educational Technology Research and Development, 38*(3), 5–13.

Scanlan, J. M. (1993, November). *Education for women in development.* Paper presented at the meeting of the Association for the Advancement of Policy, Research and Development in the Third World, Cairo.

Schein, V. E. (1975). Relationships between sex role stereotypes and requisite management characteristics among female managers. *Journal of Applied Psychology, 60*(3), 340–344.

Schwab, R. C., Ungson, G. R., & Brown, W. B. (1985). Organizational/environmental interchange: A model of boundary spanning activity. *Journal of Management, 11*, 75–76.

Schwartz, F. N. (1989, January–February). Management women and the new facts of life. *Harvard Business Review, 32*, 65–76.

Scott, C. E. (1986). Why more women are becoming entrepreneurs. *Journal of Small Business Management, 24*(4), 37–45.

Scrimger, J. (1985). Profile: Women in Canadian public relations. *Public Relations Review, 11*(3), 40–46.

Scrimger, J. (1989). Women communicators in Canada: A case for optimism. In E. L. Toth & C. G. Cline (Eds.), *Beyond the velvet ghetto* (pp. 219–240). San Francisco: IABC Research Foundation.

Seideman, T., & Leyland, A. (2000, March 27). *PR Week* salary survey report 2000. *PR Week*, pp. 23–25, 27, 29, 31, 33, 35.

Sekaran, U., & Kassner, M. (1992). University systems for the 21st century: Proactive adaptation. In U. Sekaran & F.T.L. Leong (Eds.), *Womanpower: Managing in times of demographic turbulence* (pp. 163–191). Newbury Park, CA: Sage.

Selnow, G. W., & Wilson, S. (1985). Sex roles and job satisfaction in public relations. *Public Relations Review, 11*(4), 38–47.

Serini, S. A., Toth, E. L., Wright, D. K., & Emig, A. G. (1997). Watch for falling glass

. . . women, men, and job satisfaction in public relations: A preliminary analysis. *Journal of Public Relations Research, 9*(2), 99–118.

Serini, S. A., Toth, E. L., Wright, D. K., & Emig, A. G. (1998a). Power, gender, and public relations: Sexual harassment as a threat to the practice. *Journal of Public Relations Research, 10*(3), 193–218.

Serini, S. A., Toth, E., Wright, D. K., & Emig, A. (1998b, July). *An examination of managerial traits by men and women in public relations.* Paper presented at the Public Relations Division, International Communication Association, Jerusalem.

Sexual harassment of women over 50 is serious problem in the workplace. (1993, Winter). *WEPR (Women Executives in Public Relations) network,* p. 2.

Sha, B. L. (1993). *Intercultural public relations: Communicating with ethnically diverse publics.* Unpublished manuscript, University of Maryland, College Park.

Shanker, A. (1991–1992, December–January). Where we stand: Merit gets them nowhere. *AFT Teacher,* p. 5.

Shapiro, L. (1990, May 28). Guns and dolls. *Newsweek,* pp. 56–65.

Sharpe, R. (1997, November 10). Seeking a share: A female contractor often gets caught up in preference disputes. *Wall Street Journal,* p. A1.

Sheldon, K. R. (1990, August). Build bridges with a multicultural speakers bureau. *IABC Communication World,* pp. 21–23.

Shepard, S. (1985, January). Why stereotypes hurt. *Management World,* p. 44.

Sherif, C. W. (1982). Needed concepts in the study of gender identity. *Psychology of Women Quarterly, 6*(4), 375–398.

Sidel, R. (1986). *Women and children last.* New York: Viking.

Silver, L. (1990, August 27). White males still dominate top-level jobs. (Portland) *Oregonian,* p. D1.

Simeone, A. (1987). *Academic women: Working towards equality.* South Hadley, MA: Bergin & Garvey.

Simmons Market Research Bureau. (1996). *Salary survey of public relations professionals.* New York: Public Relations Society of America.

Simon, H. (1953). Notes on the observation and measurement of political power. *Journal of Politics, 15,* 500–516.

Simpson, R. L., & Simpson, I. H. (1969). *Women and bureaucracy in the semi-professions and their organizations: Teachers, nurses, and social workers.* New York: Free Press.

Singletary, D. (1993). Developing an effective introduction to public relations for pre-college students. In *Diversity in public relations education: Issues, implications and opportunities: A collection of essays* (pp. 86–94). Florida International University, North Miami, and University of South Carolina, Columbia: Diversity Committee, Educators Section, Public Relations Society of America.

Skolnik, R. (1993a, March). The emerging firm of the 90s: Largest firms adapt to changing market conditions. *Public Relations Journal,* pp. 20–25.

Skolnik, R. (1993b, March). F-H thrives on decentralized structure. *Public Relations Journal,* p. 24.

Skolnik, R. (1993c, March). Successful firms changed style of management before recession. *Public Relations Journal*, p. 22.

Skvoretz, J., & Smith, S. A. (1990). Changing reward structures and population distributions: An aggregate analysis of earnings inequalities in the 1980s. *Social Science Research, 19,* 372–398.

Slovik, P. (1966). Risk-taking in children: Age and sex differences. *Child Development, 37,* 169–176.

Smith, J. M. (1993, July 28). Brown discusses female leadership. *Summer Orange,* pp. 1, 5.

Smith, R. W. (1968, October). Women in public relations. *Public Relations Journal,* pp. 26–29.

Snowden, S. (1986). *The global edge: How your company can win in the global marketplace.* New York: Simon & Schuster.

Sohn, A. B. (1984). Goals and achievement orientations of women news managers. *Journalism Quarterly, 61*(3), 600–605.

Solomon, C. (1992). Keeping hate out of the workplace. *Personnel Journal, 71*(1), 30–36.

Solomon, J. (1990, September 12). Learning to accept cultural diversity. *Wall Street Journal,* p. B1.

Sommer, M. (1994, June 28). Welcome cribside, Dad. *Christian Science Monitor,* p. 19.

Special report: 1997 membership survey results. (1997, July). *The (PRSA) Society Page,* pp. 1–2.

Spence, J. T., & Helmreich, R. L. (1978). *Masculinity and femininity: Their psychological dimensions, correlates, and antecedents.* Austin: University of Texas Press.

Spence, J. T., & Helmreich, R. L. (1980). Masculine instrumentality and feminine expressiveness: Their relationships with separate role attitudes and behaviors. *Psychology of Women Quarterly, 5*(2), 147–163.

Spencer, P. (1997, June 24). New dads. *Woman's Day,* pp. 77–80.

Springen, K. (1992, August). How Anita Hill got to Oral Roberts U. *Working Woman,* pp. 18, 20.

Sriramesh, K. (1992). *The impact of societal culture on public relations: An ethnographic study of South Indian organizations.* Unpublished doctoral dissertation, University of Maryland, College Park.

Statham, A. (1987). The gender model revisited: Differences in the management style of men and women. *Sex Roles, 16,* 409–429.

Statistical abstract of the United States (115th ed.). (1995). Washington, DC: U.S. Bureau of the Census.

Stead, B. A. (1985). *Women in management* (2nd ed.). Englewood Cliffs, NJ: Prentice-Hall.

Steeves, H. L. (1987). Feminist theories and media studies. *Critical Studies in Mass Communication, 4*(2), 95–135.

Stephens, A. (1993). *Wild women: Crusaders, curmudgeons, and completely corsetless ladies in the otherwise virtuous Victorian era.* Berkeley, CA: Conari Press.

Stewart, L. J. (1988). Women in foundation and corporate public relations. *Public Relations Review, 14*(3), 20–23.

Stewart, L. P., & Gudykunst, W. B. (1982). Differential factors influencing the hierarchical level and number of promotions of males and females within an organization. *Academy of Management Journal, 2,* 586–597.

Stone, V. A. (1987). Changing profiles of news directors of radio and TV stations. *Journalism Quarterly, 64*(4), 745–749.

Straughan, D. M. (1990, June). *Women and public relations careers: A not-so-tender trap?* Paper presented at the meeting of the International Communication Association, Dublin, Ireland.

Strenski, J. B. (1980, January). The top 12 public relations challenges for 1980. *Public Relations Journal,* pp. 11–14.

Stroh, L. K. (1992). All the right stuff: A comparison of female and male managers' career progression. *Journal of Applied Psychology, 77*(3), 251–260.

Struck, M. (1992). What is *Majority Rules! Majority Rules!, 1*(1), 1–2.

Sugawara, S. (1992, September 29). Study finds salary gap at associations. *Washington Post,* pp. D1, D3.

Sugg, D. K. (1995, November 8). Black doctors feel chill at HMOs. *Baltimore Sun,* pp. A1, A6.

Suro, R. (1998). *Strangers among us: How Latino immigration is transforming America.* New York: Knopf.

Survey reveals insights into attitudes and perceptions of public relations practitioners. (1991). *IABC Communication World,* pp. 11–13.

Swoboda, F. (1990a, September 23). Executive employment outlook bleaker. *Washington Post,* p. H3.

Swoboda, F. (1990b, September 30). Empowering the rank and file. *Washington Post,* p. H3.

Tannen, D. (1990). *You just don't understand: Women and men in conversation.* New York: Ballantine.

Tannen, D. (1994). *Talking from 9 to 5: Women and men in the workplace. Language, sex, and power.* New York: Avon.

Tannen, D. (1998). *The argument culture: Moving from debate to dialogue.* New York: Random House.

Taylor, A. (1986, August). Why women managers are bailing out. *Fortune,* pp. 16–22.

Tech's faded promise: Young industry, old problem. (1990, July 13). *USA Today,* p. 1B.

Teegardin, C. (1991, November 10). Study: Women bosses are instinctively better. *Tallahassee Democrat,* p. 7E.

Terpstra, D. E. (1989, March). Who gets sexually harassed? *Personnel Administration, 34,* 89–111.

Terrell, K. (1992). Female–male earnings differentials and occupational structure. *International Labour Review, 131*(4–5), 387–404.

Theobold, R. (1967). *Dialogue on women.* Indianapolis, IN: Bobbs-Merrill.

Theodore, A. (1986). *The campus troublemakers: Academic women in protest.* Houston, TX: Cap and Gown.

30th survey of the profession, Part II: Salaries, benefits, and work conditions. (1998, October 12). *pr reporter*, pp. 1–6.

Thomas, R. R., Jr. (1991). *Beyond race and gender: Unleashing the power of your total work force by managing diversity.* New York: Amacom.

Thompson, C. A., Thomas, C. C., & Maier, M. (1992). Work–family conflict: Reassessing corporate policies and initiatives. In U. Sekaran & F.T.L. Leong (Eds.), *Womanpower: Managing in times of demographic turbulence* (pp. 59–84). Newbury Park, CA: Sage.

Tiger, L. (1999). *The decline of males.* New York: Golden.

Tong, R. (1989). *Feminist thought: A comprehensive introduction.* Boulder, CO: Westview Press.

Top 5 factors in choosing a public relations firm. (1993, November 1). *pr reporter*, p. 4.

Torry, S. (1995, November 20). Voice of concern grows louder on gender bias issue. *Washington Post*, Business section, p. 7.

Tortorello, N. J., & Barnes, K. (1989, June). PRJ's fourth annual salary survey: Median salary at $39,400; gender gap still lives. *Public Relations Journal*, pp. 17–21.

Tortorello, N. J., & Wilhelm, E. (1993, July). Eighth annual salary survey: Growth stalls but firms expect improvement. *Public Relations Journal*, pp. 10–19.

Toth, E. L. (1988). Making peace with gender issues in public relations. *Public Relations Review, 14*(3), 36–47.

Toth, E. L. (1989a). Gender issues from a speech communication perspective. In E. L. Toth & C. G. Cline (Eds.), *Beyond the velvet ghetto* (pp. 59–70). San Francisco: IABC Research Foundation.

Toth, E. L. (1989b). Trends from focus group interviews. In E. L. Toth & C. G. Cline (Eds.), *Beyond the velvet ghetto* (pp. 71–96). San Francisco: IABC Research Foundation.

Toth, E. L. (1989c). Summary issues from the velvet ghetto: The impact of the increasing percentage of women in public relations and business communications. In E. L. Toth & C. G. Cline (Eds.), *Beyond the velvet ghetto* (pp. 7–23). San Francisco: IABC Research Foundation.

Toth, E. L. (1994, July). *PR salary statistics: Missing the forest for the trees.* Paper presented at the meeting of the International Communication Association, Sydney, Australia.

Toth, E. L., & Cline, C. G. (Eds.). (1989a). *Beyond the velvet ghetto.* San Francisco: IABC Research Foundation.

Toth, E. L., & Cline, C. G. (1989b). What the numbers tell us: A survey of IABC and PRSA members in the U.S. and Canada. In E. L. Toth & C. G. Cline (Eds.), *Beyond the velvet ghetto* (pp. 97–138). San Francisco: IABC Research Foundation.

Toth, E. L., & Cline, C. G. (1991). Public relations practitioner attitudes toward gender issues: A benchmark study. *Public Relations Review, 17*(2), 161–174.

Toth, E. L., & Grunig, L. A. (1993). The missing story of women in public relations. *Journal of Public Relations Research, 5*(3), 153–175.

Toth, E. L., Serini, S. A., Wright, D. K., & Emig A. G. (1998a). Trends in public relations roles: 1990–1995. *Public Relations Review, 24*(2), 148–163.

Toth, E. L., Serini, S. A., Wright, D. K., & Emig, A. G. (1998b). Unpublished raw data for the "glass ceiling study," phase 2.

Touhey, J. C. (1974). Effects of additional women professionals on rating of occupations' prestige and desirability. *Journal of Personality and Social Psychology, 29,* 86–89.

Treichler, P. A., & Wartella, E. (1986). Interventions: Feminist theory and communication studies. *Communication, 9,* 1–18.

Tribute: Annual forum established to honor Nancy Woodhull. (1997). *Freedom Forum Annual Report,* p. 76. Arlington, VA: Freedom Forum.

Tsui, A. S., & Gutek, B. A. (1984). A role set analysis of gender differences in performance, affective relationships, and career success of industrial middle managers. *Academy of Management Journal, 27,* 619–635.

Turk, J. V. (1982, August). *Women in educational communications: Profile of CASE members.* Paper presented at the meeting of the Association for Education in Journalism, Athens, OH.

Turk, J. V. (1986a). Forecasting tomorrow's public relations. *Public Relations Review, 12*(3), 12–21.

Turk, J. V. (1986b). The changing face of CASE. *CASE Currents, 12*(6), 8–20.

Turk, J. V. (1986c). The shifting salary scene. *CASE Currents, 12*(6), 20.

Turk J. V. (1992, November). *Women as managers.* Paper presented at the meeting of the Association for the Advancement of Policy, Research and Development in the Third World, Orlando, FL.

25th survey of the profession, Part I: Salaries and demographics. (1989, October 16). *pr reporter,* p. 1.

Twenty-first survey of the profession: Salaries. (1985, September 30). *pr reporter,* pp. 1–6.

24th survey of the profession, Part I: Salaries and demographics. (1988, September 12). *pr reporter,* pp. 1–6.

Twenty-second survey of the profession, Part I: Salaries. (1986, October 20). *pr reporter,* pp. 1–6.

26th survey of the profession, Part I: Salaries and demographics. (1990, October 1). *pr reporter,* pp. 1–6.

27th survey of the profession, Part II: Salaries and demographics of upper-level practitioners. (1991, October 21). *pr reporter,* pp. 1–6.

23rd survey of the profession, Part I: Salaries and demographics. (1987, September 14). *pr reporter,* pp. 1–2.

Twombly, S. B. (1993). What we know about women in community colleges: An examination of the literature using feminist phase theory. *Journal of Higher Education,* 64(2), 186–210.

U.S. Bureau of the Census. (1995). *Statistical abstract of the United States: 1995* (115th ed.). Washington, DC: Author.

U.S. Bureau of the Census. (1997). *Statistical abstract of the United States: 1997* (117th ed.). Washington, DC: Author.

U.S. Bureau of the Census. (1998, Sept. 30). The official statistics. *Statistical abstract of the United States: 1998.* Washington, DC: U.S. Government Printing Office.

U.S. Department of Commerce, Bureau of the Census. (1984). *We, the American women of the 80's*. Washington, DC: U.S. Government Printing Office.

U.S. Department of Labor. (1989, August 21). *Women and work*. Washington, DC: U.S. Government Printing Office.

U.S. Department of Labor. (1991). *A report on the glass ceiling initiative*. Washington, DC: U.S. Government Printing Office.

U.S. Department of Labor, Bureau of Labor Statistics. (1979). *U.S. working women: A databook*. Washington, DC: Author.

U.S. Department of Labor, Bureau of Labor Statistics. (1984). *Employment and earnings*. Washington, DC: Author.

U.S. Department of Labor, Bureau of Statistics. (1992a, January). *Employment and earnings*. Washington, DC: U.S. Government Printing Office.

U.S. Department of Labor, Bureau of Labor Statistics. (1992b, August 3). *News: Usual weekly earnings of wage and salary workers: Second quarter 1992*. Washington, DC: Author.

Unabridged Communications. (1991). *The invisible majority*. Alexandria, VA: Author.

Unger, T. (1992, August). Minority hiring debate heats up. *Public Relations Journal*, pp. 5, 25.

Varadan, M.S.S. (1991, March 7). What makes women managers different. *Hindu*, p. 18.

Verdugo, N. (1982). *The effects of discrimination on the earnings of Hispanic workers: Findings and policy implications*. Washington, DC: National Council of La Raza.

Wakefield, G. (1993, April). Trouble, trouble, trouble. . . . *PR update*, p. 4.

Wakefield, G., & Cottone, L. P. (1987). Knowledge and skills required by public relations employers. *Public Relations Review, 13*(3), 24–32.

Wallace, P. A. (Ed.). (1982). *Women in the workplace*. Boston: Auburn House.

Wallis, C. (1989, December 4). Onward, women! *Time*, pp. 80–82, 85–86, 89.

Walther, J. B., & Parks, M. R. (1998). *Researching personal relationships in cyberspace*. http://www.rpi.edu/walthj/inpr96.

Wann, A. (1993, December). A speech to remember. *IABC Communication World*, pp. 22–26.

Ward, J. G., & Anthony, P. (Eds.). (1992). *Who pays for student diversity? Population changes and educational policy*. Newbury Park, CA: Corwin Press.

Warner, H. K. (N.d.). *Ten challenges to public relations during the next decade*. Washington, DC: Manning Selvage & Lee.

Warnick, B. (1999). Masculinizing the feminine: Inviting women on line ca. 1997. *Critical Studies in Mass Communication, 16*, 1–19.

Webster's ninth new collegiate dictionary. (1987). Springfield, MA: Merriam-Webster.

Weick, K. E. (1979). *The social psychology of organizing* (2nd ed.). Reading, MA: Addison-Wesley.

Wellington, A. J. (1992). Changes in the male–female wage gap, 1976–85. *Journal of Human Resources, 28*(2), 333–411.

WEPR Memo. (1991). *Women Executives in Public Relations, Ad Hoc Committee on*

Sexual Harassment, Internal Memorandum. New York: Women Executives in Public Relations.

Westerbeck, T. (1992, July). Suppliers zero in on growing Hispanic market. *Public Relations Journal,* pp. 7–8.

Wetherell, B. L. (1989). *The effect of gender, masculinity, and femininity on the practice of and preference for the models of public relations.* Unpublished master's thesis, University of Maryland, College Park.

Wharton, C. S. (1994). Finding time for the "second shift": The impact of flexible work schedules on women's double days. *Gender and Society, 8*(2), 189–205.

What they're saying: Women still dominate PR classes, but that may change as other fields, such as law, even the gender ratio. (1993, July 19). *Ragan Report, 24*(7), 4.

The white face of public relations. (1993, March). *Inside PR,* pp. 25–32.

White, M. C., DeSanctis, G., & Crino, M. D. (1981). Achievement, self-confidence, personality traits, and leadership ability: A review of literature on sex differences. *Psychological Reports, 48,* 547–569.

Wilcox, D. L., Ault, P. H., & Agee, W. K. (1992). *Public relations: Strategies and tactics* (3rd ed.). New York: HarperCollins.

Wilkins, B. M., & Andersen, P. A. (1991). Gender differences and similarities in management communication: A meta-analysis. *Management Communication Quarterly, 5,* 6–35.

Williams, M. V. (1990, January). Managing work-place diversity. . . . The wave of the '90s. *IABC Communication World,* pp. 16–19.

Williams, M. V. (1991, March). Will diversity equal equality for multicultural communicators? *IABC Communication World,* pp. 26–30.

Winkleman, M. (1986, July). Percentage of professional women rises. *Public Relations Journal,* p. 6.

Wise, N. M. (1993). *The African-American woman in public relations management.* Unpublished manuscript, University of Maryland, College Park.

Wise, N. M. (1997). *The African American female public relations professional: Gender socialization and career experiences.* Unpublished master's thesis, University of Maryland, College Park.

Wolfgram, T. (1984, June). Working at home: The growth of cottage industries. *Futurist,* pp. 31–34.

Women in the workplace. (1998, Spring). *sec . . . in action!* (Publication of the University of Maryland Career Center and Its Student Employment Center, SEC), pp. 1–5.

Women managers superior. (1988, January 7). *Australian,* p. 15.

Women on top. (1999, January 18). *PR Week,* pp. 16–17.

Women slowly catching up to men in earnings. (1991, September 26). *Syracuse Herald Journal,* p. 1.

Women, blacks soar in schools. (1998, June 29). *Gainesville Sun,* p. 2A.

Woo, D. (1992). The gap between striving and achieving: The case of Asian-American women. In M. L. Andersen & P. H. Collins (Eds.), *Race, class, and gender: An anthology* (pp. 191–200). Belmont, CA: Wadsworth.

Wood, J. T. (1997). *Gendered lives: Communication, gender, and culture* (2nd ed.). Belmont, CA: Wadsworth.

Wood, J. T. (1998). Ethics, justice, and the "private sphere." *Women's Studies in Communication, 21*(2), 127–149.

Woods, J. D., & Lucas, J. H. (1993). *The corporate closet: The professional lives of gay men in America.* New York: Free Press.

Wright, D. K., & Springston, J. K. (1991, June). Gender gap narrowing. *Public Relations Journal,* pp. 22–24.

Wright, D. K., Grunig, L. A., Springston, J. K., & Toth, E. L. (1991). *Under the glass ceiling: An analysis of gender issues in American public relations* (PRSA Foundation Monograph Series, Vol. 1, No. 2). New York: Public Relations Society of America Foundation.

Wright, D. K., Lewton, K., Springston, J. K., & Grunig, L. A. (1991, March 23). *Gender survey: Internal report to the chapters.* New York: Public Relations Society of America.

Wynter, L. E. (1997, December 12). Business and race. *Wall Street Journal,* p. B1.

Yamashita, S. H. (1992). *The examination of the status and roles of Asian-American public relations practitioners in the United States.* Unpublished master's thesis, University of Maryland, College Park.

Yelsma, P., & Brown, C. T. (1985). Gender roles, biological sex, and predispositions to conflict management. *Sex Roles, 12*(7–8), 731–747.

Yzaguirre, R. (1990, September 25). *Hispanic educational trends and needs.* Speech given by the President and Chief Executive Officer of the National Council of La Raza to the Hispanic Educational Forum, Washington, DC.

Zaharna, R., Diggs-Brown, B., & Yamauchi, J. (1994). Cultural diversity in the public relations industry. *Public Relations Review, 18*(4), 13–18.

Zerbinos, E., & Clanton, G. (1993). Minority practitioners: Career influences, job satisfaction, and discrimination. *Public Relations Review, 19*(1), 75–91.

Zimmerman, J. (1986). *Once upon the future: A woman's guide to tomorrow's technology.* New York: Pandora.

Zoch, L. M., & Russell, M. P. (1991). Women in PR education: An academic "velvet ghetto"? *Journalism Educator, 46*(3), 25–37.

Index

About the Authors

Larissa A. Grunig, PhD, has been on the faculty of the University of Maryland, College Park, since 1978 and is currently an associate professor. She teaches scientific and technical writing, public relations, and communication research. In 1989, Dr. Grunig received the Pathfinder Award for excellence in research, sponsored by the Institute for Public Relations Research and Education. She was cofounder and coeditor of the *Journal of Public Relations Research* and has written more than 150 articles, book chapters, monographs, reviews, and conference papers on public relations, activism, science writing, feminist theory, communication theory, and research. She also serves as a conslutant in public relations and as a member of an international grant team, sponsored by the IABC Research Foundation, investigating excellence in public relations and communication management.

Elizabeth Lance Toth, PhD, is associate dean for academic affairs and professor of public relations at the S. I. Newhouse School of Public Communications at Syracuse University. She has published over 75 articles, book chapters, and papers. Dr. Toth co-authored *The Velvet Ghetto: The Increasing Numbers of Women in Public Relations, Beyond the Velvet Ghetto,* and the PRSA Glass Ceiling studies. Her coedited book *Rhetorical and Critical Approaches to Public Relations* won the NCA PRIDE Award, and another coedited book *The Gender Challenge to Media: Diverse Voices from the Field,* is currently in press. Dr. Toth received the 1998 Institute for Public Relations Pathfinder Award for her research on gender issues and public relations.

Linda Childers Hon, PhD, is an associate professor and graduate coordinator of public relations at the University of Florida. She also holds a UF Research Foundation Professorship. Dr. Hon is editor of the *Journal of Public Relations Research*. Her research, which has focused on public relations evaluation as well as gender and diversity issues in public relations, has been published in the *Journal of Public Relations Research*, the *Public Relations Strategist*, the *Journal of Applied Communications*, as a chapter in *Excellence in Public Relations and Communication Management*, and as a monograph from the Institute for Public Relations and Ketchum Public Relations.